From a Marxist-Feminist Point of View

Essays on Freedom, Rationality and Human Nature

Nancy Holmstrom

Haymarket Books
Chicago, IL

First published in 2024 by Brill Academic Publishers, The Netherlands
© 2024 Koninklijke Brill NV, Leiden, The Netherlands

Published in paperback in 2025 by
Haymarket Books
P.O. Box 180165
Chicago, IL 60618
773-583-7884
www.haymarketbooks.org

ISBN: 979-8-88890-538-8

Distributed to the trade in the US through Consortium Book Sales and Distribution (www.cbsd.com) and internationally through Ingram Publisher Services International (www.ingramcontent.com).

This book was published with the generous support of Lannan Foundation, Wallace Action Fund, and the Marguerite Casey Foundation.

Special discounts are available for bulk purchases by organizations and institutions. Please call 773-583-7884 or email info@haymarketbooks.org for more information.

Cover art and design by David Mabb. Cover art is an adaptation from *Luibov Popova Untitled Textile Design on May Morris Honeysuckle Wallpaper*, screen print on wallpaper, 2010.

Printed in the United States.

Library of Congress Cataloging-in-Publication data is available.

Second Printing

Praise for From a Marxist-Feminist Point of View

'Nancy Holmstrom represents a unique blend of philosophical rigor and activism rooted in genuine concern for women and LGBTQ people suffering from the ills of capitalism, racism, patriarchy and homophobia in the Global North and the Global South. Her articulation of Marx's concept of human nature is especially relevant to the current debates on queer theory and gender identity and challenges an essentialist and unchanging concept of human nature.'
—**Frieda Afary**, author, *Socialist Feminism: A New Approach*

'Holmstrom's wide-ranging essays are unified by her consistent attention to the mode of production. Using this as organizing principle, Holmstrom delivers illuminating discussions of topics such as exploitation, self-ownership, gender relations, sex work, human nature, rationality and freedom. As a whole, the book provides a powerful vision of the liberatory potential of a genuinely democratic socialism.'
—**Alison M. Jaggar**, author, *Feminist Politics and Human Nature*

'*From a Marxist-Feminist Point of View* is an essential resource for the left today. I've been reading Nancy Holmstrom's political philosophy since the 1970s and am thrilled to be able to return to them now in a single volume. These essays showcase her exceptional ability to clarify and critically assess Marxist and Marxist-feminist ideas—and, crucially, to clarify for us the political stakes.'
—**Susan Ferguson**, author, *Women and Work: Feminism, Labour, and Social Reporoduction*

'Nancy Holmstrom's articles tackle some of the most important and controversial issues in social theory. Whether the topic is the meaning of "rationality" and "freedom," the question whether unpaid care labor is exploited, or the complexities of gender and race in the capitalist mode of production, few writings better illustrate the theoretical reach of Marxist feminism. Even fewer convey more forcefully the political stakes of the theoretical debates. Even those who do not agree with me that she is right about pretty much everything will find insights on every page.'
—**Tony Smith**, author, *Beyond Liberal Egalitarianism: Marx and Normative Social Theory in the Twenty-First Century*

'This remarkable collection of Marxist/feminist essays is grounded in a critical analysis of the capitalist mode of production, and its consequences for women's life and work. Committed to human rationality and the values of freedom, justice and equality, Nancy Holmstrom persuasively argues for the need for collective anti-capitalist action to prevent climate catastrophe. The only way out is a radical social change which is at the same time feminist and ecosocialist.'

— **Michael Löwy**, author, *Ecosocialism: A Radical Alternative to Capitalist Catastrophe*

'Thanks to her consistent Marxist-feminist point of view, Nancy Holmstrom provides, in this brilliant collection of essays, invaluable insights on women's work, exploitation and struggles. For her, democracy and feminism are both ends and means of the socialist movement, which aims to put an end to capitalist irrationality and alienation, as well as patriarchal domination.'

—**Eleni Varikas**, author, *Pour une théorie féministe du politique*

'In *From a Marxist-Feminist Point of View* Nancy Holmstrom brings together decades of groundbreaking work that has shaped the field of Marxist-feminist theory. Moving from Marx's theory of modes of production to contemporary debates on freedom, rationality and human nature, Holmstrom shows how feminism and Marxism together illuminate and challenge the social relations that shape our lives. Bold, rigorous and deeply committed to social and political transformation, this volume is a vital resource for anyone committed to freedom, justice and equality—and to the struggles that make them possible.'

—**Cinzia Arruzza**, co-author, *Feminism for the 99%*

'This collection of Nancy Holmstrom's work on Marxist feminism is a remarkable testament to her brilliance, clear voice and political insight. She brings to the page her deep insight from over fifty years of political and philosophical work and articulates it without jargon or fluff. This is a book for anyone who is looking to analyze our current crises and offers inspiration for continuing the struggle.'

—**Sally Haslanger**, author, *Resisting Reality: Social Construction and Social Critique*

Contents

Acknowledgements   IX

Introduction   1
1   Modes of Production   2
2   Rationality   4
3   Freedom   5
4   Human Nature/Women's Nature   6

PART 1
Modes of Production

1   Developing Marx's Mode of Production Theory   13

2   Marxist/Socialist Feminist Theory and Practice in the USA Today   17
   1   Varieties of Socialist Feminism: One System or Two   17
   2   What Is a 'System?'   20
   3   Intersectionality   21
   4   A Framework Model—One Non-reductive System   24

3   Sex, Work and Capitalism   26
   1   Introduction   26
   2   What Is Sex Work?   27
   3   Political/Economic Context   28
   4   Empowerment vs. Power, Agency and Freedom   29
   5   A 'Work Ethic instead of a Sex Ethic?'   31
   6   Is Sex Special?   34
   7   What Is To Be Done?   39

4   'Women's Work,' the Family and Capitalism   42

5   Democratic Socialism for a Finite World   65
   1   'Democracy'   65
   2   'Socialism'   66
   3   Democracy as the END of Socialism   68
   4   Democracy as the MEANS to Socialism   70
   5   Why Democratic Socialism Is ECOSOCIALIST   72
   6   Why Democratic Socialism Is FEMINIST   74

PART 2
Rationality

6   Rationality and Revolution   79

7   For a Sustainable Future: The Centrality of Public Goods   98
     1   Rethinking Property and Rationality: From the Individual to the Collective   99
     2   Property   100
     3   Rationality   103
     4   From Common Sense to Common Practice: Struggles around Public Goods   105

PART 3
Freedom

8   Free Will and a Marxist Concept of Natural Wants   117

9   Against Capitalism as Theory and Reality   140
     1   Basic Definitions: 'Capitalism' and 'Women's Interests'   144
     2   Gender interests: Strategic and Practical   148
     3   Capitalism *in Theory*: Ideals and Limits   149
         3.1   *On Property, Ownership, and Freedom*   149
         3.2   *Political Freedom and Democracy*   151
         3.3   *Freedom, Private Property and Self-Ownership*   156
         3.4   *Self-Ownership—History and Import of the Concept*   157
         3.5   *Self-Ownership—the Contemporary Debates*   165
         3.6   *Freedom/Unfreedom in the Abstract*   169
         3.7   *Internal Obstacles*   175
         3.8   *Tests of the Analysis*   176
         3.9   *A More Ideal Capitalism?*   178
         3.10   *In Theory*   179
         3.11   *In History*   181
         3.12   *How Ideal? The Inevitability and Importance of Extreme Inequalities*   184
         3.13   *The Most Basic Inequality*   189
         3.14   *Summing Up Capitalism in Theory*   192
     4   Capitalism *in Reality*   194
         4.1   *Compared to Pre-capitalist Societies*   194
         4.2   *Capitalism as Tendentially Better for Women*   195

4.3 *With Respect to Practical Gender Interests*   198
4.4 *Compared to So-Called Socialist Societies*   199
4.5 *Gains and Losses: Sweatshops and Worse*   201
4.6 *Competitive Market Constraints*   207
4.7 *Changed Gender Roles in Context*   208
4.8 *The Global Picture*   211
4.9 *Human Interests Are Women's Interests*   216
4.10 *Constrains on Rationality*   220
4.11 *Conclusion: What Is the Alternative? And What Should Feminists Do Now?*   222

PART 4
Human Nature/Women's Nature

10   A Marxist Theory of Women's Nature   229

11   Humankind(s)   248

12   Alienation, Freedom and Human Nature   275

Bibliography   291
Index   312

Historical Materialism Book Series

The Historical Materialism Book Series is a major publishing initiative of the radical left. The capitalist crisis of the twenty-first century has been met by a resurgence of interest in critical Marxist theory. At the same time, the publishing institutions committed to Marxism have contracted markedly since the high point of the 1970s. The Historical Materialism Book Series is dedicated to addressing this situation by making available important works of Marxist theory. The aim of the series is to publish important theoretical contributions as the basis for vigorous intellectual debate and exchange on the left.

The peer-reviewed series publishes original monographs, translated texts, and reprints of classics across the bounds of academic disciplinary agendas and across the divisions of the left. The series is particularly concerned to encourage the internationalization of Marxist debate and aims to translate significant studies from beyond the English-speaking world.

For a full list of titles in the Historical Materialism Book Series available in paperback from Haymarket Books, visit: www.haymarketbooks.org/series_collections/1-historical-materialism.

Acknowledgements

Richard Smith, my husband, had been urging me to do a collection of my articles for a while. He thought 'Exploitation and Modes of Production' was particularly important, as the key to Marx's method and way of understanding the world, and the implicit organising theme of all my work. I first shared the idea of the book with my friends Laura Esikoff and Allan Scholom, both psychoanalysts in Chicago, as well as socialists, who were enthusiastic.

A few years ago I was pleasantly surprised that an Australian novelist Julienne van Loon decided to focus on my work in her chapter on work in her book *The Thinking Woman*.[1] The fact that she took such abstract ideas like self-ownership and whether labour power is a commodity seriously enough to consider, intellectually and on a personal level, what alternatives there are to alienated work encouraged me to think that they might be useful to a broader audience. A documentary filmmaker named Mary Filippo had also relied on my work on public goods in her film 'My Mis-education in 3 Graphics' about how economics is taught.

Also very stimulating to me has been the socialist feminist reading group led by Sally Haslanger of MIT. Ann Ferguson, Alison Jaggar, Robin Zheng, Mirjam Mueller, Lori Gruen, Anna Moltchanova, Ege Yumusak, Rose Lenahan, and others, from literally all over the world—Singapore, Berlin, Amsterdam, as well as the United States, thanks to the wonders of Zoom—have gathered together to discuss many of the themes featured in this collection. I sometimes sent a paper around to explain my thoughts on a topic more fully than I could at the meetings. The favourable response of members of the group, particularly Rose Lenahan, again made me think that these papers spoke to important issues today.

Meanwhile my close collaborator and real co-thinker Johanna Brenner had joined the group, and I shared with her my idea of the book. Her encouraging response and active editing advice were invaluable because she knew the field well and had done a similar collection.[2] She generously read all the articles I had organized in a Table of Contents, advised me as to what to include and in

---

1 van Loon 2019. This highly original work, intended to connect philosophical thinking and everyday experience, is a mix of memoir and interviews with six 'thinking women' (Laura Kipnis, Siri Husfeldt, myself, Rosi Braidotti, Marina Warner and Julia Kristeva) on love, play, work, fear, wonder and friendship.
2 Brenner 2000.

what order and gave me feedback on the Introduction. My daughter Alexandra Holmstrom-Smith, and my friends Laura Esikoff, Nancy Romer, Elizabeth Rapaport, Gary Young and Jane Reid, also advised me on this Introduction and some or all of the contents.

Introduction

This book consists of writing I've done throughout my career, from almost the beginning to quite current work. Until recently I was too busy going from one thing to another, from teaching to conferences to political work. When I retired I finally had time to stop and reflect on the overall sweep of my work and to ask myself if there was enough unity or interconnected themes and threads to put together a coherent book. I decided there was, centred on Marx's concept of a mode of production. As for Marx, capitalism, our present mode of production, is primarily what occupies most of my essays, but in his spirit I also contrast this mode with others that preceded, persist, and emerge alongside it. Moreover, another red thread is present, discernible throughout: the writing in this book integrates my intellectual work with the values I have been committed to all my life: freedom, justice and equality.

I have been a political activist all my life, almost instinctively Marxist before I read any Marx. I went to the City College of New York, 1964–9, which was free at the time, a marvellous public good from which I benefited immensely and always appreciated. In 2016 I was canvassing for Bernie Sanders in Harlem and frequently referred to going to City College—a campus was always in sight—when it was free. People were amazed; they never knew that it had ever been free and the idea of a tuition-free college was almost the stuff of fantasy to them, whereas of course it is common for college to be free (or at least affordable) throughout the world.

My first political involvement at CCNY was with CORE (Congress of Racial Equality); we followed the civil rights movement closely, picketing Woolworth's on 125th St in support of the lunch counter sit-ins and supported the Freedom Rides. I desperately wanted to join them, but my mother didn't let me (I was under 18 at the time). When Malcolm X came to campus to debate Herbert Hill of the NAACP, I found him so inspiring I wasn't surprised that a fellow member of CORE joined the Black Muslims. I was also active in SPU (the Student Peace Union), which, unlike other peace groups like SANE, analysed the forces in each society that propelled the arms race. I was arrested protesting Kennedy's resumption of nuclear testing in Times Square. Experiencing police brutality first-hand, and later witnessing outright lies told by cops at the trial, had an undeniably radicalising effect. I came to the conviction that it would take a democratic socialist society to realize my values of peace and freedom and justice for all. I was recruited, easily, to the Young People's Socialist League, which had been growing at the time. It attracted me because it maintained a socialism-from-below perspective, rooted in the sorts of movements that I had already been participating in. My father's life as an intellectual working-class socialist (who only finished the 8th grade, being the child of an immigrant, widowed mother) also affected me profoundly. My parents divorced when I was young but I remained close to my father, who died on welfare. No doubt bad luck and bad choices contributed, but he always seemed to me to exemplify the enormous waste of human potential that is the lot of working people in capitalism.

I went to graduate school at the U of Michigan from 1965–70 where I studied philosophy of mind and metaphysics. Analytic philosophy in those days was rigidly differentiated from history and social theory; I studied no political philosophy, carefully avoiding it, since, after all, it was liberal at best. All my political activity was outside of philosophy. When political friends asked me how I could do 'that bourgeois philosophy', I challenged them to tell me why it was bourgeois. They couldn't. I thought the kind of philosophy I did was like music or physics, that is, that they were interesting, challenging subjects although essentially apolitical. I helped to organize the Society of Women in Philosophy, along with Alison Jaggar, but I saw it as more of a movement for women philosophers, rather than a critique of the field. It wasn't until I was teaching at the University of Wisconsin in the early 1970s and radical philosophers and feminist philosophers were beginning to organize, many also from an analytic philosophy background, bringing radical and feminist ideas into philosophy, that I finally began to bring my political and philosophical interests together. This was not good for my academic career and I was denied tenure at the University of Wisconsin and moved to Rutgers University at Newark, where I also was denied tenure. However, Rutgers had a union and I fought to be awarded tenure. After 18 years as a tenure track professor I finally received tenure. In any case, I was more estranged from the academy than ever and my writing over the years reflects it.

1   Modes of Production

All my work is implicitly grounded in the concept of a mode of production. This is especially true of the articles in the first section of the book, but is the foundation of all the articles collected here. Based on Marx's social and historical perspective, the concept of a mode of production is the key to his method and his way of understanding the histories of human societies. In a paper written on the 150th anniversary of the publication of *Capital*, 'Exploitation and Modes of Production', I explored the breadth, flexibility and usefulness of the concept. By no means is the concept restricted to the economy, as is so frequently said in criticism of Marxism. Neither is it equivalent to the more vague notion of 'social formation'. There are many stages and varieties of capitalism but they all create certain potentialities and limits that are rooted in the nature of the capitalist mode of production. Earlier I had written a paper simply called 'Exploitation' that concentrated on its operation in capitalism, in which I defended what became known as a force-inclusive interpretation of the concept, and explored other related philosophical issues, such as whether exploitation was a moral concept.[1] In 'Exploitation and Modes of Production', I made clear first, that it was not only capitalism that was exploitative, a point that is frequently misunderstood because Marx's focus in Capital was capitalism, but second, that it is the particular process through which exploitation occurs in the capitalist mode of production that holds the key to understanding the system as a whole. I continue this exploration of the capitalist mode of production in the article 'Varieties of Marxist Feminist Theories', a section of which is excerpted here. I discuss dual systems theories of capitalism and patriarchy versus a one-system model, the popular concept of intersectionality, and explain how we can account for many kinds of oppression, particularly sexism, within capitalism, but in a non-reductive way, using what I call a framework model. This model regards the capitalist mode of production as foundational but not determinative.

I continue this idea that the capitalist mode of production sets the terms, if you will, of degrees of freedom and unfreedom, again in historically particular ways, different from other modes of production in 'Sex, Work and Capitalism'. Here I explore the ways in which sex work is and is not different from other kinds of work within capitalism, bringing together Marx's discussion of exploited and free work and feminist insights into sexuality and power.

The question of exploitation within capitalism was at the heart of what came to be called the domestic labour debate in which feminists sought to understand how the unpaid labour of housework, childcare, care of ill and elderly members, and so forth contributed to the social reproduction of the working class, and whether or not that labour could be best understood as exploited labour in capitalism. The paper '"Women's Work", the Family and Capitalism' remains relevant today because it is women who still primarily do unpaid care work. This fact has given rise to a new current within Marxist-feminism: social reproduction feminism. How does one understand the persistence of

---

[1] If you are interested in these issues, see Holmstrom 1977a; 1983; 1994a; 2012.

this gendered division of labour and its relation to capitalism? Is this labour exploited and if so, by whom? What strategic conclusions can we draw from its persistence?

The final paper in this section takes us to an alternative mode of production to capitalism, democratic socialism, which is conceived as rational democratic planning, a mode of production which would not be exploitative. Not all conceptions of democratic socialism stress the necessity for planning.

2 Rationality

In the next section, on Rationality, I critique the abstract individualist model of rationality dominant in economics and philosophy, which says that rational behaviour is first of all individual behaviour that aims to maximize utility. The first article 'Rationality and Revolution',[2] critiques an influential application of this to Marx, which purports to show that Marx's theory of revolution made for rational reasons, as opposed to other causes, such as coercion or emotions, is incoherent. Rationality so conceived is a prime example of an ideological theory in Marx's terms. An ideology is a set of ideas that arise from the basic economic structure of a society—in this case, the central aspect of the capitalist mode of production in which people are forced to sell their labour power to survive and must do so in a competitive labour market. Ideologies are powerful because they express fundamental relations that organize our lives, but they are wholly or partially false and function to maintain the social relations of that society, in this case by representing radical social change as either impossible or irrational, most likely requiring undemocratic manipulation or coercion. I offer instead various alternative accounts of how participation in revolutionary action can be rational. Some of my arguments remain within the individualist framework but some go beyond it, defending a social model based on the premise that individuals cannot properly be understood independent of a society. A Marxist view of rationality has primarily to do with forms of social practices and collective action rather than individual acts, does not exclude emotions, and most fundamentally is not limited to means, but is an end—that of bringing the world under conscious human control. The individualist model of rationality remains dominant, however, even appearing as common sense—despite refutation—because it reflects the realities of life in capitalist society.

---

[2] On rationality, see Holmstrom 2000; and Holmstrom and Smith 2002.

Yet individualist accounts are more than ever in need of a social alternative given the climate catastrophe on our doorstep, which can only be solved through collective anti-capitalist action. The Covid pandemic only reinforced the fact of our human interconnectedness and interdependence and the patent stupidity of relying on an individualist model of society to understand and to respond appropriately to it. 'For a Sustainable Future: The Centrality of Public Goods' argues for the necessity of reconceiving the concepts of security, property and rationality moving away from an individualist perspective—which sustains capitalism—to a social model, stressing the importance of taking public goods or commons as the default, rather than private property. This leads us to rational democratic planning—which is the only way we can stop the ecological crisis.

3 Freedom

Freedom is discussed in two areas of academic philosophy: metaphysics, where determinism and free will are debated, and social/political philosophy. Individualism is appropriate in the former domain where the question is whether freedom and determinism are compatible, i.e. can free actions be determined? In 'Free Will and a Marxist Concept of Free Will'[3] I discuss a popular theory known as compatibilism, which argues that acts can be both determined and free, but whether or not they are so depends on what they are determined by. If the causes are the agent's wants and beliefs, then the act is free. However, I argue, if they are the result of brainwashing or subliminal advertising, most everyone would agree the acts are no longer free. Then I move the discussion into the social/political domain, arguing that a Marxist analysis of capitalist society—of what causes our wants and beliefs—shows that most acts done in capitalist societies are more similar to these counterexamples than would at first appear and are therefore unfree, except in a very superficial limited sense. I stress that freedom is always a matter of degree, but that we want our acts and our society to be as free as possible since, in J.S. Mill's words '... freedom is the first and strongest want of human nature'.

I extend this argument in 'Against Capitalism as Theory and Reality', an excerpt from a book I co-authored with Ann Cudd entitled Capitalism For and Against: A Feminist Debate. Defenders of capitalism as the best political economic system overall usually do so either on the grounds of its greater effi-

---

3 On free will see also Holmstrom 1977b.

ciency at producing material well-being or its greater freedom. Efficiency and freedom are connected in that well-being, which is the result of efficiency, enhances freedom. But independently of this rationale, capitalism is alleged to be essentially freer than all alternatives; hence better for women, our focus in the book. Since Ann Cudd stresses the latter defence of capitalism both in theory and in reality, my critique of capitalism also focuses on freedom. Key questions I pose are whether capitalism is more free compared to what alternatives, and with respect to what, and which women are we looking at? Exploring freedom in general involves important philosophical issues, such as the idea of self-ownership, thought by some to be the foundation of freedom, the difference between empowerment and power and the question of whether poverty renders one less free or just less capable, as liberal philosophers often claim, in that it renders one less capable of taking advantage of this freedom. It also involves such empirical issues as the existence of sweatshops, how bad are they, and whether they are inevitable but in the long run good, the constraints of the market, and global migration, particularly of women, sometimes involving outright slavery. What is the relation of capitalism to all this? Freedom will appear again in the next section in connection with human nature, particularly in the final essay 'Alienation, Freedom and Human Nature'.

4   Human Nature/Women's Nature

The final section addresses issues related to Human Nature and (so-called) Women's Nature, discussions of which have always been a mixture of scientific facts and political assumptions. In an early article 'Do Women Have a Distinct Nature?'[4] (not included here), I argued that the question was better put 'are there sex-differentiated natures?' since there is no reason that men should be taken as the norm which is implied by the very question 'do women have a distinct nature?' The answer could not rest on their different reproductive properties because that answer is tautological. The question is whether those biological properties produce different psychological properties that lead to different behavioural propensities. A critical review of the existing literature on sex-linked psychological and behavioural differences led me to conclude that there is little evidence to support a biologically based theory of gendered 'natures' but that we should acknowledge a particular range of gendered differ-

---

4   Holmstrom 1982.

ences that we could see as 'natures' which are socially-determined, historically changeable, and limited, in the sense that women and men share a human nature despite their different gendered 'natures'. I argue that 'nature' is a theory-laden term and that a theory of gendered natures, to be adequate, would conceptualize them as dynamic rather than static and socially/culturally constructed rather than innate. In 'A Marxist Theory of Women's Nature'[5] I extended this approach, drawing on Marxist theory that stresses the importance for peoples' lives—and their very natures—of the mode of production in which they live and their place within it, most importantly their labour and the social relations in which they are embedded. I suggested that women might be said to have distinct natures given women's distinctive labour taking care of children and others. My analysis allows that not all women share this nature, whereas they all share a common human nature, and that gendered natures being, in a Marxist framework, socially constituted and historically evolving, can change. So talk of women's distinct nature in a Marxist sense is highly qualified and theory-laden and does not put limits on the extent to which the traditional gender roles can and should be altered, as do most theories of women's nature, including radical feminist ones.

The next paper 'Humankind(s)' compares the concepts of human nature, gender and race, which have all been used to explain and to justify existing hierarchies of class, sex and race and to deny that a society without such hierarchies is possible. While the biological determinist assumptions underlying the claims are all false, there are important and interesting differences in the usefulness of these concepts. I contend that Marx had a theory of relatively invariant, biologically based human nature, while also holding to historically specific forms of human nature. This is due to the fact that human beings are embodied physically, but they are also always intrinsically embedded in social relations, which change. Thus the possibility of change and variability—and liberation—is dependent on, but not determined by, our biological constitution, in particular our brain. The essentialist account of women's nature being false, it is not even clear that there are two genders except in the limited theory-laden sense explained earlier, which would have class and race variations. In a non-sexist society, the human potentialities common to all would be developed by each individual in his/her own way, including some of the ways called masculine and feminine in earlier societies. While there are two sexes that most people fall into, which is important for biological theory, there is no necessary connection between sex and gender, and the biological fact of sex carries

---

5 Holmstrom 1998 and 2013.

little importance (except in certain social/historical contexts).[6] Though the concepts of gender and race are similar in how they have functioned ideologically, race is different in an important respect; there is nothing comparable to sex in the case of race. But it would be a mistake to think that races simply disappear, once their lack of any biological basis is proved, as some infer. Race is a historical, social, political construct and has profound harmful effects on those defined as non-white. In short, it is racism that creates the group that needs to struggle against it.

'Alienation, Freedom and Human Nature' is the final article, which is appropriate in that it looks back to our discussion of freedom and sums up several themes of this book. I wrote it for a book on alienation that in the end was not published, so I am happy it will be here. In it I explain Marx's theory of alienation, a theory found in *Capital* and not just the *Economic and Philosophical Manuscripts* (as some Marxists claim) that, along with exploitation, is one of the ineliminable evils of capitalism. I address the article to radicals whose critique is not of capitalism per se, but of the current plutocratic form of it, and who think that anything more radical is utopian. Even if a more humane form of capitalism were possible, and I don't believe it is, it would still be unsustainable ecologically and would be constitutive of ongoing alienation. Alienation takes several different forms in capitalism: alienation from the product of one's labour and from the process of labour, from other people and from the fundamental character of the human species, which is free, conscious activity. I concentrate on the latter aspect of alienation as it is the most complicated and also the most controversial. Clarifying what this last aspect of alienation means and refuting arguments against its coherence and its attribution to Marx in his later work, I explain why he credits some variants of human nature as more 'truly' human than others. The reason is that it was formed and expressed in conditions of freedom as opposed to oppressive social relations. The final aspect is alienation from other people, which brings out that Marx's vision of social equality combines community and individuality. If Marx is right

---

6 I wrote 'Humankind(s)' in 1991 before transsexual/transgender issues were commonly discussed. Today Trans Philosophy and Trans Studies are found in many academic departments. While I believe that my denial that sex determines gender was fundamentally compatible with thinking about transsexual/transgender issues, and affirming the legitimacy of transgender identities, when putting together this collection I was unsure how what I had written would accord with current language and sensibilities. For useful current philosophy articles see work by Talia Mae Bettcher (Bettcher 2009) and Louise Antony (Antony 2020). The new books *Transgender Marxism* ed. by (Gleeson and O'Rourke 2021), and *Transgender Resistance: Socialism and the Fight for Trans Liberation* (Miles 2020) connect these themes with socialism.

that most people have enormous unrealized potential, which if realized would make them happier and more fulfilled, and that this realisation can only happen in an egalitarian and free society, this is a powerful moral argument in favour of such a society, and in favour of encouraging the traits of empathy, solidarity and reciprocity necessary to achieve it.

.

PART 1

Modes of Production

CHAPTER 1

Developing Marx's Mode of Production Theory

The mode-of-production concept that Marx develops in *Capital* (although the idea is present earlier) is the essential methodological tool for understanding history, different societies, and the possibilities for social change.[1]

According to Marx, exploitation was essential to all class societies, indeed *defining* class society, both in general and for each particular form. While many people think Marx's concept of exploitation was specific to capitalism, as the extraction of surplus value, he makes clear that this is just the specific form of exploitation in capitalism.

'The essential difference between the various economic forms of society, between for instance a society based on slave labour and one based on wage labour, lies only in the mode in which this surplus labour is in each case *extracted* from the actual producer, the labourer'.[2] Or, from Volume III: 'The specific economic form in which unpaid surplus labour is *pumped out of* direct producers determines the relations of rulers and ruled'.[3]

From these I infer that a particular kind of coercion and surplus extraction are connected in all class societies; indeed they are constitutive of the relations that define a given mode of production.

Exploitation occurs when producers lack control of their means of subsistence, and hence, in order to survive, they are forced, directly or indirectly, to work for others who appropriate their labour's product. In slavery and in feudalism both the force and the surplus are clear. In capitalism, less clear. Marx's specific account of how this happens in capitalism rests on the labour theory of value, but his understanding of exploitation in capitalism is broader than that. Workers, Marx says, 'agree, i.e. are compelled by social conditions, to work for others who reap the product of their labour'.[4] With or without the labour theory of value, this is true.

---

1 This chapter was originally presented as a talk on the occasion of the 150th anniversary of *Das Kapital*, at a forum organized by the Rosa Luxemburg Foundation and the Goethe Institute in New York, on 14 September 2017. It was later published by *New Politics* for its Winter 2018 issue (Vol. XVI No. 4).
2 Marx 1967, p. 217.
3 Marx 1967, p. 791.
4 Marx 1967. P. 271.

The mode-of-production analysis helps us to see that exploitation also existed in post-capitalist societies. The fundamental question is always: Who controls the means of production? In Soviet-style bureaucratic systems, it was the bureaucracy that controlled the means of production and subsistence, leaving the producers no choice but to work for them. And it was the bureaucracy that controlled the surplus for their needs and purposes.

So this allows us to see the continuity between capitalism, feudalism, slave systems, and bureaucratic systems—but the specific differences between them are equally important.

Each mode of production, as Marx understood it, has certain kinds of structures and tendencies, a certain nature if you will. In capitalism, being a kind of competitive market system, each capitalist firm must try to maximize its own profit in order to beat the other capitalists and get a larger share of the market. So each firm is compelled to grow, to expand, to revolutionize the forces of production in order to produce more while lowering costs. Other systems, pre- and post-capitalist, do not have this built-in imperative. Indeed slavery and feudalism were marked by stasis and crises of underproduction, while capitalism undergoes periodic crises of overproduction.

This concept is important for several debates, starting with what changes are and are not possible within capitalism.

Consider gender relations: In developed capitalist countries, women have become more independent from men and more equal, both legally and economically, than ever before. Nevertheless, they still are subject to sexual predation, as Trump has helped to highlight, and they still do the bulk of caring labour, whether for free or for low pay. Low-paid care work fits the account of exploitation in *Capital*, while the work women do for free does not. Feminists have often criticized Marx on this point, but since *Capital* is intended to elucidate what makes the capitalist system tick, so to speak, unpaid work is irrelevant, so this criticism is not to the point, in my opinion. Marxist/socialist feminists have, however, developed an enriched account of social reproduction, which tries to supplement the account in *Capital* by showing the importance of this work, both in human terms and for capitalism since it produces labour power.

Now the extraordinary improvements in gender relations within capitalism raise the question of whether women and men could ever be totally equal in a capitalist society. Liberals think so, and some Marxists seem to imply it by their contention that, unlike class oppression, sex and race oppression are not essential to capitalism. But while they are not *logically* essential (that is, we can *imagine* a gender- and race-neutral version of capitalism), it does not follow that they are incidental; indeed, as Marxist feminists including myself have argued, they are very likely historically, pragmatically necessary. Consider what women have and haven't achieved. What they've achieved are their basic democratic rights, which do not threaten profits, indeed may augment them. But care work in the United States is still largely a private responsibility because supporting care work as the public good it is would seriously cut into profits. In other countries with relatively more robust social welfare, the advent of global neoliberalism has meant drastic cutbacks.

The nature of capitalism thus puts constraints on gender and race equality. Today, while individual women and minorities have moved to the top ranks of society, class differences among women and among blacks have actually increased. Any movements that could reduce sex and race oppression must be based on working-class struggles, integrating other forms of oppression. Thus the counterposition of class and 'identity politics' is misleading, indeed counterproductive.

Another, and probably the most important, example of capitalist limits to change is the multiple ecological crises facing the planet, which, as Al Gore's charts show, took off with the development of capitalism. Its imperative to grow is simply incompatible with a sustainable environment. I will return to this point in a minute.

The mode of production helps us understand debates about countries transitioning to capitalism. Many post-colonialist thinkers have denied that Marxist analyses are applicable to countries like India because, they argue, India lacks key features of developed capitalism, in particular, liberal political and cultural institutions. But Vivek Chibber, using the mode-of-production analysis, clarifies that Marxism does not contend that capitalist development will be *uniform* all over the world, but rather that *certain* features of capitalism are *universal*. Capital's economic needs—the sine qua non being profit maximisation—are the defining ones; they are present in India and in fact they might be aided by the very traditional social hierarchies and oppression that post-colonialists deem to be incompatible with capitalism.[5]

The above point regarding capitalism and ecological crisis is underlined by considering the changes in the Soviet Union and China. While each country developed under Stalin and Mao, their push for development and growth was not the same as capitalism, either in scope (nowhere near the same growth) or in cause. Unless the bureaucracy decided to develop something, it did not happen; there was no *automatic* motor that drove growth as a market system does. In fact, the cause of growth was more like feudalism in that it stemmed

---

5 See Chibber 2013.

from political rather than economic needs: As feudal lords competed with each other, so these countries competed with other global powers.

Richard Smith identifies in China today a hybrid mode of production.[6] The capitalist sector of the economy has created *enormous* growth: it has a 20 percent growth rate. But the other sector, the state-owned enterprises, which includes the *commanding heights* of the economy, runs on *very different imperatives*. Many of the state-owned enterprises are justly called *dinosaurs* because they would have gone extinct in a fully capitalist economy. But the government cannot afford to let millions of people be unemployed, so they create things like ghost cities. Though totally irrational from a capitalist point of view, as Western economists never tire of pointing out, they make sense in the bureaucratic mode of production.

This combination of market-driven growth in the largest economy in the world and the lack of even the minimal political democratic checks typical of capitalism is causing what Smith has called an ecological apocalypse. Environmentalists who advocate a simpler no-growth economy are 100 percent correct, but unless they also recognize that this is impossible within capitalism they are another variety of climate change deniers.

Finally, the mode-of-production analysis also gives us the key conditions for socialism. As Marx conceived it, this is a society where the means of production are under *collective democratic control*, so the conditions for exploitation do not exist. The producers control the product of their labour and they get it all back collectively. This is expressed in this famous quote from *Capital* Volume III: 'The *producers rationally* regulate their interchange with Nature, bringing it under *their common control* ... with the least expenditure of energy and under conditions most favorable to and *worthy of their human nature*'. Beyond that is the true realm of freedom, he says. 'The shortening of the work day is its basic prerequisite'.[7]

Today it is ever more clear that, in Rosa Luxemburg's words, humanity's choice is between socialism and barbarism.

---

6   See Smith 2020.
7   Marx, 1967, p. 820.

CHAPTER 2

Marxist/Socialist Feminist Theory and Practice in the USA Today

1   Varieties of Socialist Feminism: One System or Two

I will use 'socialist feminism' to include all of these more radical versions of feminism, some of which are Marxist and some not.[1] As I define it, all socialist-feminists see class as central to women's lives, yet at the same time none would reduce sex or race oppression to economic exploitation.[2] All socialist-feminist politics have an anti-capitalist edge, not merely anti-neoliberal capitalism.[3] As we will see throughout this paper, women of colour have played an important role pushing feminist movements to the left; some identify as socialists, others do not but given that most black women are working class or poor, black feminists tend to be more radical than the average white feminist.

Which word we choose to identify ourselves *largely* depends I think, on the political context we're in, and the debates in which we're involved, as well as how we understand these categories. So the same label may not mean the same analysis—and different labels may not mean different analyses. For example, Margaret Benston[4] was one of the first Marxists to analyse women's domestic labour, back in 1969. She considered herself a Marxist, used Marxist categories, wrote in *Monthly Review*, a Marxist publication, and is described as a Marxist Feminist. In fact however, her analysis was more like that of feminists of the 1970s who were calling themselves '*Socialist* Feminist' precisely in order to distinguish themselves from Marxists. Hilary Wainwright calls herself a feminist socialist rather than a socialist feminist in order to signal her interest in bringing insights from feminism into the socialist movement and into visions of socialism. She's been arguing this since the 1970s and recently expressed her frustration that she still has to make the same argument.

---

1 This chapter constitutes an excerpt from a longer text, 'Marxist/Socialist Theory and Practice in the USA Today'. A full reference can be found in the Acknowledgements.
2 Holmstrom 2002.
3 As with any continuum, it is not always clear how to draw the lines. For example, Iris Marion Young, whom I knew for decades, saw herself as a socialist feminist but is included as a liberal feminist in an encyclopedia entry.
4 Benston 1969, pp. 13–27.

Sometimes these different labels do signal different theoretical analyses of women's oppression and capitalism. Interestingly however, as I shall discuss in the conclusion, these different theories need not entail different politics.

What are called 'dual systems theories' of women's oppression in capitalism were developed in the 1970s in response to the appalling sexism in much of the left, new as well as old, and to 'Marxist' theories which ignored or dismissed women's oppression. In the United States, Heidi Hartmann referred to the 'unhappy marriage of Marxism and feminism in which Marxism subsumed feminism'[5] contending that to understand women's oppression in capitalism, we must theorize it in terms of another system, patriarchy, existing before and after capitalism. Though unfortunately few American activists follow developments outside of the United States, it happened that across the ocean, similar dual system theories were developed, most notably by Christine Delphy. They accepted Marx's critique of capitalism but contended that it must be supplemented *and significantly revised* in order to understand women's oppression.

It is easy to show that sexism—and racism—increase the rate of exploitation in Marx's sense, as women and racial minorities are typically confined to the lowest paid work or paid less for the same work. But dual systems theorists say this benefits male workers as well as capitalists and should be seen as a function of patriarchy as well as capitalism—and that these two kinds of inequalities have equivalent importance. (Notice that the oppression or exploitation is part of the material base if one wants to speak in those terms.) Many feminist critics also charge that it was sexist of Marx to focus so exclusively on wage labour in capitalism and to ignore all the unpaid labour done by women in the home, again very material. Indeed, they find it particularly insulting that, according to Marx's analysis, this labour is not 'productive' labour. Surely, they contend, much of this labour is absolutely necessary for the reproduction of the work force, both biologically and in the sense of getting the worker to the factory door every day. Hence it is not only necessary for life in general, but for capitalism as it provides the basis for all work. Other feminist critics like Christine Delphy,[6] however, reject this focus on capitalism; instead they theorize a domestic mode of production alongside capitalism in which men exploit women's labour.

I will address these two points in turn. It was not sexism, nor an oversight, I contend, that led Marx to exclude household labour from his category of productive-in-capitalism, though of course it is productive in a general sense;

---

5 Hartmann 1979.
6 Delphy 1984, 1992.

production of people is obviously essential in all times and places and modes of production. Marx restricts the definition of productive labour as he does, in order to 'express[es] precisely the specific form of the labour on which the whole capitalist mode of production and capital itself is based'.[7] Hence the concept is the key to understanding the 'essence' of capitalism, and to understand the limits to which it can be reformed. As Rosa Luxemburg said: from the standpoint of capital, 'The dancer in a café, who makes a profit for her employer with her legs, is a productive working woman, while all the toil of the women and mothers of the proletariat within the four walls of the home is considered unproductive work. [This] sounds crude and crazy but it is an accurate expression of the crudeness and craziness of today's economic order ...'.[8] Note that the labour of a male carpenter who works for the state is equally unproductive in this sense.

Though domestic labour does not produce surplus value, capitalism and the constraints it poses are still important for understanding its persistence. The more labour done in the home for free, the less capitalists have to pay labour; hence their desire to push it onto the individual family. This helps to explain why women in the United States were able to win legal equality, but why caretaking is still largely a private responsibility.

But men also benefit from women's unpaid labour in the home, feminists rightly insist. Even if most men do not benefit from this gender system since it benefits capitalism, they certainly benefit in the short run. They have a shorter workday! And even though domestic labour does not produce surplus value, this does not mean that women are only oppressed in the home, but not exploited. As Delphy points out, exploitation is a broader concept than extraction of surplus value. Marx himself said clearly that this is simply the form that exploitation takes in capitalism. The unpaid surplus labour women have no choice but to do in the home[9] is exploited labour. Whether it is husbands, or men in general, or both capitalists and men who exploit domestic labour is too complicated to resolve here, but I am inclined to say that there is *no one* answer to this question. Rather, it depends on the details of the family, in particular just how much nonwage work a woman does and whether or not this is on top of wage work—which most women in developed capitalist countries are doing. So I think a theory of a domestic mode of production is less plausible today if it ever was. Marxists need not claim, however, that capitalist class relations are the *only* important social relations, or indeed the only class relations that exist

---

7   Marx 1963.
8   Luxemburg 1912, p. 21.
9   For a powerful demonstration that women do not freely choose their lot, see Mathieu 1990.

in capitalism. In fact, other modes of production, e.g. slavery, have often coexisted with capitalism, and hierarchies based on race/ethnicity and nationality have thrived within capitalist societies. So, even if the idea of a distinct patriarchal mode of production, with men and women forming two classes, is not, as I shall argue, the best way of illuminating sexism and capitalism, it is not inherently inconsistent with Marxism.

2   What Is a 'System?'

What *would* require a significant revision of Marxism is the claim that these two systems of capitalism and patriarchy are of equal explanatory weight for understanding our current system, its history and its trajectory. While this can be further researched, the idea raises a number of thorny methodological issues:

1) If it is necessary to postulate a distinct system of equal importance to understand how sexism works within capitalism, then why only two systems? In addition to these two, there is racism, there is heterosexism, ageism, ableism. Racism in particular has played a critical role in the history of US capitalism, but all are relations of power and unjust privilege. Does it mean we should theorize them as systems? This leads to the question:

2) What exactly constitutes a system? While I have no definitive answer, capitalism is clearly a system; its constitutive elements give it powerful tendencies that work across time and place, whatever their variations. A necessary condition for the transition from feudalism to capitalism in England centuries ago was the separation of producers from their means of subsistence and the amassing of wealth by others; today we see the same process of primitive accumulation in Russia and China as they have transitioned from the Soviet system to versions of capitalism.[10] Descriptions of factory conditions in the developing world today could be taken directly from Engels' descriptions from the nineteenth century. The drive to turn everything into a commodity has penetrated areas of the globe, of our bodies and our minds, in ways few could have imagined. Most significantly, the need to develop the productive forces, to grow, to accumulate on an ever-expanding basis is so powerful that it now threatens the very basis of human life on this planet.[11] Now that's a system!

I do not see sexism having anything like this kind of explanatory weight. What we see are *descriptions* of multifarious ways in which sexism operates

---

10 Holmstrom and Smith 2000, pp. 1–14.
11 See works by Marxist ecologists such as Ian Angus, John Bellamy Foster, Michael Lowy, Andreas Malm, Richard Smith, Chris Williams.

in capitalism and in other modes of production, how it has changed, even lessened within capitalism, but persists. While it has some autonomous causal efficacy, struggles against it have succeeded *only within the terms set by capitalism*. Thus we now have women at the highest levels of society, but the majority are disproportionately poor and becoming poorer. (Increased class differences are even more pronounced in the case of race in the US). For understanding capitalism, it is essential to see how deeply sexist—and racist—it is, but this does not entail that sexism and racism constitute 'systems' in anything like the sense in which capitalism is a system.

3) If we do take them as distinct systems, involving two sets of classes, men and women, and capitalists and workers, (or more to deal with race), how these 'classes' interrelate is complicated. Some women exploit both other women and also men—both in capitalist terms and in familial terms—and as I indicated, the class divide is increasing. How do the classes formed by capitalism and patriarchy (and racism) interrelate? Sex and race hierarchies definitely exist, but it is clearer in my opinion to see them as existing *within* socio-economic classes rather than as distinct *kinds* of classes (thus, for example, within the working class, whites tend to be better off than blacks, men better off than women). These hierarchies can therefore create conflicts of interest among working-class men and women and between black and white workers, even though they would all benefit from an end to capitalism, (an implication that is controversial among Marxists). Keep in mind, however, that gender inequalities today are significantly less in the US than class inequalities, as two recent sex-discrimination lawsuits reveal. A bond-saleswoman at Morgan Stanley sued because her salary of over a million dollars/year was much lower than her male colleagues'; women at Walmart sued because their annual salary was $1100 lower than the men's, but the average pay for *all* Walmart employees is only $10/hour. Despite these gender inequalities, the woman bond salesperson was still really rich, and the male Walmart worker quite poor.

3   Intersectionality

The popular concept of 'intersectionality' might seem to answer the question of the relationship among these different kinds of oppressions. The term 'intersectionality' is credited to Kimberlé Crenshaw,[12] an African American law pro-

---

12   Crenshaw 1989, pp. 139–67.

fessor who introduced it in 1989, but the idea has been around for longer; we see it in socialist women in the nineteenth century who focused on working women's distinct struggles, and is found in Marxist feminists like Alexandra Kollontai. But most importantly in the United States, the concept goes back to the groundbreaking Combahee River Collective Statement[13] of 1977. Drafted by a group of radical black feminists, it brought together not only sex and class but race and sexuality. They wrote from their specific identities as black lesbians of working-class origin who had found the male dominated black liberation movement (especially its nationalist wings)[14] and the mainstream white feminist movement unwelcoming or downright hostile. Though they collaborated well with socialist feminists they wanted to make clear what they thought was their unique perspective—and they did. Their manifesto argued that black women's unique experience of oppression was erased as they were put into either the category of race or of sex; nor can these two identities simply be 'added on' because they are so interrelated. The manifesto made the radical claim that because these multiple kinds of oppression are so interwoven, it will be impossible to free oneself from one without dismantling them all. Explicit socialists, they insisted that a socialist revolution must also be a feminist and anti-racist one. They identified as third world women, expressing solidarity with anti-imperialist struggles and they suggested that their position at the bottom might be used to 'make a leap into revolutionary action. If Black women were free, it would mean that everyone else would have to be free since our freedom would necessitate the destruction of all the systems of oppression'.[15] The radical Black Feminism of the Combahee River Collective Statement has been extremely influential in current movements, as I shall discuss later. Thus, the concept of intersectionality is extremely valuable for understanding the specificities of the position of American Black women, but also more broadly, as an analytic and strategic insight. In political practice it is extremely important to emphasize the intersection of different kinds of oppression, or else we risk the false counter-position of class politics and what are dismissively labelled 'identity politics'. Since working-class women's lives and oppression do not begin at the door to the factory or office (likewise for non-white working-class men) socialists wanting to organize working-class women and men of differ-

---

13   Combahee River Collective Statement originally appeared in Eisenstein 1979, pp. 362–72. It has been reprinted many times most recently in Taylor (ed.) 2017, pp. 15–27. One of its members, Barbara Smith, is credited with founding the academic field of Black Feminism and retains her commitment to socialism.
14   Mullings 2002, pp. 313–35.
15   Taylor 2017, p. 23.

ing race/ethnicities have to recognize this, and they increasingly do so, though there is still much room for improvement.[16]

However, turning back to the abstract question of one-system or two (or more) systems, the concept of intersectionality in itself does not *explain* on a theoretical level exactly *how and why* different kinds of oppression relate as they do. Moreover, the notion of intersectionality does not commit us to two or more systems, as we could just as well be exploring the intersection of *different aspects of the one system of capitalism*. In fact talk of a *distinct system of patriarchy* tends to obscure the integration of sexism with capitalism and to encourage people treating them as distinct autonomous systems. Thus, for example, Ann Cudd, my co-author of the recent book *Capitalism For & Against: A Feminist Debate*,[17] blames patriarchy for women's lower pay and absence of childcare—but not capitalism, though it is obvious that capitalists benefit from the lack of childcare and from women having lower salaries. My concern is that if we proliferate systems of equivalent importance that we lose explanatory coherence and end up with simple pluralism.[18]

Nevertheless there are several reasons why dual or triple system models are more attractive to many than a unitary model. As discussed, there is the political importance of an intersectional approach, the fear—based on all too many historical examples—that sex and race oppression will be subsumed by class, and the fact that sex oppression and race oppression *seem* distinct, and are experienced as distinct, from class oppression. For these reasons theorists have continued to work to develop intersectional theories, which are seen by many to support dual or triple system analyses. A recent sophisticated version is that offered by French theorist Danièle Kergoat[19] who wants to capture the interplay, the dynamic social and historical character of gender, race and class rather than seeing them as abstract and distinct elements that are added together in a geometric way. To do so, she borrows the term 'consubstantiality' from theological debates regarding the unity and difference of the three elements of the Trinity. Gender, race and class are each held to be a relation of production involving exploitation; thus there is no difference of substance between the three (problematic assumptions, but I will ignore this). By co-forming and mutually determining one another, they constitute a unified

---

16 For further Marxist discussion of intersectionality, see Brenner in Holmstrom 2002, pp. 336–48. A recent symposium on Intersectionality in the Marxist journal *Science & Society* (2018) 82 #2, April takes a more critical stance on the very concept of intersectionality.
17 Cudd and Holmstrom 2011.
18 Iris Marion Young 1997, pp. 95–106, made something like this point.
19 Kergoat 2009.

system of three systems of equivalent importance. The theory of consubstantiality is an intriguing attempt to understand differences within a unity, which makes it a definite improvement over additive models and would be attractive to many American socialist feminists though, regrettably, few are familiar with work done in non-English-speaking countries. However, the unity provided by the concept of consubstantiality is not really a coherent one because given the equal importance of the three, their unity cannot provide an explanation of *how, when and why* the elements interact as they do. The relation is ultimately mysterious, like the Trinity, as Cinzia Arruzza wittily puts the point.[20]

4   A Framework Model—One Non-reductive System

If we conclude, then, that a two- or three- (or more) system model cannot give us the coherence and unity we want in order to understand the system in which we live, then we need to find a one system model that can accommodate differences. The system in which we live is capitalist and patriarchal and racist and heterosexist ..., but to leave it at that description does not tell us how and why they all work together—and how this is different from simple pluralism. Instead of a multi-system model, I think we need a model that gives primacy of explanation to capitalism, but—and I stress this—which is not reductive. There are different ways of expressing this: recall Engels' Letters on Historical Materialism where he clarifies that all he and Marx ever said was that the economic was '*ultimately decisive*' or determining '*in the long run*', etc. Such phrases help to dispel misinterpretations of the theory, but they do not get us very far. Better, I think, is what has been called the framework model, based on Marx, in which explanation is contextualist, rather than atomist.[21] The idea is that different modes of production like capitalism and feudalism have structures that make possible different causal relations. Capitalism is then understood to be the context or framework within which other relations of oppression operate, with more or less salience in different times and places. So this gives capitalism a primacy in explanation, but it does not rule out other causes. Rather, in fact, it helps to explain *how and why other causes operate*—both material and non-material causes. Thus, while capitalism did not create male dominance, it uses it; capitalism's essential nature allowed for male dominance to lessen in certain ways but sets obstacles to its complete eradication. In the

---

20   Arruzza 2014.
21   This is developed by Fisk 1989, chapters 2 and 3.

1960s and '70s, political and economic conditions led many more women to higher education and the paid work force, and lowered fertility rates. Inspired by the civil rights movement which had successfully challenged allegedly biologically based subordination and led to anti-discrimination laws, women now had both the impetus and the opportunity to join together to challenge the patriarchal gender order. While they succeeded in dismantling restrictions on abortion, discriminatory laws and policies in the public and the private sphere, nevertheless women still do the bulk of the caretaking labour today. (This will be explored further in later sections of the paper).

Analogous questions regarding capitalism and racism have arisen among Black radicals, who range from nationalists (analogous to Radical Feminists) to liberals and social democrats to Black Marxists, like C.L.R. James. Although James was known for his powerful critiques of racism and colonialism and his defence of Black Power, he accepted something like the one system framework model I have proposed, as seen in this quote from his masterwork *The Black Jacobins*. 'The race question is subsidiary to the class question, and to think of imperialism in terms of race is disastrous. But to neglect the racial factor as merely incidental, is an error only less grave than to make it fundamental'.[22]

---

22   James 1963, p. 283. The Black Marxist tradition is less well known than other varieties of Black radicalism in the United States, but it was substantial and still is, as documented in a recent collection: Johnson and Lubin (eds.) 2017. It is alive and well today in such younger writer/activists as Cedric Johnson, Touré Reed, Keeanga-Yamahttta Taylor and others.

CHAPTER 3

Sex, Work and Capitalism

1   Introduction

The current debate regarding sex work is frustrating, which is one of the reasons I am writing this article.[1] Counter-posed positions are a good way to generate debate, but when they are false counter-positions, it is not likely to be a fruitful debate. The title of this symposium Sex Work: Emancipation or Oppression is an example of this, but unfortunately it reflects the discussion. Actually this is not a new debate but harks back to debates among feminists in the 1980s and resembles debates that went on in the nineteenth century.[2] Recent legal changes regarding sex work in some countries and under consideration elsewhere have given the debates a practical focus and a feeling of urgency. Unfortunately the 'sides' in this debate seem so solidified, it is difficult to trust a lot of what is written, as writers pick cases and evidence that fit their perspective.

Most feminists now agree that sex work should not be criminalized; this just drives it underground and causes further hardship to those doing the work. However, this position does not take us very far, as there are countless public and private actions which might be morally/politically problematic, but where legal prohibitions would be impractical, intrusive or counterproductive. Socialist feminists need to say more about the nature and context of sex work, the effects of different legal policies on women and to analyse these within our anti-capitalist and anti-patriarchal values.[3] In this paper I will

---

1 This chapter was first published in a 2014 issue of *Logos*, and was originally going to be co-authored with Johanna Brenner. For reasons of space, different foci and somewhat different conclusions, we decided to do separate articles. But her contribution was invaluable throughout the writing of this article. I also wish to express my thanks to the following for their helpful suggestions and comments: Alexandra Holmstrom-Smith, Laura Esikoff, Jan Haaken, Meena Dhanda, Eleni Varikas, and Elizabeth Rapaport.
2 See *The Economist* 2014; Gira Grant 2014. Some reactions include Politt 2014 and Sarah Ditum 2014. For the earlier debates, see Ferguson, Philipson, Diamond and Quinby, Vance and Barr Snitow 1984; Walkowitz 1983.
3 I am using 'socialist feminist' to include anyone trying to understand women's subordination in a coherent and systematic way that integrates class and sex, as well as other aspects of identity such as race/ethnicity or sexual orientation, with the aim of using this analysis to help liberate women.

primarily be focusing on the political philosophical issues central to the debate, but in conclusion I will indicate the practical directions to which I think my analysis points. Others will be addressing different programs and policies in detail.

2 What Is Sex Work?

'Sex work' can be conceived broadly or narrowly. Women's bodies are objectified and commodified throughout our capitalist and patriarchal society. Whether the commodity is toothpaste, cars, clothes, music or food, women's bodies or body parts are used to attract buyers and excite or calm customers. (I once had to wear an abbreviated leopard print outfit for a waitress job.) So even many 'normal' jobs done by women could be seen as being to some extent sex work. Then there are the jobs more usually understood as sex work, which are quite varied, from stripping, pole dancing or lap dancing, 'dirty-talking' conversation, erotic massage, fetish work, pornographic modelling or acting, and selling sexual services. So the category of sex work should be seen as a continuum.

There is no question these are all work and should be recognized as such. However, although it is useful politically to unite all sex workers, for this paper I will concentrate on the sale of sexual services, usually called prostitution, as the paradigm case of sex work. It is the most stigmatized and also the most controversial and problematic from a feminist moral/political point of view. It is imperative in the discussion that we recognize and keep in mind the huge variations within the business of prostitution, depending on whether it is part time, occasional or full-time, whether it is in hotel suites or on the streets, whether it is high paid and relatively safe or highly dangerous and poorly paid, whether the prostitute is an adult or very young, addicted or not, subject to direct coercion or not, and so on. When we are urged, therefore, to consider the experience of prostitutes themselves, it is important to know who it is that is speaking. But leaving aside these differences for the moment, all forms of prostitution—by definition—involve 'payment for unilateral use of a woman's body without desire or erotic attraction on her part'.[4] I am limiting my discussion to the sale of sex by women to men, as women make up 80% of 'the commercial sex workforce' and men are the vast majority of buyers of

---

4 Pateman 2007, p. 227.

sex from men as well.⁵ Transgender people appear to be over-represented in prostitution, perhaps because their access to other employment is limited by transphobia. (Despite these clear gender patterns, an odd feature of some of the debate is that it is carried on in gender-neutral language!) What I have to say about prostitution should apply to the other occupations on the sex work continuum to a greater or lesser extent depending on their proximity to prostitution.

3   Political/Economic Context

We live in days of hyper-charged global capitalism with greater inequality globally and domestically than at any point in history. Neo-liberalism has meant cutbacks in already meagre or non-existent social supports. Some have profited enormously in this environment, some a little, and others not at all. Women are disproportionately among the latter group. Everywhere peoples' aspirations are higher. This political/economic context has created both a greater supply and a greater demand for sex workers. Women now make up half of the world's migrants, legal and illegal. Some women migrate in order to become sex workers, some are recruited and helped to get into the business, often under false pretences, and others are trafficked by criminal gangs—and these should not be conflated.⁶ Undocumented immigrants, often racialized, are particularly vulnerable to abuse. The newly rich in some countries buy a night at a brothel for colleagues and friends the way one buys a round of drinks; most men working in a globalized industry can now afford a prostitute. Sex is a multi-billion dollar growth industry globally, and it is a central piece of many developing countries' economies. Our pensions may be invested in huge 'entertainment' and 'hospitality' corporations where sex is available for purchase. At the lowest end of the industry, the women are literally enslaved.⁷

---

5   *The Economist* 2014.
6   For example, the English anti-trafficking law does not require that a person is trafficked for sex against their will or with the use of coercion or force. Simply arranging or facilitating the arrival in the United Kingdom of another person for the purpose of prostitution is considered human trafficking. This is not helpful to those who have been coerced or deceived into becoming sex workers.
7   See Bales 1999 for a horrific discussion of the lowest end of the industry. Bales, one of the world's experts on slavery, estimates that there are a half million to a million prostitutes in Thailand of whom one in twenty is enslaved. (Slavery is not limited to the sex industry. His conservative estimate is 27 million people.)

4 Empowerment vs. Power, Agency and Freedom

To say that all kinds of sex work are work, as they certainly are, says nothing about their voluntariness (after all, slaves work), or about what moral value we should place on this work. These are the questions to be addressed next.

The word empowerment is often used in this discussion, and it is important to distinguish it from actual power. Empowerment refers to a psychological quality of an individual. Power, on the other hand, can be used to apply to individuals or very large groups, but it refers to objective, not subjective phenomena. Note that something could be 'empowering' for certain women, but dis-empowering for women in general. Also note that if something is empowering for an individual, it does not follow that they have more power. In the literature about sex services there is a lot of ethnographic evidence that prostitutes have different kinds and levels of negotiating power. Some have little or none and others have more, for example, whether or not they can refuse to work with a particular customer or refuse to do certain acts. One study of prostitutes in New Zealand found that many said that the new law, which makes it illegal to purchase sex without a condom, had increased their ability to force clients to wear them.

Along with empowerment, the concepts of agency, emancipation and free or voluntary choice are employed in this debate, but often in unclear ways. Acts and choices are not simply free or unfree. Rather, freedom is always relative, on a continuum, in a context. So to counter-pose oppression and empowerment, as so many writers do, is misleading. An act/choice could be more free than the alternatives, it could be an expression of agency and personal empowerment to that extent, but still be profoundly unfree because of the paucity of choices that the agent would prefer.

A poignant and extreme, non-sexual, example of this point is found in the prize-winning book *Behind the Beautiful Forevers* about life in a Mumbai slum: Meena, a young woman who is forbidden to go to school, often beaten, facing an arranged marriage in a village, has a friend Manju whom she only talks with at the public toilets. 'The minutes in the night stench with Manju were the closest she had ever come to freedom'. Shortly thereafter she eats rat poison ...

> 'She wasn't acting out of anger ... She'd thought it through—had consumed two tubes of rat poison on two other days, but had started to vomit, which led her this time to mix the poison with milk. She hoped the milk would keep the poison in her stomach long enough to kill her.
> This was one decision about her life she got to make. It wasn't easily shared with a best friend'. In hospital she says 'I decided for myself' ...

'She was fed up with what the world had to offer', the Tamil women concluded. Meena's family, upon consideration, decided that Manju's modern influence was to blame'.[8]

If Meena had chosen to run away and become a prostitute the same point would apply; an agent can judge an option to be the best of the available options and choose it carefully and deliberately; hence the act could be said to be free, or empowering, or an expression of agency—but only in the most minimal sense—because at the same time, a choice is profoundly unfree if it is merely the least evil of the options available.

Consider an example further towards the free end of the continuum, of poor single mothers who choose sex work 'not simply as a survival strategy; [but] as an *advancement* strategy'.[9] They believe that sex work will be more lucrative than factory or domestic work, especially in a sex tourist destination like Sosua, Dominican Republic. Seeking to escape not only poverty, but the machismo of their countrymen, their goal is to find a tourist who will take them out of the country. In most cases, that hope turns out to be illusory and they return home as poor as when they left; this is true even for the ones who do manage to get a visa. Faced as they are both with capitalism and patriarchy, their carefully thought-out strategies, which the researcher takes pains to stress, can take them only so far. Again, this example shows there is no inconsistency between saying people are exercising resourcefulness and agency, attempting to maximize their possibilities, but within very oppressive constraints.

Thus, the conditions under which people choose determine to what extent their choices are free; these conditions can pose obstacles to doing something or they can enable them. More precisely, to say one is free is to say one is free *from* an obstacle preventing one from doing something; one is unfree *to do* something because an obstacle prevents one from doing it. Thus one can be free to do something with respect to one obstacle and unfree to do it with respect to another obstacle. The obstacles may be physical or may involve persons in some significant way. Thus legal restrictions have been obstacles to women living their lives as they want, as has direct force or threat of force, both of which count as coercion. But people can limit others' freedom in less overt ways. Certain kinds of proposals or offers can also prevent someone from acting freely.

---

8   Boo 2014, pp. 185–8.
9   Brennan 2002.

For example, if an employer offers a dangerous and low paid job to someone whose only alternative is starvation for her and her family, this should count as a 'forcing offer'.[10]

Not only individuals, but social institutions may limit someone's freedom. This can be missed if we focus only on individuals. The absence of childcare can prevent a woman from taking a job and the need for medical care can force someone to take a dangerous job they hate. More generally, lack of money functions as an obstacle to people acting freely, despite the opinion of many learned philosophers to the contrary.[11] Certainly, it is experienced as such. Finally, internal obstacles (often caused by the external constraints) can limit one's freedom: mental illness or addiction, or lack of self-confidence, fears, patriarchal ideas of gender roles, guilt or shame.[12] All these kinds of obstacles would have to be eliminated for women to choose more freely whether or not to be prostitutes.

5   A 'Work Ethic instead of a Sex Ethic?'

Calling prostitution work is an attempt to remove it from sexual moralising and from the picture of all prostitutes as victims, thereby opening up possibilities for prostitutes to organize for rights as workers. But some critics, in particular, Kathi Weeks and Peter Frase, have argued that calling prostitution sex work buys into a different morality, the work ethic, claiming legitimacy by association with traditional work values. And this ethic must be resisted by radicals.[13] From their perspective, the problem with sex work is 'not the sex, but the work'. Frase quotes a sex worker who says yes, it's degraded; but so is all work in capitalist society. While this anti- (or post-)work politics has some political validity, we think it is over-simplified and unhelpful in this debate. After discussing work in general we turn to the question of sex work in particular.

If selling sexual services is work, how should we understand that work? To address this question it is worth a detour into Karl Marx's rich discussions of work/labour, which I believe are unrivalled in their subtlety, but which have often been misinterpreted. As readers know, Marxists contend that all wage

---

10   Ezorsky 2007.
11   John Rawls is among those who deny that lack of money is a limitation on freedom, though he says it may affect the 'worth' of someone's liberty. See Rawls 1971. Also see Pettit 2001, which groups poverty with 'natural limits' on freedom like illness.
12   Holmstrom and Cudd 2011, pp. 145–85.
13   See Weeks 2011, and Frase 2012.

labour involves exploitation and alienation and that this is a chief reason why capitalism should be replaced by 'a higher form of society', as Marx often put it. In capitalist societies, workers are free of legal bonds but also free of any means of subsistence. Hence they have no choice but (i.e. they are forced) to work for the owners of the means of production who control the labour process and the labourer and who get to keep the product of their labour. This—in great brevity—is exploitation and also alienation.[14]

Defenders of capitalism describe the situation differently, of course. In capitalism they say, everyone owns something, even if it is only 'themselves', and hence their own labour power, and therefore that the wage relation is a voluntary exchange between two individual commodity owners, simply a buyer and a seller. The two principal classes that constitute capitalism, with their vastly unequal power vis-a-vis this 'transaction', disappear. But to call either labour or labour power a commodity is essentially a legal fiction (like declaring corporations persons). Certainly labour power is unlike other commodities; unlike other things I 'own', it can't be stolen or left on the bus! This is because it consists of mental and physical energies, capacities, potentials, and hence cannot be separated from the labourer to whom they belong, but exist only in 'his living self', Marx says. Labour is the expression of these.[15] Wherever my labour power/labour goes, I have to go with it; whatever is done to it, is done to me. So the worker who 'sells their labour power' is selling their selves to the owner, albeit with temporal and other limitations.[16] The domination of capitalists over workers due to their monopoly of the means of production is continually reproduced and increased through the process of production.

Behind Marx's condemnation of wage labour as exploited and alienated is a very different view of what human labour can and should be. In a very early work, *The Economic and Philosophical Manuscripts* on alienation, Marx says 'The whole character of a species—its species character—is contained in the character of its life-activity; and free, conscious activity is man's species character'.[17] Thus one aspect of alienation is alienation from the human species

---

14 Holmstrom 1977a.
15 In his early work Marx talked of workers selling their labour; later he changed this to labour power. Though the distinction is crucial for the theory of surplus value, it is not important to us here.
16 The illusion that labour power is an entity separable from the person may have come to seem more plausible after Descartes' separation of the mind from the body and his identification of the self, the 'I' with the mind. This entails both an ontological and conceptual separation of the body from the person, along with the devaluation of the body, leading to intractable sceptical problems.
17 Marx 1975a, pp. 276–7.

character. This view of the special character of human labour is elaborated upon in a much later work *The Grundrisse*, where he criticizes Adam Smith's account of work as sacrifice, saying that while this is true of exploited work ('external, forced labour'), this is not true of work as such. Yes, work always involves some external goal, he says, but overcoming obstacles can be liberating when they are goals set by the individual; then work is *'self-realization, objectification of the subject, hence real freedom, whose action is, precisely, labour'*. In the same passage he criticizes the utopian socialist Fourier, whose views sound like the anti-work writers. In contrast to Fourier's vision of labour in a socialist society as essentially play, Marx says *'Really free working, e.g. composing is at the same time precisely the most damned seriousness, the most intense exertion'* (emphasis mine).[18]

In *Capital* Volume III Marx distinguishes different kinds of necessity and different kinds of freedom. He distinguishes a realm of necessity and a realm of freedom. In any society, he says there will always be some labour required by physical necessity—but this, he says, is consistent with a different kind of freedom:

'Freedom in this field can only consist in socialized man, the associated producers, rationally regulating their interchange with Nature, bringing it under their common control, instead of being ruled by it as by the blind forces of Nature; and achieving this with the least expenditure of energy and under conditions most favourable to, and worthy of, their human nature. But it nevertheless remains a realm of necessity. Beyond it begins that development of human energy which is an end in itself, the true realm of freedom, which, however, can blossom forth only with the realm of necessity as its basis. The shortening of the working day is its basic prerequisite'.[19]

This account of freedom within necessity as consisting of rational collective control underscores the connection between Marx's view of human nature and his commitment to a radical democratic vision of socialism.

So in Marx's view labour (work) is not inherently oppressive. In fact, when it is determined by an individual's wants, needs, passions, it is free in the fullest possible sense. When on the other hand, the work is required by the facts of nature, (i.e. what satisfies our physical needs requires work to get it), it can still be free in a more limited sense, if it is *we who* decide how to do it. Finally, within wage work, though always exploited from a Marxist point of view, there

---

18   Marx 1986, p. 530. This example shows that Marx's conception of humans' distinctive kind of productive activity is not limited to material production and is in no way 'productivist'. It is strikingly similar to what some contemporary psychologists call 'flow'.
19   Marx 1998, 867.

are many variations which make the work better or worse for the worker: the amount of control exercised by the worker, how direct is the capitalist's control over the worker/work, the remuneration and respect accorded to it, how intrinsically attractive or repulsive the work is to the worker, how difficult and how dangerous it is, physically or emotionally, and so on.

Marx's accounts in *Capital* of the degradation of work as capitalism developed, of the loss of all 'charm' and 'interest', making the work a kind of 'torture', of the de-skilling of the worker, of transforming the worker into 'an appendage of the machine', are eloquent testimony to his appreciation of this fact (as is the participation of Marxists in struggles for better working conditions.) Some workers in capitalism enjoy their work, believing it to be worthy work, some few are even fortunate enough to do for pay what they would want to do anyway. Thus Marx's general account and condemnation of wage labour as exploited and alienated in no way denies these qualitative and quantitative differences—which we will draw on when we discuss sex work in particular. But his concluding line in the quote above about the necessity of a shorter work day reaffirms that we all need more time to pursue the activities we most care about, 'really free working', whether these be composing music, teaching children or working on machines. We also need more time for 'eating, sleeping, procreating', but these activities do not have the same *distinctively human* importance for Marx.

Notice that this critique of wage labour is distinct from a critique of the work itself. A great deal of the work done in capitalism would not be done in a socialist society (e.g. wasteful production of junk or products designed for obsolescence, figuring out how to get people to buy things they don't need or manufacturing instruments of torture). On the other hand, much other work that is done today would be necessary in any society, including an ideal non-capitalist one, although it would be done in humane and environmentally sustainable ways. The latter point entails that there would have to be *substantially less* production of things altogether. This eco-socialist argument dovetails with the goal of the anti-work writers. Meanwhile, however, an anti- (or post-)work politics should not be used to deny the important qualitative and political differences between types of work or the importance of the struggle for better jobs. Therefore we can ignore this perspective in our analysis of sex work.

6   Is Sex Special?

Most prostitution, and sex work in general, is exploited in a Marxist sense in that pimps, brothel owners, and perhaps multi-national corporations are making a profit from the sale of the prostitute's labour. But if this exploitation were removed because the prostitute worked for herself, as some do today, or for a sex workers' cooperative, would it still be problematic? In other words, does the moral/political objection to prostitution go beyond the exploitative character of most of the work? If it were de-criminalized, should it be seen as similar to any other service work? *The Economist* recently editorialized for just this position with a cover depicting a sexy young woman cutting her ball and chain, and some feminists agree. The key to her freedom according to *The Economist* is the Internet, allowing her to transact freely with prospective clients, negotiate the services and price and pointed to web sites where clients can evaluate their experience, like on Trip Advisor, and sites where prostitutes can expose bad clients, e.g. Blacklist. The web service would be something like Task Rabbit, but instead of selling babysitting, shopping, housework, painting, paper work, etc., the services would be sexual intercourse (anal intercourse at a higher price), fellatio (without a condom a high price), spanking or heavier S&M (also more expensive), masturbation, etc.[20]

Though the precarity of the working conditions are similar and perhaps the average pay might be the same (because so many can enter the business so easily), or better, I do not think that the latter commodified sexual services are the same as the service work done by the Task Rabbits. This opinion is not based on sexual prudery (on the contrary), on outdated romantic notions, or on the belief that all prostitutes are victims (though many are). In part, my judgment regarding most instances of prostitution is based on the political economic context discussed earlier; economic pressures put the choice to do this work decidedly on the unfree side of the free/unfree continuum for the great majority. However, even for those in a situation allowing a greater variety of choices that are not totally awful, I believe that prostitution is not 'simply a kind of service work' and is not work that feminists should regard as unproblematic.

What is the prostitute selling? Certain sexual services. But just as rape is not primarily about sex, prostitution is about more than that. For most individuals, sexual satisfaction is, after all, as Carole Pateman has pointed out, always 'at hand'. And sexual services cannot be separated from the sale (or rent) of the body that supplies those services.[21] The client is buying the right to use a woman's body as he wishes, without any desire on her part. Once she has contracted to provide a particular service—assuming she has this power to set

---

20 This is based on the extensive survey of sex work advertisements reported in *The Economist* 2014.
21 Gira Grant insists that the prostitute is not selling her body but selling sexual services. See Grant 2014, p. 94.

limits—she has to allow him to *enter into* her body, her vagina, her mouth, her anus, to put his hands all over her body, and she must do whatever she has contracted to do to his body with her hands and mouth. This is domination at a most intimate level, whether or not he plays the dominating role in the interaction; it may be he who wants to be penetrated or spanked. It is the client's power to determine that and how he gets sexual satisfaction from a prostitute that makes male domination central to prostitution, not a male desire to dominate.

And, except at the lowest end of the business where there is no pretence, she must pretend to be enjoying it; the interaction, therefore, is always a charade, a performance on the prostitute's part. Thus what the client is buying (renting) is not only her body, but the (appearance of) her emotions. If she just lies there and looks at her watch, he will not be satisfied; an important part of what he is buying is the appearance of her pleasure. His motivation may be to dominate a woman, to affirm his masculinity to himself or others, to have (particular kinds of) sexual experiences because he cannot get them without paying for them, or he may be looking for bodily/emotional connection (kissing costs more too), or to have a 'girlfriend experience' without responsibilities. Whichever it is, the prostitute is selling him the right to use her body in this way. This indicates an important difference from the employment contract, as Pateman has pointed out. What the capitalist is paying workers for is to use their bodies to make products, and workers' bodies can be replaced by machines. Not so in prostitution

Of course, 'emotional labour' is not unique to prostitutes. Arlie Hochschild's work has shown how much work today, especially by women, involves emotional labour, where workers pretend to feel what they do not feel because delivering the service in a certain way is part of the service.[22] She shows that there is a serious cost: the alienation of workers from their feelings. The flight attendant becomes estranged from her smile, she says; it is not hers anymore. Hochschild's powerful work illuminating the emotional dimension of most prostitutes' work, but it does not convey the half of it since other emotional labour jobs do not involve letting a client use her body as he wishes. While Pateman's distinction between the employment contract and the prostitute/client relationship is less true of service work, many services—from bank tellers to sales people to financial planners—are now self service through machines and the Internet. Even flight attendants, because of speed up and feminism, are no longer required to give such personal feminized service.

---

22   Hochschild 2012.

It is because human sexual experiences are highly intimate and both physical and emotional that they can range from ecstatic to horrific and everything in between. Only with great effort of dissociation is sex ever *purely* physical, which can be a useful defence, but this often takes a psychic toll. Consider the fact that prostitutes, especially street prostitutes, as well as soldiers and war victims, often suffer from PTSD, whereas other low status, dangerous, physically demanding jobs don't have that particular effect, which is due to its emotionally damaging experiences, as much as violence and fear of violence.[23] The body is where we experience pleasure and pain. Indeed, it is the original site of emotions, of our very selves. Research has shown that babies who are not picked up and held are damaged emotionally and may 'fail to thrive' physically, even when their basic physical needs are met. So the right kind of physical contact is crucial to emotional and physical well-being. On the other hand, the wrong kind of physical contact can be traumatic. Even when conscious memory is gone the body retains experiences, e.g. of abuse, which is why abusers were usually abused as children. That's why we tell children that they should decide if they want to be touched and how. Thus selling sexual services is not like selling other services. Selling intimate bodily experiences is a kind of ultimate alienation (which has degrees, as discussed above).

In a non-patriarchal, non-capitalist society, would this still be true? Yes and no. Since human beings are simultaneously physical and emotional/social beings, the body and its experiences, early and throughout life, including how an individual decides to use it, would still be crucial to that person's physical and emotional well-being. In the absence of patriarchal and capitalist pressures to use their bodies in dangerous and degrading ways, some women might nevertheless choose to provide sex to strangers without desire on their part. (Let us take at face value their answer to the question of why they choose this).

---

23 Empirical research on these matters is difficult to do and more difficult to assess, particularly since so much of the work is clandestine, especially at the low end of the industry, including the not-insignificant number of prostitutes working in slavery-like conditions. Hence their experience at the low end of the business will be under-represented in the data. Nevertheless the data show that prostitution is dangerous, but that the conditions under which it is done can either heighten or minimize the dangers. Street workers are at greater risk of violence from clients, but 17% of indoor workers had experienced attempted rape. Hardly a normal service job. Church, Henderson, Barnard, Hart 2001, pp. 524–5. Other researchers show high rates of PTSD even among indoor sex workers. Farley *et al.* 2003, pp. 33–74. How much this would change with legalization is debated. Prostitutes' protection against AIDS is likely enhanced by legalization as it increases their ability to insist on the use of condoms. However, since *The Economist*'s survey showed men will pay more for sex without condoms, this could act like the 'forcing offer' described earlier.

Some might even choose to do it as a regular thing, as a service to those who were unable to satisfy their sexual and emotional needs through personal relationships. But if so, that would be more like being a sex therapist than what is understood today as a prostitute (consider the film The Sessions) The crucial point is that the power relationships of the society at large and between the two people would be totally different—and hence both its nature and its effects, both individually and socially, would be different.

My description of sex in prostitution as ultimate alienation is similar to sex in patriarchal marriages in that husbands control when and how they have sex with their wives. (Consider how recently the very concept of marital rape was considered incoherent.) Sometimes women do not get to choose their husbands in the first place or they do so for financial reasons. Thus socialist feminists have always been fierce critics of traditional marriages. Emma Goldman referred to 'prostitution—public and private', saying '… it is merely a question of degree whether she sells herself to one man, in or out of marriage, or to many men …'. From the 19th and early 20th century figures like Emma Goldman and Alexandra Kollontai to socialist feminists today, the central goal has been sexual liberation: the freedom to choose if and when and how and with whom to have sexual relations. Women should be free to choose whatever partner, male or female, they want and to have sex for love, for lust, for friendship, for fun, for procreation, for comfort or whatever else the lovers want. Fortunately, in developed countries especially, women and men are more and more able to form personal relationships based on love and friendship rather than direct coercion from families and the law.[24] Same sex couples are a dramatic example of the enormous expansion of human freedom and personal happiness that this has brought.

The fiction at the heart of capitalist ideology that one can sell parts of one's self without selling oneself, and that doing so is an exercise of freedom rather than domination has led to the commodification of everything that people do not resist in defence of other values, intruding into the most intimate areas of our lives.[25] Libertarians see nothing wrong with selling one's organs. But while that may be all a person has to sell, this should never be construed as a free act. The same is true of sex; it may in fact be the only 'commodity' a woman has

---

24 Whether these are legalized as 'marriages' or not is not so important as the fact that increasingly numbers of people today are in long term intimate relationships based on mutual desire and respect. Thus 'marriage' has been able to be fundamentally reformed in a way that prostitution cannot be, though the conditions may be somewhat improved. See Pateman 2007, p. 227.
25 Anderson 1990, pp. 179–205.

to offer on the market, but this should be understood as an expression of the poverty of her choices in our capitalist patriarchal system.

7 What Is To Be Done?

Given our global political/economic system, both the demand for prostitutes and their supply are not likely to be eliminated anytime soon. The challenge for socialist feminists therefore is how to support women working as prostitutes without giving up our critique of the work and the institution of prostitution. But support for the women in the business must always be conjoined with struggles to change the political economic conditions that push so many into it. We should fight for jobs with living wages, affordable housing and childcare, substance abuse programs, help with immigration problems and whatever else sex workers say they need.

A first step is recognising that prostitution is work and that those in the business deserve the same protections as citizens and as workers as everyone else. Egregious conditions sometimes exist in the industry, including debt bondage and other slavery or slavery like conditions. However, these are neither inherent nor unique to the sex industry. Women and men are trafficked or caught in debt bondage to work in agriculture, manufacture, carpet weaving and as domestics. But of these super-exploited people, prostitutes are the only ones who are also criminalized, depriving them of what international and local legal protections exist. Though not enforced as they should be, these conventions provide some basis for pressure by those affected and by their supporters. Therefore all laws against the selling of sex should be removed. Then prostitutes will be free to organize and work with other sex workers and activist organisations to improve their conditions and those in other industries. Given their limited options some women will choose prostitution as the best available option; indeed some go to great lengths to get into the industry. They should not be deprived of their right to make this choice.[26]

In recent years other legal changes have been put into effect that seek to protect prostitutes and promote feminist goals. In 1999 Sweden adopted a law decriminalising the selling of sex, but criminalising the client, the pimp and the brothel owner. It has since been enacted elsewhere and has become known as the Nordic model. I am sympathetic to their goals of protecting the women in

---

26 This is the strong position of Anti-Slavery International which argues that it is prostitutes' exclusion from society that encourages slavery and slavery-like conditions. See Holmstrom 2002.

the trade, but reducing the number of women choosing it, which, they argue, is in the best interests both of prostitutes and women throughout society (and ultimately of men as well).[27] However, I have some doubts about the model. If in fact prostitution is the best option for a woman given her particular circumstances, then criminalising her clients will make it difficult for her to do the job. Sweden's social support system gives women better choices than in most countries. However even there it is not clear how the law has worked. (I leave others to examine this question in detail.) In poorer countries, and less generous countries like the United States, such a law would be counterproductive to prostitutes' interests. They are doing the work because they feel they have to.

A variant of the Nordic model that would not have this disadvantage is more attractive to me: decriminalising both the selling and the buying of sex, but criminalising pimps and brothel owners. The reasons are simple. First, no one should be allowed to profit from the labour of prostitutes except prostitutes themselves. Second, the profitability of the sex business creates an enormous incentive to recruit women into the business. Such a law would help to eliminate that incentive. One line of objection to this proposal would be that prostitutes need the protection they get from pimps and brothels. My response is that prostitutes could organize to provide for themselves whatever benefits they may sometimes get from pimps and brothels. They can hire someone as a driver or bodyguard, they can rent an apartment from which they can work and organize the work themselves in a cooperative way. Another objection would be that such a law could expose friends, relatives, employees and landlords of the prostitute to arrest because they are mistaken as pimps and brothel owners. This is possible, just as innocent parents are occasionally arrested for child abuse. This shows the importance of careful crafting of the law to minimize the arrest or harassment of those who are not pimps or brothel owners. It also would require education and training of the police and active involvement by prostitutes' organisations to monitor the effects of the law.[28]

I offer the above proposal in a very tentative way. I am far from an expert and the crucial question is how it would work in practice. At this stage I think we need to experiment with different legal and social models and see what works

---

27 Ekman 2014.
28 The Red Umbrella Project (www.redumbrellaproject.org) is the kind of organisation I have in mind. It works to 'amplify … the voices of people in the sex trades through media, advocacy and storytelling programs'. They helped change the law allowing police to use a woman having condoms as evidence of her engaging in prostitution and they have observed and done a report on New York's special Anti-Trafficking Courts to see how they have worked in practice.

and what does not, working towards best practices to advance the interests of those in the sex business and support those who wish to leave. Whatever legal changes and social policies are considered vis-a-vis the sex industry, the organisations of sex workers themselves should be given a central role in formulating and implementing them. But finally, legislation should never be the central part of the discussion.

CHAPTER 4

'Women's Work', the Family and Capitalism

It is striking that just when women are becoming an increasingly important part of the paid work force (43% in the U.S.),*,1 theoretical debate has centred on their work within the family. Some of the discussion of women's domestic labour seems shockingly out of touch with the dramatic change in their working lives. This lack of awareness is evident in reference to domestic labour as 'women's work'. Nevertheless, as many feminists have vigorously argued, women's lives are still dominated by their role in the family, even when they are also wage workers. The question arises as to whether and how far this fact can change. Can women be integrated into the workforce on an equal basis with men? What impact would equality in the workforce have on their role in the family? Can the family be eliminated under capitalism?

Before any of these questions can be answered, the role of the family within capitalism has to be understood. If only because the family has survived, albeit battered and changed, it is widely assumed that it is in some way beneficial to capitalism. But exactly how and what follows from this has not been clear. A central aspect of the question of the relationship of the family to capitalism is the question of the relation of domestic labour to capital. It is primarily this aspect of the question on which I will focus in this paper. Questions about the relation of the family and domestic labour to capital frequently underlie serious political/strategic disputes within the women's and socialist movements, and hence are of more than theoretical interest.

This chapter shares the view that women's labour in the home is critical to capitalism as well as to women's role in society and that one of the key reasons the family has survived is that domestic labour benefits capitalism. However, I argue, as have others, that domestic labour does not benefit capitalism by producing surplus value or value and I explain both why it is a mistake to try to make these concepts fit domestic labour and why people have been led to these mistaken views. Rather, domestic labour benefits capitalism by reducing the value of labour power. Although this does not mean that it is most benefi-

---

* I wish to thank the following people. whose discussion of the issues whose comments on an earlier draft were helpful to me: Kathy Blee, Robert Fitch, Alan Schiffman, Anwar Shaikh, Erik Olin Wright, and the editors of Marxist Perspectives.
1 Bureau of Labor Statistics.

cial to capitalism for women to remain in the home full time, it does limit the extent to which they can be fully integrated into the workforce. Another factor that maintains the family is the importance of women's super-exploitation as wage workers and the obvious benefits of this to capitalism:[2] I also contend that despite the fact that women in the family do not produce surplus value they are exploited in Marx's sense of the term, primarily by capital, although men in general share in this exploitation to some extent. On the other hand, the household does not constitute a mode of production nor do women constitute a class in Marx's sense of these terms, and there are not good reasons to revise the concepts. Along the way an effort will be made to indicate the political/strategic implications of these issues.

∴

Margaret Benston was one of the first writers in recent years to stress women's production within the family as critical to capitalism and to their position within capitalism.[3] According to Benston, the fact that a massive amount of socially necessary labour gets done in the nuclear family for free is one of the primary ways in which the traditional social/sexual arrangement is so beneficial to capitalism. Benston identifies the fact that this production is for use rather than exchange as the material basis for the inferior status of women in capitalist society. 'In a society in which money determines value, women are a group which works outside the money economy'.[4]

---

2 I am not saying that domestic labour, the family, and the associated sexual/social relations exist because they are beneficial to capitalism. Fortunately not everything that happens is beneficial to capitalism. And it would be quite miraculous if their benefits to capitalism were the cause of their existence. They existed long before capitalism. Hence I am not (intentionally at least) offering a functionalist argument. What I am assuming is that in the context of a capitalist mode of production, and barring some significant social struggle, the usefulness of something to capitalism explains how it functions, how and why it changes, and why it continues. Cf. Fisk 1981 for a valuable discussion of these points. I also do not mean to imply that these are the only ways that the family benefits capitalism nor that the capitalist class is the only beneficiary of the family. I agree with Humphries (1977) that the role of working-class struggle in maintaining the family has too often been ignored in an emphasis on the needs of capital. However, I take this point as an addition to, not a negation of, the arguments developed here.
3 Benston 1969. Benston in fact *defines* women as 'the group which is responsible for the production of simple use values in those activities associated with the home and family'.
4 Ibid., p. 202.

Some feminists argue that this is merely apparent. Mariarosa dalla Costa[5] and other proponents of this view[6] argue that the absence of a wage hides the real economic position of the housewife in capitalist society. In fact, they argue, '... domestic work not only produces use values but is an essential function in the production of surplus value'. This because on a daily and a generational basis, the labour of housewives 'serves the reproduction of labour power',[7] the commodity whose use produces surplus value.

If we stick to Marx's definition of productive labour, which these writers claim to be using,[8] their position is simply incorrect. Productive labour in a general sense is the production of use values. In this sense domestic labour is certainly productive. However, Marx says that 'this method of determining, from the standpoint of the labour process alone, what is productive labor, is by no means directly applicable in the case of the capitalist mode of production'.[9] 'Productive labor, in its meaning for capitalist production, is wage labor which ... reproduces not only "the value of its own labour power, but in addition produces surplus value for the capitalist"'.[10] Since only labour which is directly exchanged with capital can produce surplus value, domestic labour cannot be productive labour.

Dalla Costa and the others who share her position mistakenly assume that if labour is necessary for the production of surplus value it therefore produces surplus value.[11] Marx, however, rejects the notion of labour that is 'indirectly productive of surplus value'. Much of the labour Marx classifies as unproductive is necessary for the production of surplus value, e.g., most supervisory labour. Surplus value could not be produced without a whole army of people whose function is, in Marx's words, to exercise despotic control over the workers. It does not follow that this control produces surplus value. Rather, it 'belongs to the incidental expenses of production in the same way as 9/10 of the "labor" occasioned by the circulation process'.[12]

---

5   Dalla Costa and James 1972.
6   Larguia and Dumolin 1972.
7   Dalla Costa and James 1972, pp. 30–1.
8   E.g., Ibid., fn. 12, p. 52.
9   Marx 1970, p. 181.
10   Marx1969, p. 152.
11   Cf. Larguia and Dumblin 1972, who say, 'It is only with these hours of invisible labor that the proletariat can produce surplus value in the economy. It can therefore be said that women's labor in the home is *transferred into the creation of surplus value through the wage labor force*'.
12   Marx 1969, Vol. 3 p. 505; Vol. 2, pp. 355–6.

Marx also excludes as unproductive some labour that would be necessary in any system. For example, the labour of a cook employed by a private individual is not productive because the individual buys his or her labour 'not as a value-creating element but purely for the sake of its use value'.[13] Once again, to be productive in the context of capitalism, labour must be wage labour, exchanged with capital, and moreover 'only that wage labor is productive which produces capital'.[14] Whether it is necessary, in this or any other system, is another question. Rosa Luxemburg expressed this well when she said that from the standpoint of capital:

> the dancer in a cafe, who makes a profit for her employer with her legs, is a productive working woman, while all the toil of the women and mothers of the proletariat within the four walls of the home is considered unproductive work. [This] sounds crude and crazy but it is an accurate expression of the crudeness and craziness of today's economic order.[15]

Some of those who argue that domestic labour is productive are aware of what Marx meant by productive labour but believe that the notion has to be broadened in ways that would include housework. It is sometimes said to be a sign of sexism that 'women's work' is unproductive in Marx's schema. Some argue that the distinction should be eliminated although they wish to remain within Marx's theoretical framework.[16]

If we consider the reasons for Marx's restrictions on the concept, it should be clear that it is in no way sexist, and that it is futile to alter the concept and try to retain the framework. Calling it apologist, Marx ridicules the view that all labour is productive in capitalism with an amusing discussion of the productivity of the criminal.[17] To understand capitalism requires understanding what is productive from the point of view of capitalism as a specific mode of production. Although commodities must have some use value in capitalism, this is not why they are produced. The aim of production in capitalism is the creation of surplus value, the self-expansion of value, and this has its source in labour power. This is why Marx says:

---

13 Marx 1969, Vol 1, p. 165.
14 Ibid., p. 152.
15 Luxemburg, 'Women's Suffrage and the Class Struggle', in Holmstrom 2002, p. 21.
16 For example, Gough and Harrison 1975; or Harrison 1973b. Michael Kidron 1974, says of Harrison's definition of all labour performed in capitalism as productive, 'Not even the most dyed-in-the-wool of the system's trusties would say that when sober'.
17 Marx 1969, Vol. I, pp. 387.

Productive labor is only a concise term for the whole relationship and the form and the manner in which labour power figures in the capitalist production process. The distinction from other kinds of labor is, however, of the greatest importance, since this distinction expresses precisely the specific form of the labor on which the whole capitalist mode of production and capital itself is based.[18]

Given the centrality of Marx's concept of productive labour to his whole theory, the restrictions he puts on it are not arbitrary but essential. It is impossible to eliminate the distinction and retain the rest of the framework.[19] Thus to call labour unproductive in Marx's sense is hardly to say something disparaging about it. If domestic labour is not productive it does not follow that it is unproductive. Labor directly exchanged for money as capital is productive; labour directly exchanged with revenue, that is, wages and profits, is unproductive.[20] We have the latter kind in the sphere of circulation,[21] in public employment, and in the purchase of someone's services merely for the sake of those services.[22] Labor must have a certain relation to capital if it is to be either productive or unproductive. The labour of housewives is neither because it is not exchanged either for money as capital or for money as money.[23]

Some writers, e.g., Secombe,[24] argue that housewives do have this relation to capital, but that it is hidden. He argues that, despite appearances, the wage pays for the labour of the housewife as well as the wage worker. Hence her labour is exchanged with money as revenue and she is a productive worker. However, it is only wage workers who directly exchange their labour power for money, and this is a necessary condition for labour to be productive. The housewife and her labour are supported by a wage, but although she does some of the same things they do, she is not a maid, cook or prostitute. The economic and social relationships (the 'exchanges') are quite different. In the labour done in

---

18   Marx 1969, Vol I, p. 196.
19   Behind some of the arguments for the productivity of domestic labour because it is 'truly necessary' may be a notion similar to Baran's revised concept of 'productive labor': labor is unproductive if it would not be necessary in a socialist society. This is a different notion from Marx's. Just because it would not be necessary does not mean it is not necessary in capitalism. Baran 1975.
20   Marx 1969, Vol. I, p. 157.
21   Marx 1974, Ch. 16 and 17.
22   Marx 1969, Vol I, p. 403.
23   Smith 1978/9 and Terry Fee 1976, also argue that housewives are neither productive nor unproductive workers.
24   Secombe 1973.

the home, the worker '... belongs to himself, and performs his necessary vital functions outside the process of production'.[25] Hence it is neither productive nor unproductive.

Another point of view[26] is that although domestic labour does not produce surplus value (for the reasons given above), it does produce value, not simply use value, because it produces the commodity labour power. The value of this commodity is the amount of simple, abstract, socially necessary labour that goes into producing and reproducing labour power, some of which is embodied in commodities like food and clothing. However, in most cases, additional labour has to be expended on these commodities in order for them to contribute to the reproduction of labour power. For example, the food that is bought must be cooked and served. This labour 'becomes part of the congealed mass of past labor embodied in labour power. The value [the housewife] creates is realized as one part of the value labour power achieves as a commodity when it is sold'.[27]

Because it is necessary for the production and reproduction of labour power, housework is 'a factor in the production and reproduction of capital'.[28] However, it does not follow that housework forms part of the value of this commodity. According to Marx's theory, only that labour which is embodied in commodities required for the production and reproduction of labour power forms the value of labour power. The reason he does not include as part of its value the additional labour often required to convert these commodities into means of subsistence is that he analyses capitalism from the point of view of capital. Given that capitalism is a system devoted to the production of surplus value, the key categories have to be understood in relation to this process. What is relevant to capital in the value of labour power is how much capital has to be paid to workers. This depends on the labour embodied in the commodities they have to purchase. Whether fifteen minutes or three hours go into preparing workers' dinners, whether they are TV dinners or gourmet dinners, is irrelevant to capitalists because this labour does not affect surplus value. Hence it is not part of the value of labour power.[29]

---

25   Marx 1970, p. 571. Marx calls this labor 'individual consumption' as opposed to 'productive consumption'.
26   For example, Secombe 1972; also Gough and Harrison 1975.
27   Secombe 1972, p. 9.
28   Marx, 1970, p. 572.
29   Gardiner 1975; and Coulson, Magas and Wainwright 1975, offer other arguments for the same conclusion.

Other writers have argued that housewives can be compared to simple commodity producers[30] who also are neither productive nor unproductive.[31] Simple commodity producers produce commodities that they then sell on the market, and the amount of labour embodied in them determines their value. Like simple commodity producers, housewives do not sell their labour power to capitalists. However, the analogy stops there. Unlike simple commodity producers, housewives do not produce a commodity and then sell it on the market. They produce use values which contribute to the (re)production of wage workers and their capacity to labour. This labour power becomes a commodity only when it is sold to capitalists on the market. Even if we consider the housewife the producer of labour power we cannot say she produces it/or sale on the market; nor can we say she owns it and then sells it to the capitalists as simple commodity producers do with their products. And only by unreasonably bending the word 'produce' could we say that housework produces labour power. As Gough and Harrison argue, this 'is like saying that a capitalist who produces food and clothing which workers consume is in fact producing labour power. This is quite untenable'.[32]

∴

Thus far I have argued mainly in the negative. The explanations cited of the relationship between domestic labour and capitalism fail because they attempt a Marxist explanation but misuse key Marxist terms. This is not scholastic quibbling. What we are dealing with are paradigmatic examples of what philosophers of science call 'theory-laden' terms. Hence extracting them from the theory or changing them but trying to keep the theory otherwise unchanged cannot be done without theoretical incoherence. Nevertheless many of the substantive statements made in the analyses presented thus far have validity and do point toward more adequate explanations of how domestic labour is beneficial to capitalism.

The labour that is done in the home is necessary, is productive of use values, and contributes to the production of surplus value. For the reasons already explained, this is not the same as being productive of surplus value. However,

---

30 Gerstein 1975 takes this position; Saffiotti 1975; Gardiner 1975; and Coulson, Magas and Wainwright 1975 argue well against this analogy.
31 'They [simple commodity producers] confront me as sellers of commodities not as sellers of labor and this relation therefore has nothing to do with the distinction between productive and unproductive labor ...': Marx 1969, I, p. 407.
32 Gough and Harrison 1975, p. 39.

these facts do make domestic labour beneficial to capitalism. This is because the existence of domestic labour lowers the value of labour power by lowering the cost of reproduction to the capitalist. If all the labour done in the home had to be purchased on the market, capital would be forced to pay a higher percentage of the social cost of reproduction of labour power. The value of labour power would be higher even though the total labour time involved in its (re)production would not have changed. The value of labour power consists in the labour time embodied in the commodities that go into maintaining and reproducing labour power. Thus, although domestic labour is not part of the value of labour power its existence means an increase in the ratio of surplus to necessary labour. Domestic labour allows a higher rate of surplus value because this socially necessary labour is either free or very cheap. An analogous gain accrues to capitalists who require workers to clean and repair the machines on their own time. If capitalists have to pay workers to do the cleaning and repairing of the machines, the costs of reproducing the means of production are higher and therefore their rate of surplus value lower. In both cases capitalists are spared some of the costs of reproducing the means of production. Domestic labor also provides a backup for times when the wage falls below the value of labour power. Housewives can sew clothes or repair old ones rather than buy new ones, provide all the meals at home and use fewer prepared foods, and so on. The fact that domestic labor can expand and contract and take different forms according to economic conditions allows a flexibility to the wage without dramatic social consequences.[33]

It does not follow that a system in which women are full-time domestic labourers is necessarily most profitable for capitalism. On the contrary, the traditional nuclear family with the husband the only wage worker is not most beneficial for capitalism. If women are full-time domestic workers, wages have to be higher because the value of labour power has to include the costs of (the commodities required for) the maintenance and reproduction of two adults rather than one. The wage is then a family wage. If most women as well as men are wage workers, the value of labour power is lower. The wage need support only part of the family. This means that somewhat less socially necessary labor can get done privately and this has to be compensated for by the purchase of commodities on the market. This exerts an upward pressure on the wage. Therefore women becoming wage workers seems to exert two opposite pressures on the value of labour power. However, even when women are full-time wage workers, most of the family's needs are satisfied by domestic labor. The

---

33   See Weinbaum and Bridges, in Eisenstein 1979, and Milkman 1976.

upward pressure on the wage because women are not available to do domestic labor full time is more than compensated for by the downward pressure on the wage because it need not support a whole family. Thus capitalists profit more by having women become wage workers as well as domestic workers, as evidenced by the fact that over 43% of the work-force in the U.S. is now composed of women. The deepening crisis of capitalism makes it unlikely that the family wage can be reinstated. More women are also available for wage work today due to the women's liberation movement and changing demographic patterns. Combined with the increased number of 'women's jobs' in today's economy, it seems likely that women will be an increasing and permanent part of the workforce.

This fact, plus the growth of industries like fast foods designed to meet the needs of working women, raises the question of whether domestic labor could be phased out altogether in the future, with all or almost all the socially necessary labor now done in the home purchased on the market instead. This would benefit those sectors of the capitalist class that produce socially necessary consumer goods. However, this is not the most numerous or significant sector of the capitalist class overall. To see why, it is important to distinguish two questions. One is the question of whether and how far the number of full-time domestic labourers can decrease. This is essentially the question of whether the traditional one-wage nuclear family can be eliminated under capitalism. The other question is whether and how far the amount of domestic labor can decrease—in other words, whether domestic labor can be completely capitalized and purchased in the form of commodities. My answer to the latter question is that there are substantial limits to how much domestic labor can be reduced. Yet this fact also limits somewhat the extent to which the number of full-time domestic labourers can be reduced. Having women do wage work as well as domestic labor lowers the value of labour power. However, if all domestic labor were eliminated this would raise the value of labour power. The wage would have to be considerably higher so that the goods and services previously provided for free could be purchased on the market. This would increase the amount capitalists spend on reproduction, thereby reducing the rate of surplus value. It would not be in the interest of capitalists, therefore, for domestic labor to be reduced beyond what is necessary to enable women to also do wage labor.

Furthermore, one major area of domestic labor poses severe obstacles to capitalisation—child care.[34] This is because it is so expensive. The ratio of

---

34   Socialization under socialism is another question.

worker to child in day-care centres just cannot be that much different from what it is in the home, especially if the centres are expected to do all the care and training that mothers do at home; moreover, there are also the additional costs of the facilities. Hence it costs less to care for a child privately. Since domestic labor cannot be eliminated under capitalism, full-time domestic labourers cannot be totally eliminated. By and large preschool children will have to be cared for by full-time domestic labourers. This is indicated by the fact that mothers in the work force for the most part have school-age children.[35]

The arguments just given explain how domestic labor and some full-time domestic labourers serve to benefit capitalism; as a result it is hard to see how they can be eliminated within capitalism. The arguments do not explain why most of the domestic labor should be done by women. Here it seems the explanation has less to do with benefits to capitalism than with benefits to men.[36] It is surely a matter of indifference to capitalists who does the labor in the family, while it is not a matter of indifference to men. It is certainly true that men care who does most of the labor in the home and, abstractly, it is true that capitalists do not care. However, at this point we have to look at the relationship between women's role in the family and their position in the work-force. This will reveal another way in which a family with full-time domestic labourers is in the interests of capitalists and not men.

Although it is likely that women will become an increasing and permanent part of the work-force, it does not follow that they will be integrated into the work-force on an equal basis with men. At present women in the US earn 57% of what men earn. The gap in earnings between the sexes has increased substantially since 1955,[37] while the percentage of women in the workforce increased dramatically during the same period. What helps maintain this situation of unequal pay for equal work and, more significantly, unequal work for women, is their role in the family. Thus, another (and perhaps the most crucial) way in which the family benefits capitalism is that it helps sustain women's

---

35 Bureau of Labor Statistics. Some writers have argued (Himmelweit and Mohun 1977), that another area of domestic labour that cannot be socialized or capitalized under capitalism *is* the actual physical reproduction of children because this would be incompatible with the class of free labourers, which is a defining characteristic of capitalism. I do not think that physical reproduction should be considered a kind of domestic labour; people *do* lots of things, like eating and sleeping which are necessary for capitalism but which are not kinds of *labour*. However, capitalism requires a class of free labourers and the family continues to be the primary way the reproduction of the species is organized in capitalism. Cf. Smith, 1977 for a development of this point.

36 This point was pressed on me by Sandra Bartky.

37 *New York Times* 29 November 1976.

super-exploitation as wage workers. It does this in manifold ways: the family is used as an ideological justification for discrimination in the work-force; the family hides the unemployment and underemployment of half the population; the family limits women's equal participation in the work-force in both objective and psychological ways, including the formation of personality structures appropriate to 'male' and 'female' jobs.[38]

It might be argued that what is beneficial to capitalism is low paying jobs, whether or not women are used to fill them. Of course this is true—abstractly—and women are not the only category of low-wage workers. But the question is, what propels a particular group into the worst job categories? Although abstractly it might be possible for unequal jobs and unequal pay for equal jobs to be distributed on a totally random basis, it would be difficult to obscure and justify such inequality. When the discrimination goes along with an ideology and a complex system of social roles such as those of the traditional family, it is easier. Even if fewer and fewer families today conform to the 'ideal' one-paycheck model, the existence of the model and the fact that most people are in such a family for at least part of their lives helps sustain the idea that women do not really 'belong' in wage work.

Furthermore, the privatized and hierarchical structure of the family is congruent with the individualistic structure of capitalist society. The family both reflects the larger society and makes it easier for people to conform to it.

Once again, this is not to say that sexism came into existence because sexism is useful to capitalism. The precise origins of sexism is a topic beyond the scope of this paper, but it certainly antedates capitalism. Since until recently women spent much of their productive lives pregnant or with small children, it is 'natural' that it should be women as a group and not men who play the social role they do in capitalism.[39]

Thus the family and the sexual roles of the family benefit capitalism, but they are also undermined by capital's need for women in the work-force. The short-term effects of these contradictory tendencies in capitalism are apparent; how they will be resolved remains to be seen.[40]

---

38   Regarding the importance of women's role in the family for male/female personality structures, see Chodorow 1979, and Dinnerstein 1976, for valuable though overly psychoanalytic perspectives on this question. I also discuss this question in 1982.
39   Cf. Saffiotti 1978, for a similar argument.
40   Zaretsky, in his justifiably popular book, *Capitalism, The Family and Personal Life* (Zaretsky 1976), correctly stresses the integration of the family into the capitalist mode of production. Some of what he says sounds like the analysis I have just given. However, he does not discuss the theoretical issues with which I am concerned in sufficient detail to make clear

Thus far it has been argued that domestic labour does not produce surplus value or value, and another explanation of the relationship of domestic labour and the family to capitalism has been projected. It is now appropriate to consider why people were led to these views and whether it isn't possible to credit some of their instincts and insights without making the same theoretical mistakes. One reason why people argue that domestic labour produces surplus value or value is that domestic labour seems to be indispensable, or at least highly beneficial, to capitalism, and the claim that it produces surplus value or value is an attempt to explain just why this is so. We have just seen that we can explain how domestic labour benefits capitalism without revising Marx's basic concepts. If the revisions proposed were correct, housewives would be more central to the struggle for socialism (perhaps even as important as industrial workers) because they would have more social importance and power than they had previously been thought to have. This, perhaps, is the theoretical basis for the wages-for-housework movement.

According to Marx a theoretical analysis of the social order is essential as a guide to revolutionary strategy. However, the relationship between theory and strategy is not as direct as this. In Marx's conception of social revolution every oppressed sector of the population can make a contribution to the transformation of the social order. Yet, even if housewives' labour did produce surplus value, it would not follow that they were of equal importance to industrial workers in the struggle for socialism. Being productive of surplus value is only one of the factors traditionally used by Marxists in determining those sectors of the working class likely to play leading roles in creating a socialist revolution. Although there is no uncontroversial list of characteristics, I think we can consider the following critical: centrality of the work to the economy; size, concentration, and location of work places; degree of unionization; traditions of militancy; intersection with other kinds of oppression. Domestic labour meets only the last criterion; it meets none of the others even minimally. So the strategic conclusion that priority should be given to organizing housewives around the demand for wages for housework would not follow even if the theoretical premises were correct.

There are other objections to the wages-for-housework strategy aside from the theoretical confusion behind it. It is reactionary in that it accepts the sexual

---

just where he stands on them. For an interesting debate on capitalism and the family, see Smith 1977; Bruegel 1978; and Smith 1978/9.

division of labour; it looks to the state for material support that would only serve to reinforce the sexual division of labour and further extend the penetration of people's lives by capital and the state. There is nothing in the strategy that would lead women out of their oppression and confinement in domestic labour. In fact proponents of wages for housework argue against the traditional socialist demands of reintegration of women into the paid work force and the socialization of domestic labour. While correctly pointing out the limitations of these changes under capitalism, they tend to glorify pre-capitalist modes of production.

Another basis for the theoretical positions we have discussed is the strong and correct sense that housewives are in some sense being 'ripped off', or to put it in Marxist terms, that they are being exploited. The question is, what does this mean and how can it be justified? Equating the situation of the domestic labourers with that of the wage workers is a mistake. The inference frequently drawn from this is that housewives are not exploited in a Marxist sense; Secombe, arguing against James and dalla Costa, says: 'The housewife, in Marxist terms, is unexploited because surplus value is not extracted from her labour the housewife is intensely oppressed within the nuclear family under capitalism but she is not exploited'.[41] Secombe is right that housewives are oppressed and that they are not exploited in the way in which James and dalla Costa think. However, it does not follow that they are not exploited in Marx's sense. This is why the dalla Costa position is unnecessary as well as mistaken. Although in Capital Marx first explains the concept of exploitation with reference to capitalism, he does not say that exploitation is unique to capitalism. In fact he says, 'The essential difference between, for instance, a society based on slave labour, and one based on wage labor, lies only in the mode in which this surplus is in each case extracted from the actual producer, the laborer'.[42] Unlike feudalism, where it was apparent that the serfs were forced to perform surplus labour which was unpaid and whose product was not under their control, exploitation is hidden in capitalism and had to be discovered by science, specifically through the discovery of surplus value. So although housewives do not produce surplus value they are exploited if they are forced to perform surplus labour for which they are not paid and whose product is not under their control.[43] I think most domestic labour meets these conditions of exploitation.

---

41   Secombe 1973, p. 11.
42   Marx 1970, p. 217.
43   Cf. Holmstrom 1977, for an elaboration of this interpretation of Marx's concept of exploitation.

According to Marx, work that is necessary for the workers' own maintenance is basically for the workers themselves and cannot be said to be forced.[44] Single wage workers with no dependents generally do little more than the minimum domestic labour. Because they control and consume the products of their domestic labour they can be said to be 'paid' for it.[45] They lose control of one of the products, their labour power, only when they sell it to the capitalist. Therefore the domestic labour of single workers with no dependents does not meet the conditions of exploited labour.

However, the nature of most domestic labour is very different from this. Consider the full-time housewife. Some of the labour she does is necessary to (re)produce her own labour power. However, she does more: she does much of the labour required to (re)produce the labour power of her husband and the next generation of wage labourers. This is surplus labour, so one of the conditions of exploitation is present. Married women wage workers with children do less domestic labour than full-time housewives, for various reasons, but certainly more than is necessary for their own (re)production. But can this surplus labour be said to be forced? After all, housewives (supposedly at least) love their families, whereas wage workers seldom love their employers. Her feelings about her family are irrelevant, however, because the economic and social realities impose this labour regardless of her personal inclinations. Someone has to do it, and ideology, traditions, and the power relations in the family ensure that the wife does most of it. In some states the law requires it as well. Thus she is forced to perform surplus labour.[46] And while she controls some of the products of her labour (at least to a greater degree than wage workers control their products), she does not control what is economically the most important (indirect) product: her husband's (and then her children's) labour power. Because her husband's wage supports her some of her labour is paid labour. However, the wage covers only her necessary labour (plus costs involved in the labour done for the rest of the family, i.e., the cost of the groceries, etc.). The surplus labour she does is not covered by the wage.[47]

Thus the conditions of exploitation are met in the case of most domestic labourers. They are forced to do unpaid surplus labour, whose product they do

---

44   How 'necessities' are determined *is* irrelevant to this discussion.
45   Cf. Holmstrom 1977 for a discussion of this point.
46   The exceptions are no more refutations of this claim than the argument that because some people 'choose' to go on welfare or steal rather than work is a refutation of the claim that social conditions compel people to sell their labour power.
47   By and large, women whose portion of the wage covers more than this are wealthy enough to avoid domestic labour.

not control. How much they are exploited will vary just as the rate of exploitation of wage labourers varies. Although housewives' exploitation cannot be measured precisely, how much they are exploited depends on whether or not they have families, the size of the families, how much help they get from others, their income, etc.

In contrast to most exploited wage labour the surplus domestic labour that women do under capitalism is socially necessary labour. According to Marx even under socialism there has to be some surplus labour.[48] In addition to what is necessary for their own individual (re)production, people have to perform labour necessary for social (re)production. The question arises, is the situation of domestic labour much different under socialism? If not, the force of the criticism of this aspect of capitalism diminishes. However, a critical difference is that the criteria for exploitation are not fulfilled in a socialist society.[49] Since labour and products are under the conscious control of the workers, who are paid in accordance with their labour, several of the conditions of exploitation are absent. In addition, the amount of surplus labour, of whatever sort, that anyone has to perform greatly diminishes since only socially necessary labour is required. However, since the surplus domestic labour presently done in individual homes is socially necessary, it is imperative that it be socially organized. Otherwise, since attitudes take a long while to change, it is likely that women will do a disproportionate share of society's labour. For this reason Marxists have always considered the socialisation of socially necessary labour an essential condition for the liberation of women. When this is achieved, women will do the same amount of unforced surplus labour as men. None of the conditions of exploitation will be present even if for a while there is still some sexual division of labour and women are disproportionately represented in areas of work that (re)produce labour power.[50]

If domestic workers are exploited under capitalism, who exploits them? The answer depends on the questions of who forces them to labour, who benefits from it, and who controls the products. Since they do not have a direct relationship to any particular capitalist it seems that no particular capitalist

---

48 Marx 1974, p. 820; *Critique of the Gotha Program*, in Tucker 1978, p. 525.
49 By 'socialist society' I mean a society controlled by the working class where production is under conscious collective control rather than determined by the law of value. When societies are called socialist which do not meet these conditions, they usually do fit the conditions of exploitation, although the mode of extraction of surplus labour differs from that of capitalist society.
50 Aside from the question of how it is organized it is interesting to compare the amount of labour that would be required for (re)production of labour under capitalism and socialism.

can be exploiting them. Nevertheless we know that one of the things that distinguishes the relationship between exploited and exploiter in capitalism (as opposed to previous class societies) is that the relationship between individuals is less important. In slave and feudal societies the workers is tied to a particular person, whereas in capitalism this is not the case: workers are the slaves of a class. When the individual worker contracts with an individual capitalist, Marx says, he is 'compelled by social conditions'. Domestic labourers are similarly compelled by social conditions to do surplus, unpaid labour. These social conditions are controlled by capitalists who benefit from domestic labour in the way we have seen. Thus we can say that it is capital (the capitalist mode of production) that forces domestic labourers to do surplus, unpaid labour, whose product they do not control. Hence domestic labourers are exploited by capital.

Are they also exploited by their husbands? Husbands and men in general derive some benefit from women's oppression, specifically from the role of women in the nuclear family. Although this benefit is superficial and more harmful than beneficial in the long run, it remains true that in the short run, men benefit from women's oppression. However, it seems to me that men participate to only a minimal extent in the exploitation of housewives. They benefit from women's domestic labour, but this is not sufficient to make them exploiters, unless one wants to claim that children exploit their parents because they are both a cause and a beneficiary of much of their parents' labour. Unemployed women have to do this labour for husbands and children, in part because there is no one else to do it: finances are limited and the men do full-time wage work. It is very difficult to measure the amount of time that must be spent on housework. It is not under direct control like wage work, and varies greatly according to the degree of mechanization, the size of the family, and other factors, Some studies estimate that more time is spent on domestic labour than on wage work.[51] However, since wage workers also need to travel to and from work and since other family members usually do some domestic labour and domestic labour is usually less intense than wage work because it is self-controlled, it is difficult to judge whether, in general, full-time housewives do more or less surplus labour than their husbands.

On the other hand, women wage workers still do most of the housework and thus do both more labour and more surplus labour in toto than their husbands. They both work more and are more exploited than their husbands. These differences in the labour of husbands and wives cannot be explained simply by

---

51 'It has been calculated in Sweden, that 2340 million hours a year are spent by women in housework compared with 1290 million hours in industry. The Chase Manhattan Bank estimated a woman's overall working week averaged 99.6 hours' (Mitchell 1971, p. 102).

the sexual/social division of labour. They are the result of the ideology of sexism and the power relations within the family. It is men in the home rather than capitalists who are the most immediate cause and beneficiaries of the surplus domestic labour of women wage workers. If housework were shared equally, men in the home would be the immediate losers. However, in the long run, capitalists would lose more and men would gain as a result. This is because of the relationship between women's role in the family and their superexploitation in wage work which was discussed earlier. It is women's role in the family that sustains their inequality in wage work, and as long as they are unequal in wage work it is difficult to equalize relations in the family.[52]

My conclusion, therefore, is that while in most of the domestic labour that women are forced to do husbands are neither the primary source of the compulsion nor the primary beneficiaries,[53] they participate in and benefit from some of their exploited labour, at least in the case of married women wage workers. This is one of the ways men benefit from the family and one of the reasons why married men tend to be happier than unmarried men and married women.[54] Nevertheless it is capital that is the primary exploiter of domestic as well as wage labour. More important benefits that men derive from women's oppression (even if counterbalanced or outweighed by losses) lie elsewhere, beyond the scope of this paper.

---

52 In Sweden there have been many attempts to equalise relations between the sexes in the family but progress remains slow. This seems to have something to do with the fact that sex segregation in jobs has continued and even worsened in recent years. Swerdlow, (ed.) 1980.

53 The argument that capitalists are the primary cause and beneficiaries of women's domestic labour rests on women's role in the family and their superexploitation in wage work; this obviously benefits capitalists. It might be objected that men benefit from women wage workers' superexploitation too. This cannot be argued in the long run since superexploitation helps sustain capitalism, which is not in most men's interest. The short run question is too complicated to be dealt with adequately in this paper. Similar questions are whether white workers benefit from racism and whether workers in imperialist powers benefit from imperialism. However, the case of men and women is different from either of these since men and women workers tend to live together whereas white and black workers do not. The whole family suffers from the lower wages of women workers, not just the women themselves. It would be hard to prove that male workers benefit from the superexploitation of women wage workers even in the short run, although, unfortunately, male workers have not always recognized this fact. And if they do benefit in the short run, this is only because of the competitive position capitalism puts them in; capitalism would thus still be the more fundamental cause and beneficiary.

54 'The Paradox of the Happy Marriage', by Jesse Bernard, in Gornick and Moran 1971; and Veroff and Feld 1970.

On the basis of the points just discussed and others, Sheila Rowbotham[55] and John Harrison[56] argue that housework constitutes a mode of production. Both contend that it is a distinct though subordinate mode of production called the family or household mode of production. The question, of course, depends in part on how one understands the concept of a mode of production, but I would argue that this is not the clearest and most useful way of understanding the concept. Their argument rests on the difference between the labour conditions and social relations of domestic labour and those of the labour typical of capitalism, i.e., wage labour.[57] In housework there is a low degree of socialization, division of labour, specialization, and (relatively) little mechanization. Production is for use, not exchange, and the producers have immediate control over their own labour and the means of production. The relationship between husband and wife is mediated by custom, feelings and the marriage contract rather than exclusively the 'cash nexus'. What this amounts to, as Gough and Harrison point out, is a definition of a mode of production as 'any set of social relations within which production takes place'. Thus the typical 'capitalist' society actually consists of two modes of production, capitalist and domestic, but called capitalist because it is this mode of production which most determines the social formation as a whole. The domestic household mode of production is in fact 'a truncated mode of production with an unusually complex, symbiotic relationship to capital'.[58]

Given this complex and subordinate relationship to the capitalist mode of production, what is to be gained from calling housework a distinct mode of production? It only obscures this relationship and deviates from Marx's usage of the concept.[59] Only what Harrison calls the dominant set of work relations is a mode of production in Marx's usage. Only those relations of production have distinct laws of development and determine the rest of the social formation by creating a superstructure.[60] Other sorts of work relations can and usually do exist within a given mode of production, usually as remnants of

---

55 Rowbotham 1973.
56 Harrison 1973b.
57 Their position also rests on the belief that housework is productive labour, although they do not hold that it produces surplus value. Since I have already considered this, and in any case it is not relevant to whether the family is a mode of production, this point will be ignored.
58 Harrison 1973b, p. 39.
59 Ennis 1974, in a review of Rowbotham, points this out.
60 No monocausality is implied by this.

earlier modes. In fact a mode of production could be defined as 'an integrated complex of social productive forces and relations linked to a determinate type of ownership of the means of production'.[61] In periods of transition more than one relatively autonomous and vertically differentiated set of work relations coexist. Otherwise, the dominant mode of production undermines the autonomy and the superstructures of the other sets of work relations. As Saffiotti argues:

> Once the juridico-political and ideological instances of the pre-capitalist modes of production have been destroyed, these modes no longer survive as such. What remains are pre-capitalist work relations, which now have different connotations ... The re-defined pre-capitalist work relations thus become an integral part of the capitalist social formation and thereby further the accumulation process.[62]

The family constitutes such a set of work relations, bearing the historical marks of an earlier domestic mode of production but totally integrated into the capitalist mode of production.[63]

Underdeveloped countries provide fascinating examples of the complex and 'dialectical' relations between the capitalist mode of production and the pre-capitalist work relations. Even in advanced capitalist countries, however, it is worth noting that if we followed Harrison's definition of mode of production there would be more than two. The working conditions and relations of self-employed professionals, state employees, and petty commodity producers are also quite different from those of wage labourers. It would be a very complicated picture if we called all of these work relations modes of production. Furthermore, it would obscure their relationship to capitalism. As Gough and Harrison point out, it is not what words are used to define the household but the substantive question of its relation to capitalism which is of primary importance. However, their terminology obscures the answer to the substantive question.

∴

---

61   Laclau 1971.
62   Saffioto 1975, pp. 61.
63   Whether the relations in the family are called 're-defined pre-capitalist work relation' or are simply said to be non-capitalist work relations which bear the marks of an earlier mode of production seems to me a trivial verbal question.

This issue has another significant political/strategic implication. If housework is a distinct mode of production, then it follows that housewives constitute a class. Gough and Harrison endorse this implication of their position; Rowbotham does not, but this is a troublesome inconsistency in her position. (It also follows that husbands exploit their wives, but neither Gough and Harrison nor Rowbotham accept this implication of their analysis, at least not in so many words.) Gough and Harrison go further and argue that women constitute a class, which does not follow from the position that housework is a mode of production. Benston, we recall, offers a similar analysis by defining women as 'the group which is responsible for the production of simple use values in those activities associated with the family'. The view of women as a class is usually associated with radical feminists; it is a confused, confusing and dangerous position for a Marxist to take.

The political/strategic implications of the radical feminist perspective are clear: men are the enemy; socio-economic and other differences are all less fundamental than the sexual difference. Hence all women must struggle against all men. This, of course, is not the view of the writers we have been discussing. Their analysis of women as a class must be integrated into their analysis of capitalism as a class system. But how exactly is this to be done? If the 'family mode of production' is taken to be a subsidiary of capitalism, then socio-economic classes presumably would be more fundamental than sex classes. But the precise relationship between the two, and indeed whether a coherent synthesis is possible, remains unclear. Calling the household a mode of production obscures its relationship to capitalism; calling housewives or women a class obscures their relationship to capitalism. In Marx's sense of the word class, housewives and women come in all classes.[64] All women suffer oppression as women, but they do not all suffer it in the same way or to the same degree. Working class women are super-exploited in their wage work and exploited in their domestic work.[65] In other ways as well they suffer more from sexism

---

64 Some Marxists have unnecessarily confused matters by equating the working class with the workforce, or, worse yet, a certain sector of the workforce, usually productive workers. These usages imply that full-time housewives cannot be working class, that people change class just because they grow up and get a job or lose their job or retire or when they switch from public employment to private employment. Aside from deviating from Marx's usage, this is unnecessarily complicated and counter-intuitive. There is also no adequate account of the class position of those people ordinarily considered working class who do not happen to be in that sector of the workforce. According to my usage (and Marx's), when a housewife gets a job she is not (usually) entering the working class or changing her class at all; she is simply entering the workforce.

65 The claim that women workers are super-exploited means that they are paid less than the

than do middle- and upper-class women. They have less reproductive freedom in that they have less access to abortion, contraception and child care, and are often subject to sterilization abuse. They are also more subject to sexual abuse on the job and in the streets. Hence the interests of working class women are more consistently opposed to sexism as well as capitalism, than are the interests of middle- and upper-class women.

Given the theoretical confusions of the analysis of housework as a mode of production, the political/strategic implications of the position are also unclear. In the stronger version of Gough and Harrison, which is some kind of amalgam of radical feminism and Marxism, a movement of women of all (socio-economic) classes would seem to be called for, but it is unclear how it would relate to a movement against capitalism, which presumably is also necessary. Rowbotham believes that the strategic implication of her position is that an independent working-class women's movement is necessary as one wing of a united working class movement against capitalism. However, even though she has drawn back from some of the implications, her analysis of housework as a mode of production undercuts any basis for optimism about the possibility of such a development.[66]

This chapter has discussed some aspects of the relationship between women's oppression and capitalism. Although the analysis given here is incomplete and although theory cannot provide a simple formula for practice, I think it can help us to draw some general political/strategic conclusions. Women's oppression neither began with capitalism nor does it end with the end of capitalism.[67] However, according to Marx, exploitation also existed prior to capitalism,[68] These general trans-historical truths are of little value in understanding the nature and source of women's oppression or of exploitation in a given society. To do this we have to understand how they operate in that system. Women's super-exploitation as wage workers and their exploitation and oppression in the family and society at large cannot be understood in isolation from one another or in isolation from capitalism. Nevertheless we cannot be sanguine that the success of a socialist movement would automatically end women's oppression (or indeed that it could succeed if women were not equal parti-

---

value of their labour power, which follows from the Marxist theory of wages and the ratio of women's wages to men's. Hence the concept of super exploitation does not apply to domestic labour.

66   This problem is addressed by Rapaport 1974 in her review of Rowbotham.
67   Few would credit the claim that in the so-called socialist countries women suffer no oppression as women.
68   *Capital*, I, p. 217.

cipants in the struggle). As Eleanor Marx said of women, extending her father's famous dictum, 'their emancipation must come from themselves'.[69] We need, therefore, an independent working class women's movement as one wing of a united working-class movement.[70]

The strategic and tactical question, then, is how to build such a women's movement and how to link it to a united working class movement against capitalism. I think that the traditional socialist support for the reintegration of women into social production and a strategic emphasis on women workers rather than housewives remains correct. This is not simply because housewives do not produce surplus value; not all women wage workers do either and even if housewives did, it would not make them strategically central, as has already been argued. Most housewives are also wage workers now, and as wage workers they have more feminist[71] as well as class consciousness. The further question of whether there are certain categories of women wage workers who would be more militant and more conscious than others is beyond the scope of this paper. It would require both a detailed analysis of where women work and an analysis of the implications of those employment patterns. What strategic implications follow from the fact that women workers are found to a disproportionate extent in unproductive jobs, e.g., the public sector and the sphere of circulation, in unorganized and in highly competitive industries? Analysis of these question would be useful but the value of such an abstract analysis should not be overestimated. Aside from the importance of various conjunctural factors, we are not simply talking of workers in particular job categories but women in those jobs. Their oppression and their needs as workers cannot be separated from their oppression and needs as women. Our expectations and strategies have to be informed by both aspects of their oppression.

Although a detailed discussion of strategy would be inappropriate here, this analysis suggests that building a working women's movement can best be approached from two directions: through issues and movements especially related to their oppression as women, which will not necessarily be 'work-place' issues, but will include such questions as control over their reproductive lives; and through issues that affect them primarily as workers, Since the former issues also affect working class women who are not workers and middle class

---

69   Aveling 1972.
70   This is Rowbotham's strategic conclusion as well but I think that my analysis provides a more consistent basis for it. A revolutionary organization is necessary in addition, and not counterposed, to a united working-class movement and independent organizations of the specially oppressed, such as women, but this question is beyond the scope of this paper.
71   Ferree 1976.

women as well, the organizational forms these struggles take will have to reflect this. Given greater time and other advantages middle class women will often be in the leadership of these struggles. However, in view of the differences in, as well as the commonalities of, interests between working class and middle class women, the special needs of working women need to be given priority by socialists working in such movements. Similarly women workers need to unite with male workers on issues that affect them both, but they need some organizational autonomy within a united movement if they are to ensure that their special needs are met. Especially important to building a working women's movement are those issues where the women's movement and the workers' movement can make common cause. An example is the danger on many jobs to women's reproductive capacity which could unite feminist reproductive rights groups, health and safety groups, trade unions, etc. Socialists need to find ways to creatively link these struggles if we are to build a movement that can end both women's oppression and capitalism.

CHAPTER 5

Democratic Socialism for a Finite World

'Democratic socialism' is in the air in the United States for the first time in a very long time, a surprising and happy fact for those of us who identify with that label.[1] But there is little clarity as to what the concept means. In fact it means many different things to different people. In this paper I will defend a conception of democratic socialism as Marx understood it, and explain why it is inherently feminist and eco-socialist.

Democracy is such an appealing concept that it is appropriated and applied to systems that are not remotely democratic, e.g. the German Democratic Republic. Only slightly more plausibly, we hear that capitalist societies—and only capitalist societies—will necessarily be democratic. Yet it is also said that democracy is both the end and the means to socialism. How do we sort out these contradictory claims? What exactly do 'democracy' and 'socialism' mean?

1   'Democracy'

The root meaning of 'democracy' is rule by the people—but which people? and what do they get to rule over? The definition entails that democracy admits of degrees according to 2 measures: 1st, how inclusive the category of 'the people' is, and 2nd, what the people get to decide. By the first measure democracy in the United States has clearly expanded. In those capitalist societies that are politically democratic (not all capitalist societies, we should note) all citizens get to vote. However, this hardly happened from the beginning, by 'nature', as supporters of capitalism seem to believe; indeed it has been a long heroic struggle by working-class people, women and racial minorities. Initially, only a tiny percentage of the population had the vote; property qualifications for male voters were not removed throughout the US until the mid-nineteenth century, while women won the right to vote less than one hundred years ago. African-Americans were effectively denied the right to vote in the South until the Civil Rights movement won the Voting Rights Act of 1965, and they still face struggles over felon disenfranchisement and voter ID.

---

1   This chapter first appeared as an entry in Thompson and Zucker 2019.

Even at its most inclusive, however, the formal equality of democracy in capitalism (or any class society) is undermined by economic inequality; those with more economic power simply have more influence over political decisions. Extreme inequality, the influence of money in elections, and the peculiar institution of the electoral college, further limit US political democracy.

Even more important, however, is the 2nd measure of degrees of democracy, viz, that *the range of issues on which voters in capitalist societies have power is extremely limited*. Both before and after capitalism political and economic power were fused. In feudalism and in the Soviet style systems those with political power and economic power were one and the same. With capitalism, however, the 'economic' and the 'political' became separate for the first time, and real social power rests in the economy. As Ellen Meiksins Wood has argued, this made political democracy both more possible but also less important. The most crucial decisions affecting us all: what to produce (gas-guzzling and driverless private cars versus buses and trains), how to produce (fossil fuels or renewables), and the all-important question of *how much* to produce are not up for a vote; they are made by capitalists who are unelected. A full-scale economic democracy, where these decisions would be made democratically, is simply incompatible with capitalism.

Small countries, more subject to global capitalist powers, have even less ability to govern themselves. Pushed to austerity and anti-ecological decisions, democratically elected governments are fragile, as people get frustrated with 'democracy' and can turn to authoritarian leaders. This shows why it is so important to focus on the constraints on democracy *posed by capitalism*.

Aristotle, who opposed democracy, defined it very clearly as a constitution in which 'the free-born and poor control the government—being at the same a majority', whereas in an oligarchy 'the rich and better-born control the government—being at the same time a minority'. By these definitions, we live in an oligarchy not a democracy, despite universal suffrage. And how could it be otherwise given the extremes of inequality? Noam Chomsky has a nice acronym to describe our system of political democratic institutions within an oligarchy—he calls them RECDS (really existing capitalist democracies).

2 'Socialism'

'Socialism' has been applied to an even wider, indeed incompatible, variety of societal models with little in common except a vague commitment to 'the social' or some state involvement in the economy. Not even anti-capitalism is a common denominator. Throughout history many have put forward collectivist models, most never realized, some attractive, others positively dystopian. More importantly, consider the actually existing models called socialist: local governments that pursue public welfare policies, such as a sewer system (hence the description 'sewer socialism'), capitalist countries called socialist because they have a large state sector including generous welfare measures, like Sweden. This social democratic model of capitalism is probably what most proponents of democratic socialism in the US today, like Bernie Sanders, mean. On the other hand, we had the Union of Soviet Socialist Republics and the countries in the USSR's orbit, which are very different from the former model, being neither capitalist nor politically democratic. The means of production were owned collectively rather than privately, but by the government not the people. Hence a good term to describe them is bureaucratic collectivist.

These two major kinds of societies called socialist are typically differentiated as reformist versus revolutionary or democratic versus dictatorial. Although those words apply, a more illuminating way of dividing up the many types of 'socialist' societies is provided by Hal Draper in his seminal essay 'The Two Souls of Socialism'. He contends that the fundamental divide between all these visions of socialism is between 'socialism-from-above' and 'socialism-from-below'. A surprising implication is that the supposedly 'opposite' models of social democracy and bureaucratic collectivism, as well as the utopians, all belong in the same category: 'socialists-from-above'. Despite their differences, they all believe that socialism is to be handed down to the people by a ruling elite, whether the Communist Party or a Parliament or a utopian thinker.

In contrast, what unites 'socialists-from-below' is the belief that socialism can only come into being through the self-activity of the masses of people 'from below'. This is expressed in the first principle of the First International Workingmen's Association written by Marx: 'the emancipation of the working class must be the act of the working class itself'. In addition to Marx and Engels, the most famous socialists-from-below are Rosa Luxemburg and our own Eugene Victor Debs. Unfortunately, Draper admits, it is socialism-from-above that has been more influential historically and still today, but the seeds of the alternative are found wherever masses of people struggle to take control of their destiny, from the Paris Commune to the Russian Revolution, Hungarian Revolt in 1956 to the Arab Spring and today's revolts in China by workers and students.

Once we have the idea of socialism from below, the inextricable connections between socialism and democracy become clear: as the slogan says, *democracy is both the means and the end of socialism*. To see why, we should start with the end, the vision of socialism—and then turn to the means. This is because *ends determine means*; first we have to know what we are aiming for in order to know what are the best means to get there. Different ends require different means. It is also true that *the means determine the ends*; if we want to create an egalitarian democratic end we cannot use cruel and undemocratic means.

3   Democracy as the END of Socialism

Marx and Engels did not write a great deal about what socialism would look like. In my opinion this is unfortunate. A clearer idea of what they were hoping for and expecting would have forearmed us better against the hideous equation of socialism with what existed in the Soviet Union, China et al which has been so damaging to the cause of socialism. And it might have helped us in arguing for and experimenting with transitional models. Their reticence came from their critiques of the utopians, who created models of socialism in their own heads, 'from-above', without an analysis of existing society and how and by whom socialism could come into being. Instead Marx and Engels saw themselves as developing a scientific theory of modes of production, in particular capitalism, which predicted that capitalism would end and be replaced by socialism. This would not happen automatically, but by human action, in particular through class struggle. And then the working class, the principal agents of the transformation and the dominant power in the new mode of production would themselves determine collectively the forms of this new system.

Nevertheless we know some things about their vision of socialism based on its core difference from capitalism and also from their response to the Paris Commune. The Commune was established in 1870, at the end of the Franco-Prussian War by the workers of Paris who refused to surrender to the Prussian Army after the French forces had capitulated. In his pamphlet *The Civil War in France*, Marx vividly described their heroic story. Since, in their view, a state is always the instrument for the rule of the most powerful class, Engels wrote 'Look at the Paris Commune. That was the Dictatorship of the Proletariat'.[2] Except for the Commune's mistake of not seizing the Bank of France, their measures expressed the crucial insight that the working class could not just take over the existing capitalist state institutions; they had to devise new ones suited to protect their own very different interests. Hence they abolished the old repressive machinery of government, replacing the army with a National Guard consisting of all citizens capable of bearing arms, and they separated church and state. To protect against the development of a new repressive force, they limited their own pay to that of the average worker's and made them-

---

2 Marx 1978, p. 629.

selves subject to immediate recall. Various measures on behalf of working-class interests were put into effect, most important, converting all closed factories into cooperatives to be united into one big union, a measure Marx believed would have led to a full scale socialist society. Although the Commune lasted only from Sept to May before it was brutally crushed, we see similar political forms wherever the working class has come to power like Russia in 1917 or Hungary in 1956. (Marx describes the Commune as elected by universal suffrage, but in fact it was universal *male* suffrage; as women were very involved and revolutionary processes have a momentum of their own it is highly likely that this would have been corrected.)

Whatever the exact policies decided upon by a particular workers' government, we can infer crucial general features of socialism simply by the very different class relations that constitute it. In capitalism and all class societies, those who own/control the means of production force (directly or indirectly) those who do not to work and to produce a surplus that the ruling class appropriates. This is true in feudalism, slave societies and the bureaucratic collectivist modes of production. In capitalism it appears to result from free contractual agreement, but Marx stresses that 'in essence it always remains forced labour'.[3] This is exploitation, which would not exist in socialism because the producers are the owners; the means of production are no longer in others' hands, but are owned and controlled collectively by the working class. Production is not for profit or for increased power of the bureaucratic class, but for need. What, how and how much is produced would be determined democratically according to their assessment of their needs. Labour would still however be necessary to satisfy human needs but this does not make it the forced labour inherent in class societies. In this inevitable realm of necessity, Marx says,

> Freedom can only consist in the associated producers rationally regulating their interchange with Nature, bringing it under their common control, instead of being ruled by it as by the blind forces of Nature, and achieving this with the least expenditure of energy and under conditions most favorable to, and worthy of, their human nature... Beyond it begins that development of human energy which is an end in itself, the true realm of freedom, which, however, can blossom forth only with the realm of necessity as its basis. The shortening of the work day in its basic prerequisite.[4]

---

3   Ibid. p. 440.
4   Ibid. p. 441.

In short, Marx's vision of socialism is collective ownership with democratic planning (freedom within necessity) allowing for maximum time for creative expression (true freedom). (Note that *collective* property involves the *individual* right to enjoy and to share the control of the property.)

Just how would such a society be organized? We cannot say for sure in any detail, but this is not unique to socialism. Before capitalism came into being, no one could have said exactly how it would work or how it would evolve. Certain principles, and particular measures that transcended pre-capitalist society gave an idea but it was worked out in historical practice, through confronting new challenges, and through struggle and that's all we can be asked to do to make a vision of socialism plausible. The key to what it would look like is the class nature of those making the decisions, as we saw in the case of the Paris Commune.

A central debate is whether there a place for markets in democratic socialism. Proponents of 'market socialism' think so. Proponents of democratic planning say maybe, but the key question is the status of the market within the society. Even if we are talking of worker-owned enterprises in a post-capitalist socialist society, so long as socialism is conceived as *basically a market system*, then it cannot resolve the multiple ecological crises we are facing. Worker-owned enterprises are constrained by the same political and economic forces of the market to continue producing the same stuff in the same way. *Thus whatever markets there are in socialism have to be brought under the control of institutions of rational democratic planning.*

At what level should the planning be done? That all depends ... Many experts stress the importance of keeping the planning small because local knowledge is bound to be more reliable than far away experts' and people can develop trust and abide voluntarily by rules they themselves develop. Due to lack of knowledge and cooperation, regulation by central governments has often led not to conservation but to destruction of natural resources. This advice is very important, though our discussion of ecology will force us to qualify it.

4 Democracy as the MEANS to Socialism

> The emancipation of the working class must be the act of the working class itself.
>
> KARL MARX, First International Workingmen's Association

∴

> Without the conscious will and the conscious action of the proletariat there can be no socialism.
> ROSA LUXEMBURG, *Die Rote Fahne*

∴

> Too long have the workers of the world waited for some Moses to lead them out of bondage. He has not come; he never will come. I would not lead you out if I could; for if you could be led out, you could be led back again. I would have you make up your minds that there is nothing you cannot do for yourselves.
> EUGENE V. DEBS, Speech, New York 1905

∴

It is difficult to separate a discussion of democracy as the ends and as the means of socialism as they are so interconnected. The struggle for reforms is key to creating socialism but not because socialism is simply the accretion of reforms as some non-Marxist socialists have argued. It is the process of struggling to transform capitalism that develops the experience, the vision, the organisation and the capacities of working people to resolve the new challenges of a fundamentally different mode of production. This was Rosa Luxemburg's reply to Edward Bernstein in *Reform and Revolution*.

Debate and experimentation are an essential part—hence the importance of individual rights and political freedom. The gross limitations and hypocrisies of capitalist democracies lead some on the left to reject totally the limited institutions of political democracy we have or even disparage the concept of democracy. This is mistaken and was never Marx's position; starting with his first published article in defence of freedom of the press against all government censorship he never wavered in his commitment to these principles. In our RECDs, we cannot only talk, but organize around concrete issues that challenge vested interests like fossil fuel corporations. Sometimes we even win.

More important than specific wins, we should struggle to put these decisions under popular democratic control, thereby deepening democracy. Open public discussions are essential, with mechanisms in place that allow people to indicate what they want, but along with institutions that enable them to have *control*, not just consultation, over the representatives they choose to carry out their decisions. An exciting experiment of bottom-up and creative alternatives to capitalism is the new kind of party in Barcelona that emerged from social movements that 'crowd-sourced' its code of ethics and uses new 'digital-technological means of developing democratic experiments at the local and regional scale'.[5] Of course, they are still operating within a capitalist system that limits what they can do, but they give us ideas of what is possible.

Whether it is social movements against imperialism and war or focused on women's issues, anti-racism, or environmental or labour struggles, democratic socialists use a rank-and-file strategy and attempt to integrate the issues within an anti-capitalist perspective. Mistakes will be made. But as Rosa Luxemburg said, 'Mistakes committed by a genuinely revolutionary labour movement are much more fruitful and worthwhile historically than the infallibility of the very best Central Committee'.[6]

5 Why Democratic Socialism Is ECOSOCIALIST

Rosa Luxemburg's statement on the eve of World War I that the choice is between socialism or barbarism was never more true. But today our struggle is about our very existence. The latest IPCC report on climate change stresses that we are on a collision course with the limits of our planet. 'To prevent widespread misery, humanity must practice a more environmentally sustainable alternative to business as usual', including 'reassessing … the role of an economy rooted in growth'.[7] Since Al Gore's 'An Inconvenient Truth', the problems have gotten much worse very rapidly. The reason is that an even more inconvenient truth than global warming is that the standard measures proposed will do very little to stop the threats to the planet's ecosystems as long as capitalism exists. For capitalism is—for better and for worse—an economic growth machine. The world economy now produces in less than two weeks the equivalent of the entire physical output of the year 1900, and global economic output now doubles every twenty-five to thirty years. China's transition to a global capitalist economic power and its lack of democratic controls threaten ecological apocalypse.

Although some capitalist politicians and even corporations have recognized the urgency of the problems and the need for radical measures, capitalism 'just can't help itself'. The basic problem lies in the conflict between the individualist rationality enforced by the competitive market system and what is

---

5 Charnock Ribera-Fumaz 2018.
6 See Draper 1970.
7 IPCC, 2018: http://report.ipcc.ch/sr15/pdf/sr15_headline_statements.pdf.

rational from a social point of view. Each firm is compelled to act to maximize its own individual interests, and it goes on and on ... though the results are catastrophic. One would think that self-destruction would be a refutation of this individualist model of rational economic behaviour, but it is too deeply rooted in capitalist ideology for mainstream economists to give it up.

A democratic socialist society, on the other hand, would be governed by a broader social understanding of rationality. When there is a conflict between what is rational from an individualist point of view and the collective, the latter has to take priority. Given Marx's vision of the 'associated producers rationally regulating their interchange with Nature, bringing it under their common control, instead of being ruled by it as by the blind forces of Nature, and achieving this with the least expenditure of energy and under conditions most favourable to, and worthy of, their human nature', the recognition of the constraints posed by our finite planet would be fundamental.[8] The list of products produced because they are profitable but which are worthless, wasteful and damaging to the well being of people and the rest of the planet is long. Most or all weaponry, toxic endless iterations of i-things, and gas hog cars, products designed to become obsolete so they have to be replaced after a short life... And then there is the issue of quantity... To live within our planetary means would not be a sacrifice, but liberation, as research has shown that past a certain minimum, people are not happier because they have more money and more stuff. Free time and relationships are more important for happiness.

Our multiple ecological crises force us to recognize that while planning should be kept local whenever possible, many things simply cannot be accomplished in towns, or cities or regions. We need national clean air regulations or else states will compete for business by lowering environmental standards, and the same is true on an international level. This is why climate scientists call for *planet-wide* curbs on emissions and ocean scientists say we need a Five-Year plan to save the oceans 'plundered by overfishing'. Nor do the human and political problems engendered by climate problems stay within national borders. Consider unemployment due to depleted resources, wars over scarce resources and the millions of refugees fleeing across the globe as a result.

Thus socialism would need more institutions of international governance, that is, planning and regulation, such as a United Nations of socialist societies, as well as local, regional and national institutions. The issue is not primarily whether planning is local, regional, national or even international, I contend,

---

8 Marx 1967.

but *what kinds of institutions enable rational democratic control from below and effectively address our environmental crisis*. Our urgent task in this period is to create a global network of these grassroots institutions.

6   Why Democratic Socialism Is FEMINIST

As feminists have often observed and critiqued, wage labour, specifically labour that produces surplus value, is not the only form of labour that exists in capitalism, yet it is the only form of labour that Marx concentrates on. Indeed, they find it particularly insulting that, according to Marx's analysis, this unpaid caring labour done mostly by women, is not 'productive' labour. Not only is it necessary for the reproduction of the workforce biologically but in the sense of getting the worker to the factory door every day. Hence it is not only necessary for life in general, but for capitalism.

This is true. However, Marx restricts the definition of productive labour as he does, in order to 'express[es] precisely the specific form of the labour on which the whole capitalist mode of production and capital itself is based'.[9] Hence the concept is the key to understanding the 'essence' of capitalism, and to understand the limits to which it can be reformed. As Rosa Luxemburg said: from the standpoint of capital, 'The dancer in a café, who makes a profit for her employer with her legs, is a productive working woman, while all the toil of the women and mothers of the proletariat within the four walls of the home is considered unproductive work. [This] sounds crude and crazy but it is an accurate expression of the crudeness and craziness of today's economic order ...'[10]

Though not a valid criticism of Marx, the stress by feminists on the importance of non-waged labour done largely by women is undeniable; indeed it is the labour that makes all other labour possible. Marxist/socialist feminists, particularly those espousing what has come to be called social reproduction feminism, have attempted to develop a complete story of labour in capitalism, some waged, some not. Their conception is of a single system of species reproduction, always involving a division of labour, but one that takes different forms related to changes in the capitalist economy. Neither the relations of production nor of reproduction are given by nature but are the result of gender and class struggles. Demands have been made by feminists in the United States to support caregiving as a public good, as it is in many countries with stronger

---

9   Marx 1963, p. 396.
10   Luxemburg 2002, p. 21.

social democratic traditions. Even there, however, neoliberalism, a response to the ongoing crises of capitalism, has led to cutbacks in every field of social reproduction. Thus socialist feminists should make these crucial demands, but they should be recognized as transitional demands in the sense that they are not all winnable securely under capitalism but rather, point us toward a different society. A society that gave equal value to non-waged caring labour would be socialism, not capitalism.

In a socialist mode of production dedicated to the satisfaction of need, not profit, the constraints of this 'crude and crazy' economic system of capitalism would not apply. On the contrary; because what drives the two systems is different, what counts as productive and unproductive would be different. Instead of 'productive' being defined in terms of what is productive of profit, it would be defined in terms of what is productive of well-being. Hence all the non-waged caring labour that is done 'for free', out of love, that is necessary in all societies, would be recognized as the essential productive labour that it is. And consider the scientific and creative work that is not done because it is not profitable but would enhance our lives in manifold ways. Unproductive in capitalist terms but productive in socialism. On the other hand, much of the labour that is 'productive-in-capitalism' would be rightly recognized as unproductive, as has been discussed in the section on eco-socialism.

Overall then a democratic socialist society would have more leisure time, hence more time to spend with our friends and families. This has always been a foundational value of feminist thinking.

A democratic, feminist, eco-socialist society would rest on a foundation of true security. In the US after 9/11 security is conceived exclusively in terms of protection against intentional threats to our safety and well-being, which entails that they are threats by individuals or nations. And we respond in kind. Indeed aggression by the United States was crucial to causing 9–11. As Bishop Desmond Tutu said, 'you don't get true security from the barrel of a gun'. There is a broader meaning of security, (social security, security blankets), usually associated with women, in which it means protection against threats of all kinds, intentional or not. Whether threats come from environmental disasters or wars, no one can be truly secure in the world as it is organized at present. Increasingly the world's people are all interconnected and ultimately one, so our planetary resources must be seen as a common treasury to be managed rationally and democratically. Marx said in *The German Ideology* that socialism in one country was impossible. How much clearer that should be today!

PART 2

Rationality

∴

CHAPTER 6

Rationality and Revolution

The question of an action's rationality has two aspects: 1) the 'appropriateness' of the action given the beliefs held and 2) the 'reasonableness' of the beliefs themselves or of holding those beliefs.[1] The former involves questions of motivation, the latter epistemology. This paper will concentrate on the former aspect of the question.

One way of understanding rational motivation is so widely accepted as to seem incontrovertible to many of its proponents. This is the sense of rationality as maximisation of utility. Although individual action is motivated by many things, the claim is that when behaviour is rational it can be understood as an attempt to maximise utility. Rationality in this view has solely to do with means, not ends. The only restriction on an agent's ends is that they form a coherent set and whatever the content of the utility at which the agent aims, it is presumed to be open-ended. The theory is descriptive in that it says that (normal) people act this way most of the time and also normative in that behaviour which does not fit the model is judged irrational.

This conception of rationality is the basis of rational choice and game theory, is fundamental in much of economic theory and in many ethical, social and political theories as well, Rawls1 work being the most important recent example. Though the individualist rationality theory says nothing about peoples' ends, the general assumption usually made is that the ultimate end of individual acts is always some (presumed) good of the agent. However, since the view of human beings as utility maximisers is strictly separable from the egoistic theory of the nature of their utility, I will not take egoism to be part of the theory.[2]

This conception of rationality generates problems regarding collective action—how it ever happens and whether it can ever be rational. In his highly

---

[1] Rawls 1971, pp. 60–8. For criticisms of Rawls' use of the concept of rationality, see Gibson, 1976. Schwartz, 1973. Braithwaite 1955. For criticism of Braithwaite's approach, see Lucas 1959. Sen 1970.
[2] In my opinion, egoism as a general theory of human motivation was long ago shown to be either false or tautological. The locus classicus of this critique is Butler 1950. A contemporary philosophical discussion is Nagel 1970. Whether egoism is even true as a theory of economic behaviour is also questionable. See also Sen 1976. Hollis and Nell 1975. Luce and Raiffa 1975. These last three grant the assumption of rationality is a tautology but hold that it is a useful one in their abstract theory.

influential book, Mancur Olson sharply poses the problems.[3] He criticises as a common fallacy the assumption that if something is in the interests of a group it is therefore rational for the individual members of the group to contribute to that end. In his view, groups are just collections of individuals and group interests are the aggregate of individual interests. Hence, it is only rational for a group to do something if it is rational for the majority of members individually. Where the success of the effort does not depend on a single individual and where an individual will get the benefits of success regardless of whether or not he contributed to the effort, it is not rational for him to contribute. Yet if many act rationally the result is that no one will get what would benefit them all. Such goods are called public goods and the problem of social coordination to which they give rise is called the 'free rider' problem. The problem does not exist for small groups, according to Olson, because each individual's contribution is more likely to affect the outcome. However, he claims that the 'free rider' problem holds regardless of the content of the individual's utility, specifically whether behaviour is selfish or unselfish.

One implication that Olson draws, developed by Allen Buchanan in 'Revolutionary Motivation and Morality', is that people acting rationally would never engage in revolutionary action, i.e., would never struggle to overthrow a socially dominant class.[4] Hence, Karl Marx's vision of a socialist revolution made by masses of working-class people acting to further their interests is a utopian vision. According to Marx the emancipation of the working class would and must be the act of the working class itself, not any elite manipulating or coercing them. The dynamics of capitalism, he held, in particular, capitalist crises are such that workers' interests—indeed their very survival—lie in overthrowing capitalism. The fact that workers in advanced capitalist countries have not made a successful revolution, and have seldom even tried, is usually explained in two ways: either 1) contrary to Marx's predictions, capitalism has reformed itself to such an extent that it is not rational for them to overthrow capitalism; or 2) while it is still rational for them to revolt, they do not recognize this or simply cannot act according to their true class interests. They have false consciousness. According to Olson and Buchanan, however, both sorts of explanations are seriously off the mark. In their view, workers' failure to make a revolution is due to the predominance of rational thinking. Socialism, in the Marxist vision, is a public good in the sense explained and hence, they argue, insofar as workers are rational, they will not make a socialist revolution. While they might

---

3   Olson 1965.
4   Buchanan 1979, p. 65. Olson 1965, p. 64.

be coerced or manipulated or moved by moral convictions to do it, these kinds of reasons are fundamentally different from the reasons that Marx thought would motivate people to become revolutionaries. The conclusion they draw is that Marx had an inadequate—indeed, incoherent theory of revolutionary motivation. If valid, this criticism is quite devastating to the Marxist theory of social change. In this paper I will discuss what Marx could say in defence of the rationality of socialist revolution. This discussion will serve to illuminate the differing conceptions of rationality found in different social/political theories.

Marxists would grant that the theory has a lot of evidence on its behalf. Most of the time workers seem to act just as the theory describes—i.e., as non-revolutionary individual utility maximisers. This, Marxists would say, is to be expected in a competitive society where individuals' interests are often opposed to each other. However, on the other hand, sometimes workers do act collectively; sometimes they even make revolutions. Though utility theory does not say that no collective action is ever possible, it explains it in one of two ways: either 1) as due to the movements' ability to offer selective incentives, thereby changing the individuals' calculation about participating.[5] Or 2) as due to non-rational factors such as force and emotion. The latter movements, in Olson's view, are irrational, while the former are rational, but only because, for extrinsic reasons, they are individually rational.[6]

I will argue that revolutions in Marx's sense cannot be understood in the terms provided by the utility maximising theory of human behaviour. On the one hand, I will explain how to some extent, in some of its phases, revolutionary activity is rational in the individual utility maximising sense, but on the other hand, I will argue that an adequate explanation of revolutionary motivation must go beyond the narrow mould provided by the utility maximising model. It must be granted right at the outset that Marxists do not have a theory of revolutionary motivation in the sense of a set of conditions that are sufficient for revolutionary action.[7] Since, according to Marxists, it would always be in the interests of the working class to revolt against capitalism yet they only occasionally do so, these interests cannot be a sufficient condition for revolution. Nevertheless, the classical Marxist position is that when the

---

5 Selective incentives are benefits and costs that affect individuals selectively according to whether or not they participate. For example, Olson explains the development of large scale union organisation in the United States as primarily due to their success in winning the closed shop, which gives workers the choice of joining the union or losing their job. This is disputed by, among others. See Booth 1978.
6 Olson 1965, pp. 108–9.
7 Buchanan seems to assume that this is required. See Buchanan 1979, p. 72.

working-class revolts, they do so primarily because they recognize it to be in their interests. Certainly more work needs to be done to explain just what brings about this recognition and the will to act on it. And even Marxists at this point in history should have a certain amount of scepticism mixed with their optimism. However, to demand a set of sufficient conditions and to accept nothing less as an explanation seems rather arbitrary. Such explanations are not available for most behaviour, much less for significant social behaviour. What Marxists should be expected to do is to give an account of the sorts of interrelated conditions which make it probable that workers will engage in revolutionary struggles. Though the classical Marxist theorists have somewhat different emphases at different times, seeing revolution as more inevitable or less so, they are all committed to the rationality of a socialist revolution for roughly the same reasons. I will discuss the sorts of factors they held that moved people toward revolutionary action, in the absence of which they would expect workers to behave in various ways, some of which might be understood quite adequately along utility maximising lines.

In the last part of the paper I will discuss what follows if revolutions cannot be explained in utility maximising terms. This involves a consideration of utility maximisation as a normative model of rationality. Many of the fundamental assumptions of this model are rejected by Marxists. I will explore these assumptions and the alternative assumptions of the Marxist approach. In examining the question of the rationality of revolutionary action I will concentrate on the rationality of the motivation of revolutionaries and—somewhat artificially—ignore the issue of the rationality of their beliefs.

Allowing that much of the time peoples' behaviour can be understood as attempts to maximise individual utility, the situation where participation in revolutionary struggle is most likely is that in which the free rider problem does not hold because there appears to be no conflict between individual interests and group interests. Marxists hold this is true of many cases of revolutionary struggle and simple class struggle. There are public evils as well as public goods—that is, ills that befall every member of a group regardless of what he/she has done, or, that will fall, though not on every member, indiscriminately on many members. Take a dramatic case like the repression—even slaughter—of masses of people if a movement is defeated or if certain forces come to power. In most such cases only collective action has any chance of preventing the evil. If there is little chance of avoiding the evil should the effort fail, then there is little chance of maximising individual utility except by furthering the group's utility. While such struggles start out defensive they are frequently forced to become more far reaching and positive—more revolutionary. As revolutionary movements get underway and individual and group interests tend to converge, individual solutions are less possible, which is one explanation of the momentum movements frequently generate.

However, people sometimes engage in revolutionary activity when individual 'outs' are possible. What explains their participation then? What individual utility theorists claim to be the most common 'solutions' to the free rider problem, viz., selective incentives, are generally unavailable to revolutionary movements. Aside from the fact that this would hardly fit Marx's conception of a socialist revolution as the self-emancipation of the working class, the ability of revolutionary movements to offer bribes or coercive incentives is negligible compared to the ability of their opposition to do the same. Another frequently mentioned solution is what are called 'in-process benefits', goods that are part of the contribution and offset the costs. Revolutionary and pre-revolutionary political/economic struggles often provide for the participants goods that are missing from most peoples' lives: a sense of comradeship, meaningful activity, an understanding of their society and the world and a sense of agency, of taking some control of their lives and affecting the world. However, while these goods may play some explanatory role (particularly in the case of long-time revolutionaries), they are not fundamentally decisive in explaining revolutionary motivation in that some of the goods can be gotten elsewhere and some depend on other factors to be explained.

To understand the motivation of revolutionaries we have to move away from the static and artificial approach of Olson and Buchanan. They pose the problem almost as if workers go from ordinary life to revolution in a single bound. Totally absent from their picture is the long process of struggle that precedes any major social revolt. Though less dramatic and less newsworthy, the many small struggles, made for various reasons, with differing consciousness, are, according to Marxists, critical for the development of working-class consciousness, commitment and organisation. In her classic work, The Mass Strike, the Polish revolutionary Rosa Luxemburg remarked that, 'The most precious, because lasting, thing in this rapid ebb and flow of the wave [of struggles] is its mental sediment: the intellectual and cultural growth of the proletariat ...'.[8] One of the crucial changes brought by collective activity is the trust workers develop that others will join with them, and not leave them out on a limb. The more experience they have of common sharing of risks, the more confidence—

---

8   Luxemburg 1925, p. 35. The recent events in Poland provide a clear example of this in that struggles in 1956, 1970 and 1976 were crucial to the successes in 1980–1. The current defeat will nevertheless provide lessons for the future.

and more basis for confidence—each person has that acting in a collective way will produce the best results and hence that it is rational to take the risk. Organisation can help to sustain this trust.

This is true even on individualist assumptions. It is analogous to games like the Prisoner's Dilemma where a cooperative response from both players yields the best results overall, but where non-cooperation is the most individually rational response if a player cannot be sure of the other's cooperation. Experiments show that in repeated playings of such games cooperation increases, and is more rational because the possibility of communicating the intention to cooperate increases.[9] Since the findings indicate that this is even more likely when the payoffs for cooperation are high, this is particularly applicable to revolutionary action since the participants believe they are likely to be crushed if they do not cooperate but they have a world to win if they do.

Joining together in collective struggle also gives people the recognition of themselves as a collectivity and the tremendous social power the collectivity has—power that led a journalist to describe the leader of the 1980 strikes in Poland as the most powerful man in Poland. They have no sense of this in quiet times because as individuals they have no such power. By coming to realise they have the power to affect society, individuals come to realise that their goal is more possible and their action less risky than they had previously thought. Hence it is more rational from an individualist point of view.

Emphasising that revolutionary action is not a single example of collective action but a process involving many smaller less significant collective actions shifts the question of the rationality of revolution to the rationality of those contributory and constituent actions. Since Olson allowed that in small groups where each individual can rightly feel that his/her contribution can make a difference to the outcome, shifting the problem in this way reduces the free rider problem.

On the other hand, most of the considerations I have advanced for the individual rationality of revolutionary action apply most readily to participation in struggles that are already underway. They apply less readily in most cases to the early stages and to the initiators of struggles. Sometimes something about a situation—sudden deterioration of living conditions, repression or the opening up of new possibilities—can indicate that others will be willing to take similar risks.[10] If so, the initial actions of a struggle could be individually rational as well. However, while the arguments I have given show that in most cases

---

9   Rapoport and Chamman 1964. A. Rapoport 1974. Mathew Edel uses these results to explain how working class actions can be individually rational. See Edel 1979.
10   Edel 1979, p. 755.

there is at least some measure of rationality in the individualist sense to participating in revolutionary action, and in some cases a very high measure, I do not think that such considerations would usually be sufficient to explain why individuals engage in revolutionary action. Even in cases of near coincidence of individual and group interests, it is difficult to say for sure that no individual solutions are possible and there are always some 'free riders'. And as I have emphasised, a revolutionary process consists of many different stages and phases in most of which the risks to the individual of cooperating are greater than of not cooperating. A more adequate account of revolutionary motivations, I believe, has to include factors that do not fit the utility maximising model.

The fact is, even in laboratory situations people do not always choose what is individualistically rational over what will be best overall. In games like the Prisoner's Dilemma, some people cooperate even in the first game and it begs the question to interpret this as game theorists tend to do, as due to the individuals' lack of intelligence. Cooperation of this kind is more likely when there is a sense of identification between people. Capitalism provides the basis for this among workers in that it creates common interests for them as well as what might be called a collective interest. What I mean by workers' collective interest can be seen by contrast with peasants, who Marx believed could not acquire class consciousness and be a revolutionary class despite their common and extreme oppression. Peasants need one another in order to fight their common oppressor, the landlord. But their goal is an individual one—to control their own self-sufficient plot of land. The objectively individualised condition of their lives and their individualised needs create an individualist consciousness. The situation of the working class is quite different. They are concentrated together and, through the interdependent division of labour, are forced into manifold relations with one another. In advanced production processes they compose one collective worker. In addition to sharing oppression and needing one another as a means to overcome it, their goal of controlling their work and their lives cannot be accomplished on an individual basis but is a collective end. Workers cannot control their means of production individually, as can peasants.

Identification has several aspects. In part it involves taking others' concerns as one's own, aiming at a group utility rather than an individual utility. But this is not an adequate characterisation of identification. When people identify with others, they think in terms of 'we' rather than 'I', of 'what should we do?' rather than 'what should I do?' Actions taken on the basis of this kind of identification may or may not be individually rational, but this is not why they are done.

In everyday life in capitalist society this kind of identification is strongest within small units like a couple or a family. Within the working class as a whole there is a basis both for individualism and competitiveness and for commonality. It is especially in times of capitalist crisis when workers can protect themselves only through collective action that the individualist side of their consciousness begins to break down and the collective side of their experiences and consciousness develops and deepens. Unlike economic behaviour in the marketplace or political behaviour in the voting booth, people involved in these kinds of radical economic and political struggles are not isolated atoms.[11] Each individual's action will usually affect the actions (certainly the morale) of at least a few other people—family, friends, immediate co-workers—and vice versa—and their actions will in turn affect the actions of a few others and so on. Because each action usually has these kinds of reinforcing and ripple effects, the individual cannot so readily imagine the result as independent of what he/she does. When people act as a collectivity they begin to think as a collectivity and in the process often begin to see one another as 'brother', 'sister', and 'comrade'. The other aspect of this identification is moral convictions. People feeling this kind of identification with others feel they ought to help if they are going to benefit, and they feel a sense of shame if they 'let the others down'. Other moral principles may play a motivating role as well. While many people might assent to the principles 'no one should go hungry while others are rich', 'people should not be treated like commodities', 'those who produce should control production', they are not usually moved to action by them. Individuals feel—correctly—that they can't do anything about it anyway. But when, through collective action, it seems possible to realise those principles, the commitment to do so can help move people to action and make them willing to take risks—even many who might not even have assented to them before. People are also more likely at these times to feel anger at the violation of their principles—and anger can be a very potent motivating force.

Olson claimed that the 'free rider' problem holds whether behaviour is selfish or unselfish. He is right if 'unselfish behaviour' means individual behaviour directed at a group utility. Each rational individual would calculate either others will contribute enough to achieve the end (the utility of the group) without my effort or they won't. In either case my effort would be a waste. However, if Olson is not committed to psychological egoism it is not clear why 'unselfish behaviour' must be so interpreted. If 'unselfish behaviour' means actions based on identification with others ('what should we do?') or action

---

11 Actually it is questionable whether utility theory can explain even this. See Sen 1970, p. 195.

based on moral principles, then the free rider problem does not hold for unselfish behaviour. Whether or not it is utility maximising, this is not why such behaviour is done. Hence to the extent that revolutionary activity must be understood in these terms the free rider problem is not a problem.[12]

Desires are also more motivating when they seem possible. When people want something but think it is impossible, they usually do not dwell on it; in fact they may not even realise they want it. Similarly, if something painful and onerous seems inevitable, people usually resign themselves to it as much as they can. But such 'survival mechanisms' disappear when suddenly it seems possible to realise the desires or end the pains. What once was hard but could be borne becomes an intolerable weight; what once was a utopian fantasy to be ignored becomes a marvellous possibility.[13] Combined with the previously discussed greater basis for confidence, these feelings that come with a changed sense of possibilities must be part of what explains the euphoria often reported and, what Marxists call, the 'qualitative leaps in consciousness' that occur so frequently in revolutionary struggles, where the goals of the struggle change from reformist to revolutionary almost overnight.[14]

The account of revolutionary motivation I have given emphasises the long process of struggle that leads up to and is part of a socialist revolution as Marx conceived it. The motivation of participants is varied, as are the struggles, and each individual's motivation is probably a slightly different mixture.[15] I have explained various ways and conditions under which involvement in revolutionary and pre-revolutionary struggles can be rational from an individualist point of view. However, I have also argued that this cannot provide a complete explanation and advanced several other factors as important to the explanation. Rosa Luxemburg expressed the inadequacy of an individualist utility

---

12 Engaging in collective action out of moral conviction could be understood as individualistically rational if the person's feeling of self-satisfaction for acting and guilt at not acting provide sufficient selective incentives. However, if we interpret 'selective incentives' so broadly, the theory explains everything and hence nothing. For this reason Olson does not include such factors as selective incentives. So actions taken because of moral convictions do not fit the model of action motivated along individualistically rational lines.

13 See Moore 1978. One might question how one could say that they wanted it If they did not know that they wanted it, but their response when they judge it to be at hand shows that they had wanted it all along. See Brandt and Kim 1969.

14 For example, the initial demand of the Polish strikers in August 1980 was to lower the price of meat and ended in demands that amounted to fundamental restructuring of the society. In Russia in 1917 and in France in 1968, protesters began with economic demands and within a week were calling for the overthrow of the government and for socialism.

15 One problem with the arguments of Olson and Buchanan is that they seem to assume that Marx must have a single factor theory.

approach to revolutionary motivation and the transformative effect of mass action upon individual consciousness as follows:

> ... the revolution brings such an enormous mass of people upon the stage that any computation or regulation of the cost of the movement such as can be affected in a civil process, appears to be an altogether hopeless undertaking ... At the moment that a real, earnest period of mass strikes begins, all these 'calculations' of 'cost'' become merely projects for exhausting the ocean with a tumbler. And it is a veritable ocean of frightful privations and sufferings which is brought by every revolution to the proletarian masses. And the solution which a revolutionary period makes of this apparently invincible difficulty consists in the circumstances that such an immense volume of mass idealism is simultaneously released that the masses are insensible to the bitterest sufferings. With the psychology of a trade unionist who will not stay off his work on May Day unless he is assured in advance of a definite amount of support in the event of his being victimised, neither revolution nor mass strike can be made. But in the storm of the revolutionary period even the proletarian is transformed from a provident 'pater familias' demanding support, into a 'revolutionary romanticist' for whom even the highest good, life itself, to say nothing of material well-being, possess but little in comparison with the ideals of the struggle.[16]

If participation in revolutionary activity cannot in general be explained as individually utility maximising, the conclusion drawn from the normative side of the theory is that such action is irrational. This is the issue to which we now turn.

Now the fact that results that are best overall cannot always be achieved by individualistically rational action is widely acknowledged and hardly peculiar to revolutionary activity. As two well known authorities on game theory put it, in certain situations, 'two 'irrational' players will always fare better than two 'rational' ones'.[17] Since most people find unsatisfactory the conclusion that pursuing the best overall results is irrational, different ways of avoiding this conclusion have been attempted. Some reject the model of rationality as utility maximisation altogether. Others wish to retain the identification of rationality and utility maximisation but revise the individualist model for situations

---

16   Luxemburg 1925, p. 51.
17   Luce and Raiffa 1975, 94–102.

where the actions of individuals affect one another, and hence where some form of agreement and cooperation is in order. Game theorists attempt to devise formal models of such decision-making situations, the closest to our case being n-person cooperative games under uncertainty. However, there is no formal solution to this problem at present which can be applied to any social issue even close to the complexity we are dealing with in this paper.[18] David Gauthier argues that because a straightforward policy of individual utility maximisation does not always yield optimal results, this view of rationality is inadequate.[19] However, he still identifies rationality with utility maximisation. For interdependent action, he contends, it is sometimes rational to agree not to act according to a policy of individual utility maximisation in that agreement will produce an outcome with greater utility for everyone than acting individualistically. He calls this the condition of agreement-constrained maximisation and argues that, while not rational in the traditional (individualist} sense, it follows from this sense.

Gauthier's approach seems applicable to our problem since revolutions involve just such interdependent actions. Since collective action is necessary to achieve the goal of a revolutionary transformation of society, it seems that it would be rational, in Gauthier's sense, for those who share that goal to agree not to act according to individualistic criteria. So long, that is, as they can be assured that others will do the same, but we have seen how this confidence can develop. However, in revolutionary activity the chance of losing one's life is significantly higher than in most forms of collective action. There would then be no benefit for that individual to offset the cost of contributing to the action and Guthier's conception requires that each individual benefit from agreeing not to act individualistically. Whether such action could still be rational in this sense would depend on the estimate of the probability of that outcome, but even a low probability makes it more difficult to justify the action along individual utility maximising lines.

Whether or not it is possible to apply this sort of extended utility maximising approach to revolutionary action1 my account of revolutionary motivation included elements that do not fit a utility maximising model. If those elements are essential to the motivation of revolutionaries then their actions cannot be understood as rational in the utility maximising sense. In what follows I would like to discuss what, from a Marxist point of view, are faulty assumptions in this model of rationality.[20]

---

18   Ibid., p. 115.
19   Gauthier 1974.
20   Some of these points are specifically Marxist; others would be more widely accepted.

According to Marx, although there are some {few} transhistorical features of human beings, such as rationality in the most general sense of intelligence, human nature as a whole changes according to different social and historical conditions. Most important is the different forms of labour people do. Marx says 'By thus acting on the external world and changing it, [man] at the same time changes his own nature'.[21] Theories about human behaviour and motivation ('human nature') also change and, though presented as having universal validity, actually reflect the social/historical conditions in which they emerge. The same is true of many of our basic normative concepts regarding behaviour, such as 'just' and 'rational'. This is what is called Marxist historicist approach.[22] From a Marxist point of view, the identification of rationality with utility maximisation (particularly combined with psychological egoism), reflects the conditions of life in capitalist society. Because capitalism as a system is directed towards maximising profits, peoples' behaviour in capitalist society is closer to that norm than in previous times. It therefore seems plausible as a general descriptive theory to people in capitalism, whereas it would not, e.g., in feudalism.[23] Similarly, since success in capitalist ventures is measured by this criterion, the normative side of the theory seems plausible. Though the theory has greater descriptive validity when relativized to capitalist society, it is not totally accurate as a general theory even there. Revolutionary action is only one example of behaviour that cannot entirely be understood in utility maximising terms. Rationality as utility maximisation (particularly combined with psychological egoism, as it usually is), is a prime example of an ideological theory in Marx's terms, the criteria for which are: 1) it is caused by the socio-economic structure; 2) it wholly or partially distorts the conditions which cause it, and; 3) it functions to maintain the social (i.e., power) relations of that society. Utility maximising theory fits the third condition by presenting radical social change as either impossible or irrational, most likely requiring undemocratic manip-

---

21   Marx 1967, p. 177.
22   '... even the most abstract categories, despite their validity—precisely because of their abstractness—for all epochs, are nevertheless, in the specific character of this abstraction, themselves a product of historic relations, and possess their full validity only for and within these relations' (Marx 1973, p. 105). One problem with Buchanan's discussion of the historicist reply is that he imagines it as only directed against the concept rationality and argues correctly that the problem of explaining revolutionary activity remains. However, the historicist critique also applies to the descriptive theory.
23   Gauthier agrees that this conception of rationality emerged in the modern period but it is not clear what he thinks accounts for the historical change: see Gauthier 1974, p. 43.

ulation or coercion. This critique of utility maximisation as a descriptive theory suggests elements of an alternative descriptive/normative conception of rationality.

One problem in the Olson-Buchanan approach, from a Marxist point of view, is the rigid exclusion of emotions and moral convictions from rational motivation.[24] Marxists' conviction that workers would come to see that it was in their interests to overthrow capitalism and would act on that basis does not exclude workers' emotions and moral principles from playing a motivating role, even an essential motivating role. In their view, moreover, emotions can be reasonable, e.g., anger at oppression. Emotions are rational when they are based on (or can be influenced by) rational beliefs. What Marx rejected in 'moralising socialists' was abstract morality and moral judgments separated from an analysis of peoples' interests, of the conditions being criticised and of how to change them and make possible the realisation of those moral principles. Because utopian socialists had no such theory, they appealed in the name of morality to those whose interests were opposed to change as well as to those whose interests required it. Marx referred to workers' recognition that their alienation from the products of their labour is improper and forcibly imposed as an enormous advance in consciousness. He did so in part because this moral conviction involved, in his view, a correct perception of workers' interests and also because he assumed their awareness would help bring an end to their alienation. So far from interest and moral motives being mutually exclusive, the realisation of this moral principle is an essential interest of workers and can be among the interests (though not material interests) of non-working-class socialists as well.[25]

Most fundamentally, Marxists reject the utility theorists' basic assumption that the concept of rationality is primarily ascribed to the individual, and only in a derivative sense to an action or a society. While Gauthier is correct that this presupposition does not imply that our conception of a rational individual is of someone capable of existing independently of other persons or society, it does imply that the individual can be properly understood independently.[26]

---

24 Olson 1965, p. 108. Buchanan 1979, p. 74.
25 Buchanan also argues that if Marxists wish to give some role to moral principles in their account of revolutionary motivation, they 'must produce an adequate moral principle or set of principles' (Buchanan 1979, p. 81). This is mistaken. The question we have been addressing in this chapter is whether the motivation of revolutionaries in Marx's sense is rational (a question of rational agency). The question of the rationality of Marxist beliefs is a distinct though related question. For a challenge to the usual counterposition of rational and moral considerations in the acceptance of hypotheses, see Gaa 1977, p. 44.
26 Gauthier 1974, p. 412.

Else why should the individual be the conceptual or analytical starting point? That he can be so understood is what Marx denies. Starting from a very different perspective—a social one, Marx describes the human being as an animal which can individuate itself only in the midst of society. The most basic form of human interaction with nature is the production of necessities. And Marx stresses—against the Robinson Crusoe idylls of his day—that production is always social production, calling production by an isolated individual as absurd as the development of language by an isolated individual. Through this interaction, which constitutes a whole 'mode of life', human beings transform nature and themselves. Since Marx was interested in explaining social change and isolated individuals are fairly irrelevant to this, he does not make such individuals the starting point of his theory. '… individuals are dealt with only insofar as they are the personifications of economic categories, embodiments of particular class-relations and class-interest'.[27]

Although individuals are always interdependent, the nature of their interdependence and the relationships between the individual and the group undergo change. Marx says that the further back in history you go the more integrated the individual appears with the social whole—the family, the clan, communal society. In feudalism, for example, the family was the collective unit of production and individuals had no mobility. However, with the rise of competitive capitalism, which involves more developed social relations than ever before existed, individuals acquire greater mobility and the concept of the isolated individual emerges and moves to centre stage. The shift in perspective is seen in all intellectual disciplines, from economics to philosophy to literature. Though the individual assumes this independence only given the context of a particular kind of social organisation and connectedness, this is lost sight of. This individual appears 'not as a historic result but as history's point of departure'.[28] And the point of analytic departure for philosophy and economics as well.

Being primarily about social practices and collective action, the Marxist conception of rationality is more general in character than the utility maximising conception in two respects: it neither applies primarily to individual persons nor to individual acts.[29] Marx's move is analogous to Wittgenstein's move in epistemology and philosophy of mind away from the approach that starts 'from the inside' or 'from one's own case' to behaviour and forms of life. It is not

---

27   See Marx 1974, p. 84. Marx 1978, pp. 150, 157. Marx 1967, pp. xix, 177.
28   Marx 1973, p. 83.
29   Generality could be achieved simply by requiring that rationality be evaluated in terms of rules rather than acts. Though this would be more consistent with Marxism with respect to generality, it would not be consistent in other respects.

implied that individuals do not feel pains or do not behave (ir)rationally, but that the way to understand this is to start with social forms of action. Only with the social context as background is the individual case intelligible. For Marx, however, as opposed to Wittgenstein, the 'social context' is the historically evolved socio-economic structure.

Other fundamental aspects of the view of rationality as utility maximisation that Marxists reject have to do with its means-end approach. Here it is important that utility maximisation not be confused with the simpler notion of instrumental behaviour. That human beings are capable of instrumental behaviour and are rational in this more general sense of intelligence is not at issue. It is the specific assumptions of the utility maximising reconstruction of instrumental behaviour that are rejected, for example, the assumption that all sorts of different ends can be compared meaningfully along a single, quantifiable and open-ended dimension of utility. Utilitarianism has often been criticised on this point. Marxists would add that this idea could only seem plausible in a system—capitalism—where all different sorts of products made by all different sorts of labour are compared along the single and quantifiable dimension of value for the single end of profit maximisation. Thus, the famous statement by a GM spokesman that 'Our business is not to make cars but to make profits'. If they could make more profits by producing hula hoops they would do so.[30] On the other hand, in a system devoted to the satisfaction of human needs, rather than the maximisation of profits, it would be clear that hula hoops and cars are not interchangeable. Needs are specific and require specific goods which require specific forms of labour and materials. Marxists would also challenge the assumption that whatever utility is, it is always rational for a person to want more of it.[31] While this is true of capitalists' need for profits, it is not true of all human wants. Furthermore they would deny that means can always be separated from ends. If the goal is socialism, which is a society organised along democratic and cooperative lines, then the means must also be democratic. In part an empirical issue of the most effective means to the end, this also brings out the point that the means can be a constituent of the end. Collective action is not only instrumentally necessary to achieve the good which is socialism, like the good of clean air, but a certain kind of collective action is an end itself.

---

30   U.S. Steel recently demonstrated this point when they used the money they had gotten from concessions granted by U.S. steelworkers to save their jobs to buy Marathon Oil Company.

31   See Cohen's critique of Max Weber's making of capitalism's preference for output into a canon of rationality. Cohen 1978, p. 320.

Thus, Marxists reject the consequentialism of the utility maximising approach. They would also question some of the technical definitions and assumptions regarding preferences.[32]

Most importantly, Marxists reject the fundamental assumption that rationality has solely to do with means, that, no matter how silly and destructive the end, an act is rational so long as it is an efficient pursuit of that end. From a Marxist point of view, there are deeper senses of rationality than utility maximisation in which rationality is a feature of the society at which they aim. Rationality in a basic sense refers to the exercise of human power and agency. Rational behaviour in this sense is conscious deliberate action, a more rational person one whose actions are the result of his/her conscious decisions, desires, beliefs, etc., and a more rational society one in which more of the basic features are the result of social decisions.[33] In this fundamental sense of 'rational' socialism is rational, capitalism irrational. In socialism production is under conscious collective control, whereas capitalist production is under control of a market which functions 'independent of the will, foresight and action of the producers'; hence it rules the producers instead of the reverse.[34] The only way working-class people can exercise rationality in this sense is collectively; since they have no power to affect society individually, rational behaviour for them necessarily is collective behaviour. To act to further this end of rationality would be rational behaviour in a more fundamental sense to Marxists than the purely instrumental utility maximisation. Revolutionary action would be highly rational because it involves taking the fundamental structure of society as an object of will and acting to transform it. Thus, both the end and the means of revolutionary action are rational.

Rationality is a feature of socialism and irrationality of capitalism in an epistemological sense that follows from the previous point. In brief, Marx's theory

---

32   See Sen 1977. Gauthier 1974.
33   On the Marxist view consciousness has its origins in the social forms of production; when the latter is under conscious collective control, so to that extent will the former. This is developed in my essay on Free Will and a Marxist Concept of Natural Wants. See Holmstrom 1973.
34   Though this is a point well worth developing, I have nothing particular to say here about the method of determining social preferences in socialism/communism except that 1) the Marxist view is that social choice is connected to individual preferences (though exactly how is complicated); 2) Marxists' critique of what they call 'bourgeois democracy' is not so much a critique of its formal system of collective choice—majority rule, (though there might be better mechanisms), as a charge that the issues decided by voting, how the voting is organised, and of course, the power relations make the system *de facto* one of *minority* rule. For Marx's view of 'rights' (restrictions on majority rule), see *The Critique of the Gotha Program* in Tucker. Marx 1978. Marx 1967, 11, 315, 75.

of ideology holds that capitalist society is inherently and systematically mystifying to the people who live in it. Because it is an exploitative society in which production is regulated by a market, the apparent relations between people and between people and production are not the real relations. Marx's theory of surplus value is required to reveal, among other things, that the apparent free and equal relations between individuals are actually relations of class domination, by means of which capitalists extract unpaid labour from workers. Though capitalists have an interest in obscuring the facts, the source of the problem lies deeper. Given capitalist social relations, the illusions 'appear directly and spontaneously as current modes of thought'; hence only revolutionary action can end them. (Capitalist interests are the direct cause of more mundane kinds of mystification e.g., regarding the worth and safety of consumer products.)[35] On the other hand, in a society where production is socially planned and democratic, i.e. where production is rational in the previous sense, the relations between people are 'transparent' and 'intelligible'. This unity of social theory and social practice is a constituent of the 'revolutionised rational world' which is the outcome of successful revolutionary action.[36]

Capitalist society furthermore hinders the development and exercise of rationality even in the utility maximising sense of efficient pursuit of a coherent set of ends (whatever they are). As Mary Gibson argues, basic institutions in capitalism foster inherently conflicting desires in many people so that it is impossible for them to carry out a rational life plan, obstruct much of the knowledge necessary for such a plan, and often make it very difficult to successfully satisfy one's ends by requiring conflicting actions.[37] The 'free rider' problem is an instance of this. In an exploitative and competitive society it is often in one's individual interests to act in a way that conflicts with one's interests as a member of a group, e.g., the working class. The result is that one loses whatever one does. Gibson therefore suggests that 'the only rational course of action for the worker is to reject and abolish the institutional framework which gives rise to this predicament'.[38]

To summarise, Marx's view of rationality differs from the utility maximising conception in the following ways: The latter excludes emotions and moral convictions from the realm of rational motivation whereas Marxists do not. While

---

35   Marx 1967, 542.
36   See 'The Withering Away of Social Science,' Appendix in Cohen 1978. For discussion on forms of consciousness and modes of production, see Sohn-Rethel 1978.
37   Gibson 1967, 213.
38   Ibid., p. 217. This critique is developed in the context of discussing Rawls' use of the (supposedly) 'value-neutral' utility maximisation conception of rationality.

on the utility maximising view rationality is primarily ascribed to individuals, for Marxists it has primarily to do with forms of social practices and collective action. The utility maximising conception of rationality as solely the efficient pursuit of any (coherent set of) ends is, to Marxists, only a very limited sense of rationality. More fundamentally to them rationality is an end—that of bringing the world under conscious human control and thereby establishing a coherence between social practices and the understanding of those practices. Thus from Marx's perspective the idea that rational actions could lead to socially non-optimal—indeed disastrous—results is a *reductio ad absurdum* of the individual utility maximising conception of rationality. And the social arrangements that systematically set up conflicts between peoples' interests as individuals and as members of the working class are obviously irrational.

Marx contended that until socialism the progress of the human species occurs to a large extent at the expense of the individual. Slavery helped to advance Greek and Roman civilisations. Capitalism is historically so progressive for Marx because through the worldwide development of productive forces, it makes possible for the first time in history a society geared to the satisfaction of human needs. To get there requires collective action aimed at that collective end; actions that are merely individually rational will not suffice. Though what is rational from a collective point of view necessarily is in the interests of the majority of individuals in the group, it may or may not be in the interests of each individual. That depends on whether there are ways for a person to maximise his/her individual interests other than by acting for the group's interests. Until society is structured so that there is a coincidence of individual and social interests, what is rational cannot be shown to be always in the interests of each individual working-class person. Only when there is such a coincidence of individual and social interests will the flowering of each individual's potentialities that is preached in capitalism actually be possible.

But if these are just such different conceptions of rationality, how can one decide between them? My aim in this paper was not to produce a theory of rationality but merely to show that the question of the rationality of revolutionary motivation cannot be settled by assuming the descriptive and normative adequacy of the economic model of rationality. Revolutionary action, I argued, is only a dramatic example of behaviour that does not fit the model. Moreover, it cannot automatically be concluded from this that Marx was wrong in believing in a revolution done for rational reasons. Marxists reject many of the fundamental assumptions of the model of rationality that is prevalent in modern Western political theory and have a distinctly different conception.

In conclusion, however, I will offer one consideration in favour of some sort of social conception of rationality. First of all, an empirical supposition: that if the world continues in its present antagonistic, competitive way, nuclear war and ecological disaster are inevitable or at least highly probable. Then we will all have literally nothing to lose. Only some kind of very elaborate social cooperation will prevent this. A critical empirical question is whether this is possible so long as capitalism exists. Marxists believe it is not. (Here is where we need to integrate the motivational and the epistemological issues of rationality.) In any case, using the individualist utility maximising conception of rationality and accepting the free rider problem that arises from it, the social cooperation necessary to avoid disaster cannot be achieved rationally. Rational behaviour, then, will lead to the destruction of the species.[39] Though this is not a logical refutation of this conception of rationality, it seems to me that self-destruction ought to count as some sort of pragmatic refutation.

---

39   Whether some non-individualist but still utility maximising approach would be sufficient to solve this is a further question.

CHAPTER 7

For a Sustainable Future: The Centrality of Public Goods

The most recent report of the UN's Intergovernmental Panel on Climate Change (IPCC) makes it absolutely clear that ways of living in the twenty-first century must be premised on the existential threat to our survival posed by multiple ecological crises. Indeed it could all be over before the end of the century. If we do not radically suppress global CO_2 emissions, global warming will rise to the point where it cannot be stopped. While not long ago the word 'catastrophe' seemed hyperbolic to many, today few could deny it is fitting. Melting glaciers, rising sea level, drought, fires, and flooding all over the world and the resulting migration are catastrophes for those who suffer them—and give us a taste of far worse catastrophes to come. Already the World Health Organization (WHO) estimates that there are 150,000 excess deaths per year due to climate change, likely to double by 2030.

After the 9–11 attack on the World Trade Centre we heard the word 'security' incessantly, almost always invoked as *intentional* threats to our safety and well-being, which of course means they are threats by people, whether they be individuals, groups, or nations. Global warming, on the other hand, is a threat from nature that is an *unintended* result of human action—not what is usually intended by a 'security' threat, and it does not grip our imagination and fears in any way proportional to its severity. But it is not only intentional acts that can threaten our safety and well-being. Once threats to our security are conceived more broadly, consider the greater dangers from unclean air and water and contagious diseases, whatever the mix of intentional and unintentional acts that created the problem.

The narrow conception of security may be beginning to change as the threat from climate change becomes more apparent to more people. Bernie Sanders said in the announcement for his 2020 campaign for President that the greatest security threat we face is global warming. Even while the US spends over three billion dollars on the military (as Desmond Tutu once said, 'you don't get true security from the barrel of a gun'), a broader understanding of the meaning of security has become more common.[1] Since the economic crisis of 2008, amidst

---

1 For an analysis of where tax dollars go in the United States, see research and infographics

ongoing austerity and inequality, there have been more references in the mainstream US press to the number of Americans who are 'food insecure'. Indeed, even the 2019 Worldwide Threat Assessment, issued by the Director of National Intelligence, brings the two ideas of (in) security together in their warning that 'climate-driven food shortages could increase the risk of social unrest, migration and interstate tension'.[2]

While the Pentagon has said repeatedly that climate change is a national security threat, what they have in mind is that climate change is likely to destabilize some countries, threatening US military installations and leading to mass migration, intra-state conflicts, and terrorism, thus threatening 'national security'. So the concept of security is still understood in these warnings simply as protection against intentional threats by other people. While we used to worry about intentional threats only from criminals, now more and more people have to carry, even to wear, ID cards, big concrete blocks line the sidewalks of many of our streets, and our access to countless public buildings is tightly controlled by phalanxes of security guards and video monitors. But most people pay little attention; the possibility of terrorist attacks has been normalized.

The left's most urgent ideological task in the face of this, as well as the environmental crisis itself, is to make people see the world and themselves in broader and more inclusive terms. As Dr Robert Bullard, often called the father of environmental justice, once put it: 'There's no Hispanic air, no African American air, or white air, there's just air. ... if you're concerned about the quality of that air, I would consider you an environmentalist ... you just might not know it'.[3]

1 Rethinking Property and Rationality: From the Individual to the Collective

The concepts of property and rationality are foundational to the way we think about society and about ourselves. The predominant ways these are commonly

---

produced by the War Resisters League, available online (www.warresisters.org/resources/pie-chart-flyers.com). The 2020 figures show 1.7 trillion dollars going to the military, a figure obscured by the official government calculations.
2   Davenport 2019. Oftentimes these warnings focus on population growth as the principal cause, which then are used to justify strict population control measures focused on women in the Global South. For a critique see Silliman and King 1999.
3   Akuno and Nangawa 2017, p. 217.

understood serve to support capitalism. If we are to have a sustainable future, making an appreciation of public goods and a new understanding of 'the commons' central to a transformed 'common sense' understanding of security, we need to start by transforming the meanings of property and rationality.

Unlike the technical definition of mainstream economists, by public goods I am referring to goods that all can share because they are not privately owned; they are not commodities. My enjoyment of them does not preclude your enjoying them as well. Some goods are public because of their intrinsic nature, like air, others are public because their nature makes it too inconvenient to make them private (a lighthouse), and still other goods like education or health care are public—if they are—only because people have struggled to take them out of the private for-profit sector and make them available to all.

Public goods satisfy universal needs, though the importance of their being public varies. Even for the intrinsically public goods, whose importance is universal, there are still class variations. If water is unclean, some people can buy it, but most cannot. Air has not yet been commodified, but if air is not clean, the rich can buy gas masks or move; hence the thousands of middle-class Chinese fleeing the country. But this is obviously a very poor substitute. Though society as a whole benefits from good systems of public education and medical care, their importance to individuals varies greatly by class. They provide far better education and medical care than most everyone can achieve on their own, but the rich do not need them. Public parks provide what only the very wealthy can provide for themselves. Moreover, public goods are interconnected; people without one tend to be deprived of others.

2 Property

When can we say of something that 'it's mine?'—that it belongs to me, that it's my property? Leaving aside our bodies and body parts, which are inseparable from us, there is one kind of property everyone has.[4] It might be as little as the clothes on one's back, or a bicycle, some furniture, and a modest pension plan, or for the more fortunate among us, several houses filled with furniture and clothing along with cars in the garage and a great deal of money set aside for retirement. Whether a bare minimum or a great deal, if this property is all just

---

4   Whether individuals can in some sense own themselves has been much debated among political philosophers. For arguments that this idea of self-ownership functions as a defence of capitalism and that it is not a helpful way for the left or for feminists to claim individual rights, see Holmstrom and Cudd 2011, pp. 167–73.

for one's personal use, then it should be called *personal* property. On the other hand, if the cars were part of a taxi business, or the houses part of a real estate development, then they are not for personal use but function as capital because they are used to make more money. In this case, they are not personal property but *private* property. This is the kind of property Marx defined as depending on the non-existence of property in the hands of the majority—and which thereby allows the capitalist to subjugate the labour of others—while pointing to the abolition of private property as required to overcome this.

Note: *first*, that property is a right not a thing and *second*, that the key to having both personal and private property is the right not only to use the property, but also to exclude others' use of it, and to sell or otherwise dispose of the property. They are essentially rights of exclusive use on the part of the property owner and exclusion of all others. In contrast, common or collective property (whether called public goods, or the commons), such as a public park, is by definition open to all. Every individual has a right to use the park. Thus—a *third* essential point—common property involves an individual right to property just as much as private property does. This fact is usually overlooked, because of the equation of an individual right of property with private property.[5] The difference between these kinds of individual rights to property is simply that common property does not entail a right of exclusion. Historically, in England, 'the commons' referred to land on which commoners had the right to graze their animals, forage for wild food, and collect firewood, rights they lost in the enclosure movement at the beginning of capitalism. Not surprisingly, the commoners saw the enclosures as theft of their land; each one lost his/her right to use the land. Similar processes occurred around the world then—and continue today—as people lose access to lands that had been held communally for centuries. This happens wherever capitalism extends its reach into non-capitalist regions, whether in a geographical sense or into new sectors of society.[6] Laws are then changed or reinterpreted to lend legitimacy to the theft.

Today the term 'commons' is used more broadly than it once was, not only for land and other natural resources, but for the cultural/intellectual sphere as well—radio waves, the Internet, scientific knowledge, etc. All are part of our common human heritage, created by countless people around the globe, throughout human history, building one upon the other. Hence they are all

---

5   Compare Macpherson 1962.
6   Capitalism has also expanded into post-capitalist societies. See Holmstrom and Smith 2000; Qinglian 2000. David Harvey's influential concept of 'accumulation by dispossession' includes capital's geographic expansion to commodification of things and services that had formerly been free to large capital's taking over small capital. See for instance: Harvey 2003.

collective human products, whatever particular individuals have contributed most recently. When something that was or could be accessible to all is made private, whether it is water or seeds, medicine or music, or education, this privatisation can be conceived as an enclosure too. The fundamental question is who should have the right to use and control these goods? Why should some have the right to exclude everyone else?

Across the political spectrum in capitalist society the default is private property. *Our task as socialists is to turn that capitalist assumption on its head and make public goods/the commons the default.* The pragmatic reason for this is that this is the only way common goods can be protected from profit-driven development.[7] Logical, moral, and political reasons also argue for making common property the default. Hence it is privatisation, taking away the right of use, that should have to be justified.[8] Furthermore since all human beings are equal from a moral point of view, the basic assumption should be in favour of equal access to the Earth's resources and to collective products of humankind—and also equal right to decide how they are used. So again the burden of justification should be on those who would exclude, i.e. on claims to private property. This prioritisation of common property provides a philosophical justification of civil disobedience in defence of the environment.[9]

In the case of natural resources, speaking in terms of property *of any kind* is problematic. Marx suggested that one day the idea of ownership of the Earth would seem as morally repugnant as the idea of owning another human being. Better, he suggested, to see humans as caretakers of the Earth for future generations; as Native Americans believe, 'for the seventh generation'.[10] Stewardship rather than ownership as the proper relationship between humans and the natural world is a common tenet of most of the world's religions, showing the

---

7   Contrary to the 'tragedy of the commons argument', long exposed as a fallacy, there are countless cases of resources held in common that have been managed in sustainable ways, sometimes for centuries. Nobel Prize winner Elinor Ostrom's work on 'common pool resources' shows that groups as well as individuals can cooperate and plan, and negotiate and abide by rules that they devise. See Ostrom 1990.
8   Compare to Anton 2000.
9   Recent court cases in the US appealing to the public trust doctrine (which says that the government is responsible for protecting natural resources) have presented protestors as law-*enforcers* rather than law-*breakers*. Several cases on behalf of children against the US government for promoting fossil fuels and thereby de-stabilizing their future environment have been allowed to proceed in the courts despite vigorous opposition from both business and government. See: *Juliana v United States of America*, and others on the state level, including *Aji P v State of Washington*.
10 Marx 1967, p. 776.

potential for the broadest of coalitions to fight for taking our natural resources out of the hands of capital and putting it under popular democratic control.

3   Rationality

According to the individualist model of rationality that is dominant in the social sciences and philosophy, as well as being the modus operandi of capitalism, fully rational behaviour can lead to the destruction of the species. How could such a bizarre conclusion follow?[11]

Given the importance of public goods—even sometimes life and death importance as in the case of clean air and water—it would seem the most rational thing in the world to work together to achieve them. But according to the dominant model, known as Individual Utility Maximization (IUM), which is supposed to apply to persons, organisations, including corporations, or countries, it is not. When an individual's behaviour is rational, she aims to maximize her own utility, *whatever* that might be. Offered as both a descriptive and a normative theory, IUM is inadequate on both counts. Allowing no judgment as to the ends themselves, it reduces them all to the one quantifiable end of utility and assumes we want to maximize them all. Not only does this fail to do justice to the diversity of our goods; it is particularly dangerous because it lends ideological support to capitalism's endless growth machine. Certainly many times human beings do act as the theory describes, especially in our society, but the fact is that people do not always choose what is individually best rather than what is best overall, even in laboratory situations, and it begs the question to say that their behaviour is therefore irrational. Human choices and preferences are far more complex than IUM allows, as has been shown a long time ago.[12]

In the real social world IUM generates puzzles as to how collective action, e.g. working in an environmental group, ever takes place and how it could be rational. Since, according to IUM, groups are only collections of individuals, it is only rational to do something if it is rational for the majority of individual members. But since each individual could get the benefits of a clean environment without contributing, it would be irrational for them to do so, a conclusion known as the free rider problem. Though they might do so out of moral conviction, emotion, or coercion, this would not be rational. However, if

---

11   The following rests on earlier work: Holmstrom 1983. I cannot do justice in this chapter to the very technical literature on rational choice theory (including by some writers sympathetic to Marxism).
12   Sen 1977, pp. 317–44. Kuttner 1997.

many act rationally they will not get what would benefit them all, even their own self-preservation. Certainly, building the solidarity necessary to override the free rider problem is a challenge, but it happens and it is not therefore irrational. Nor must rational behaviour be devoid of moral conviction or emotion, as Hume and Aristotle recognized. The most fundamental problem with IUM is that it starts from the assumption that rationality is primarily ascribed to the individual and only derivatively to the group or a society. This implies that the individual can be understood independent of society, a highly dubious assumption since the very notion of an isolated individual only arose in the context of a very particular kind of social organisation. Instead, rationality should be looked at first from within a social context, and if there is a conflict, the social point of view should take priority.

Because individuals can identify with others and have irreducibly social goals as well as egoistic ones (a fact omitted by IUM), sometimes the distinction between behaviour that is individually and collectively rational is not clear. But when the distinction is clear, e.g. if I want to dispose of my company's waste into a stream because it is most convenient and cheaper, and because I can get away with it, IUM would say that is the rational choice (even if it is immoral) and it would be irrational not to do so. On the other hand, from a social model of rationality, which involves taking a long-term perspective, it is very irrational. Note that if one were to say that there are simply two perspectives on what is rational (a relativist position), this suffices to refute the IUM claim that cooperative behaviour is irrational (or could be rational only under special conditions e.g. with material incentives to cooperate). However, I suggest that the relativist position is too weak; rather than being neutral we can say that taking the long-term social point of view is simply more rational, as well as the right thing to do from a moral or political point of view. After all, 'short-sighted' is practically synonymous with 'foolish', 'far-sighted' with 'rational'. Thus if our polluter were to switch from the individualist to the social perspective, it is not just a *different* outlook but also an *advance* in consciousness. A society that disallowed production of designed-obsolescent products would be more rational than one that encourages throwaway products because they are more profitable. For consider the function of rationality. Clearly it is the chief evolutionary advantage humans have, giving us control over the world, including ourselves, which we would otherwise lack. Our ability to think, discuss, plan and cooperate with others for long and short-term ends extends this advantage. After all, not all our goals can be accomplished individually no matter how rational we are. When people cooperate to achieve some common goal, e.g. to shut down a nuclear plant, or when they join together in a union or a political group, their individual capabilities become collective capabilities, allowing them to achieve what they could not otherwise. Since prioritising long-term interests gives people greater control over their world—the way rational behaviour is supposed to do—it is reasonable to consider this *an expansion of rationality*.

That thoroughly rational behaviour would lead to the destruction of the species is the *reductio ad absurdum* of the IUM perspective. It remains dominant only because it fits so well with capitalism. It is long past time to replace the individualist utility maximisation model with a social model of rationality that will facilitate the creation of a sustainable future.

4 From Common Sense to Common Practice: Struggles around Public Goods

'When Did The Common Good Become A Bad Thing?' stood out among the many wonderful creative signs from the Occupy Wall Street protests. The central focus of socialist strategy in the twenty-first century should be protecting and radically expanding public goods/the commons. We should use every means we can to raise peoples' understanding that public goods/the commons, especially natural resources 1) are the only basis of real security; 2) should be accessible by all as a right, and hence no one should be excluded by the alleged rights of private property; and 3) are foundational to the most rational way to organize society. Making those re-conceived collectivized concepts of security, property, and rationality central to our organising is a way to resist capitalism and can help to inspire more radical visions and strategies. I will discuss examples based in the US that fit this approach, though clearly the principles must be taken to the international level.

Since auto-related emissions are the lion's share of emissions in the US, let us compare the radical liberal environmentalist position with that of the eco-socialist. Most proposals for a massive switch to electric cars, away from fossil fuels, are advanced without calling for cutbacks on growth. This is completely insufficient. First of all, most of the pollution from producing *any* car comes before it gets on the road. Second, producing electric cars is even more polluting than producing gasoline-powered cars. Thirdly, much as we would like to have it all, we can't; growth simply must be curtailed. So what is to be done? Eco-socialists reject market solutions like carbon taxes which leading oil companies actually support because they just add a cost to their business (which can be passed along to consumers) and do not put any limits on growth. Moreover, they have not worked, since they were always too low to make a difference.

While the scientific facts and the daily news reports of 'extreme weather incidents' have been most crucial in creating a new sense of urgency, socialists have an important role to play combatting ideological resistance to governmental action and helping people to see that it is their right to decide what to do regarding this existential threat. We must always stress the necessity of democratic control. There are risks to almost everything we humans do and we often have competing goals. This means that complex decisions and often trade-offs have to be made, and no one is in a better position to make these decisions than the people who are most directly affected. Bhopal and Chernobyl remind us of the dangers of undemocratic control, whether private or public.

However, to translate these ideas into social power the support of the labour movement is crucial. They should be allies and leaders in this struggle since, as the slogan goes, there are no jobs on a dead planet. But that is the long run. Meanwhile, most unions see their principal task as defending the immediate interests of their members; thus, the AFL-CIO Energy Committee, dominated by the building trades and utility company unions, followed their short-term interests and rejected the Green New Deal. However, some more far-sighted unions like the National Nurses Union and the American Transport Union have signed on, and some locals have supported it, like the Los Angeles United Steelworkers local—whose resolution was endorsed by the LA Central Labour Council, the second largest in the country. Clearly this will be a critical struggle; to take the position that is in their members' *long-term* interest, the major labour unions in the United States will have to be convinced that their members will be protected in the transition while being pushed from below and outside to be sure that this happens.

The recent battles in the US for public education are very significant and inspiring for the broad solidaristic politics they have manifested, and could be a model for a revived labour movement. Words are important. Not only were their demands broad and inclusive, but they also said explicitly that they were striking for the common good. Over time, that kind of solidarity is the best way to overcome distrust and change minds. Public employees combining with those they serve is a huge step forward and hopefully can be emulated in other sectors.[13] Too often workers and consumers are pitted against one another—and workers with some benefits and protections are pitted against those who lack them. Public employees are especially vulnerable to this kind of divisive

---

13   For example, transit workers' unions could reach out to riders about common interests, like better staffing. For a more radical strike tactic, bus drivers could not collect fares. Hilary Wainwright's work details several such examples. Too often public employees' unions, including teachers, have had a narrow trade union orientation that alienated them from the public they serve. See Wainwright 2003.

anti-working-class ideology in the United States because it is taxpayers who pay their salaries, and fewer and fewer workers in the private sector have union protections.

Meanwhile, faced with closures of several auto plants in the US and Canada, and the loss of 14,000 jobs in Michigan alone, some movement along eco-socialist lines has sprung up among autoworkers. Instead of struggling vainly to keep the plants open making ever more cars, a number of radical autoworkers have campaigned to convert the plants to producing wind turbines, electric buses, trains, and any elements of the infrastructure that needs to be rebuilt. Back in 2008 when the US government bailed out General Motors, a group calling itself the Autoworkers Caravan went to Washington, calling for the nationalisation and conversion of the US auto industry. It got little attention—but today a bit more so, as Congresswoman Rashida Tlaib and the Detroit branch of the Democratic Socialists of America (DSA) now back it. Such a conversion is definitely doable from a technical point of view; it was only months after Pearl Harbor that auto plants were making planes, tanks, guns, and ammunition. As a Swedish autoworker and union leader stressed, autoworkers have the tacit knowledge of both mass production and the potential for change: '… the auto industry is not a coalmine. It's a flexible machine that society can use to make almost anything on a large scale. Send us the blueprints for socially useful stuff, and we'll make it'.[14]

The importance of models should never be underestimated; they build experience, capacities, and serve as examples for other initiatives. The Plan developed by rank-and-file workers at Lucas Aerospace in 1976 for the conversion of their largely military production to socially useful production was hugely influential in the '70s and '80s, even being nominated for the Nobel Peace Prize. Workers came up with 150 doable ideas, relying on their tacit knowledge of the production process. Such a model of worker-controlled production for social good rather than profit is frightening not only to the capitalists, but also to mainstream trade union leaders and the Labour Party—as seen by their tepid support. Unfortunately this potential was killed by the rise of Thatcherism, but the Lucas Aerospace Plan still inspires activists.[15] In times and places with greater acceptance of government involvement in the economy, and with

---

14   Henriksson, 2015. For how a conversion could happen under public ownership see Gindin 2018. The Autoworkers' Caravan is part of the Detroit Green New Deal Coalition, along with DSA and community groups. They propose a Great Lakes Authority modeled after FDR's Tennessee Valley Authority to 'make the Rust Belt Green'. See Fernandez-Silber 2019, pp. 10–11.
15   Smith 2014.

some supporters in the government—and yet more climate disasters—such ideas might have a better chance, starting perhaps at a local level. Since this is a broad issue affecting not only workers, they could try to organize councils including the community and the anti-war and environmental movements.

Cooperation Jackson (Mississippi) provides another kind of exciting model that is compatible with this.[16] A local community network connected to the Our Power Campaign of the Climate Justice Alliance, influenced by the radical black nationalist tradition, along with Marxism and anarcho-syndicalism, Cooperation Jackson is explicitly anti-capitalist and eco-socialist, carrying forward the vision of Mayor Chokwe Lumumba, after his untimely death in 2013, to establish a network of living/working self-sustaining cooperatives along with decision-making Peoples' Assemblies. By reducing reliance on fossil fuels, producing renewables, and reducing consumption, they aim to create an ecological city resting on economic democracy and black self-empowerment. However, being a small and very poor city, they desperately need capital and have not yet been able to build a sufficient number of cooperatives to equal 10 per cent of the city's GDP, which was their goal at this stage. Cooperation Jackson thus shows the strengths and weaknesses of a local community-based approach. They are well aware that their success will depend on larger political forces. The US does not have a radical party that could give them the kind of support they need, but should the Green New Deal come into existence they could benefit.

But cooperatives can end up just competing with one another. To avoid this tendency, they need to encourage broader goals, connect with other small-scale efforts and make connections with eco-socialists and labour groups. A network of radical municipal initiatives around the world, such as the exciting experiment of a new kind of bottom-up party in Barcelona would be an important goal.[17] As Hilary Wainwright has argued: 'In many diverse locations, grassroots trade union and community alliances have been a driving force in the defence and improvement of public services or utilities in the face of privatization'.[18] Since Americans in particular are facing what can be definitely be called a crisis of social reproduction, perhaps that conceptualisation, popular among socialist feminists today, will prove to be a useful way of bringing together diverse struggles. But socialist feminism has always stressed that the lives of working women do not begin and end at the workplace and so it is necessary to bring together issues affecting their families and their communities. Beyond

---

16   Akuno and Nangwaya 2017.
17   Charnock and Ribera-Fumaz 2017.
18   Wainwright 2016, p. 94.

education and health care, there is no issue more important for communities today than the ecological one. The rational transformation of our global economy of the magnitude and scale that is necessary for genuine security may seem impossible. But the visionary yet practical examples now coming forward, such as from Canadian postal workers' campaign 'Delivering Community Power' point to what an eco-socialist future could look like.[19]

The Labour Network for Sustainability (LNS) and Trade Unions for Energy Democracy (TUED) are trying to make this happen. LNS, whose mission 'is to engage workers and communities in building a transition to a society that is ecologically sustainable and economically just', has recently issued a report called 'Clean Energy Future' that offers an optimistic approach to the jobs vs. environment conundrum, contending that there are jobs in protecting the environment.[20] Sean Sweeney of TUED has argued that because renewable energy is not sufficiently profitable at this stage for private enterprise to make the conversion, it requires public ownership or government loans along the lines of Roosevelt's Rural Electrification Administration.[21] Although this does not address all the other industries heavily dependent on energy, it's an important point that could be repeated for other industries. The LNS report is along the lines of the Green New Deal, and Jeremy Brecher, the LNS's Research and Policy Director, has drawn up a detailed prescription of how a Green New Deal could be enacted.[22] Yet while stressing the importance of labour activism and community and environmental groups—not least in terms of strengthening the left of the Democratic Party—there is no mention of capitalism.

Alexandria Ocasio-Cortez's Green New Deal proposal has definitely opened the conversation about climate change, and pushed it away from sole reliance on market-oriented solutions. But it contains no explicit call to stop the endless growth of the economy, does not explicitly call for shutdowns of any industries, and does not propose nationalisation. However, all of these would seem to be entailed by the call for 'de-carbonization'. How else could this be accomplished? While also starting from the example of FDR's command and control economy, in which he ordered auto makers to produce tanks, planes, etc. instead of private cars, Richard Smith has gone further in proposing 'a strategy of rationally planned, democratically managed transition to renewable energy that avoids economic collapse and guarantees re-employment for the affected workers'. Smith's specific proposal is based on four points:

---

19 Canadian Union of Postal Workers 2023.
20 Brecher 2019.
21 Sweeney 2019.
22 Brecher 2019, Brecher, Blackwell and Uehlein 2014.

1. Declare a State of Emergency to suppress fossil fuel use: ban all new extraction, ration gasoline, ban production of new fossil-fuel vehicles. Nationalize the fossil fuel industry to phase it out. We propose to do this by means of a government buyout at fair value (fair to both owners and society). Nationalize downstream fossil fuel industrial consumers ... whose business is irreversibly based on fossil fuels and which without a government buyout would be bankrupted.
2. Institute a new federal Public Works Administration-style jobs program to re-employ every worker in the fossil fuel-related industries at equivalent pay and benefits in other useful but low-emission work.
3. Launch an emergency state-directed program to phase-in renewable electric generation, replace fossil-fuel powered transportation with electric propulsion, discourage individually owned vehicles, and encourage public transit, shared vehicles, bicycles and other non-fossil fuel modes of transportation.
4. Develop emergency plans to phase out wasteful, destructive and polluting industries from arms production to needless toxics, designed-to-be-obsolesced iPhones, cars etc. Develop emergency plans to shift from fossil-fuel dependent factory farms to fully organic agriculture.[23]

Smith calls de-carbonisation a 'self-radicalizing transitional demand'. The immensity of the full political, economic and social transformation required need not lead to fatalism; on the contrary facing head-on what is needed to avoid catastrophe can be highly motivating. As 16-year-old Greta Thunberg said to world leaders at Davos: 'I don't want your hope. ... I want you to panic. I want you to feel the fear I feel every day'. The activism by millions of children on this issue is the brightest spot on the horizon. Perhaps some modest victories, even if inadequate, combined with the continuing ecological crises, will help to build a movement that can push beyond to the kind of vision eco-socialists put forward. We also cannot ignore the historical lesson which tells us that, in conjunction with policy proposals, more radical disruptive direct action tactics along the lines of the Sunrise Movement and the Extinction Rebellion will be necessary.

In response to an Intergovernmental Panel on Climate Change (IPCC) report, UN Secretary-General Antonio Guterres warned world leaders to 'Do what the science demands before it's too late'.[24] Yet the impossibility of doing this within a capitalist system, where profit maximisation through economic growth must

---

23   Smith 2019. Smith 2016. Skandier 2017. Skandier 2018. Gowan 2018.
24   Sengupta 2018.

be systematically prioritized, has become ever clearer with each passing decade of unimpeded global warming.[25] Humans have always taken things from nature and transformed them for sustenance, but capitalism's relentless transformation of nature as part of its accumulation strategy (Marx refers to fish as a productive force in the fishing industry) has led to depletion of what's needed for human sustenance. This same imperative for growth explains the attack on the public sector. Capitalism needs to search out ever new areas of profitability, both geographically and in non-capitalist areas of society, by commodifying what had been free, whether parts of nature like air and water, labour (care work for example), or public services. Capitalist globalisation has meant deregulation and privatisation of public goods all over the world. The effect has been, predictably, disastrous for the majority of the world's populations, especially the poorest. As Elmar Altvater succinctly puts it: 'Social, economic and political security depend on public goods being readily available'.[26]

Deregulation and privatisation are exactly the opposite of what we need. Instead we need to move to a radically different system with more ecologically sustainable production and consumption patterns and lifestyles. This requires planning. At what level should the planning be? Local knowledge tends to be more reliable, as Ostrom's work shows, but many things cannot be accomplished at a local or even a countrywide level. The whole planet shares the air. The issue is not primarily whether planning is local, regional, national, or even international, but *what kinds of institutions enable rational democratic control from below and effectively address our environmental crisis*. Whatever markets there are should be embedded in the larger social economy. But the very word 'planning' brings massive opposition from all quarters, because planning is equated with the centralized command planning of the Soviet system that did not work. Elmar Altvater and others explain this failure by the absence of democratic feedback needed for corrections, innovation, and dynamism, as well as the inertia and paralysis at the centre, and the alienation of working

---

25 System Change not Climate Change 2023. www.SCNCC.org. Not all critics of growth agree that a socialist alternative is desirable or necessary. Herman Daly in the United States and the decroissance school in Europe seem to believe that growth can be a choice. If it should turn out that capitalism could be reformed so as to become sustainable, it would be such a radically transformed system that it is not clear it should be called capitalism.

26 Altvater 2004, p. 1. Altvater 2002. She shows that growth has also failed to solve the problems of unemployment, inequality and economic instability that mainstream economists claimed for it.

people.[27] Their unutilized capacities and tacit knowledge, however, would be liberated in a genuinely democratic system'.[28]

Marx's vision of socialism, as rational democratic planning, shows that planning and democracy are not counterposed. In *Capital* Volume III, he says that while after capitalism, in a new 'higher form of society', i.e. socialism, there will always be material production:

> Freedom in this field can only consist of ... the associated producers, rationally regulating their interchange with Nature, bringing it under their common control ...; and achieving this with the least expenditure of energy and under conditions most favourable to, and worthy of their human nature. But it nonetheless still remains a realm of necessity. Beyond it begins that development of human energy which is an end in itself, the true realm of freedom, which, however, can blossom forth only with the realm of necessity as its basis. The shortening of the workday is its basic prerequisite.[29]

If we add 'consumers' to the 'associated producers', we have a vision of a radically democratic society where we can choose if, where, and how we want to grow. Whereas in capitalism, every technological advance in production leads to more production (the Jevons paradox), in socialism we could take advantage of technological progress to produce less and work less. Unlike capitalist democracies, the most crucial decisions affecting us all: what to produce (gas-guzzling and driverless private cars versus buses and trains), how to produce (fossil fuels or renewables), and the all-important question of *how much* to produce would be decided democratically, most likely by councils of producers and consumers. Expertise is only required to lay out the implications of different options and then to figure out how best to implement their decisions.[30] This of course does not entail that producers and consumers will always make the right decisions, but without the built-in pulls in other directions (as in capitalism), and because of the fact that it is they who will bear the consequences, mistakes are less likely and would be corrected. This illustrates the point that

---

27 Altvater 1993.
28 Wainwright 2018, p. 183.
29 Marx 1967, p. 820.
30 Goldsteen and Schorr 1991. After the near-meltdown at Three Mile Island one woman said that if they had just explained the possible consequences of relying on nuclear reactors to get cheap energy, she would have preferred to hang her clothes out to dry. If the community's values had been in place, they would not have come to a near-catastrophe.

different modes of production will have different measures of efficiency and different rationalities.[31]

That we cannot have socialism in one country is even more apparent when we are talking of eco-socialism. Based on a global commitment to public goods/commons as the default and a social rationality we can aim for the '*buen vivir*' for all. To achieve that we need to contract in the over-producing/consuming countries of the North and expand (sustainably) in the South, thus leading to a contraction and convergence. An important step in that direction would be something like the Green New Deal on a global scale, including a commitment to regenerative agriculture.[32] This all would require more institutions of international governance, that is, planning and regulation, such as a United Nations of socialist societies, as well as local, regional, and national institutions. This now seems impossible, but if civilisation is to survive the twenty-first century, we have to do our best to make it begin to seem inevitable.[33]

---

31 Holmstrom and Smith 2007.
32 Ries, 2019.
33 Lowy 2006; Smith 2017, pp. 283–304.

PART 3

Freedom

∴

CHAPTER 8

Free Will and a Marxist Concept of Natural Wants

Most philosophers today would probably hold that freedom is compatible with determinism. This position is known as compatibilism.[1] I will first explain the version of the theory I find most persuasive and then attempt to show that the theory is inadequate unless it is supplemented by some distinction between wants that are truly the person's and those that are not. I will then explain Marx's account of consciousness and human nature on the basis of which a distinction can be drawn between natural or truly human wants and false or artificial wants. Using Marx's distinction in a revised version of compatibilism one can understand and see the justification for Marxists' claim that almost no act done in a capitalist society (or any other class society) is free in the most basic sense.[2]

The version of compatibilism I find most persuasive rests the notion of freedom on the notion of what a person has the power to do, which in turn rests on the notion of a person doing what he/she wants to do.[3] Compatibilists often appeal to what are taken to be clear cases of free acts to support their analysis, such as going to the movies, ordering coffee, taking a walk. Circumstances in which we. would be inclined to say that they were not clearly free are those in which there is evidence that the. cause was something other than the agent's

---

1 Representative of contemporary 'compatibilist' approaches· but somewhat different and less adequate, I think, than the view I expound are Schlick 1966. Hobart 1966. Earlier versions are found in Hill 1872. Hume 1956.
2 I am treating wants and desires as mental entities of some sort. If this is incorrect and wants should be conceived in some other way, e.g., behaviouristically or as a kind of connection between reasons and actions, I do not think this would call for *substantive* changes in what I am concerned to argue. This approach bypasses the alleged distinction between so-called positive freedom and negative freedom. It emphasizes the person's ability to do certain things (so-called positive freedom). However, a person's ability to do anything clearly depends upon and so 'includes and implies the absence' of various restrictions (so-called negative freedom). The only difference that can intelligibly be made between these 'two kinds of freedom' is one of emphasis. I emphasize the positive aspect because it seems to me that the desirability of being *free from* constraints is owed to the ability it gives one to do the things one wants to do.
3 The model actually is that of a continuum with clear cases of free acts at one end and clear cases of unfree acts at the other with many or most acts in between.

desire. An act is free if and only if it is caused by the wants of the agent.[4] Acts which are clearly unfree are done against one's desires; they are compelled.[5]

The compatibility of freedom and determinism follows from: this definition of a free act. To say that an event is determined is simply to say that it is caused, i.e., it is described by the consequence of causal law. Free acts are acts which are determined primarily by the wants and desires of the agent.[6]

One might think that this account of free acts applies to a drug addict taking his drug and a kleptomaniac's stealing. These acts issue from desires and hence would be free. Yet drug addiction and kleptomania are physiological and psychological compulsions, respectively, and acts resulting from compulsions are unfree. Examples like these, however, are not counterexamples to compatibilism because they are not examples of the sorts of acts done out of desire that the compatibilist has in mind.[7] If the causes of the drug addict's taking drugs and the kleptomaniac's stealing should properly be called desires or wants at all, which is dubious, they are certainly unusual ones. The person may want very much not to have that want, in fact these wants may be totally in conflict with all the rest of the person's wants, values, beliefs, attitudes and character and yet these wants still determine the person's acts. So if such acts are the expression of a want they are also in conflict with a greater number of integrated wants. They may even be in conflict with the want that the agent wants to have and with which the agent has thereby identified him or herself.[8] Both these factors would give sense to the claim that the act did not proceed from the self as a free act must.[9] 'Wants' such as these can also be called cravings or compulsions.

---

4 I am using 'wants' and 'desires' interchangeably. There is a sense of 'want' that is considerably weaker than 'desire' but I am ignoring this sense and using the sense of 'want' in which they are equivalent.

5 I am taking acts to be a certain subset of events in which persons are involved. A further specification of the subset is beyond the. scope of this paper.

6 I am assuming that laws explaining much of human behaviour will either (1) make reference to wants and desires, (2) be translatable into or reducible to others that either (a) do make reference to wants and desires or that (b) will be true if and only if some law that does make reference to wants and desires is true.

7 We consider the man to be more or less unfree, and hold him less accountable, because we rightly view the influence of the drug as 'external' even though it is found within the body; *it prevents him from making decisions in the manner peculiar to his nature'.* Schlick 1966, p. 59. I take these remarks of Schlick to be suggestive hints in the direction I develop.

8 This way of putting the *point* and the general importance of '2nd order volitions' was brought home to me by Frankfurt 1971.

9 In fact it might even be argued, with some persuasiveness, that the implication. holds in the other direction as well, that if an act proceeds from the self it *is* free. Thus, e.g., if an act was not caused by a desire but was caused by a sense of obligation, would it be free? We would

There are many difficulties with compatibilism, one of which I will take up in the remainder of the paper. I think that compatibilism is still the most interesting theory to discuss in part because it is presently the most widely accepted theory but for more important reasons as well. Whether or not determinism as a general thesis is true (and it would seem safer to bet that it is) the same problem is posed by any particular determined act—and it is fairly certain that some exist. In addition there are difficulties with incompatibilism whether of the libertarian or the hard determinist variety.[10] The libertarian has to make intelligible the notion of an uncaused act as well as explaining how we could hold an individual responsible for an act he/she did not cause. Hard determinists obliterate the distinction we ordinarily make among acts and thereby violate our ordinary concepts of (un)free, (in)voluntary, (un)compelled. More important in my opinion is the fact that hard determinism implies that so far as his or her freedom is concerned, it makes no difference whether a person is healthy or psychotic, lives in a totalitarian or a free society, is a slave, or a master. A sense of freedom according to which such distinctions are irrelevant is not a sense that can be relevant to human beings and leads to reactionary, anti-human conclusions. If there is such a sense I am simply not interested in it.

The objection I want to develop to the analysis of a free act as one caused by the agent's wants is that it is insufficient. Consider the case of a person who is brainwashed for a month by the forces of a government with which he is in violent disagreement as a result of which he accepts all their moral, social and political beliefs, values and attitudes. He agrees to spy on his native country because he wants to help this other government. His spying would be caused by his desire. Hence, given the above analysis, his actions are free. Yet if the circumstances under which he acquired the want leading to the acts were known he would not be held responsible for his actions.

Consider another example. The message 'Buy popcorn' is flashed on a movie screen intermittently at a level below our conscious awareness. This produces a strong desire for popcorn in most of the audience and even people who never bought popcorn buy some. The acts of buying popcorn were caused by the

---

    naturally speak in such a case of 'having to do it' or of 'being compelled by one's sense of duty' and hence it could not be free in any full sense. Nevertheless, being compelled to do an act because of a sense of obligation is clearly different from being compelled to do an act out of fear. The former is certainly more free than the latter because it proceeds from a part of the self.

10   The reactionary implication of a hard determinist position comes out clearly in the work of B.E. Skinner.

desires of the agents for popcorn. Hence they are free according to the version of compatibilism I have described. Again I think they would pretty clearly not be considered free.

Now there is a sense in which we could even say of the person who had been brainwashed that his actions of spying were free or voluntary but the major point in saying this would be to make clear that he was not, e.g., following orders given at gunpoint nor was he under some psychological compulsion. This use of the words 'free' and 'voluntary' is a negative, contrastive use. An act which is only free in this sense is unfree in a more important and more fundamental scene. This much I take to be incontrovertible. What the difference is between those acts which are free because they are caused by wants and those acts which are caused by wants and yet are unfree remains to be investigated and we will take up this question in part 3 of this paper.

∴

Now Marxists would hold that most of the actions called free that are done in societies that are non-socialist and non-communist are free only in a similarly limited sense.[11] Consciousness of a class and of individuals is determined by the material conditions of their existence. 'The mode of production in material life determines the general character of the social, political and spiritual processes of life'.[12] 'Consciousness is thus from the very beginning a social product and will remain so as long as men exist'. This does not preclude the resultant ideological spheres from in turn affecting the material spheres but these causes are never the decisive ones, according to Marxists. In any conflict between directions, posed by the material conditions and by elements in the superstructure, the former will always in the long run be decisive.[13]

In any epoch the class which is dominant materially controls the production and distribution of ideas as well as the production and distribution of material goods. 'Each new class which displaces the one previously dominant ... has to give its ideas the form of universality and represent them as the only rational,

---

11 By a socialist society I mean one that is controlled by the working class; by a communist society. I mean the classless society envisaged as evolving out of socialism. (Applying these interpretations to the world there turn out to be no genuinely socialist or communist societies in existence.)
12 Marx 1904, pp. 11–12.
13 Marx 1967, p. 442. Engels 1959, p. 395.

universally valid ones'.¹⁴ Marx is not saying that the reason why 'the ruling ideas of each age have ever been the ideas of the ruling class' is simply; or even most importantly, that the ruling class deliberately deceives people through its control of the means of dissemination of ideas.¹⁵ Although this is often true, it is not the fundamental cause of false consciousness. The capitalist form of social life itself is the fundamental cause of the ideology of capitalism (which constitutes false consciousness) because under capitalism these false ideas 'appear directly and spontaneously as current modes of thought'.¹⁶ In other words the dominant ideas of a period are simply the expression in ideas of the actual material relations that hold between people and thus are the expression of the domination of the ruling class.¹⁷

This means that at any given time in a class society the vast majority of the people (i.e., everyone not in the ruling class) accepts ideas which are false and which are the expression and instrument of the material conditions and relations of their own domination. These ideas are of all kinds: ideas about the metaphysical, religious, and scientific nature of reality, ideas about what kinds of character traits, activities, and objects are worthy of pursuit and possible of achievement and so on. Members of both the ruling class and the working class have false consciousness in this sense because the real nature of social relations is hidden to both. They do not understand the real motive forces in history and have a distorted view of peoples' relation to arid places in history and society. This will be so in all class societies short of socialism since in all these societies the majority is dominated by the minority and the consciousness which is an expression of those material and social relations must serve to hide that fact. (There are other senses of 'false consciousness' that we will discuss later.)

True consciousness is the absence of false consciousness. People with true consciousness would see beneath the forms or appearances to the real relations that hold in their society. Since the mistaken perceptions 'appear directly and spontaneously as current modes of thought, the real relations must first be discovered by science'. Marx thought that he had done just this—laid bare the

---

14   Marx 1967, 439.
15   Marx and Engels 1959, p. 26.
16   Marx 1961, p. 542. See also Mepham 1972.
17   '... This domination of relationships (that material dependence which ... changes *into* determined personal states of dependence) itself appears *in* the consciousness of individuals as a domination of ideas; and since the belief in the eternity of these ideas, i.e., of these. material states of dependence, is of course, confirmed, nourished and inculcated by the ruling classes' (Marx 1971, p. 73).

hidden realities of capitalism—through his discovery of surplus value. Wages appear to be an exchange of equivalents but this conceals the fact that wage labour includes surplus, i.e., unpaid, labour. '... history took a long time to get at the bottom of the mystery of wages ... On the surface of bourgeois society the wage of the labourer appears as the price of labour; a certain quantity of money that is paid for a certain quantity of labour ... [but] wages are not what they appear to be, namely, the value, or price of labour, but only a masked form for the value or price of labour power ... it was made clear that the wage-worker has permission to work for his own subsistence, that is, to live, only in so far as he works for a certain time gratis for the capitalist ... the system of wage-labour is a system of slavery ... whether the worker receives better or worse payment'.[18] True consciousness requires that the real relations beneath the appearances be laid bare in this way. However, given that under capitalism these false beliefs 'appear directly and spontaneously as current modes of thought', it will be impossible to completely get rid of false consciousness so long as capitalism remains. These appearances are real appearances.

'True' and 'false' in 'true' and 'false consciousness' are also used in a different sense not referring exclusively to beliefs.[19] False consciousness of a class or an individual in this sense is consciousness that is the expression in ideas and the instrument of the material conditions and relations of its own domination. True consciousness would be the expression in ideas of the material conditions and relations that constitute its fulfilment and realisation or the struggle for such conditions and relations.

The ruling ideology promotes the rule of the ruling class over the working class. Thus this ideology constitutes false consciousness for the working class in that it is false to their class interests. These ideas promote their own domination by another class. A ruling class cannot have false consciousness in this sense because the ideology serves their class interests. However, members of the ruling class (as well as the working class) can have false consciousness in the sense that they accept ideas that are against their interests as human beings. They accept ideas that are the expression and instrument of their own alienation. As Marx expressed it, 'The propertied class and the class of the proletariat

---

18   Marx 1967, pp. 540, 535. Marx 1970, p. 29.
19   'True' and 'false' are used both in the cognitive sense and in another sense. The latter use of the word 'true' and its connection with the concepts of freedom and the expression of human nature is found in such passages as: 'Suppose we had produced things as human beings ... labour would then be *true, active,* property... it is then only a *semblance* of an activity, only a *forced* activity, imposed on me only by *external* and accidental necessity and *not* by an *internal* and *determined* necessity' (ibid., p. 281).

represent the same human self-alienation. But the former feels comfortable and confirmed in this self-alienation, knowing that this alienation is its own power and possessing in it the semblance of a human existence. The latter feels itself ruined in this alienation and sees in it its impotence and the actuality of an inhuman existence'.[20] Ideas and wants not predicated on false consciousness would be ideas and wants that are the expression of the true humanness of a person and would not be superimposed from without by the class nature of their society.[21] They would be what a person truly and naturally wants as opposed to what a person as distinctly human wants. False consciousness in this sense as well cannot be eliminated within class society because in Marx's view alienation is intrinsic to class society. Within a class society, however, the most advanced and conscious individuals may understand the source of their consciousness and hence recognize it as false consciousness. They may also understand their own class position, the direction in which history will move and their role in making it more that way. This increased understanding is an aid to achieving freedom (it is what makes revolution possible) but it does not constitute freedom. They will not be able to fully rid themselves of false consciousness.[22]

Marxists' characterisation of consciousness as true or false in the last sense rests on a certain conception of human nature. Marx and Engels spent a great deal of time throughout their lives arguing against the idea of a fixed human nature which was very prevalent at the time, trying to show that as material conditions changed so did human nature. There are many remarks to the effect that it is ahistorical to pick on a particular mode of behaviour and consciousness as revealing the essence or true nature of human beings. If human beings acted aggressively and greedily, this merely proved that they would act this way under certain conditions. Given other conditions they would act without aggressiveness and greed.

There are other key discussions, however, which suggest a different view of human nature. Marx and Engels were objecting to the making of charac-

---

20   Ibid., p. 367.
21   'The overcoming of private property means therefore the complete *emancipation* of all human senses and aptitudes, but it means this emancipation precisely because these senses and aptitudes have become *human* both subjectively and objectively', (Ibid, p. 308) Also: '... the realm of freedom actually begins only where labour which is determined by necessity and mundane considerations ceases ... beyond the realm of necessity begins that development of human energy which is an end in itself, the true realm of freedom ...' (Marx, 1967, p. 820.)
22   The question of consciousness under socialism and communism will be discussed in section v.

teristics due to particular conditions into essential characteristics of human nature. Among the more famous examples of this are Hobbes' and Lockes' reading of individualistic, competitive, and aggressive traits fostered by capitalism back into the state of nature. However, although they held that different conditions produce different behaviour and character traits, they did not view all these possible ways of behaving and all these different character traits as on an equal par. Nor did they view the conjunction of them as collectively constituting human nature. The behaviour, character traits and consciousness that were manifested under certain conditions were more expressive, indeed constitutive of the essence of human beings than that manifested under other conditions. 'Communism [is] ... the actual appropriation of the human essence through and for man; ... only here has the natural existence of man become his human essence and nature become human'.[23] This means that if it is true that given certain conditions human beings will be a certain way then one could say that it is natural for them to be that way, i.e., it follows from certain scientific laws describing human behaviour. However, the quotation makes clear that, for Marx, to say that a mode of existence is natural in this sense is not to say that it is expressive of a truly human nature (which is what I mean by 'natural' when I speak of a natural want). Only under certain conditions, which are realized under communism, will the natural (i.e., lawful) mode of existence coincide with the truly human mode of existence. Marx took the form of activity characteristic of a species to be its nature or essence. 'In the mode of life activity lies the entire character of a species, its species-character; and free conscious activity is the species character of man'.[24] Until socialism this human nature is not realized because in class societies individuals produce under necessity, in ways and towards ends that they themselves do not set. The development of the human productive forces which Marx refers to as "the development of the richness of human nature as an end in itself will, however, reach a point at which, given the social relations of socialism and. communism, this nature will finally be realized. in the individual. In Marx's words, '... although at first the development of the capacities of the human species takes place at the cost of the majority of human individuals and even classes, in the end it breaks through this contradiction and coincides with the development of the individual'.[25]

---

23 Marx 1967, pp. 304, 306.
24 Ibid., p. 294.
25 Marx 1963, p. 117. Again, in another later work, Marx says [Even] 'the overcoming of obstacles may ... constitute an exercise of liberty, ... these external purposes lose their

However, this talk of a human nature or essence should not be taken to imply that there is an individual human essence independent of society, which would be quite contrary to Marxism. Human nature, for Marx, consists of a certain form of life, and activities which necessarily involve relations between and interactions with others. 'As human nature is the *true common life* of man, men through the activation of their nature create and produce a human common life, a social essence which is no abstractly universal power opposed to the single individual, but is the essence or nature of every individual'.[26] 'But the human essence is no abstraction inherent in each single individual. In its reality it is the ensemble of the social relations'.[27]

Now if individuals rarely engage in free conscious activity in class societies how can Marx say that is their nature? If and when individuals do engage in this form of activity then that will be their nature but not before then. In other words, why should we say that the human nature manifested in socialism and communism although different and perhaps preferable to earlier forms is more truly human than earlier forms? The answer is partly just terminological. Marx, as we saw, designated as the nature of a species the form of activity characteristic of, i.e., peculiar to, that species. Only human beings have the capacity to engage in free conscious activity although until socialism few individuals are able to exercise this capacity. Marx believed that human beings had all sorts of capacities and potentialities that had not yet been realized in any society. These as yet unrealized potentialities included different personality and character traits, wants, needs and even the development of different physical senses. Marx envisaged 'the complete emancipation of all human senses and attributes', with the emphasis on the word 'human'.[28] What makes the senses of humans different from the senses of animals is not something that is simply given by nature. Rather, "only through the objectively unfolded wealth of human nature is the wealth of subjective human sensibility either cultivated or created ... a musical ear, an eye for the beauty of form ... in short, senses capable of human gratifications, senses confirming themselves as essential human capacities'.[29] Marx's whole theory is a justification of the claim that all human

---

    character of mere natural necessities and are established as purposes which the individual himself fixes. The result is the self-realization and objectification of the subject, therefore real freedom, whose activity is precisely labour ... Really free labour, the composing of music for example, is at the same time damned serious and demands the greatest effort' (Marx 1973, p. 124.)

26   Marx 1967, p. 271.
27   Marx 1967, p. 402.
28   Marx 1967, p. 308.
29   Ibid.

beings have these capacities and that they are going to be developed. Even before they are developed, however, human beings have the capacity to develop in that direction. It is fundamental to a dialectical approach to see reality not as merely a static given but rather to see the existents at any time as containing capacities and potentials for certain kinds of change, growth and decline. These are as real, according to Marxists, as the things that exist at any given time. The human nature which will be manifested under socialism and communism is a more developed form of human nature than that realized under feudalism or capitalism. This claim is intended first of all in the straightforward sense in which we say that the chimpanzee is a more developed animal than the cow and the human is a more developed animal than the chimpanzee. It is a more developed form of human nature, i.e., it is more fully or truly human, because it is a further development of what is peculiar to the human species. It is a greater differentiation of the human from the rest of the animal world. The human nature of socialism and communism is the realisation of the potential inherent in earlier forms of human nature. It seems quite reasonable to me to identify the most fully developed and distinctive form of a thing with that which is most truly; that kind of thing. There is also another, more specific reason why Marx saw the human nature of socialism and communism as more truly human which we will get to in the middle of section 4.

Marx, of course, was not a neutral spectator of this process of historical development. He was actively involved in trying to bring about what he predicted. This involves no inconsistency because he believed that history was going to go in a certain direction only because people in specific historical circumstances were going to act in certain ways. What human beings did would determine what is true of them. Human beings were going to make it true that this is their true nature by bringing this nature into being. Marx's work, including his descriptions of the potential of human nature, were part of the process of making it true. This active hortatory aspect of Marx's work does not make it unobjective. In Gramsci's words, 'it is absurd to think of purely 'objective' prediction. Anyone who makes a prediction has in fact a program for whose victory he is working and his prediction is precisely an element contributing to that victory'.[30] Although I would not endorse this statement unqualifiedly, it seems very appropriate on this point.

Given Marx's concept of human nature a distinction can be drawn between wants based on true consciousness and wants based on false consciousness. I will call the former real, natural or truly human wants. An act is only truly or

---

30   Gramsci 1971.

most fully free which proceeds from a natural want, very few of which will be found outside of socialist or communist society.

This distinction between natural and unnatural wants entails that a person does not always know what he or she really wants.[31] There may be a distinction between what one thinks one wants, what one pursues and may in fact superficially want, and, on the other hand, what one really wants. What one really wants is identified with what one would want if one's wants were not determined by the class society in which one lives or by other external constraints. Although we do not know in detail what such wants are we can rule out wants that are solely the product of class societies.

∴

Let us look now at the question of how a philosopher accepting compatibilism who is not necessarily a Marxist would try to distinguish those acts which are free because they are caused by wants and those acts which are unfree despite being caused by wants. Then we will see that a distinction must be drawn between wants that are truly the person's (natural wants) and wants that are imposed on the person and are not his or her true or natural wants. This is the Marxist distinction which most Anglo-American philosophers would prefer not to have to recognize.[32] Then we will see whether the same criteria which apply to the wants in our examples of unfree acts caused by wants do not also apply much more generally.

---

31 The consequence, that one often. does not know what one really wants, that one's choices are only a reliable guide to one's preferences and superficial wants, is consistent with ordinary and. psychological thinking about wants. Since Freud we have come to realize that a person is not always the best judge as to his or her wants. Evidence of certain kinds could contradict a person's opinion about his or her own wants. The psychoanalytic view and the Marxist view both involve views of human nature on the basis of which they interpret behaviour and ideas as neurotic or based on false consciousness. According to both theories the causes of most of our: actions are unknown to us.

To the extent that our ordinary thinking about wants is distinct from psychological thinking about wants, it too recognizes that a person does not always know; what he or she wants. For example, we believe it to be true about wanting that 'If, given that x had not been expecting p but now suddenly judged that p would be the case, x would feel joy, then x wants p' (see Brandt and Kim, 1967). If the condition mentioned were not realized, then a person might want p but not know that he did. This example is particularly relevant to Marxism. We are not experiencing socialism or communism and most people do not expect that they are soon to be realised. Hence many people may want things that are only features of life under socialism or communism but not realize that they do.

32 Nielsen, 1971.

If the above examples of the spy and the popcorn buyers are accepted as showing the inadequacy of compatibilist analyses to date, then being caused by a want is not sufficient to make an act free. We have to consider what it is about the wants in the above examples or the manner in which they were acquired that makes us say that the acts resulting from them are unfree. What seems crucial is that measures were taken by others to induce the wants, which would probably not have existed if these measures had not been taken. The desire to spy on his native country was the result of brainwashing done by others in order to instil that desire. The desire would most probably not have come into existence (at least at this time) if it had not been for the brainwashing. Likewise the subliminal advertising was done in order to induce a desire for popcorn.

Another feature of the wants in the above examples that would seem significant is that the person having the wants had no power over the measures taken to induce the want in him. In the case of the want produced by subliminal advertising the person was not conscious of what had caused his or her want; the person being brainwashed may have been aware of what was being done to him but it was against his will. Thus for an act to be free it must not be the result of wants or desires caused by measures taken to induce the want, which were either unknown to the agent and/or against his/her will.[33]

These criteria that we used (not as Marxists) to distinguish examples of unfree acts caused by wants from acts which are free because they are caused by wants, form the basis for a distinction between real or natural and false or unnatural wants. The manner in which the wants producing the unfree acts were acquired makes it reasonable to say that they were (1) not really the person's wants at all, or, they were (2) not the person's real wants. They did not proceed from the person but were imposed by others. The person had no control over or perhaps even awareness of the source of these wants. On the other hand, wants that did not come into being because of others' attempts to instil in them a way that deprive the person of control over their acquisition seem to have the person as their source and hence to be more real or true or natural wants. So in the attempt to distinguish these two types of examples we are lead to make the same sort of distinction that Marxists make and which many non-Marxists find very objectionable.

The only basis for calling wants unnatural that we have come up with thus far is the manner in which they were acquired. This has the consequence that the same want might be natural in one person and unnatural in another person

---

33   For obvious reasons, we cannot further specify whether one person's 'will', i.e., their desires regarding these measures are natural or unnatural.

because they had acquired the want in different ways. This result is unobjectionable in the case of many wants. Some wants, however, seem to be unnatural in anyone regardless of how they were acquired. Can this be justified or is it simply intuition or prejudice? The judgment could be tested if we had some developed theory. Lacking a theory, however, we might suggest one criterion to the effect that if achieving the object of a want invariably does not lead to the agent's pleasure or satisfaction, caeteris paribus, even though the agent is still in a position to achieve satisfaction from it, then the desire for that object is false or unnatural. In fact we might reasonably say that the lack of satisfaction would show that the person did not really want whatever it was but only thought he/she wanted it. This condition, however, is not a necessary condition. Obtaining the object of a want, even if the want was unnatural, might very well lead to at least a temporary satisfaction. In some cases, the fact that the agent achieved satisfaction upon attaining the object of his/her want might only further confirm our judgment that the want was unnatural. Such a case might be the desire to hurt people. It is possible as well that such a want be in perfect harmony with the rest of the person's wants. We might question whether the person really was satisfied by achieving the object of that want but the problem of distinguishing true and false wants reappear as the problem of distinguishing genuine and ungenuine satisfaction. It might be that the only basis for seriously denying that the person was satisfied and justifying in our judgment that the want is unnatural would be a theory which we do not as yet possess.

However, there is a sense in which we might say that the satisfaction was false while not denying that the person really felt satisfied. Satisfaction or pleasure always involve some beliefs and if those beliefs are false then according to Plato it makes sense to say that the satisfaction or pleasure is false.[34] For example suppose a man feels satisfied because he has made a woman feel inferior. For him to feel satisfaction he must believe he has made her feel inferior and this makes him satisfied only because he believes that this makes him superior. If either of these beliefs is false then his satisfaction can be said to be false. For this reason all satisfaction deriving from sexism, racism or any other kind of false consciousness would be false.

It might be objected that my conditions are not sufficient to make a want unnatural. The fact that a desire was acquired by a person by measures deliberately taken by others to induce the want which were unknown to the person

---

34 See 'Plato's *Philebus* and "False Pleasures"', in Thalberg 1962 for an explanation and defence of this position.

and/or against his/her will need not make the desire an unnatural one. Our conception of a natural want, it might be claimed, is independent of its source. For example, the desire for friends or for intellectual stimulation seems a natural (i.e., truly human) want regardless of how it was acquired. It might be possible (even necessary?) to instil such wants through some sort of social engineering but this would not make them unnatural.

To some extent it is an empirical question as to just what sort of wants can result from deliberate measures taken by others that are not known and/or against a person's will. However, I am inclined to think that this objection separates too much the process of acquiring desires and the desires themselves. It is a much more integral process than is implied by the objection. Furthermore we cannot say that a desire, e.g., the desire for friends, in and of itself is a natural desire. Different people at different times and in different circumstances have the desire for friends. One person's desire at a given time may be healthy and another's may be neurotic. We would need a lot more information to decide. I think it unlikely that}: desires we would feel to be natural could come about in ways that fit my conditions for an unnatural desire. However, I won't rest everything on this doubt. I would be willing to call a desire natural even if it fit the conditions I have given for an unnatural desire only if it could have arisen without such conditions. In other words there must be non-coercive conditions that would have been sufficient for the person to have acquired the desire even though these conditions were not fulfilled. If we have reason to believe that this is the case and if the person appears to achieve genuine satisfaction from satisfying the want then I would judge the want to be a natural one. I think it is because we believe this to be true of the desires for friends and for intellectual stimulation that we think them to be natural wants. I cannot conceive of calling a desire a natural one (either for an individual or the species) that can only be acquired through coercive measures.

We have come up with two conditions which are sufficient to determine a want or desire to be unnatural. If a want was acquired by a person by measures taken to induce it which either were unknown to the person and/or against his/her will and if the want would not have arisen if measures of that kind had not been taken, then the want is unnatural. If people are consistently unsatisfied by achieving the objects of a certain desire then the desire for that object is unnatural.[35] The converse of these conditions are two necessary conditions

---

35 One might suspect that these criteria are not really distinct because one might suspect that wants for objects that do not bring satisfaction were all acquired under the conditions set out by the first criterion—even if this could not be decisively shown at a given time.

for a want being natural. However, we do not have a sufficient condition for a want to be natural if we would not want to call the desire to hurt others even if the want does seem to have been acquired in the above ways and if the person does seem to achieve genuine satisfaction from hurting others.

∴

Marxists would claim (and many non-Marxists would agree) that many or most of the actions that people do are not done because they really want to do them, although they might have preferred that option to the others they had. This puts such actions on the unfree side of the continuum. Marxists go on and applying similar criteria to those used in the examples of the spy and the popcorn buyers, judge that even most of the actions in non-socialist and non-communist countries that are supposedly done because the agent wanted to do them are not fully free or are only free in a superficial and. limited sense. What Marxists are saying is that the ordinary distinction between free and unfree only takes in a segment of the continuum. Those acts ordinarily called free are further along toward the free end of the continuum than are the acts ordinarily called unfree. However, we can look more deeply and see that they are still quite far from acts that would be most clearly free.

On the Marxist analysis of how consciousness is produced, most of the wants that we have in class societies are wants that are due to material conditions and relations over which we have no control and which serve the ruling class of the society. Many (though not all) of these wants are deliberately and consciously produced, e.g., the desires for most of the commodities on the market in capitalist countries. These wants would not have arisen if it were not for the measures taken to instil them (or equivalent measures), nor do these measures simply amount to exposing the person to the object or experience in question.[36] Hence by the criteria we established before, these wants are not natural wants-and acts resulting from them are not free. They do not proceed from the self. Some of the wants for products are not so much unnatural as they are distortions or perversions of natural wants. It is a natural want to want to be able

---

36   I am not denying, of course, that in many cases simply exposure to these products plays some part in producing desires for them. However, even in these cases we would not have been exposed to them if desires for them did not serve the interests of the ruling class. Moreover, we are not *simply* exposed to them but exposed to them in certain ways, under certain conditions the sole end of which is to produce desires for them. And it is also frequently the case that simply being exposed to them would make it less likely that we would desire them.

to get from place to place as conveniently and pleasantly as possible. If one is living today in a place where public transportation is poor, it might very well be a natural desire to want an automobile. (It would not be a natural want to want to own an automobile but it would be natural to want to have use of it whenever one wanted.) Although this desire might not be a primary one it could still be a natural desire In capitalist society this natural desire is distorted into a desire to own dangerous, unnecessarily expensive, extravagant vehicles even when no private vehicle at all is needed.[37] The desire for an automobile would in some cases have arisen even if there had not been the influences from those who profit from the buying of automobiles. However, there would not be as many desires for automobiles, nor desires to own them nor would there have been desires for these particular kinds of automobiles. Examples could be multiplied but I will mention just one more very basic one. The natural desires for love and security are perverted in a society in which people are atomized, insecure, in competition with one another and think in terms of ownership. The love relationship is corrupted by the unnatural desires to possess and have power over others.[38] These wants would not have arisen in a society where there was no ruling class whose interests encouraged them. Hence the acts caused by these wants are only free in a superficial sense.

Another feature of those wants which cause unfree acts was that the person was unaware of the measures taken to instil the wants and/or the measures taken were against his or her will. A non-Marxist might use this as a basis for distinguishing actions that resulted from wants instilled by subliminal advertising from actions that resulted from wants instilled by ordinary advertising or simply through socialisation. But is it really more than a matter of degree—at most? Although people are conscious of the existence of most advertising

---

37 I claimed that the general want to get from place to place as conveniently as possible is a natural desire. If the only way to do this in our society is to own dangerous extravagant automobiles it might seem that it would be a natural desire to want to own them. This is mistaken. If the condition mentioned is satisfied, it does not even follow that one will desire to own them. The context is referentially opaque. Nor would it follow even if one knew that this was the only way to satisfy the desire. Furthermore, even if one did have the desire for them it does not follow that that desire would be a natural one (although it need not be *unnatural* either). Take a different example: if one is lost in the Andes and knows that the only way to satisfy one's sexual and emotional needs is with a llama, it does not follow that the desire to have a llama for a lover is a natural desire. (This example was suggested by Haskell Fain and seems to convince people unconvinced of the invalidity of the inference in the case of the automobiles, suggesting something about the nature of most peoples' basic assumptions). I realize the problems involved here about individuating desires but do not have the time or space to go into them further in this paper.

38 Marx 1967, p. 303.

that they encounter, they are not conscious of how the advertising works to instil wants in them. They are not aware of exactly what it is that causes them to desire what is being advertised.[39] They did not choose the desires nor did they choose to have these measures taken to instil the desires; in fact it is probably against their will that they encounter most of the advertising that they do. It also may be against their will that they come to have the desire that they do. Socialisation can be broken down into large numbers of acts which function to instil a certain consciousness, even if these acts were not done with this conscious understanding. Innumerable actions of parents, teachers, religious and political figures, writers, among others (not to mention those who pay their salaries) fall into this category. Where wants are not instilled in us by any human actions they are nevertheless the result of the social system over which most people have little or no control and the real nature of which is obscure to them. In class societies the consciousness people acquire will be determined by the interests of the ruling class, even though this consciousness will not always be the result of deliberate attempts to produce it. Individuals have little if any control over their socialisation, little knowledge of how they are being socialized or why they are being socialized the way that they are. They are, to a large extent, merely passive victims of their social system.

The second criterion we set out earlier for a natural want was that it consistently lead to satisfaction (or at least not be consistently unsatisfying). Most of the wants that people have in class societies do not fit this criterion.[40] There are widespread signs of discontent among the bourgeoisie who have supposedly gotten what they want in capitalist societies. These signs range from political protest among those who are more conscious of why they are discontent to suicide, alcoholism and widespread use of dangerous drugs, increased reliance on all forms of psychotherapy, respectable and not, sexual promiscuity, and a turn to mysticism. There are also less dramatic signs of dissatisfaction. The desire for commodities found in most people in advanced countries seems to have no end in that each commodity acquired only produces a desire for still another commodity. Since there is no biological basis for it as in the case of food, this suggests that acquiring the commodity did not give the person satisfaction and

---

39 Advertising 'employs techniques designed to reach the unconscious or subconscious mind because preferences generally are determined by factors of which the individual is not conscious' (Packard 1957, p. 7).
40 A memorable example is found in Harvey Swados' *On the Line* which recounts the story of a young auto worker whose job is made almost enjoyable by planning to get a fancy car but which turns out so disappointing that he sells it and then quits the job which has lost the only thing making it tolerable.

perhaps that the person did not really want the commodity at all. This kind of consumerism is analogous to nymphomania but about as widespread as the common cold. Marx also develops the idea that the greater the wants for commodities the more dependent a person is. By this standard most people today are extremely dependent, hence unfree. Most of the actions which result from wants in class societies are not free in the fullest and most fundamental sense, because they do not proceed from natural wants as determined by the criteria we set out.

Other wants that people have in class societies are not due to measures taken by others to induce them but nevertheless are equally external to the person. Economic scarcity, regardless of the social arrangements, would mean that in some instances not everyone will get what they want and need.[41] An individual wants enough for his or her family. A consequence of that individual getting it is that others will not have enough. This does not necessarily entail that the individual would want the others not to have enough. However, the individual might come to have such a want in part as a survival mechanism. Such a want would be natural in the sense of lawful. Given these conditions, some people at least will have this want. However the want would clearly be the result of conditions external to the person and not the expression of his/her nature. He might even want not to have that desire. Remove economic scarcity and the want would be removed although perhaps not immediately. Many wants that people have are due to these kinds of conditions and hence the acts resulting from them are unfree.

∴

I have tried to determine when the causes of wants can be considered coercive. When a want is caused by coercive conditions, then acts caused by that want are not free. That want is not a true or natural want. Now it might be wondered whether the criteria I have used to pick out these wants have not been so far extended that next to no act—even in a socialist or communist society—would be judged free by those criteria. What is the basis for the distinction between the wants acquired in socialist and communist societies and the wants acquired in non-socialist and non-communist societies such that Marxists claim what most acts resulting from the former are free while most acts resulting from the latter are unfree? Marxists would agree that wants are always going to be determined—in large part by the material and social condi-

---

41   The importance of this type of example was suggested to me by Gary Young.

tions of peoples' lives. 'Our wants and pleasures have their origin in society.' This will be true in socialist and communist society as well. However, the nature of the material conditions and relations that cause the wants would be different in socialist and communist society in ways that lead Marxists to say that the causes would not be coercive and hence that the wants people would acquire are (on the whole) natural wants.[42]

Socialism can only exist in conditions of material abundance. Hence consciousness will not be determined by conditions such as economic scarcity. Although moving in that direction, a socialist society is not yet a classless society. Therefore there is a ruling class whose interests determine consciousness. However, there are crucial differences between socialism and all other class societies. It is the first time the ruling class is the majority. For the majority of people, then, the situation with respect to the source of wants is not very different under socialism from what it would be under communism. The consciousness of the majority is determined by their own class interests, and hence is not false consciousness in the sense of promoting the rule of others. Although some false consciousness remains from previous class society, other elements of false consciousness will have been overcome or else capitalism could not have been overthrown. In societies where a minority dominates the majority, consciousness serves to hide that fact. Many of the wants that people have then, are the result of ignorance and confusion concerning the real nature of social relations in their society. In a socialist society a major source of false consciousness will have been eliminated and hence wants will not be the result of ignorance and confusion, another reason for saying that under socialism wants are not acquired under coercive conditions. Under socialism those who are socialized and those who are responsible for socialisation are of the same class. Although not everyone in this majority will be in the institutions of government or in the leading party everyone will participate in this common control at some level. Another crucial point is that the only way a socialist society can come into being is by a socialist revolution. Marx's conception of a socialist revolution is as the self-emancipation of the working class. A socialist revolution so conceived requires self-activated masses of people moving in a conscious struggle to take control of their lives. Hence socialism comes into being with the majority of people already aware, critical, self-moving individuals having collectively created a new society. People in a socialist society are no longer passive victims of their social system. Rather than merely being products of the society that

---

42   'From this relationship one can thus judge the entire level of mankind's development'. (Marx 1967, p. 303.)

they (unconsciously) create, they become critical self-determining individuals as society and history come under conscious social control.[43]

Communism is the further development of conditions that begin in socialism. It is also only possible in conditions of abundance and sees elimination of all vestiges of false consciousness. In a communist society by definition-there is no ruling class. Hence consciousness (which includes wants) is not determined by the interests of a ruling class. Measures are not taken that are unknown and/or. against peoples' will to create wants in them. Since there is no distinction between rulers and ruled there is no one who would be able and have reason to take such measures. Wants that consistently failed to bring satisfaction upon attaining the object of the want would not remain wants for long since there would be nothing to sustain them as there is today. Furthermore, having experienced a long transitional period of self rule brought into being by their own collective action, people would have fully developed into critical, discriminating beings.

For all these reasons Marxists would claim that the grounds for saying that wants are determined coercively or externally in class societies are not present in a communist society and are present only to a very small degree in a socialist society. Hence most wants acquired in a communist or socialist society do not meet the criteria of wants that produce unfree acts. What is true of wants is true more generally of all the modes of behaviour and consciousness that constitute the socialist and communist forms of human nature. The fact that human nature is not determined in an external coercive way in communist society is another reason for Marx's designating the communist form of human nature as more truly human. It is what human nature is naturally, i.e., without external constraints and coercions. The socialist form of human nature is close to this form and evolving in that direction.

Another possible line of objection to what I have said is that Marxists' claim that most every action in class societies is unfree really makes no sense. After all, the objection might proceed, we use the words 'free' and 'unfree' to distinguish among acts within given societies in order to determine for which acts an agent can be held responsible. The purpose of giving an analysis of the concepts of free and unfree is to explain the basis of the ordinary distinction among acts that we do in fact make. It may be that there are somewhat fewer acts on the free side in one society, but it makes no sense to say that there are almost no free acts in a society. There is a distinction between free and unfree acts in every

---

43 MacIntyre 1929. This point also fits well with Frankfurt's article in which he argues that the criterion of being a person that is of most philosophical interest is the having of second order volitions, i.e., control over one's wants.

society and we would defeat our purposes if we judged all acts in a society to be unfree. This argument is mistaken. First of all it does make ordinary good sense to say that in some given society next to no act is free. This might be conceded most readily in a very primitive society where almost every action is dictated by necessity and the people have very few real options. The same would be true in a totalitarian society. A free action is not simply the most preferred action among the available options. Some of the actions within such an unfree society might be free in the negative contrastive sense. If the society distinguished such acts from the others and called them free, we could understand the basis of this distinction but still understand that the acts are all unfree in a more important sense.

Other societies, even though class societies, have a somewhat greater number of acts that were done (we would say) because the agent wanted to do them. However, if Marxists are right then most of these are done because of wants predicated on false consciousness. To say of a society that most of the acts done in it are unfree it is not necessary to contrast the society with another existing society. We have a certain idea about what a free act in the fullest and most important sense is and it may be that no existing society has very many such acts. The question of whether the concept of unfree needs a contrast is irrelevant because it has one. Unfortunately, Marxists claim, it is not realized in any existing society.

I have argued that philosophers who accept the compatibilist view that a free act is one that is caused by a want of the agent need to go further. They have to distinguish among the wants that cause action because not every act caused by a want of an agent is free. The criteria used to distinguish wants amounts to or at least comes close to a distinction between natural and unnatural wants, wants that are truly the person's and wants that are imposed on the person from without. This is a distinction found in Marxism which many non-Marxists would reject but it is unavoidable if one is to go beyond an inadequate and very superficial position on the free will problem. Marxists believe, moreover, that the same criteria reveal that most of the acts that are said to be done because the agent wanted to do them are unfree (i.e., are on the unfree side of the continuum). Many or most of the acts that we do everyday, such as putting on our shoes, closing the door, etc., cannot sensibly be said to be either free or unfree. Hence they belong in the middle of the continuum or not on the continuum at all. The claim that is being made here is that many more important acts which are said to be done because the agent wanted to do them are on the unfree rather than the free end of the continuum where they would be placed by the standard compatibilist theories. Marxists explain why this is so by their analysis of what determines wants and by their extension of the criteria used to pick out wants that cause unfree acts. The other side of this claim about class societies is an account about how human freedom could be enhanced. Presumably non-Marxists would disagree with the Marxist analysis of the determinants of wants and/or with their extensions of the criteria. What extensions have been made seem to me minor and quite reasonable. Presumably non-Marxists would find them unreasonable. To such a philosopher just the differences in degree make the difference between a free act and an unfree act. So even if Marxists' analysis of how wants are required were accepted, it would not be accepted that most acts done because of wants are unfree.

What is the basis of the disagreement? What would move someone to choose one side or the other? I am inclined to think that the underlying difference is a political one. The rejection of the more extended criteria that the Marxist uses is based on a difference in philosophical purpose which reflects a difference in political perspective. The position that the purpose of giving an analysis of the concepts of a free and an unfree act is merely to represent the ordinary distinction that we draw between acts is a conservative one—in effect if not in intention. Similarly, the claim that while it might make sense to say that most of the acts in some particular society are unfree, it does not make sense to say this of the freest societies in existence seems to reflect a contentment with the status quo or a somewhat improved status quo. In any case, regardless of the motivation, the function of this point is to discourage a critique of the status quo. To take as the paradigm of a free act ordinary acts in class societies that are said to be done because the agent wanted to do them reflects a lack of commitment to the expansion of human freedom and the absence of any account of how this can be accomplished. The resistance to talk of (un)natural wants comes from the same conservative philosophical/political position. The distinction between (un)natural, true and false wants leads to the possibility of a fundamental critique of bourgeois society while the denial of the meaningfulness of such a distinction cuts the ground out from under such a critique.[44]

The Marxist perspective, on the other hand, is a revolutionary one. Historical materialism sees societies and social systems as stages through which history passes and would never consider any existing society as the standard or absolute to which others must be compared; Marxism is interested in the direction in which history is going (and in helping it to go that way) and in the society and human beings that will come into being in the course of making that history. Consequently it is interested in the fullest and most fundamental sense of human freedom. A person is most free when they are closest to themselves

---

44 Nielsen 1972.

and to their true nature as human beings. This means that a person is most free when he or she has the greatest number of options which would most fully satisfy his or her natural wants. In societies that are not socialist and communist our actions cannot be free in the most basic sense because even those actions that are caused by wants are caused by unnatural wants or distorted natural wants.[45]

---

45   Nielsen 1975.

CHAPTER 9

Against Capitalism as Theory and Reality

When we started on this project in 2006, capitalism seemed to be bigger and stronger than at any point in history. It was truly a global system, fulfilling—for better or worse—Karl Marx's description in *The Communist* Manifesto of 1848: 'The need of a constantly expanding market for its products chases the bourgeoisie over the whole surface of the globe. It must nestle everywhere, settle everywhere, establish connexions everywhere ... In one word, it creates a world after its own image'.[1]

The fall of communism in the Soviet Union in 1989 led market enthusiasts to proclaim that liberal capitalism was 'the end of history;' the free market approach to capitalism had been hegemonic in the United States for over a quarter century, President Ronald Reagan having declared in 1981 that 'Government is not the solution to our problem; it is the problem'.[2] Although the dot.com boom of the late 1990s was over, there was the new housing boom. A financial crisis had exploded in Asia a decade before, but the West had weathered the storm, and it only confirmed the experts' conviction that the Keynesian approach of mixing government spending with the market, more typical in Asia, was bad for the economy. Whatever its validity, Keynesianism was defeated politically. The European model of capitalism, sometimes called social welfare capitalism because of its extensive government spending on social services, (or branded as 'socialism' by adherents of the free market), was under heavy pressure due to global competition with the more market-oriented approach of the Americans, known as neo-liberalism. This was true throughout the developing world as well, as international agencies like the World Bank insisted that as a precondition for loans, countries must cut public spending. Although some critics pointed to fundamental problems in the system, and some protested against the effects of the free market model on the working class and the poor throughout the world, this was undoubtedly a triumphalist period for capitalism.[3] Margaret Thatcher, Prime Minister of Eng-

---

1 *The Communist Manifesto*, in Tucker (ed.) 1978, p. 476f.
2 Fukuyama 1989.
3 Robert Brenner, for example, pointed to a steady decline in the real economy since 1973, calling it 'the long downturn' (Brenner 2006). Aside from Marxists like Brenner, very few foresaw the current crisis. An exception was Nouriel Roubini in a speech to the International Monetary Fund in 2006. See Mihm 2008.

land during the 1980s, famously declared 'there is no alternative', repeating it so often that the doctrine became known simply as TINA.

How very different today! Indeed, it would be difficult to overstate how different the economic landscape looks in 2009. The *biggest financial institutions in the world failed*, and survived only with massive government, i.e. taxpayer, assistance (but never called 'welfare'). Blue chip stocks fell in value to less than a dollar. Nobel Prize-winning economist Paul Krugman described recent economic numbers from around the world as 'terrifying', writing 'Let's not mince words: This looks an awful lot like the beginning of a second Great Depression'.[4] Some have managed to stay rich or become even richer through the crisis, but most people throughout the world are suffering.[5] Most mainstream economists and the press advocate some variant of Keynesianism as the only way to prevent 'Great Depression II' and to managing capitalist economies beyond our immediate crisis, (although academic economists remain resistant to questioning the fundamentals of their free market theory).[6] The majority debate in the public sphere concerns *how much* and *where* to put the government aid and *how much government control* there should be over it. The February 16, 2009 cover of *Newsweek* magazine proclaimed 'We are all socialists now', meaning simply that everyone favoured more government involvement in the economy, i.e. Keynesianism and the widely respected Rasmussen Poll of April 2009 showed that only 53% of Americans say capitalism is better than socialism— a particularly striking figure in a country which has no socialist or even labour party and where liberal capitalists are considered the 'left'.[7] Some people are even saying that Karl Marx's thought is more relevant today than when he wrote.[8] The question implicit in these reactions is whether our current crisis is simply a crisis of the financial sector, or of neo-liberal capitalism generally, or is it, most fundamentally, a crisis of capitalism?

---

4   *New York Times*, 5 January 2009.
5   On the same day the *NY Times* reported that bonuses for employees at financial companies on Wall St were the sixth largest on record and on the opposite page was an article by Rebecca Cathcart, entitled 'Burden of Debt Weighed on Family in Murder-Suicide', 29 January 2009. The same divide into winners and losers is happening on a global level; there is a virtual epidemic of suicide among impoverished Indian peasants. On 12 September 2009 the *New York Times* reported that the 30,000 employees of Goldman Sachs were on track to earn an average of $700,000 this year. 'A Year After a Cataclysm, Little Change on Wall St'.
6   Patricia Cohen, 'Ivory Tower Unswayed by Crashing Economy', *New York Times*, 5 March 2009.
7   The Rasmussen Reports, 'Just 53% say that Capitalism is Better than Socialism', Rasmussen Reports, http://www.rasmussenreports.com/public_content/politics/general_politics/april_2009/just_53_say_capitalism_better_than_socialism [accessed September 25, 2009].
8   The cover of *Courier International No. 924 du 17 au 23 juillet 2008* was entitled 'Marx, le retour', with abstracts from articles published in *The New York Review of Books*, *The Financial Times* of

I cannot predict how things will look when you are reading these words. Will capitalism have managed to stabilize itself, and the preceding paragraph sound like hysterical ranting? If it stabilizes itself, on what basis will it have done so? Since the crisis is global, how would Keynesianism be applied beyond the nation state? Will it work? if so, for how long? Will the crisis be resolved only through an even bigger crisis, with a massive restructuring and shake out of low profit firms and a lowering of wages—which is what happened in Asia after their recent crisis? Who will have paid, in other words, for the crisis? Or will the crisis be ongoing, with what political, economic and personal effects on people throughout the world, or will it be resolved, but then reappear? And if so, what other alternatives will be proposed, either within capitalism, or going beyond? Or, by the time you read this, could the whole economy have been reconfigured, as the economies of Eastern Europe were in just a few years time? In their case, of course, the change was toward capitalism, but their story illustrates *just how rapid social economic transformation can be* when conditions are right. At the very minimum, we can conclude from this crisis that the economics experts at the highest levels of the United States government and universities and financial institutions—the so-called 'best and the brightest'—did not know what they were talking about and that capitalism has shown itself to be what critics have always said it is: A highly volatile, crisis-ridden system with devastating effects on the most vulnerable. But today this is exponentially more true as the economic problems of the United States spin around the globe with untold consequences for the globe itself; poor countries that had nothing to do with the causes of the crisis are seeing their economies shrink.[9] The many trillions of dollars sent to aid financial institutions also put the lie to the claim that 'there just isn't enough money' which was used to justify lack of public spending on health care, education and other public goods needed by the majority, particularly the most vulnerable. It is now completely transparent that the real question is *how resources are distributed and who gets to decide this*.

What does all this imply regarding whether or not capitalism is good for women? That is our concern in this book: to examine capitalism *from a feminist point of view*, that is, examining it with a special concern for the interests

---

London and elsewhere. In March 2009 an article in the British *The Independent*, 'So Karl Marx was right after all', reported that most newspapers have had articles on him in their Business pages and he was on the front page of *The Times*. More startling is that in 1997 before the crisis, *The New Yorker* issue devoted to 'the next' of everything in the twenty-first century had an article describing Marx as 'the next thinker'. John Cassidy, 'The Return of Karl Marx', 20 October 1997.

9   Edmund L. Andrews, 'Report Projects a Worldwide Economic Slide', *New York Times*, 9 March 2009.

of women. As there is no one feminist perspective on capitalism, (or almost anything else), a case has to be made. However, I am taking as a premise that feminists should be concerned with ending the oppression of women whatever the causes, be they sexism, racism or economic, or some combination difficult to disentangle. A feminism only concerned with ending the oppression of women *based on gender* would be a very limited version, far from the emancipatory vision at its core. Positions on capitalism among feminists range from apparent indifference since they ignore it, to support for capitalism with various degrees of criticism, to opposition. Indifference is not a responsible position given the enormous and ever-increasing impact of the system in which we all live on all domains of our lives, even the most intimate.[10] Instead, a feminist position on capitalism should be based on whether or not capitalism is good for women. Since capitalism is not the same in all times and places, indeed is constantly changing, we cannot limit our inquiry to any particular form in which it is realized. To see the possibilities capitalism might have to offer, we have to examine both its ideals on the one hand, and on the other, the fundamental structure and tendencies inherent in capitalism in all its manifestations. Many of its abstract ideals are very attractive, so in theory capitalism has much to recommend itself for all individuals, including women. As a historical reality also capitalism has tendencies that are liberatory for women. However, other fundamental features and tendencies are arguably at odds with these liberatory aspects. So ultimately, the question of whether capitalism is good for women has to rest on capitalism as *an actually existing, historically evolving political economic system, not just a logically possible system. To focus on capitalism as an idea—without powerful arguments to show that it is also feasible—would be to make an apologia for capitalism.*[11] In any case, a political/economic system cannot be willed into existence. It comes into existence through a complicated social historical process of evolution and/or revolution and its nature depends both on how it came into being and what it is replacing. Thus an examination of an abstract model, or what can be called the ideal or optimal version of a political economic system has some value, but this value is quite limited.

Therefore my principal concern in this debate will be on whether capitalism as an actually existing system is good for women. We will find, however, that there is no simple yes or no answer to this question; it depends on how we

---

10   One theorist describes capitalism as 'the most totalizing system the world has ever known' (Meiksins Wood 1995, p. 2). Also see Hochschild 2003; Hochschild 2003.
11   See Mills 2004. For a general philosophical argument for the importance of situating and evaluating abstract norms in the real world, see Antony 2000, pp. 103–37; as applied to questions of justice and poor women, see O'Neill 1993.

answer these crucial sub-questions: compared to what? which women?, with respect to what aspects of their lives?, in what time frame? I will argue in what follows that while capitalism creates favourable possibilities for women it also puts limits on these possibilities. Overall, I contend, the respects in which capitalism can be said to be good for women are more limited than those in which they are bad. Women do not tend to be the 'winners' in the brutally competitive system which is capitalism; indeed they are among the poorest and most vulnerable people on earth, particularly dependent on public goods. Therefore feminists truly committed to women's well-being—dare I say 'women's liberation?'—should oppose capitalism.

1 Basic Definitions: 'Capitalism' and 'Women's Interests'

But what exactly is capitalism? Not only has capitalism as a system evolved and taken various forms at different times and places, but theories of capitalism—regarding what it is, and what it could be and should be—have also evolved and they vary today as well. Sometimes it is not entirely clear just what its proponents mean by it. However, we need a minimal working definition to proceed and readers need to understand how I understand the concept. Common to almost all definitions of capitalism are the following: 1) the bulk (or the most important segments) of the means of production are privately owned, 2) wage labour is the most important form of labour. 3) production is primarily for a market rather than directly for the needs of the producers. 4) the point of production is to maximize profit. Despite #3 and #4, it is alleged—most famously in Adam Smith's 'invisible hand' argument—that selfish pursuit of individual profit is in fact the best way to satisfy the social good.[12] The validity of this claim will be a central issue in our debate.

To clarify further the meaning of private ownership it is important to distinguish 'private property' from 'personal property', which is individual property simply for one's own use. A society could have personal property but collective ownership of the means of production. With collective or common property, e.g. public parks, every individual has a right to use the park; hence common property involves an individual right to property just as private property does. The difference between the two forms of individual right to property is that, by definition, common property is not exclusive; no one has the right to exclude others from using the park. In contrast, if the land were privately owned by

---

12 Smith 1937.

a resort, the owners could exclude everyone else from using it. Hence private property—which can be small scale or truly vast in scale—is essentially a right of exclusion. In capitalism, the owners of the means of production have the exclusive right to decide what to produce, and where and how to produce it.

This definition of capitalism allows for significant differences among capitalist societies with respect to government's role in the economy. As I have already mentioned, the specific form that any given capitalist economy takes is a function of many things, not only during its existence, but how it developed (evolution or revolution) and the specific history, class structure and culture of the social formation from which it developed. In theory, a society could be purely laissez faire, (free market), with no state intervention in the economy. (It is important to note, however, that even in such a hypothetical system a state, with its monopoly of force, would be necessary to *uphold* private ownership. Hence government plays an essential role in *all* economic systems.)[13] No society in history ever fit this abstract free market model, (nor could it, I will argue), but some come closer than others. The United States, for example, has public education, roads, sanitation systems, etc., but is the only developed country in the world that does not government-funded universal health care but leaves health to the market. Not only do many governments provide more social welfare than the US, but in many capitalist countries the government owns banks, railways and airlines, radio and TV stations, and it directs much investment. For example, scholars have shown that government direction of investment was crucial in developing the economies of the so-called 'Asian Tigers'.[14] Capitalist societies have gone through cycles of government regulation and de-regulation. In the United States many industries were de-regulated in the past few decades, including the banking industry in 1999 which allowed new financial 'products' like derivatives which contributed to the collapse of the industry. It is likely we will see a turn back to regulation in the coming period. Some writers refer to societies based on private property but with greater state ownership and direction of investment as 'social welfare capitalist' or 'state capitalist', but this variant is nevertheless capitalist so long as our criteria above are met (private ownership of the most important means of production, wage labour, most production for profit). At times the fundamental long term goal of maximising profit is best served by government taking over a particular industry—temporarily or permanently—and

---

13   Except conceivably communistic anarchism, without private property, but an adequate discussion of this alternative is not possible here.
14   Johnson 1982; Amsden 2007; 2001.

sometimes popular pressure wrests more support from the government. Pres. Obama recently described health care reform as 'not only a moral imperative but a fiscal imperative'. Automakers in the US may be wishing that instead of employer-based health care, our government provided health care as this would reduce their costs and make them more competitive. To call societies socialist just because the state plays this kind of role in the economy is to mistake the abstract model for reality and to misunderstand the nature of capitalism.

Before we can address whether such a system is best for women, some methodological difficulties must be addressed. How can one judge what's good for women? We can say, initially, that what's good for women is what advances their interests, but what are their interests? Is there even such a thing as 'women's interests?' And how do we judge them? Does it depend simply on their preferences? The most abstract concern, coming from postmodern thinkers, is that women's well-being is not an objective matter of fact but depends on interpretation and language. What this means is not entirely clear. If the claim is interpreted in a very strong way, then no evaluations are possible and thus the feminist enterprise is doomed. However, we can recognize that facts are not transparent, that language and interpretation are inevitable, without giving up. If we are talking about the interests of particular women, then we must include how they perceive and evaluate their interests, what they do and what they say. This involves language, certainly, but language is not an abstract structure separate from real women, but rather it is how women explain how they perceive things, and why they do what they do. Thus language and interpretation do not pose an insuperable epistemological barrier to ascertaining women's interests, but is simply one of the best ways we have for ascertaining them.[15]

A related objection that would derail our efforts here is that each woman's identity is too complicated to make any judgments about what she wants or needs. In addition to being a woman, she has a class, a nationality, a race/ethnic group, a sexuality, marital status, health status, etc. etc. It is naïve, some claim, to make any inference from her social location in this nexus of social groups to her interests and identity. But this would be to give up all social science and history. Reliable inferences about interests and identity must be based on as much information as we can get, without reducing anyone's identity to only one dimension, and, of course, they are subject to counter-evidence, like any scientific claim. But if we know anything, we know that social location—being

---

15   Scott 1988; Tilly 1989. Varikas 1995.

a man or a woman, rich or poor, Afghani or Swedish—is 'causally relevant' to the experiences she/he will have. And *these experiences, in turn, are causally relevant to identity*.[16]

On a somewhat less abstract level: when we try to judge what conditions are good or bad for women, we often seem to be caught in a dilemma. On the one hand, to ignore women's subjective satisfactions or preferences seems arrogant and runs a high risk of bias. Who are we to second guess what a woman says she wants? How can someone else know what she wants better than she does? On the other hand, to rely only on preferences ignores the reality of adaptive preferences (the 'sour grapes' phenomenon) and gives up all chance of an objective assessment of peoples' lives. A fascinating book called *The Good Women of China: Hidden Voices* by Xinran illustrates the problem of relying on felt satisfaction as a measure of women's condition.[17] In the final chapter the author introduces us to women living in a remote area in the most extreme poverty the author had ever seen, in complete ignorance of the outside world, in ill-health and in total subjugation to all the men of their community. The women are property, breeding machines, whose existence is justified only by their utility. Yet as striking as the awful conditions of their lives is the fact that of all the women we meet in the book, they are the only ones who told her they were happy. The author reports how deeply shaken she was by her visit. This example illustrates the fact that felt satisfaction and objective well-being are not necessarily correlated nor is domination always perceived; a happy slave is possible. There are objective matters of fact regarding human health and capacities and freedom and therefore, the extent to which particular practices enhance or limit them. Independent of any subjective (dis)satisfaction, we know the dreadful physical effects on women of very early marriages and multiple children, for example. It makes sense therefore to say that it is in women's interest to end these practices. Though felt satisfaction and preferences cannot be ignored, if we stop there, we lose the opportunity for any moral and political assessment. At a minimum, as John Stuart Mill implied, satisfactions and preferences formed in total ignorance of alternatives or in disbelief that any alternatives are possible should not be the standard. Given the high risk of bias, however, we should approach these judgments with as much information as possible and with considerable care and humility.

---

16   Moya 1997.
17   Xinran 2003.

2 Gender Interests: Strategic and Practical

On the premise therefore that we can—and must—speak of how capitalism affects women, let us explore further the concept of women's interests, a highly contested concept.[18] Using the concept in an unqualified way seems to imply that despite the many diverse causes of women's subordination and the extreme differences among women, that there exists a homogeneity of interests for all women. This, however, is definitely problematic. Maxine Molyneux, a comparative sociologist specialising in developing countries, suggests that we speak instead of gender interests, which she defines as the general interests women (or men) have in common by virtue of 'their social positioning through gender attributes'—which can take many forms. She distinguishes between what she calls *strategic gender interests* and *practical gender interests*, a distinction that is particularly useful for comparing how women fare in different societies and how they themselves are likely to assess their situation.[19] It also helps to illuminate why women sometimes seem to acquiesce to arrangements that would appear, at least to outsiders, to be against their interests.

Strategic gender interests are those goals that are in fact necessary for women's liberation. Legal equality, reproductive freedom, dismantling of the sexual division of labour disrupt the institutions that reproduce women's subordination, and hence there will be no liberation of women unless they are achieved. These are the kinds of strategic goals usually identified as feminist goals, that feminists claim to be in women's objective interest—and they are.

But women have other interests based on their immediate needs that do not challenge the existing gender order, but instead, that arise from that gender order. Molyneux calls these *practical gender interests*. For example, since women everywhere are primarily responsible for the care of children and households, women have special interests in protecting them. Molyneux notes that it is such practical, rather than strategic, gender interests which women are most likely to identify as their interests and to act in defence of, e.g. in bread

---

18   See Anna G. Jonasdottir, 'On the Concept of Interest, Women's Interests, and the Limitations of Interest Theory', in Kathleen Jones and Anna G. Jonasdottir, eds. *The Political Interests of* Gender (London: Sage Publications, 1988) pp. 33–65.

19   Maxine Molyneux, 'Mobilization Without Emancipation? Women's Interests, State and Revolution', *Feminist* Studies 11 (2) 1985: 227–254; a shorter version 'Conceptualizing Women's Interests', is reprinted in Holmstrom (ed.) 2002. Molyneux's distinction has been extremely influential and also critiqued, for example by Ann Ferguson who conceptualizes strategic as 're visionary' gender interests and practical gender interests as needs, in Jones and Jonasdottir 2008.

riots that women have engaged in throughout history. Women will also prioritize them over strategic gender interests if they perceive a conflict. Note that practical gender interests are decidedly not universal to all women since they overlap with class interests. Marie Antoinette did not need to riot for bread.

3 Capitalism *in Theory*: Ideals and Limits

3.1 *On Property, Ownership, and Freedom*

With these clarifications of the key concepts we now turn to examining whether or not capitalism is best for women. Keeping in mind the caveats I have offered about abstract models of political/economic systems, our focus in this first section will be on capitalism *in theory*, its ideals and, as I will argue, its limits. Proponents of capitalism often equate capitalism with modernity and see it as the vehicle for realising the values of the modern (western) world: liberty, equality and fraternity (or solidarity in gender-neutral terms). But when focusing specifically on capitalism as an economic system they most often cite two values in its behalf over all alternative systems: greater efficiency at producing material well-being and greater freedom. Related to the second is the alleged tendency of capitalism towards equality of individuals. This would seem to have particular importance for women and will be discussed in some detail in the latter part of this article. The two primary values of efficiency and freedom are connected in that well-being enhances freedom, but independently of this, capitalism is alleged to be essentially freer than all alternatives. Many think that capitalism is also a just society, but the principal argument that it is *more just than alternatives* rests on the claim that it is more free (this is the theory that calls itself libertarianism), so by addressing freedom, I will be addressing the latter claim regarding its justice indirectly.[20] Other possible values of a political economic system, such as material equality and community, are seldom professed by capitalism so will not be discussed in this section. If I can succeed in showing that capitalism does not realize its own most important professed values, my critique will be that much stronger.

---

20 Other defences of capitalism as just tend to rest on the denial of any viable alternatives to capitalism, not that it is in principle more just than all other possibilities. John Rawls' theory of justice, for example, defends abstract principles of justice not any particular economic system. Hence if capitalism met his principles of justice better than any alternative, as he seemed to believe, then it would be just, but if in fact a different system fit them better, that other system would be most just: Rawls 1971. F.A. Hayek even warns against attempting to defend capitalism on the grounds of justice (Hayek 1988).

Whether capitalism provides more material well-being than alternatives is largely an empirical question, not an abstract one, and hence will be addressed at length in the following section on Capitalism *In Reality*. Here I will just say that this question is more complicated than is apparent from most discussions. To evaluate it, there are many issues to keep in mind. First we have to recognize that what counts as efficient or inefficient (wasteful) depends on what one is trying to achieve; in short, *efficiency does not exist in and of itself*, but is always relative to our goals. Political/economic systems are likely to be efficient and wasteful in different ways given their different goals and structures, so we have to decide which of our goals are most important and how to balance them. Only once we decide this can we judge the efficiency of how we are setting to achieve them or the efficiency of a given economic system in achieving them. A goal of maximum output per hour is likely to yield a different judgment of efficiency than a goal of maximum health and happiness. Hence efficiency should not simply be conflated with maximisation of output as is so often done. We also have to consider how material well-being is distributed in a society, not simply the absolute amount, and we have to be sure that all the dimensions of material well-being are included, not simply material goods. A certain amount of unemployment and underemployment are highly efficient from a capitalist point of view and therefore inherent in all capitalist societies; indeed economists talk of a 'natural' level of unemployment, 'currently thought to be 4.8 in the United States'.[21] But unemployment—now officially more than double that— is highly wasteful from a human and social point of view.[22] Our evaluation of efficiency must always be sure to include the long run, not just the short run, whether we are considering the efficiency of a product, method, policy. This is also true for a mode of production as it is possible that a particular feature of a system is a virtue at one stage of history and not another. I will argue that this is true of capitalism's tendency to growth. Finally, and perhaps most important, we have to be sure to consider all genuine alternatives. When these considerations are kept in mind, we will see in the next section that capitalism is not in fact more efficient at producing material well-being in all its dimensions for the majority of people in the long run than all alternatives to capitalism. A political/economic system that was genuinely democratic, economically as well as politically, would do better for *all* its members, particularly the more vulnerable members of society like women and children, the elderly and the disabled.

---

21   Krugman 2009, p. 38.
22   The rate is 11% if it includes discouraged workers and those only marginally attached to the labour force. 'Out of Work, and Too Down to Search On: Millions of Americans Left Off Jobless Rolls' *New York Times*, 7 September 2009, p. 1.

Freedom has been the object of dreams and of struggle throughout the ages by individuals and by groups, large and small, and it has many dimensions and degrees. Whether capitalism provides more freedom than all alternatives must ultimately be answered at the level of reality, not simply ideals and abstract models. However, in order to assess whether a given political economic system provides more or less freedom than another, we have to be clear as to just what freedom is, what conditions enhance it or limit it, and for whom. These are the kinds of questions we will address in this section on capitalism *in theory*. Women have sought liberation as individuals and in organized groups for eons; in fact Orlando Patterson has argued that women played a crucial role in the origin of personal freedom.[23] So if capitalism does indeed provide more freedom than alternatives, this would be an enormously important point for feminists in favour of capitalism as the best system for women.

3.2   *Political Freedom and Democracy*

One important dimension of freedom that people have struggled for, and millions of people around the globe are still deprived of, is political freedom. Capitalism is usually discussed as if all capitalist societies were political democracies, hence free from a political point of view with each citizen enjoying basic political rights and liberties, with elections, an independent judiciary and a multiparty system. Indeed oftentimes the phrase 'a free society' is used as equivalent to capitalism as when the United States is called the leader of the 'free world', though its allies include dictatorships, (their actual criterion being freedom *of the market*, not political freedom). It is true that representative systems of government came into existence with the rise of capitalism, and many theorists see a special affinity between political democracy and capitalism. Even Marx agreed. Nevertheless, the connection was hardly automatic. At the beginning of capitalism, only large landowners, a very small percentage of the population, had the vote; property qualifications for male voters were not removed in all of the United States until the middle of the nineteenth century and women have had the vote for less than 100 years. Each extension of political rights was won only after long and intense struggle. African Americans were effectively denied the right to vote in the Southern United States until the Civil Rights movement won the Voting Rights Act of 1965 and their struggles continue today over such issues as felon disenfranchisement and voter ID. In the modern period the fact is that capitalist economies have existed with a variety of forms of government,

---

23   Patterson 1991.

from representative democracies like those of the United States and Western Europe, to dictatorships like Nazi Germany or most Latin American countries throughout the twentieth century.

Milton Friedman, a principal theorist of free market capitalism, contends that political democracy and freedom can only exist in a capitalist economy.[24] However, one of the 'purest', i.e. most free market forms of capitalism existed in Chile under the Pinochet dictatorship that the United States helped to bring to power, overthrowing the democratically elected socialist government of Salvador Allende. Ironically, given Friedman's claim, Pinochet acted under the guidance of followers of Friedman known as the Chicago School of economists. Today in China we find an increasingly capitalist economy coexisting with a Communist political system. Leaving aside the special case of China, I see no way of denying that these other dictatorships were capitalist societies except by some question-begging definition of capitalism that restricts it to political democracies. Dictatorships cannot be declared to be non-capitalist simply because of greater government involvement in the society since, as already discussed, capitalist democracies also vary a great deal as to the amount of government intervention in the economy, both in terms of ownership, investment and social welfare. Thus capitalism is demonstrably not *sufficient* for political democracy and has not been shown to be *necessary*. Of the many dimensions of freedom, the only freedom that is *definitional* of capitalism, and therefore part of *all* capitalist societies, is market freedom: the freedom to buy and sell what one likes, especially labour, to contract as one likes, without needing anyone else's permission (though this too is subject to some restrictions in every capitalist society). Nevertheless, for purposes of this discussion of freedom and capitalism, I will restrict myself to the idealized version of capitalism which is politically democratic, i.e. free from a political point of view.

The democracy characteristic of capitalism is, however, quite limited. The literal meaning of 'democracy' is 'rule by the people' and admits of degrees along two dimensions: how many are included in 'the people' and how much they get to rule over. Although democracy within capitalism has gradually, with struggle, become more inclusive, the range of issues over which the voters have power is extremely limited, however, as it is restricted to the political sphere.[25] The best one can do is vote for a viable candidate and *hope* that he or she institutes the economic policies one prefers. Ellen Meiksins Wood has made

---

24 Friedman 1962.
25 Marx and Engels famously argued that political power reflects economic power, hence governments in capitalist societies were no more than 'executive committees of the bourgeoisie'.

the case that with the rise of capitalism political democracy simultaneously became possible and greatly de-valued. The reason is that in capitalism the 'economic' and the 'political' become separate for the first time, and real social power rests in the economy rather than the state.[26] Wood contrasts democracy in its original meaning as it existed in Athens in the third century BC with democracy as it was re-conceived in the last couple of centuries, particularly in the United States. Although Athens is credited as the birthplace of democracy in standard Western accounts, contemporary sensitivity to the importance of slavery and the domination of women in Athens has resulted in less attention being paid to the unique character of its democracy. Wood argues that its peasant citizens, based in the deme (village), were a social formation never seen before or since. Democracy—rule by the people—was understood by all to be a constitution in which, (as Aristotle put it), 'the free-born and poor control the government—being at the same time a majority' as distinct from oligarchy, in which 'the rich and better-born control the government—being at the same time a minority'. That peasants and shoemakers should have more political influence than the rich, who had the leisure to contemplate goodness and engage in politics, was anathema to thinkers like Plato and Aristotle who were explicitly and unapologetically anti-democratic. With the demise of Athens, democracy disappeared from the historical stage for over two thousand years.

In the early days of capitalism it was still possible to echo publicly Plato's sentiment that property-less people who work with their hands were unfit to be full citizens. However, this became increasingly difficult, especially in the founding days of the United States with its politically active citizenry, its experience of being a colony and of fighting a revolution against the British crown. The Constitutional debates carried out in the *Federalist Papers* reveal how fearful the Founding Fathers were of Athenian-style democracy, which they equated with mob rule, and how they advocated instead a republic modelled on Rome. But given the political climate of the time, 'they had to reject the ancient democracy not in the name of an opposing ideal, not in the name of oligarchy, but in the name of democracy itself'. Although the Federalists had contrasted democracy to their preferred model of the Roman republic, they ended up christening their model 'representative democracy', a novel conception Wood describes as, 'the

---

26 Meiksins Wood 1988, and 'The demos versus 'we, the people:' from ancient to modern conceptions of citizenship' in Wood 1995, 204–37. C.B. Macpherson focuses on how the system of political parties prevented universal suffrage from resulting in the domination by the numerically more numerous working class, as opponents of universal suffrage had feared. See Macpherson 1977, p. 64 ff. Aristotle *Politics 1290b*, quoted in Wood 1995, p. 220.

populus or *demos* with rights of citizenship but governed by an aristocracy'.[27] (It goes without saying that this aristocracy was understood to be exclusively white and male.)

It is important to see that the issue is not simply one of size, nor of representation as such. Some form of representative system would likely be required with a large population, but a representative system need not be opposed to democracy in its original literal sense. The two could be combined (especially in the days of the Internet!). Imagine a representative system of government in which 1) the representatives earned the average of those they represented and 2) they were subject to immediate recall. Just these features were part of the Paris Commune of 1870, which Marx called the first workers' government.[28] But the motivation of the Founders and hence their particular conception of that representation was opposite to that of the Communards. As Madison opined in *Federalist No. 10*, the advantages of an extensive representative system were that the views of a great many ordinary men would have to go through a small 'medium of a chosen body of citizens' and Hamilton, in *Federalist No. 35*, echoing Plato on the unsuitability of mechanics and such for political rule, considered 'merchants ... the natural representatives of all these classes of the community'.[29] The general understanding of democracy today around the globe as it developed from this foundation is even further from its original literal meaning of rule by the people and instead has become associated with the ideas and institutions of limited government. The role of ordinary people is a passive one, to enjoy its benefits simply as independent individuals. So while the political freedoms of limited government are certainly very important, just how much actual freedom and power they give to people depends on the social structure of which they are part. In capitalist democracies, where political democracy is compatible with the rule of the rich, their value is distinctly limited.

Political freedom is also much less than is touted. That there was no freedom of speech in the Soviet Union was transparent; anyone who criticized the official government line, for example, who described the Soviet presence in Afghanistan during the 1980s as an 'invasion', was arrested or sent to a mental institution. In the United States we are free to criticize government policy without fear of these consequences. Yet as Noam Chomsky has documented, it is a striking fact that during the Vietnam War the word 'invasion' was not used

---

27 Wood 1995, pp. 224–5.
28 Karl Marx, *The Civil War in France* in *The Marx-Engels Reader*, Tucker (ed.) 1978. These have also been features of the workers' councils that sprang up during the Russian Revolution and the Hungarian Revolt of 1956.
29 Wood 1995 pp. 215–16.

by the mainstream media. Journalists learn to censor themselves. Those who take a more radical perspective are effectively marginalized.[30] A clear example from academia is the economics profession in the United States where critics of the reigning free market are found in only a handful of universities. And note that these criticisms come *from within a framework supportive of capitalism*; more radical perspectives that challenge the system of capitalism are simply beyond the pale of what is considered rational discussion.[31] The domination of the political sphere by business is clear in the current discussions—or non-discussion—of health care reform. Despite polls showing that a clear majority of physicians, nurses and the general public favour a single payer plan (also known as improved Medicare for all), the Senate Finance Committee discussing the issue have ruled it 'off the table'. (The committee Chair Sen. Max Baucus is one of the largest recipients of donations from pharmaceutical companies.) When physicians and other advocates stood up at a recent hearing to ask why it was off the table, they were removed by Capitol police.[32] It is not only the dependence of politicians on campaign donations that business interests exercise their domination of politics. In the age of agile, mobile capital, liberal politicians dropped their support for social programs for fear of losing business abroad.

Our discussion above of the limitations of democracy within capitalism brings out a crucial aspect of freedom that is omitted from most discussions of freedom that focus entirely on the freedom of individuals. Individualism is completely appropriate in the context of the metaphysical question of whether or not human beings have free will. It is also a crucial aspect of the social political question of whether a society provides freedom for its people. It is not, however, the whole story. The analysis of the concept of freedom that I will offer below is applicable both to individuals and to groups. For individuals have, or lack freedom, not only *as individuals*, but *as members of collectivities*. Therefore the fact that in capitalism there is no economic democracy, that is, working class people do not get to decide directly where society's resources should be invested, nor do they decide it indirectly via the political process since government is dominated by the rich, entails that the majority in capitalism lack freedom in this crucial respect.[33] Since women tend to be clustered at the bot-

---

30   Herman and Chomsky 2002, McChesney 1999.
31   Cohen 2009, C1.
32   Ralph Nader, 2009.
33   While some writers talk of personal autonomy versus political autonomy, this is not exhaustive. The economy is rendered invisible, perceived as natural background conditions. Other writers use the terms civic freedom or democratic freedom, but these do not clearly bring in the economy either.

tom of the economic ladder this is especially true of them; and women higher up the ladder are still under-represented relative to men of their class in the centres of economic and political power. (Further implications of the limits of the individualistic model of freedom prevalent in capitalism will be explored at a later point.)

Let us turn now to freedom in a general and abstract sense. Some supporters of capitalism, like economists Friedrich Hayek and Milton Friedman and philosopher Robert Nozick, argue that the more pure (free market) a capitalist society is, that is, the less government is involved in the economy, the more free it is *overall*, not only from a political point of view. Though conceding that great inequalities exist, such theorists claim that capitalism is characterized by equality of opportunity, rather than results, and that freedom has a higher value than equality. As already discussed, this perspective has been very influential in the last few decades in the United States. But this is not the only view among supporters of capitalism. Others argue that fewer inequalities would make for a more ideal form of capitalism, defending this position on various grounds: the greater economic and social stability of such a society, the greater happiness and/or freedom for the majority or in terms of its greater justice. In this section we will examine these claims and consider their relevance to the question of whether capitalism is good for women.[34]

3.3   *Freedom, Private Property and Self-Ownership*

As discussed, common to all definitions of capitalism is that the bulk of the means of production is privately owned. Those who own are a small minority of the population while the majority own nothing. Radical critics of capitalism contend that this inequality of property entails lack of power and freedom for the majority and allows the former to live off the labour of the latter.[35] Defend-

---

34   I focus more on Nozick in this section since he rests his case entirely on freedom while Hayek and Friedman and indeed the majority of so-called libertarians mix in utilitarian considerations which Nozick explicitly eschews. I am saving the empirical issues for the *In Reality* section.

35   In *The Communist Manifesto* Marx and Engels say, 'You are horrified at our intending to do away with private property. But ... private property is already done away with for nine-tenths of the population; its existence for the few is solely due to its non-existence in the hands of those nine-tenths. You reproach us, therefore, with intending to do away with a form of property, the necessary condition for whose existence is the non-existence of any property for the immense majority of society'. *The Communist Manifesto*, in Tucker (ed.) 1978, p. 486. This inequality of property and power is the basis for the twin evils of capitalism as they see it: exploitation and alienation, the precise analysis of which is not necessary here.

ers of capitalism leave vague the question of how numerous are the owners of the means of production, seeing it as not essential to the definition of capitalism, but many theorists insist that individuals in capitalist societies all do own something, viz. themselves.[36] And they see this as the foundation of freedom. The notion of 'propriety in one's person', or self-ownership, is very old and has resonance not only among defenders of capitalism but among many of its critics, including feminists, so it is worth pausing to explore just what it means, how it connects to freedom, and whether it should be part of any theory committed to a better society, particularly one that is better for women.

3.4 Self-Ownership—History and Import of the Concept

Do individuals own themselves and what exactly does this mean? The concept is a complicated and contested one with an interesting and illuminating history. To appreciate its connections to private property, and the debates surrounding it then and now, an historical detour is warranted. The concept of 'self-propriety' was first articulated in the seventeenth century in England, a revolutionary period when feudalism was giving way to capitalism, common land was being enclosed thereby depriving ordinary people of their hereditary rights to the commons, small property owners were contending with the rising capitalists and wage labour was becoming the dominant form of labour.[37] King Charles I had his head cut off for raising taxes for military ventures without the approval of Parliament. The slave trade was thriving. Moderates and radicals were united in the struggle against the monarchists, but there were deep differences between them and differences among the radicals as well. Those who called themselves the True Levellers, also known as the Diggers, were the most radical of the radicals.[38] They supported universal male suffrage and protested not only against tyrannical laws but also against private property, seeing the enclosure movement, (the forcible privatisation of what had been common

---

36   Nozick; Philippe Van Parijs 1995, p. 3.
37   This transition is called 'primitive accumulation' by Marx, referring to the process by which the necessary conditions of capitalism were established: on the one hand there must be 'the owners of money ... and on the other hand, free labourers ... free in a double sense: legally free and free of any means of production of their own; primitive accumulation is ... nothing else but the historical process of divorcing the producer from the means of production'. *Capital* Vol. I, in Tucker (ed.) 1978, p. 432.
38   They were called the Diggers because in 1649 they undertook to peaceably 'dig up, manure and sow corn upon George Hill in Surrey' (and other commons land around the country) which they intended to work and live collectively. Similar actions have been undertaken in recent years by landless peasant movements in Latin America, particularly the MST (Landless Peasants Movement) in Brazil.

land), as theft. They proclaimed 'In the beginning of time, the great creator Reason made the Earth to be a common treasury, to preserve beasts, birds, fishes and man, the lord that was to govern this creation ... And the reason is this, every single man, male and female, is a perfect creature of himself, and the same spirit that made the globe dwells in man to govern the globe'.[39] It is not clear whether their idea that each individual was 'a perfect creature of himself' should be expressed in terms of self ownership but if so, it had a radically different meaning from the way others understood the concept. For the Diggers believed that no one had the right to own another person's labour; 'neither take hire nor give hire'.[40] The natural rights they proclaimed were both individual and communal; each individual had a right to partake from this common treasury, but not to exclude others. Enclosure of land into private property by some individuals makes everyone else 'servants and slaves' they said, proclaiming that 'those that buy and sell land, and are landlords, have got it either by oppression or murder or theft;' hence private property has no moral validity.[41] True liberty was incompatible with private property; until the earth is 'free and common for all, to work together and eat together', they proclaimed, England would not be a free land.[42]

The more moderate and better known radicals of the period were the Levellers, such as Richard Overton, who wrote *An Arrow Against All Tyrants* in 1646 from prison. He began by saying 'To every individual in nature, is given an individuall property by nature, not to be invaded or usurped by any: for every one as he is himself, so he hath a selfe propriety, else he could not be himself ....: No man hath power over my rights and liberties, and I over no man's'. He goes on to say 'Every man by nature being a King, Priest and Prophet in his owne naturall circuite and compasse, whereof no second may partake, but by deputation, commission, and *free consent*'.[43] (my emphasis) The gender ambiguity in the above is clarified by Leveller Richard Lilbourne Overton's statement, 'Every particular and individual man and woman that ever breathed ... are and were by nature equal and alike in power, dignity, authority and majesty'.[44] The Levellers

---

39 Winstanley 1973, p. 77.
40 Ibid., p. 89.
41 Ibid., p. 85.
42 Ibid., p. 89. The best history of the radical ideas and movements of this period is Hill 1972. Peter Linebaugh's *The Magna Carta Manifesto* (Linebaugh 2008) traces the history of struggles for rights to the commons from the thirteenth to the twenty-first century, making a powerful case that economic rights are essential to political freedom.
43 Aylmer (ed.) 1975, pp. 68f.
44 Quoted in Elizabeth Potter 'Locke's Epistemology and Women's Struggles', in Bat-Ami Bar On (ed.) 1994, p. 31.

supported a broader franchise than the moderates, but far from universal manhood suffrage. Unlike the Diggers, they took 'self-propriety' to entail a right to private (not merely personal) property as essential to freedom, and they accepted wage labour. But the property they supported was a limited property and they railed against the 'greedy usurpers' who wanted more. Thus the concept of self-propriety was used by the Radicals to express a belief in peoples' natural freedom and natural right against tyranny, though the Levellers and the Diggers disagreed as to whether this included an individual right to (limited) private property.

The concepts of self-propriety and legitimate rule requiring free consent were picked up—appropriated, one could say—by the social contract theorists. Thomas Hobbes used the premise to argue in *Leviathan* in favour of an absolute form of government and John Locke's *Second Treatise on Government* of 1690 offered a defence of limited government based on a right to unlimited private property. Locke's *Treatise* is usually seen as a reply to Robert Filmer who defended absolute monarchy and to Thomas Hobbes.[45] But other scholars of the period have argued persuasively that Locke is equally or primarily concerned with responding to the radicals, indeed, that the radicals set the terms of the debate.[46] I focus on Locke because his theory is foundational for our system of limited government resting on the right to unlimited property.[47]

As a social contract theorist Locke sets out to justify his preferred form of government by arguing that it would arise from agreement (contract) amongst free, equal and rational individuals in a state of nature. His theory is particularly powerful in that it purports to demonstrate that free, equal and rational people would *freely consent to loss of freedom and equality*. In his lengthy chapter on Property, Locke makes some momentous moves: from a right to common property to a right to limited property to a right to unlimited private property—which property is then taken as a reason and as a basis for a government. Until there are large accumulations of wealth, he says, there is no need of govern-

---

45 Despite Hobbes' enduring philosophical importance, scholars have shown that Filmer, an influential figure at the time, is the more likely target of Locke's criticism of absolute government. Locke's *First Treatise* is devoted to refuting Filmer's defence of absolute monarchy on Biblical grounds and in the opening chapter of *The Second* he pointedly distinguishes political power from patriarchal power which Filmer conflates.
46 Meiksins Wood and Wood 1997; Hill 1972; MacPherson 1962.
47 Some, for example Carole Pateman, have argued that this is simply because Hobbes's theory is more naked in its analysis of the power relations inherent in a market system.

ment.[48] Starting from the premise (almost word for word from radical texts), that God has given the Earth, its fruits and its beasts, to mankind in common, he remarks that some have wondered how then private property could be justified. In response, he first makes the valid point that individuals must be able to appropriate some of it for their own use or they would starve. Furthermore, he writes, 'every man has a *property* in his own person; this nobody has any right to but himself. The *labour* of his body, and the *work* of his hands, we may say, are properly his. Whatsoever then he removes out of the state that nature hath provided, and left it in, he hath mixed his labour with, and joined to it something that is his own, and thereby makes it his *property*'. But he adds the explicit limit that there must be 'enough, and as good, left in common for others', on top of what would appear to be the implicit limit in the 'mixing one's labour principle' (how much, after all, can one mix one's labour with?).[49] He goes on to state an additional limit to the right of individual property that it must be put to some use before it spoils.

Thus far then, Locke has justified a right to very limited private property. But these limits disappear one by one as he progresses through the chapter. Elaborating on the idea that an individual has a right to what he has mixed his labour with, Locke says 'Thus the grass my horse has bit; the turfs my servant has cut; and the ore I have digged in any place, where I have a right to them in common with others, become my *property* ... the labour that was mine, *fixed* my *property* in them'. So 'he' has as much right to the product of his servant's labour, as that of his own labour or his horse's. But why doesn't the servant have the right to the product of his own labour, a right Locke has just enunciated? The only answer is that Locke understands the premise that each person has a property in his person and therefore in his labour to entail a right to sell that property. The person who buys the labour then has a right to the product of that labour ('my' servant, 'my' horse, 'my' turf). Here Locke simply assumes that the 'property' in one's person should be conceived of as an alienable commodity. This assumption *transforms ownership to non-ownership for those who sell their labour*. As wage labour was becoming dominant, and the more radical Levellers also accepted wage labour, he could presume that his readers would share this assumption. In this passage we can also see a move from a right to property

---

48 'The equality of a simple poor way of living, confining their desires within the narrow bounds of each man's small property, made few controversies, and so no need of many laws to decide them, or variety of officers to superintend the process, or look after the execution of justice, where there were but few trespasses, and few offenders'. Section 107, p. 57.
49 Locke 1980, p. 19.

based on labour to a right to property based on the productive *use* of labour by its owner.[50] Since there is no limit to how many 'servants' (the seventeenth century term for wage earner) one can employ, the right to wage labour erases, on the theoretical level, one implicit limit to the right to private property, and in actual history, leads to the concentration of property.

The 'no spoilage' limit disappears from Locke's justification of property because of what he calls the 'tacit' and voluntary agreement to introduce money, which does not spoil. 'And as different degrees of industry were apt to give men possessions in different proportions, so this *invention of money* gave them the opportunity to continue and enlarge them'.[51] Thus although Locke stated at the beginning of the *Treatise* that men (*sic*) are naturally equal, now he contends that natural differences in 'industry' will result in unequal property. (Quite different from the Diggers' story of murder and theft as its origin!)[52] And this allegedly all happens by consent. The very limited private property which Locke has justified early in the chapter has become considerably less limited. It is not yet unlimited, though, so long as 'there must be enough and as good left in common for others'.

While this last limit on the right to private property is never explicitly rejected, it disappears. Locke seems to believe it remains in spirit, however, as can be adduced from his claim that 'he who appropriates land to himself by his labour, does not lessen, but increase the common stock of mankind: for the provisions serving to the support of human life, produced by one acre of inclosed and cultivated land, are (to speak much within compass) ten times more than those which are yielded by one acre of land of an equal richness lying waste in common. And therefore he that incloses land, and has a greater plenty of conveniences of life from ten acres, than he could have from an hundred left in nature, may truly be said to give ninety acres to mankind'.[53] Thus starting from a premise of *self ownership*, Locke's theory justifies a right *to unlimited private property*. Purely in a state of nature some people would acquire large accumulations of property which would then generate the need for a government to protect it. This is the foundation for the kind of limited government he defends. Since the purpose of government, as he says repeatedly, is the protection of

---

50 '… the activity of labour and all its attendant virtues are attributes of the master … It is a short step from here to the eclipse of labour altogether by the economic activity of the capitalist' (Meiksins Wood 1995, pp. 157–8).
51 Locke 1980, 29.
52 Karl Marx agreed, referring to accounts like Locke's as 'childish idylls … In actual history it is notorious that conquest, enslavement, robbery, murder, briefly force, play the great part'. *Capital* Vol. I, in Tucker (ed.) 1978, p. 432.
53 Locke 1980, pp. 23–4.

property, it would be a contradiction to suppose that those with property had not explicitly consented to government. And if the government fails to fulfil its side of the contract, citizens have a right to revolt. This is the politically liberatory aspect of his philosophy which is rightly celebrated.

On the other hand, those without property cannot be said to have *explicitly* consented to government, Locke says, but only *tacitly*, like visitors from foreign countries, and hence they are not to be full citizens of civil society.[54] Then what is left in his theory, one might ask, of the original freedom of the majority? The answer lies in his assumption that those who make the laws do so for everyone's best interests, so the majority *subject to law* but *without the right to make law* can still be said to be free, in his view, since 'that ill deserves the name of confinement which hedges us in only from bogs and precipices'.[55] A happy conclusion for all, in Locke's eyes, but far from freedom as most of us would understand it.

It should be pointed out that Locke's rationale for abandoning his 'enough and as good left in common for others' limit on the right to private property functioned as an important justification for taking the land of Native Americans, and moreover, it does not actually satisfy his condition. First of all, he assumes that the only alternative to private property is land left to waste in common, whereas common land may be developed as productively as enclosed and private land. Secondly, greater productivity does not automatically mean that people will have their needs met. The crucial question is whether they have *access* to what is produced—and this depends on the system of property and rights in place. As Amartya Sen has pointed out, millions of people have died in famines not because there was not enough food; the problem was that they had neither land to produce the food themselves nor the money they needed to buy it in a market system.[56] This point is particularly apparent today as we see food riots around the world caused not by lack of food but because of price increases, due not only to more hungry mouths coming onto the market, but to the desire of the wealthy of the world to burn up for fuel what could be food.[57]

---

54   Section 119–22. In some of his other writings, Locke is more explicit in his view that those without property do not have the requisite rationality for this responsibility, though it is unclear whether he thinks this is by nature or due to the circumstances of their lives. He proposes that any unemployed person (female or male) without property over the age of three years of age (!) should be made to work: Macpherson 1962, pp. 222–38; Nancy Hirschmann has a thorough discussion of this issue in Hirschmann 2008, pp. 80–106.
55   Section 57.
56   Sen 1981. Sen also makes this point in other writings.
57   Patel 2007.

Where do women fit into this story? What did the debates about property in early capitalism imply with respect to women and their rights and interests? And what does this suggest about capitalism and women's interests? Though I have been using the gender neutral language typical of political theory, it would be ahistorical to assume that all our writers intended their principles to apply universally. The Levellers did advocate equal civil liberties for everyone regardless of sex or wealth or employment status, a very radical position at the time, and Leveller women were very active as preachers, traders, petitioners and protestors to Parliament.[58] Nevertheless, the Levellers did not demand political rights for women for the same reason they did not include servants or those accepting charity in the franchise. Wives' dependence on their husbands, servants' dependence on their masters (employers), and the dependence on charity of the impoverished caused each group to lose the natural freedom Levellers believed all human beings had by birth. Their political rights were presumed to be transferred to their husbands or masters.[59] The Diggers supported universal male suffrage, the most radical position at the time, not to be realized for more than three centuries, but they did not think to extend it to women, though it is not clear why, since they expressly said that male and female were 'perfect creatures of himself' with the capacity of Reason. As for Locke, one can infer that women were not included among the individuals who are said to be naturally equal. For he says that in marriage 'the last determination, i.e. the rule ... naturally falls to the man's share, as *the abler and the stronger*'.[60] Despite this, he contends that 'the conjugal society, [as he calls marriage], is made by a voluntary compact between man and woman' which exists in a state of nature.[61] But there is an inconsistency here that rests on the meaning of freedom. If women were equal to men and could acquire property, why would they agree to become subordinate to a man and lose all rights to property, even what they had before marriage? On the other hand, if they are not equal and need the support and protection of a man, is the conjugal contract really based on their voluntary consent? Unlike Hobbes, Locke distinguishes between agreement based on superior force and genuine consent, so it is hard to see how the 'conjugal contract' between unequals could be said to be an example of genuine consent. Thus in Locke's story, all women, like landless men, freely agree to unfreedom, both in an imagined state of nature and in civil society.

---

58 'The Reactions of Women, with Special Reference to Women Petitioners', in Manning (ed.) 1973.
59 Macpherson 1962, pp. 143–6, 296.
60 Locke 1980, p. 44.
61 Locke 1980, p. 43.

An interesting alternative perspective on women's rights in marriage is provided by Locke's contemporary Mary Astell who pointed out his inconsistency: 'if Absolute Sovereignty be not necessary in a State, how comes it to be so in a Family? Or if in a Family why not in a State? ... If all Men are born free, how is that all Women are born slaves?'[62] Today we would infer from her acute observation that absolute sovereignty is justified neither in the family nor the state but, interestingly, Astell eliminated Locke's inconsistency in the opposite direction. Combining radical feminism with religious and political conservatism, she argued that there was no right to rebel in either case; absolute monarchy was founded on God's will and if a woman chose to marry then she chose to obey her husband even if he was stupid and cruel (analogously, she says, if someone agrees to work for a pig farmer, then they are obliged to shovel pig manure). Her radical feminism is reflected in her low opinion of most men and her consequent advice to women not to marry but instead to seek a community of like-minded women. Thus both in its more conservative and more liberal versions, classical liberal theory defended a property form and marriage based on that form that necessarily put limits on women's rights and freedom. As we will see, this has changed in some respects and not in others. Would it be possible to rewrite his story to allow for equality between men and women as today's liberal feminists would like to do? No, for as Lorenne Clark explains, 'One of Locke's major objectives was to provide the theoretical basis for the absolute right of the male to pass his property to his rightful heirs'.[63]

Returning to the notions of self-ownership and freedom, we can see how dramatically different Locke's conception was from that of the Diggers and Levellers. The specific kind of freedom associated with capitalism came into existence and was theorized in the context of a struggle against broader more radical visions of freedom. Against these visions, Locke promotes a *limited* kind of freedom—freedom from arbitrary rule by a monarch—for a *limited* class of individuals—large landowners—and *subordination for the majority in the name of freedom*. All women are among the subordinated majority. The discrepancy between the words and the reality behind Locke's theory is revealed even more blatantly by his involvement in the slave trade, which played so prominent a part in the rise of capitalism.[64] Although there was no chance in that

---

62 Astell 2000, p. 48.
63 Clark 1979, p. 27. The father's right to pass his property to *whomever he wished* persisted in English law until 1939. See also Carole Pateman 1988 for a powerful argument that the social contract is a sexual contract and Nancy Hirschmann 2008.
64 Combining philosophical argumentation and historical documentation, Charles Mills

historical period for the radical democratic forces to prevail, their alternative visions make clear the limitations of Locke's view of freedom, and are especially important today when it is possible, even necessary, I will argue, to realize the most radical visions.

3.5   *Self-Ownership—the Contemporary Debates*
Whatever its historical genesis, is the notion of self-ownership a useful one for liberatory purposes? What sort of conception of a person is implicit and is the concept even coherent? Certainly ownership of self or body, and by extension one's labour, is rather different from owning other things. I can lose, sell or destroy my house, my car or my stocks, without losing, selling or destroying myself or my body. If what I own is small enough, I can forget it on the bus! The point is that owner and owned are distinct. On the other hand, if it even makes sense to say you lose your body or your self, then you are lost too. If you destroy your self or body totally, you are destroyed along with it. If, on the other hand, you *sell* your body or your labour, there is still you—but you go with it. What's done to it is done to you. And it is the owner who gains its use value, all its creative potentials, while the seller necessarily loses them. In this unique and peculiar case where owner and owned are one and the same, the ownership conception seems to many critics to introduce a radical split within the person. Alienability, arguably, implies alienation, a separation from self. Alternatively, however, critics might say that this split is only metaphoric. In reality if one sells one's labour one is selling oneself, even if the sale is subject to temporal and other restrictions. It is these differences between self-ownership and ordinary ownership and the moral concerns that accompany the differences that lead many to put limits on it, or to conceive it in a radically different way from the Lockean conception—or to reject the notion entirely.

Contemporary political philosophers in the liberal and analytic tradition, including some critics of capitalism sympathetic to Marxism, are divided over the idea that each person has property in her or his person and what moral and political conclusions would follow if they do. Feminists have engaged in similar debates regarding the meaning, utility and implications of the idea of self-ownership, seeing the question as an especially salient one for women. Though the debates are quite parallel, it is striking how little interchange there is

---

demonstrates that social contract theory is also a theory of racial contract: Mills 1997. Karl Marx writes of the transition of feudalism to capitalism, '... the veiled slavery of the wage workers in Europe needed, for its pedestal, slavery pure and simple in the new world' (*Capital* Vol. I, in Tucker (ed.) 1976, p. 760; Eric Williams gives a detailed account of this relationship in Williams 1966).

between the two. Robert Nozick, like Locke, made self-ownership a key premise of his philosophy believing that it justified a right to unlimited private property even if, unlike Locke, this meant that others would starve. While Nozick is an extreme economic conservative, some liberal and left philosophers also accept the premise of self-ownership but they interpret it more weakly or in other ways try to forestall Nozick's extreme conclusion. There has been much discussion of whether this is possible,[65] and whether Marx accepted the premise of self-ownership.[66] Feminists, naturally, have debated the question with specific reference to its implications for women. Many believe the notion of each individual having property in her/his person is critically important for women because they see it as the basis of each individual woman's rights over her body.[67] Thus they see it as the necessary ground for the right to free expression of sexuality and the right to abortion. Jennifer Church, for example, treats a woman's rights over her body as immediately following from the 'fundamental fact that it is hers', which she takes to be equivalent to saying that she owns her body or that she has property in her body. Some liberal feminists believe that self-ownership also entails a right to sell the use of one's body for sexual services or for procreation, on the grounds that since one owns it, one should be able to do with it what one likes.[68] To deny this, they contend, would be to deny the individual her sexual autonomy. Most feminists disagree with this inference; they believe that even though one owns one's body, it is not like all other property and in particular should not be sold.[69] (Similar arguments occur regarding whether we should have the right to sell our bodily organs.) Margaret Jane Radin, a noted legal theorist of property, argues that certain things should not be available for sale within a market system. After considering prostitution, baby-selling and commercial surrogacy, she concludes that because of their importance for personhood, the latter two should not be permitted. While sympathetic to the view that sexual services should not be commodities either, she argues that in our present world of economic and gender inequality, to ban prostitution would be worse for poor women than to allow it. However, she advocates various legal restrictions to reduce its inherent exploitation.

---

65 Cohen 1995. Van Parijs 1995; Arneson 1991, pp. 36–54.
66 Warren 1994, pp. 33–56; Holmstrom 1997, pp. 583–6.
67 Donna Dickensen supports contract theory for feminists in Dickensen 1997; Church 1997.
68 Radcliffe Richards 1980; Lehrman 1997.
69 Radin 1987; Church 1997. Elizabeth Anderson argues that neither sexual services nor women's (procreative) labour are appropriately thought of as economic goods because to do so would violate other human good: Anderson 1990a, pp. 179–205; 1990b, pp. 71–90.

On the other side of this debate, Carole Pateman is strongly critical of the very concept of self-ownership, denouncing it as inherently masculine, individualistic and capitalist.[70] Selves and bodies are inseparable and bodies are sexually differentiated. Thus a woman cannot simply sell her body, or sexual or procreative 'services', without also selling her self. Pateman makes the same point about the sale of labour power, a concept she calls a political fiction. However she contends that prostitution is different from and worse than wage labour, even poorly paid and subordinate forms, in that ordinary labour can be replaced by machines, but in prostitution what the customer buys is the direct use of *a woman* for sexual purposes. In commercial surrogacy, a woman conceives, carries and bears a child but has contracted to give it to the man whose semen has been implanted in her. To call her the 'surrogate' mother and to give all rights over the child—who has for nine months literally been a part of herself, only gradually becoming an 'other' being—to the father, reveals fully the classical patriarchal and capitalist nature of this arrangement. To make a part of a woman's body, her uterus, and her labour, into property that a man can contract to buy and then claim the product of these, the baby, as properly his is the ultimate form of exploitation and alienation. In sum, Pateman believes it is deeply mistaken for feminists to try to use the language of ownership and contract for their ends, as the 'power and genius of contract ... proclaims that a contract of subordination is (sexual) freedom'.[71]

Socialist feminist Rosalind Petchesky has a distinct and interesting position. While agreeing that self-ownership is very important for women, and does not entail the right to sell one's body, she casts her position in a more general discussion of the many meanings of property and ownership. Arguing that both sides to the feminist debate about self-ownership accept a narrow Lockean interpretation, she seeks to restore the historically earlier understandings of the concept found in the Diggers and Levellers, as discussed above, and current elsewhere around the world. She cites examples of people claiming their 'self-propriety' to assert their rights against state harassment and their freedom to be sexual as far back as the seventeenth century. This assertion of inalienable personal autonomy was not entirely individualistic, she argues, as many radicals of the time did not make a sharp distinction between self and com-

---

70   Pateman 1986. See Pateman and Mills 2007, for further discussion and debate over the utility of contract theory for liberatory purposes.
71   Pateman 1986, p. 200. She expands her critique to the 'global racial-sexual contract' in Pateman and Mills 2007, p. 159.

munity. She also cites examples from parts of the world where they use a word translated as 'own' which really means 'has responsibility for', and which does not imply that one has exclusive rights over, especially not the right to sell. In our own society too, she notes examples of mixed property forms, of rights and relationships that lie between private and common property such as 'coops, condominiums, residents-only parks and beaches, guardianships and foster care'.[72]

Given that people of varying political persuasions use the concept of self-ownership, but interpret it so differently and draw such radically different political conclusions from it, self-ownership does not seem to me a helpful way of expressing the moral and political ideas that its users intend by it. All want to claim that individuals have some basic moral rights over their bodies. That is, each individual should be free to do what she or he likes (within certain constraints) with her/his body. The debate is over whether these rights include the right to alienate it, that is, to sell it, to profit from it as one can with any commodity in a capitalist system.[73] If one does not accept this implication, it is not clear what is added by saying that one *owns* one's body. The moral questions regarding what rights one has over one's body should be debated on their own without connecting them to the notions of property and ownership. Given the ubiquity of the market system and the dominance of private property, connecting the question of rights to ownership and property tends to pre-judge the moral debate. Granted, there are broader meanings of ownership, as Petchesky argues and I have discussed above, but as the concept has developed, in current usage ownership is *contrasted* with relationships such as responsibility and caretaking that in some cultures are called ownership. For example, we expressly deny that parents 'own' their children, even if granting them many rights over their children, and many people concerned about the environment would be sympathetic to Marx's comment that 'From the standpoint of a higher socio-economic formation [i.e. socialism or communism], the

---

72 Petchesky 1995. Petchesky's attempt to recast this right of individual control to the earlier notions of ownership is particularly tricky since some of these were committed to common property and opposed to private property. She tries to address this by arguing that these thinkers would not have made a sharp distinction between self and community. More needs to be said.

73 One approach to this debate is to distinguish two kinds of ownership: control ownership and income ownership. One can have a right to control something, and to that extent own it, but not necessarily to have a right to dispose of it and make income from it. See John Christman 1994. This distinction was customary historically in property law. Cheyney Ryan argues that ownership involves a 'bundle of rights' that do not always go together. Cf. Ryan 1977, pp. 126–41.

private property of individuals in the earth will appear just as absurd as the private property of one man in other men. Even an entire society, a nation, or all simultaneously existing societies taken together, are not owners of the earth, they are simply its possessors, its beneficiaries, and have to bequeath it in an improved state to succeeding generations'.[74] We should recognize that women have special reasons for claiming a right of control over their bodies but we do not need to describe this in terms of ownership. While this does not resolve the feminist debates as to whether there are moral or political limits to this right, for example regarding prostitution or 'surrogacy', it separates them from the distracting idea of ownership.[75]

Thus the contention that in capitalism everyone owns something, viz. themselves, cannot be sustained. Nor can we say that self-ownership is *foundational to* freedom and rights, because they come down to the same thing. The question of whether in capitalist societies each individual owns something, viz. her or his self or body, is simply the question of whether capitalism provides basic liberties and rights, control over self and body, for all individuals. *In theory* the answer is yes, though as discussed above, *in fact* not all capitalist societies do, since not all are politically democratic—and even those that are democratic do not always grant women control over their bodies. Ireland and Chile, for example, deny women the right to abortion even in cases of rape. Throughout history women have been denied their rights, and have struggled for the freedom to act as they wish. The first wave women's movement was primarily for the freedom to vote, but the second wave movement was called the women's 'liberation' movement. Given the centrality of freedom to women, we need to clarify exactly what it means before we can address how much freedom capitalism offers to women.

3.6   Freedom/Unfreedom in the Abstract

> The words 'liberty' and 'freedom' are slippery and change their meaning over time. ... one man's liberty can be another man's slavery.
> CHRISTOPHER HILL[76]

∴

---

74   Marx 1974.
75   Ann Ferguson pointed out the need for this clarification.
76   Hill 1996, p. 243 and p. 19.

Security of property! Behold in a few words the definition of English liberty!

MARY WOLLSTONECRAFT[77]

∙ ∙ ∙

Freedom is 'clothes and fire and food for the trampled multitude'.

PERCY BYSSHE SHELLEY[78]

∙ ∙ ∙

I want the same thing that I did thirty years ago when I joined the Civil Rights movement and twenty years ago when I joined the women's movement, came out, and felt more alive than I ever dreamed possible: freedom.

BARBARA SMITH[79]

∙ ∙
∙

So what is freedom exactly? Now that we have detached the notion of freedom from self-ownership, we need to clarify the concept. What are we to make of the above very disparate statements about freedom which, as Orlando Patterson has said, is 'unchallenged as ... the supreme value of the Western world'.[80] Certainly there are different interpretations of freedom, debated throughout the centuries, which have different implications for our question of whether people are freer in capitalism than in alternative systems. This therefore is a political as well as a philosophical debate. (Some conceptions of freedom are so narrow they would rule out the very question.) Who are the people who are or are not free, and in what respects are they free or unfree? For freedom comes in many *dimensions* and *degrees*, and so does lack of freedom. We need an analysis of the concept of freedom which can illuminate the controversies, how freedom can be different and also the same, as expressed in our quotations above. This is what I shall try to offer here.

---

77 Mary Wollstonecraft, *Works*, quoted in Hill 1996, p. 242.
78 Percy Bysshe Shelley, *The Mask of Anarchy*. Cf. Foot 1992, pp. 18–20.
79 Barbara Smith, *The Truth That Never Hurts*, quoted in Kelley 2002, p. 136.
80 Patterson 1991, p. ix.

Obviously one person can be free and another not, and indeed, as Christopher Hill points out above, one person's freedom, e.g. to own slaves, entails the lack of freedom of others. Just as obviously, we can be free to do one thing and not another. Also, but perhaps less obviously, we can be free to do a particular thing in one respect and not in another. More precisely, to say one is free is to say one is free *from* an obstacle preventing one from doing something; one is un-free *to do* something because an obstacle prevents one from doing it.[81] Thus one can be free to do something with respect to one obstacle and un-free to do it with respect to another. The obstacles preventing one from doing something may be physical or may involve persons in some significant way. So someone might be free to go into a particular restaurant because no physical obstacle prevents her from doing so, but un-free because it is a 'whites only' restaurant in the segregated South and she is not white. The law, backed up by force, is the obstacle to her entering the restaurant. The civil rights movement removed this obstacle, thereby expanding the freedom of African Americans. The law then became an obstacle to the restaurant owner's desire to exclude them. Prior to the U.S. Supreme Court's Roe vs. Wade decision in 1973, which the women's movement was crucial in securing, a woman was not free to get an abortion because the law forbade it. After that she would be free with respect to the law. However, government is not the only source of lack of freedom. A woman might still be unfree to get an abortion if she were poor because the Hyde Amendment of 1977, upheld by the Supreme Court in 1980, denied the use of federal funds for an abortion. In this case, lack of money is the obstacle.[82] Neither the law nor lack of money is what prevents most gays and lesbians from displaying physical affection in public, but rather negative social attitudes which could result in harassment and even death. The prevalence of violence against women, particularly rape, is an important obstacle to women moving about as freely in their daily lives as men. Their reasonable fear leads them to curtail their actions, and if they do not and something happens, then they are blamed.[83]

---

81 My account here follows MacCallum Jr. 1967, Ezorsky 2007, several articles by G.A. Cohen, especially those collected in Cohen 1988; Reiman 1987; Zimmerman 1981; and Holmstrom 1975, pp. 423–45; and 1977. Though the preceding were not written from an explicitly feminist perspective, I am gratified that they accord for the most part with Hirschmann 2003.
82 John Rawls is among those who deny that lack of money is a limitation on freedom, though he says it may affect the 'worth' of someone's liberty. Rawls 1971, p. 204. Pettit 2001 groups poverty with 'natural limits' on freedom such as disability and illness (p. 130) and argues that it is always worse to restrict people's freedom to overcome the limits posed by 'the natural order or the ways things are socially organized' (p. 132).
83 I am thinking particularly of a widespread reaction to the case of the young woman who was jogging in New York's Central Park after dark who was gang raped and almost killed.

This analysis of what it means to be free might seem to stress so-called negative liberty (freedom from interference) at the expense of positive liberty (freedom to do ...), but this is misleading.[84] As Gerald MacCallum explained a long time ago, there really is no difference between kinds of freedom; any claim about freedom involves both aspects.[85] Some writers, for example John Gray and Nancy Hirschmann, have stressed, correctly, that there are not only constraining conditions to our actions but also enabling ones and both need attention in an analysis of what it is to be free.[86] I take this important point to be included in the above analysis since the absence of positive supports can be a decided obstacle preventing one from doing something. (We will see examples of this below.) As Rhonda Copelon, the attorney opposing the Hyde Amendment before the Supreme Court argued, our 'choices are shaped, facilitated or denied by social conditions; ... to protect a 'right to choose' without assuring the social conditions necessary to foster an autonomous choice provides equality of opportunity in form but not in fact'.[87] Similarly, the absence of constraining conditions is an enabling condition. The analysis of freedom I am presenting, which combines the positive and negative, is quite compatible with a stress on the positive. Indeed this would make sense since the reason one wants to be *free from* obstacles is *in order to be free to* do things one wants to do. Liberation *from something* is necessary for liberation *for something*. Recognition of this moves us toward a conception of the fullest kind of freedom as self-determination or autonomy in both personal and political terms.[88]

Some philosophers have restrictive views about the kinds of obstacles that can limit someone's freedom. One particularly narrow view is that someone is un-free only when another person physically restrains them from doing something, (some even say it must be intentional); others take a broader view

---

84 Isaiah Berlin understood the concept of. 'positive liberty' to mean more than this, but I prefer this simpler conception. 'Two Concepts of Liberty' in Berlin 1971.
85 MacCallum 1967 says that with regard to individual freedom to act, 'such freedom is thus always *of* something (an agent or agents), *from* something, *to* do, not do, become, or not become something; it is a triadic relation ... [If any] of these terms is missing ... it should be only because the reference is thought to be understood from the context'.
86 Gray 1980, pp. 507–26, argues that MacCallum is biased towards negative freedom because he only cites constraining conditions; Nancy Hirschmann, 2003, stresses both, as I do, but interprets the distinction between negative and positive freedom as a distinction between external and internal factors that constrain or enable us, rather than simply freedom free from and freedom to.
87 Copelon 1990, pp. 38 f.
88 There is a very extensive literature on autonomy as well as freedom with different understandings of their relationship.

and allow that if a person is threatened if she doesn't do something, then she is coerced into doing it and hence is not free. While the latter view is broader than the former, both are narrower than the obstacle view of freedom presented above because they require that persons be causes of the lack of freedom.[89] Hence, as Gertrude Ezorsky explains, they cannot explain how a person *becomes free* to do something when some physical obstacle is removed.[90] For example, 'when they moved the car blocking her way, she was free to drive down the street;' this implies she was not free to drive before they moved it. So persons are not the only obstacles to freedom.

Other philosophers put moral restrictions on what counts as limiting someone's freedom. Robert Nozick, for example, contends that other peoples' actions which limit someone's opportunities do not thereby limit his or her *freedom* so long as they had the *moral right* to act as they did.[91] Thus, in the above example, if the person had the moral right to park his car in a way that blocked my car, this would not limit my freedom to drive down the block. Since this seems patently false, one might wonder why he would define freedom so narrowly. Other examples suggest an explanation. 'When she got a higher-paying job, she was finally free to take a vacation', implies that she was not free to take a vacation before that. 'Until discrimination in private employment became illegal, women and Black Americans were not free to work in many businesses', implies that discrimination limited their freedom. Since Nozick believes that employers have the moral right to pay so little that their employees can never take a vacation, and that private employers have the right to discriminate if they want, it would follow on his analysis of freedom that low pay and discrimination do not limit the freedom of the employees in these examples. But again, this is patently false. Nozick seems driven to this very restrictive definition of freedom because to allow that the ordinary workings of capitalism limit people's freedom would create a problem for his claim that capitalism is the morally best economic system *because it is the most free*. Whatever the explanation, it is unacceptable.[92] As G.A. Cohen observes, this 'moralized' concept of

---

89 This literature is vast so I will just refer interested readers to the sources found in the works I have cited elsewhere.
90 Ezorsky 2007, p. 12.
91 Nozick 1974, pp. 55, 178–82. Hayek too has a moralised understanding of freedom. See Gray 1981, pp. 73–84.
92 In the 2nd example it is the 'libertarian' or free market version of capitalism that restricts freedom, rather than capitalism per se. Some writers on freedom take existing property relations as the natural background conditions against which we judge freedom of action. This clearly is biased towards capitalism as it prevents us from even asking whether another system of property relations might provide more freedom.

freedom would entail the absurd conclusion that 'if a criminal's imprisonment is morally justified, he is then not forced to be in prison', quite rightly calling this an 'abuse of the language of freedom'.[93]

So let us assume that obstacles to someone's acting freely may be physical or may 'significantly involve persons' regardless of whether or not those persons have the right to act as they do. Now someone can limit another person's freedom in various ways, not only by direct physical force or by coercion. Certain kinds of proposals or offers can also prevent someone from acting freely. 'Forcing offers' is Gertrude Ezorsky's apt characterisation of cases like that of an employer's offer of a dangerous and low paid job to someone whose only alternative is starvation for herself and her family. In such a case the worker could say 'I had no choice; I was forced to take the job'.[94] When all the choices are terrible, freedom of choice *among them* does not mean freedom overall. Not only individuals, but social institutions, organized and maintained by people, may also limit someone's freedom. This can be missed if we focus just on individuals. Two such examples from the United States of particular relevance to women are the absence of adequate childcare and the absence of universal medical care. One woman may be prevented from taking a job she would like by the absence of childcare; another woman may stay in a dangerous low paid job she hates, even accepting worse conditions, because she needs the company's health insurance for her sick child.[95] Choices discussed above about whether or not to have an abortion provide other examples. Laws restricting abortion may leave a pregnant woman no choice but to have a child while on the other hand, the absence of social supports like childcare, medical care etc. may lead another pregnant woman to have an abortion because she feels she cannot afford to provide a good life for a child she would love to have. In all these cases, people make rational choices, and hence are free to that very minimal degree, but are nonetheless forced to do what they do. As Jeffrey Reiman has said, 'structural force can operate through free choice'.[96]

---

93 Cohen 1988, p. 256. Jeffrey Reiman 1981 also shows that Nozick's argument is circular.
94 Ezorsky 2007, pp. 29 ff. There is a large literature on the concepts of threats, coercion, offers, coercive offers by, among others, Robert Nozick, Harry Frankfurt, Roger Wertheimer, Hillel Steiner, Virginia Held and David Zimmerman.
95 Gendered expectations regarding women's roles within heterosexual relationships may also contribute to this decision, but this is not the primary explanation as single and lesbian mothers face the same obstacle.
96 Reiman 1987.

3.7   Internal Obstacles

Thus far, all the examples of obstacles preventing someone from doing something have been 'external' to the person. An adequate account of freedom I will argue would allow that the obstacles limiting someone's freedom could also be *internal* to the person.[97] As just discussed, if a woman is prevented from getting a job because the law discriminates against women, or because she has no childcare, or because the men in her family will beat her up, she is not free to work. However, suppose a woman is prevented from getting a job because she has a mental illness or an addiction, or suppose she feels that it is wrong for a woman to work outside the home, or wants to accommodate her husband who wants her home, or suppose she believes (falsely) that she is incompetent, or suppose she is afraid to travel to a job because she has been traumatized by violence? Such feelings and beliefs are widespread among women due to sexism. If there is no external obstacle preventing someone from going out to work, as in the above cases, is she simply *unable to work*, or is she also *un-free*? Many thinkers would say that she is unable to work, but she is not un-free. However, by the same reasoning used above, this seems an unreasonable restriction on what can cause someone to be un-free. The varied internal constraints mentioned above, many of which are related to sexism, can be very powerful obstacles to acting freely. As feminists from Mary Wollstonecraft and John Stuart Mill to today have stressed, women have been acculturated not only to conform to gendered expectations but *to want to do so*. Now suppose that due to cultural shifts or through her involvement in political activism or through support groups or psychotherapy, her beliefs and her feelings change such that she becomes able to work. We could also say that she becomes *free* to work. It follows that she was *un-free* until these internal obstacles were removed.[98] The constraining emotions, habits and beliefs of the past that prevented her from working have been replaced by enabling ones. This analysis accords with our common understanding that such processes and changes can be liberating, as when it is said that the cultural changes and political movements of the 1960s and 70s were immensely liberating for women or that psychotherapy can liberate us from our 'hang-ups' or 'blocks'. This is why the women's liberation movement of this period organized consciousness raising groups for

---

97   Holmstrom 1975 and 1977; Hirschmann 2003, Philip Pettit 2001.
98   This follows Gertrude Ezorsky's argument for the obstacle view of freedom though she does not extend it to internal obstacles. It can be difficult to separate the internal obstacles from the external when the internal are responses to sexism as Margaret McLaren stressed to me. Certainly the external obstacles should be eliminated but it is possible sometimes to eliminate the internal on their own.

women as well as rallies and lobbies to change laws and policies, and why there are support groups for survivors of domestic violence and rape. The problem of internal obstacles to freedom, stemming from oppression, is not limited to women. As Terry Eagleton says, 'The most efficient oppressor is the one who persuades his underlings to love, desire and identify with his power, ... any practice of political emancipation thus involves that most difficult of all forms of liberation, freeing ourselves from ourselves'.[99]

3.8   Tests of the Analysis

We started our discussion of the concept of freedom with some statements suggesting that freedom means different things to different people. And this is certainly true. For one person freedom might mean escape from a dictatorship, for another freedom is being able to openly express her sexuality, for another freedom is having enough to eat every day. Though such expressions are sometimes more literary than literal, they express something profoundly important. Can the unified analysis of the concept of freedom I have offered accommodate these differences? I think it can. Recall the quotation from Barbara Smith 'I want the same thing that I did thirty years ago when I joined the Civil Rights movement and twenty years ago when I joined the women's movement, came out, and felt more alive than I ever dreamed possible: freedom'.[100] According to our analysis, a person can be free with respect to one obstacle and not to another; for other people the situation may be reversed or they may face overwhelming obstacles in every direction. Barbara Smith's statement reflects the fact that different obstacles constrained her in different respects; in order to achieve her *single goal*—freedom as a whole person—she had to struggle to remove one set of obstacles after another.

On the other hand, what statements suggesting *differences* in the meaning of freedom express most fundamentally is that different people will experience different things either as the *most salient obstacle* to their freedom, or as the *most salient condition enabling them* to do what they want. A person who does not have enough to eat is not free to do much of anything regardless of the laws or social mores of their society. Food is freedom to the starving because it is the most salient enabling condition for them. For a person who cannot walk, freedom will be a wheel chair, elevators and curb cut-outs. For a middle class, able-bodied person living in a dictatorship, freedom will be getting away from

---

99   Eagleton 1991, xiv. Nancy Hirschmann explores the many dimensions of how this takes place, arguing that our very selves are constructed through gendered expectations (Hirschmann 2003).

100 Barbara Smith, *The Truth That Never Hurts*, quoted in Kelley 2002, p. 136.

that government. Someone living in a market society who wants to buy a book and has the money to buy it but the government forbids its sale will find this particularly galling. 'One man's freedom is another man's slavery' is literally true in that the freedom of one man to own slaves entails that others are slaves; in exactly the same way, the freedom of an employer to discriminate in hiring is the lack of freedom of others to work.

Our unified theory of freedom can also accommodate historian Christopher Hill's statement that freedom changes its meaning over time. Though not literally true as he would undoubtedly acknowledge, his statement reflects the fact that different obstacles are the focus of struggle at different historical junctures and for different groups. The change in 'meaning' may also reflect the fact that different groups have hegemony of expression at different times. In the seventeenth century freedom was associated with private property for landowners who had to fight against the monarchy and feudal restrictions. But while landowners certainly had hegemony of expression, many others expressed themselves too and private property was not all that 'freedom' meant even then. Indeed freedom was 'a continuing theme' for Gerard Winstanley, the most famous Digger, who attacked private property in the name of freedom, arguing that private property was an obstacle to freedom for all—which required communal property.[101] In the 1960s and '70s, the words 'freedom' and 'liberation' were associated particularly with movements for *national* liberation against colonial domination and this was extended to the black liberation movement and then the women's liberation movement. At that historical juncture, colonial domination, and racist and sexist power structures were seen as the primary obstacles to freedom in the eyes of the millions who suffered under them.

As we will see in the section on Capitalism *in Reality* the examples discussed earlier of lack of freedom are not simply hypothetical. Particularly relevant to an evaluation of capitalism are the external obstacles. Even in the United States, the richest country in the history of the world, people are often forced to take or keep jobs, or sometimes forced to decline jobs, because of threats and because they face terrible alternatives due to the absence of socially provided necessary goods. As documented by Human Rights Watch some workers in the United States live in conditions close to indentured servitude. Several United States Supreme Court decisions have reinforced the imbalance of power that creates this lack of freedom, most importantly, the denial that individuals have economic and social rights, and the 1915 decision

---

101   Hill 1996, p. 276. *The Law of Freedom* was Winstanley's most famous work.

which allows employers to fire workers for any reason. Though this power has been weakened somewhat over the years, non-union employees are still subject to this power (known as 'employment at will') unless they can show that they were fired for very specific discriminatory reasons.[102] In some capitalist societies around the globe, workers have won more job protection, but in the poorer capitalist countries, people live with even less freedom due to more dire choices.

3.9   A More Ideal Capitalism?

To what extent could capitalism be re-organized so that the inequalities of wealth and power that limit the freedom of the majority were removed or overcome? This has been the dream of liberals committed to genuine equality of opportunity for *all* members of society starting with John Stuart Mill.[103] Recall that on the above analysis of freedom, to say someone is un-free is not to say that she has literally no choice whatsoever. The obstacles preventing one from doing something are seldom as severe as that. Indeed unless one is physically restrained to such a degree that there is no possibility of fighting back, there is always some choice. And the choices may be perfectly rational. So it is not whether someone has or does not have choices, nor simply the number of choices, but rather *the nature of the choices* that is critical in determining the *degree to which someone is free*. Our question then is to what extent could capitalism be reformed so that so many crucial choices people make were not simply the best of a very bad lot, made in pain to avoid worse pain. In theory, capitalism could certainly be freer for most people than it is. In theory, some of the obstacles to freedom discussed above could be removed. Then people's choices could be different. If there were universal childcare, a mother would not be prevented from getting a job by the need to care for children. If there were universal medical care, no one would have to take or stay in a terrible job just because they needed the health insurance. If there were adequate subsidies for all children, no woman would have to have an abortion because she was unable to provide a decent life for her child. If the law did not allow employers to fire someone almost at will, a power that legal theorist Morris Cohen likens to absolute monarchy, then a worker would be free to protest unsafe conditions.[104] Many capitalist societies, most notably the Scandinavian countries, have gone some way in removing these obstacles to freedom. Could these

---

102   See the useful Appendix on twentieth-century US labour laws in Ezorsky 2007.
103   See his *Principles of Political Economy with Some of their Applications to Social Philosophy*, excerpted in Macpherson (ed.) 1978; and the critique in Macpherson 1977.
104   Morris Cohen, 'Property and Sovereignty', in Macpherson 1978, p. 173.

reforms be extended to our own society and to all other capitalist societies? Could they be extended even further? And how can such reforms be shown to be compatible with capitalism as a theory?

3.10   *In Theory*

These reforms can be shown to be compatible with philosophical theories in support of capitalism in several ways. One line of argument is that although in capitalism individuals have the right to own the bulk of the means of production, the very justification of this right to property assumes that there is a general right to subsistence and therefore a claim on that property. Recall that Locke starts out his argument for private property by arguing that everyone has a right to partake of the resources of the world for their sustenance. He initially puts limits on how much any individual can appropriate, saying there must be as much and as good left in common for others. Though he later drops this limit and supports a right to unlimited private property, the spirit of the limit on the right to individual appropriation remains in his claim that the greater productivity of private cultivated property can be said to give back more to mankind than if it were not privately appropriated. Though I have argued that this happy assumption does not actually meet his condition, because greater productivity does not necessarily mean that all are provided for, it can be the basis for a claim for a social minimum that stays close to this theoretical framework. Every individual has some right to the resources of the world, so if the system of property, laws and their own abilities do not allow them to appropriate it on their own it should be provided for them.[105] And indeed Locke himself insisted on a right to basic sustenance for all from the surpluses of others more fortunate.[106]

---

105   One finds this argument in Waldron 1988. It is also Philippe Van Parijs' argument for a guaranteed individual income. Whether this minimum takes the form of a guaranteed income or extensive public goods is a further issue. Supporters of the former ('left libertarians') argue that it gives more freedom of choice. Support for the latter comes from Elizabeth Anderson's argument that 'freedom of exit is no substitute for the loss of voice ...; Some forms of freedom can be secured only through institutions of voice established over goods to which public access is guaranteed .... There is a value ... in collectively taking a stand on what goods the community regards as so important that it would be a disgrace to let any of its members fall short of them'. 'Ethical Limitations of the Market', in Wilber (ed.) 1998, pp. 236 and 239.

106   Locke, *First Treatise*, sect. 42, though if one reads his policy prescriptions for dealing with the poor, one can see how incredibly meager these are. Virginia Held shows that this means Robert Nozick cannot claim to be following Locke. 'John Locke on Robert Nozick', *Social Research*, spring 1976.

Another way to justify a reformed capitalism would be to challenge Nozick's argument for the minimal state, a 'night watchman' state that provides only military and police protection. Everything else he maintained must be provided by the market and if not, then too bad. Most critiques of Nozick focus on the minimal nature of his conception of the role of government arguing for a more positive and extensive role for government, and that is certainly how capitalist societies have developed. However, it is interesting to look at the minimal state from the other side: why even this much government? In the minimal state government has the monopoly on the means of violence (and is actually a very extensive state in terms of the share of the tax budget devoted to military and policing functions in the United States). Some anarchists would find even this role for government to be too much; picture the radical right wing individualist anarchist with guns prepared to take on any threat. Nozick addresses this perspective but argues that a state would likely, or at least could, have come about from an anarchic state of nature without anyone intending it or trying to bring it about. In his story, an invisible-hand story, self-interested individuals would 'back into a state' through their need for protection against transgressors. They form protective associations, one gradually becomes dominant and becomes a de facto state.

A more plausible story would acknowledge that people have needs for protection against manifold insecurities of life, not only intentional threats to our well-being from aggressors. The classical liberal picture of Locke and Nozick of naturally independent individuals who come together by agreement is a deeply implausible one. As feminists have stressed, building on communitarian and Marxist analyses, human beings are interdependent creatures, by nature and in all societies. Nor are they only self-interested. We start out totally dependent on others, particularly our mothers, for a significant period and can become so again at any point throughout our lives. As Carole Pateman remarked, if people actually lived as the social contractarians describe, they would be the last generation.[107] Even at the height of our health and strength, we need the cooperation of others to satisfy our needs. Contrary to the Robinson Crusoe fables popular in the early days of capitalism, human beings, like those primates closest to us, have always lived in some sort of society, in families and larger communal groups, with a division of labour.[108] If a state were to have evolved out of associations, these associations would likely have had aims much broader than protecting against and punishing aggression against

---

[107] Pateman 1988, p. 49.
[108] The Robinson Crusoe story actually illustrates the reverse of the usual moral drawn from it. Crusoe is shipwrecked from a slave trading ship, sets up bookkeeping accounts, and

people and property. Hence the functions of the state would also be broader. Would every individual need and want this kind of protection? Perhaps not; no more than our gun-toting individualist who rejects the need for the military and police protection that is part of Nozick's minimal state. But this is just a story ... like Nozick's. Is it a story that is compatible with capitalist theory? Yes, though it involves a modification of the individualist model that is dominant in liberalism. One can see something more like this picture in John Rawls' conception of society as a cooperative venture for mutual advantage. At a philosophical level then, there is no inconsistency in supporting a form of capitalism that provides at least minimal welfare for its citizens—and indeed, despite the popularity of the free market model in recent decades in the United States, most defenders of capitalism defend a model of capitalism with some welfare provisions, from middle of the road liberals in the United States to supporters of more extensive social welfare as found in most European countries. Without directly challenging capitalism a number of theorists, such as Amartya Sen, Peter Singer and Thomas Pogge have argued eloquently for extending our moral duties beyond national borders to the people of the world.[109] As Onora O'Neill eloquently puts it, poor women throughout the world 'not only raise children in poverty, they raise crops and do ill-paid and insecure work whose rewards fluctuate to the beat of distant economic forces'. An *international* economic system, but only *national* systems of taxation and social supports, is a further subordination.[110]

3.11   *In History*

But these changes in capitalism will not come about, if they ever do, simply by logical argument, however persuasive. In actual history, the broadening of government functions in capitalist societies to include such things as public education, unemployment insurance, national health care (in some countries) were the result of many causes. Chief among these were the manifest failures of capitalism, particularly after the Great Depression, and the movements of working people, often influenced by communists and socialists, who were demanding these changes—or much more radical change. The Russian Revolution was even more frightening to leaders of the capitalist world than fascism,

---

establishes a master-servant relationship with the only other human he encounters. Thus he replicates the society from which he comes, rather than some 'state of nature'. According to researchers, primates closest to us even have a morality. See DeWaal 1996.

109   Probably the most relevant of Sen's many works is Sen 1999; among Singer's works, see especially Singer 2009; Pogge 2002.

110   O'Neill 1993.

despite the fact that the Soviet Union was allied in World War II with the United States and Great Britain against Germany, Italy and Japan'. If you provide not for the poor, they will provide for themselves' was the anxious thought expressed in support of what was known as 'poor relief' from the earliest days of capitalism.[111] One can see both the moral and the pragmatic strains of thought in the famous speech by Franklin Delano Roosevelt known as the 'four freedoms' speech, in which he enunciated the idea of an economic Bill of Rights.

The gains won from capitalism for working people throughout the world in this period were everywhere the result of their hard struggle. Moral arguments played a supportive role at most. The stronger and more radical the movements, the more gains they made. After World War II, powerful left wing mass movements in Europe threatened radical changes and forced the governments to provide some social supports. Though never as large or as radical as in Europe, it is clear that in the United States too, it was movements of the poor and working class, often led by socialists of all stripes, which succeeded in winning whatever social supports Americans have. Mass unemployment, and its consequent suffering was not enough, as there had been depressions in the nineteenth century which led to protests, but these were met only with repression. By the 1930s the increased size of the industrial working class and their willingness to take militant illegal actions like sit-down strikes, forceful resistance to evictions, and riots—leading in some cities to what observers called virtual class war—combined with international developments that made their protests more successful.[112]

The welfare measures at the heart of the New Deal, like Social Security and unemployment insurance, expand the freedom of the recipients. Legislation like the Fair Labour Standards Act proposed by Roosevelt in 1937 which set a minimum wage, limits on overtime, and prohibited child labour, and later, anti-discrimination laws, can be justified on the same grounds. While on the one hand, they are restrictions on freedom (the freedom of exchange), as opponents of the legislation argued vigorously, on the other hand such laws expand greatly the freedom of the many people who benefit from them. Labour unions, which were in every country so crucial to winning these gains, expand the collective freedom of those involved in that they allow them to struggle for and to achieve gains they could never win on their own, as well as adding to the freedom of all those who benefit whether they contributed or not. If freedom is a primary value one should want to maximize it, even though this entails some

---

111　Christopher Hill, Editor's Introduction, in Winstanley 1976, p. 22.
112　Piven and Cloward 1979; Bernstein 1970; 1971; Preis 1964.

limits on freedom of exchange (just as prohibiting slavery put limits on the freedom to buy and sell human beings).[113] In 1948 the United Nations adopted the Universal Declaration of Human Rights, article 25 of which states 'Everyone has the right to a standard of living adequate for the health and well-being of himself and of his family, including food, clothing, housing and medical care and necessary social services, and the right to security in the event of unemployment, sickness, disability, widowhood, old age ...'. The United States, however, has never ratified this declaration because it has never committed itself to the idea that people's basic material necessities are a *right* rather than a privilege or a hard-fought political gain.

Economists less trusting of the free market, most notably John Maynard Keynes, believe that it is necessary for government for intervene in the economy to 'save capitalism from itself'. The market is volatile, prey to bubbles and busts, and cannot be counted on to regulate itself. Alan Greenspan, who as Chairman of the Federal Reserve had led the deregulation of the US economy, admitted as much when he said that 'the whole intellectual edifice' had collapsed in the financial crisis of 2008. Just as Keynes argued in his day, suddenly, virtually all mainstream economists today are arguing for the necessity of government spending to stimulate the economy, whether it takes the form of investment in technology, roads or education or outright gifts to business.[114] In fact, despite fierce opposition to social welfare by many sectors of the capitalist class in Roosevelt's day and our own, hardly any capitalists want the government to stay out of the economy completely. They want the government to pay for infrastructure, for environmental damages due to private enterprise, and for subsidies (known as 'corporate welfare' to critics), including government bailouts of failed businesses, as we have seen so spectacularly since the fall of

---

113 By maximising freedom I mean creating conditions in which more people are subject to fewer kinds of constraints. Nozick rejects the argument for maximizing freedom because he is committed to what he calls 'moral side constraints', holding that it is always wrong to restrict individual liberty even if it would expand liberty. But this seems irrational. Moreover, he does not stick to this position in every case. Acknowledging the loss of freedoms that common people enjoyed before the transformation of commons land into private property, (e.g. the freedom to hunt and to gather), he dismisses this on the grounds that a system of private property provides so much material benefit for people. But this is a consequentialist argument justifying the restriction of individual liberties in favour of greater welfare which is inconsistent with his notion of moral side constraints. Cheyney Ryan makes this point in Ryan 1977, p. 139.

114 Most of these economists were free marketers until fall 2008. For example Lawrence Summers, Pres. Obama's economics advisor played a central role in deregulating financial institutions, allowing deposit banks to move into speculative investments previously barred by the Glass Steagall Act.

2008. The latter was the bulk of the 'stimulus packages' of both Presidents Bush and Obama. Such corporate welfare ordinarily amounts to $100 billion or so, but the recent bank bailouts amount to $2.5 trillion.[115] While philosophers like Nozick can be pure free marketeers, the opposition to government intervention of most actual capitalists is very selective; they want government action that serves their interests and they have the power to ensure this. So truly laissez faire capitalism is a utopian ideology; it has never existed and never will.

3.12 How Ideal? The Inevitability and Importance of Extreme Inequalities

But just how far from laissez faire in the direction of greater equality could capitalism go? (I am asking a purely theoretical question now, not about what kinds of changes are actually possible to achieve in capitalism today.) And is this, not just better than what we have, but rather the best humankind can do? As capitalism is a global system, the problems cannot be solved merely by changes within nations, so one would have to imagine a global social welfare system, international labour laws and so on. But for simplicity of exposition I will focus on individual societies. Reforms like the basic welfare provisions discussed above lift the floor, so to speak, so that the choices people face are not so dire. If people know they will not starve, this gives them more freedom to act. But lifting the floor does not thereby lower the ceiling; the society could still be as unequal, or more so, than one with no floor. While there have been huge controversies historically, and again today, over a very minimal, and declining, minimum wage, the idea of a *maximum* salary or a cap on income or wealth has never even been on the table in the U.S.[116]—although the wealth of today's wealthiest individuals exceeds that of many nations.[117] (Not to mention the wealth of corporations which have the status of persons under U.S. law.) Inequality is greater now than at any point in history, both globally and within the United States.

Furthermore, the kinds of inequalities inherent in capitalism should be morally problematic for capitalist theory's emphasis on the individual and its supposed commitment to equality for all. To appreciate why—even if the floor has

---

115 Folbre 2009 points out the moral double standard applied to bankers and welfare mothers. 'The top executives of banks bailed out this year—about 600 guys—received an estimated $1.6 billion in bonuses in 2007. That's a little over a third of what 1.6 million families got in cash from TANF (Temporary Assistance to Needy Families) that year'.

116 An exception, ironically, is found in colonial laws limiting wages and forbidding organization.

117 Actually, there were laws limiting income in the colonial period—but they applied to *people earning a wage*! See Piven and Cloward 1979, p. 102.

been lifted—the inequalities inherent in capitalism should be morally problematic for capitalist theory's emphasis on the individual and its supposed commitment to equality of all, it is important to recognize, first of all, that only a small part of the inequality can be explained as the result of choices individuals have made. Hence it can't be said to be 'their own fault'. Individuals do not choose the single most important determinant of where they end up materially, viz. where their parents are located in the social economic hierarchy of the globe or of their own society.[118] Nor do they choose the personal qualities (still less the luck) that make it possible for some individuals to be the exceptions to this rule.[119]

Moreover, it is important to recognize that material inequalities are also inequalities of power and freedom and general well being. The connection between general well being and material goods seems so obvious it is not necessary to elaborate except to point out first of all, that it can literally be a matter of life and death, and secondly, that material inequalities are correlated with other problems usually perceived as unrelated such as domestic violence. Feminists have stressed that this problem is not confined to particular groups but is found everywhere. But while true, this is misleading because research shows that domestic violence is seven times as likely to occur in low income than in high income households.[120] This should not be surprising when we consider the stress that financial problems bring to families. As for freedom, the more money individuals have, the more freedom they have to act in every area of their lives. And the more money individuals have, the more power they have to influence what happens in society. Though everyone is equal before the law, clearly an individual accused of a crime who depends on a public defender with a huge volume of cases does not have an equal chance in court to that of someone who has the money to buy the services of an entire law firm. Though political offices and legislation are forbidden by law to be bought and sold in a political democracy, the fact that it takes millions, even hundreds of millions of dollars to run for political office brings our system very close to this. This is all connected to the fact discussed earlier that real social power in capitalism resides in the economy not in the gov-

---

118   Ibid.
119   These two points are a foundation for Rawls' theory of justice according to which socio-economic inequalities need to be justified. What socio-economic system he thinks would best meet his principles of justice is not so clear.
120   Amy Farmer, Jill Tiefenthaler and Amandine Sambira, 'The Availability and Distribution of Services for Victims of Domestic Violence in the US', at waltoncollege.uark.edu/lab/AFarmer/services%20RR%202004.doc.

ernment. What is produced, how it is produced, where it is produced are decisions made by the owners of private property, (subject only to minimal government restrictions regarding health and safety). The power of the vast majority of individuals who do not own the means of production to influence the crucial decisions in society is therefore very limited. The bailout (some use the word 'rescue' and others 'theft') of the banks by the governments of the major capitalist powers in the fall of 2008 at the cost of trillions of dollars after decades of starving the public sector because there 'wasn't enough money' should make this clear to anyone. To what extent could these inequalities of wealth and power be reduced in capitalism? To some extent, certainly; not all capitalist societies are as unequal as the United States. But even if the degree of inequality varies, capitalism remains an inherently unequal system, materially, politically and with respect to the freedom different groups enjoy. This explains the opposition of Walden Bello and many others in the global justice movement to what might be called global social democracy, even though it would obviously be better than the current form of global capitalism.[121] Only in an egalitarian society would political freedom and democracy be maximized in that everyone would have the right to participate in collective decision making on an equal basis on economic as well as political issues.

That capitalism is inherently unequal has implications for internal obstacles to freedom as well. If human nature is not fixed, but rather evolves and takes different forms in different social structures, and different places within those structures, if society actually 'constructs the choosing subject' in Nancy Hirschmann's words, then a hierarchical society will produce people that reflect this hierarchy.[122] The groups with power control not only the means of production but the psychic means of reproduction, from educational institutions to the media. But most fundamentally, the hierarchical structure, the social relations of power, appear natural, and therefore inevitable and right (except in times of crisis and transition). Those born wealthy who receive every possible advantage tend to have the strongest sense of entitlement; 'he was born on third and thought he hit a triple' is often very apt. That women do the bulk of caring labour on top of all other labour they do, that poor and working class people work hard for little reward while others have wealth and power that kings would envy, is seen as 'just the way things are'. In capitalist society today, with an ideology of individual meritocracy, no legal barriers to

---

121   Bello 2000, and other writings.
122   Holmstrom 1984; 1994.

individual advancement based on race or sex, and the high achievements of certain individuals from oppressed backgrounds, the explanation and justification of inequality has changed from those given in the past. It is less often claimed today that the poor are immoral and lazy and more often claimed that they are unintelligent or come from dysfunctional cultures. Poverty is perceived by many as a 'natural' limitation like illness and disability, and yet at the same time the majority have the illusion that everyone can make it if they only try hard enough.[123] Thus poor and working class people, and women and racial minorities tend to internalize their oppression, which greatly increases their suffering and limits their freedom as they will be unable even to imagine a better life for themselves, or think they are entitled to one and blame themselves if they do not succeed.[124] Dorothy Allison, author of *Bastard Out of Carolina* and *Trash*, says that more important to her deepest psychic life than being a victim of incest and childhood violence or being a lesbian was being born poor in a society that despises the poor.[125]

This internalized oppression that afflicts most poor and working class people profoundly affects the form of human nature that is realized in capitalist societies. Capitalism provides opportunities for individual self development possible in few if any earlier societies. The United States, without as long a history of entrenched class privileges as most societies, and with its multiculturalism, is particularly open in this respect. But at the same time capitalism limits the possibilities for the development of most individuals' capacities. A moving illustration is provided in the film and musical *Billy Elliot* about a gifted young boy in a mining town in Northern England during the coal miners' strike of 1982 called to resist Margaret Thatcher's determination to crush the union and the national coal industry in favour of cheaper imports. Billy's gift for dance, combined with luck and the support of family and community enable him to develop the talent that gives him such joy. But Thatcher succeeded in destroying the union and mining communities throughout the country. While Billy had an exceptional gift for dance, he was not unique in having talent; almost everyone has talents and capacities that have little opportunity for development.

---

123   Pettit 2001 refers to 'the natural limitations imposed by disability, illness, poverty and the like' (p. 130). In fact, poverty is purely a social limitation and social conditions often cause or exacerbate illness and disability. (Some theorists have a social analysis of disability as well.)
124   Sennett 1972.
125   Allison 1988, reprinted in Holmstrom 2002. If she were black instead of white her race would likely be as or more salient, as she describes how determinedly poor whites of the South held on to their racism; at least they could feel they were better than some other people.

The Suzuki method of teaching violin is based on this belief and succeeds in having almost every child taught by their method playing Vivaldi by the time they leave elementary school. Only a society that was fairly egalitarian would eliminate these internal barriers to freedom and self-expression, as all groups in society would be involved on an equal basis in the institutions that shape them. Only in such a society which allowed for both personal and political autonomy would freedom as self-realisation be possible.

Thus if the material supports provided by government in many developed capitalist countries could be expanded further, this would increase the freedom and well being of those who benefit, and opponents of capitalism certainly support such reforms. But just how extensive could one envisage such changes within capitalism (leaving aside the question of whether they could be achieved)? Just *how* free, *how* ideal, could a capitalist society be? If everyone were guaranteed food, shelter, medical care and all other necessities, this would free people from the need to take dangerous low paid jobs. But in fact, if such guarantees were generous enough, they would free people from the need to work at all. That seems to me to be problematic for capitalism even in theory. While the current unemployment rates are particularly high, capitalist societies always have unemployment; in fact, economists talk about an 'ideal' rate of unemployment as 4.8%.[126] Though millions of people who want to work would be unable to find a job, this counts as full employment for them, and if it drops below this, financial and government elites take steps to restore it. The reason is that unemployment is important to capitalists because the threat of being unemployed provides a downward pressure on wages and allows for expanding the workforce when and where needed. (This may be why the government has not addressed our current crisis by providing jobs, which would seem logical in that it would not only directly help those needing work but also the economy because the employed would have money to spend.) If the guarantees provided by our ideal capitalism were generous enough so that many people would choose not to work, capitalists would not have the workers they need, or else they would have to greatly increase worker compensation which would put them at a competitive disadvantage to capitalists in less generous countries. On the other hand, if as is more likely, the supports were kept minimal enough so that almost everyone who could work would choose to, then the fundamental lack of freedom for the majority in capitalism is still there.

---

126   In spring 2009 the official unemployment rate is 8.9%, and if 'discouraged workers' and the under-employed are included, it almost doubles. In some communities, it is as much as 50%.

3.13 The Most Basic Inequality

> When I give food to the poor, they call me a saint. When I ask why the poor have no food, they call me a communist.
>
> DOM HELDER CAMARA, Brazilian Liberation theologian

⁂

Charity is good, and a capitalist society with welfare minimums would be even better. But it would still not provide genuine equality of power, opportunity, and freedom for all. The problem is the basic structure of wealth and power in capitalism, which is one of the most fundamental sources of the lack of freedom for the majority. This is what is missed by liberals who want a capitalist system with genuine equality of opportunity and freedom for all. Liberal theorists worry about the power of the state to limit freedom more than about private power because, they say, the state has the monopoly on the means of coercion, and because, unlike private powers, the state provides no exit.[127] But these differences are more apparent than real. Labour in capitalism is free in two senses, as Marx explained. Unlike slavery and serfdom, workers in capitalism are legally free to work for anyone, or for no one. This gives them the 'exit' from *any particular* private power. But they are also *free of* the means of production. This makes them economically dependent, with no choice but to sell their labour power to someone else—not to any particular person, but to some owner of means of production. By selling their labour to someone, they thereby put themselves under that person's control, (or more likely, the control of a giant corporation), acting not on their own will but that of the owner who has distinct, maybe antagonistic, ends. Selling their labour is like selling *themselves* in that respect. They are free to do so or not, but the structure of ownership and control of the means of subsistence makes them *not* free *not* to. There is no exit. Hence at its foundation, capitalism is a system of 'forced labour—no matter how much it may appear to result from free contractual agreement'. The owners determine what is produced, how much, and in how many hours of work. And with today's technology, which allows employers to monitor everything their employers do and say, they have more complete control over the labour

---

127 For example, Pettit 2001, p. 155. As discussed earlier, 'libertarians' do not even allow that private economic power limits freedom at all.

process than slave owners had over the labour of their slaves.

This is true in any system where the producers do not possess the means of production and appropriation. Consider other examples. Slavery is a system of private ownership of the means of production where people are among the means of production. By definition, slavery involves forced labour. Individuals with sufficient economic means had the power and the legal right to apply direct physical force to other individuals to make them work for them. Here the coercion is individual, direct and intentional.[128] In feudal societies the force was less ever present and direct than in slavery, but the relation between peasants and their lord was clearly one of domination. Although peasants possessed their means of subsistence within the communal setting, sometimes individually, sometimes collectively, and directly controlled their own labour process, they were required by law, backed up by brute force, either to work part of the time for their lords, or to give them some of the products of their labour. In most cases, the threat was sufficient to force the producers to do the lords' will. In the bureaucratic systems that existed in the Soviet Union, China, etc. for much of the twentieth century, the means of production nominally belonged to all the people whose power was vested in the state. But the bureaucracy, collectively, owned the state, i.e. it had exclusive monopoly control of the means of production. This compelled workers to work for the bureaucracy because they had no access to the means of production/subsistence except through the bureaucracy.

In all three of the above systems, slavery, feudalism, and the bureaucratic system, the coercion is extra-economic. Now consider a different kind of unfree labour, that of indentured servitude, which is not an economic system in itself, but an economic relationship that has existed within other systems including capitalism.[129] It lies between slavery and free labour in that the worker agrees to work for someone else under conditions set by them, usually very arduous and brutal conditions, for some specified period of time, typically seven years. Given that the choice was starvation or close to it (why else would anyone agree to such a contract?), the worker has no choice but to agree.[130] It is an example of what we have earlier called a 'forcing offer'. No direct force is necessary;

---

128   As will be discussed later, slavery can exist even without legal ownership but control through violence.
129   Some have argued that capitalism necessarily articulates with forms of un-free labour such as slave, convict, indentured and contract labour. See Miles 1987.
130   For this reason Nozick would allow that someone should have the right to sell themselves into slavery. See *Anarchy, State and Utopia* p. 133. Footnote 134 deleted. Here it is: In reality there is often not even this appearance of freedom since it is often a parent who contracts with a master for a child's labour which makes it more like short term slavery.

the force comes from the distribution of economic resources. The difference between indentured servitude and the free labour of capitalism is only a matter of the degree of un-freedom. For some people in capitalist societies, the choices are equally dire; the difference then between indentured servitude and wage labour is mostly a matter of the duration of the contract. Fortunately the choices are not nearly so dire for most people in developed capitalist societies. Nevertheless, though some people can survive by begging or stealing or opening small businesses, or after retirement from years of working in well paid jobs, the majority of those without access to the means of production and subsistence are 'compelled by social conditions' to work for others. This is why Marx refers to private property as 'the power to subjugate the labour of others'.

Feminists who have argued that marriage has not been a free choice for most women use similar notions of (un)freedom, as do feminists who argue against prostitution and (so-called) surrogate motherhood.[131] It is not necessarily particular individuals who directly force other individuals to be surrogate mothers or prostitutes, but it is the inequality of their 'bargaining positions' that allows others to take advantage of some women's position (economic and/or psychological) to secure an agreement that harms them. The social and economic context of the choice makes it not a genuinely free choice. And she cannot sell her sexual services without selling herself. But the same is true of women who do less controversial work. Women are clustered at the bottom of the economic ladder in all societies and sometimes sex work may in fact be the best of the available alternatives.[132]

The only way to eliminate the force inherent in all these economic systems is to create a system in which the producers themselves control the means of production. A possible objection to this conclusion is that on the analysis of freedom I have offered, force would be inherent in *any* economic system, including this one. Since, so the objection would go, I argued that physical conditions as well as people can be obstacles to freedom, then even in an economic system where the producers were the owners, people would not be completely free but would be forced to work to satisfy their physical needs. Plato and Aristotle used this idea to argue against democracy; anyone who was tied to physical neces-

---

131 For example, Pateman 1988; Mathieu 1990.
132 Jo Bindman of Anti-Slavery International argues against the criminalization of prostitution. '[Should we] take away their power to choose this occupation, maybe condemning them to worse conditions in another field?' 'An International perspective on Slavery in the Sex Industry' in Holmstrom 2002, pp. 209–10. Cf. Hirschmann 2003 for very sensitive discussions of the social and economic conditions in which so many women's choices are made.

sity through their need to work for a living was thereby unsuited to participate in politics.[133] As a reply to this objection, I would refer to Marx's treatment of the issue. In the realm of physical necessity, which he says would exist in every economic system,

'Freedom can only consist of socialized man, the associated producers, rationally regulating their interchange with Nature, bringing it under their common control, instead of being ruled by it as by the blind forces of Nature; and achieving this with the least expenditure of energy and under conditions most favourable to, and worthy of their human nature. But it nonetheless remains a realm of necessity. Beyond it begins that development of human energy which is an end in itself, the true realm of freedom, which, however, can blossom forth only with the realm of necessity as its basis. The shortening of the working day is its basic prerequisite.'[134]

Thus in a system where the producers control the means of production, they are not forced to work for anyone else, as there is no separate class of owners who live off their labour. The producers themselves would decide what to produce and how much of it, and how to balance leisure time and material goods. Though external conditions create the need to work, their goals, desires, values and beliefs also determine both the nature of their work and its duration. Hence a system where peoples' need to work arises simply from features of the natural world, does not involve domination by others. No one else, no other group has power *over them*, and hence they are not unfree in that crucial way. Moreover, being able to make their own decisions regarding work within the limits set by physical necessity, they would be likely to reduce the working day and expand 'the true realm of freedom'. Interestingly, this realm as Marx conceived it, would include labour; in fact, he says, 'really free labour, e.g. composing, is at the same time precisely the most damned seriousness, the most intense exertion'.[135]

3.14 *Summing Up Capitalism in Theory*

Contrary to our popular idea of property, property is not things, nor physical possession, but rights, as most writers on property recognize. Every system of ownership, every system of property involves certain rights or freedoms, and denies other rights and freedoms. Consider a system of common owner-

---

133 See E.M. Wood 1995, p. 221.
134 Tucker (ed.) 1978, p. 441. Tucker dubs this section 'The Realm of Necessity and the Realm of Freedom'. For Plato and Aristotle being constrained by material necessity, having to work for a living, is inconsistent with political freedom.
135 Marx 1973.

ship versus private ownership. A system of common ownership involves the right and freedom for all to use, enjoy and benefit from the commons. In pre-capitalist days, common people had the right to hunt, graze their animals, gather food and firewood on common land, rights that could double the income of poor families.[136] Women were and are still today around the world the principal gatherers and men the hunters. These rights/freedoms were lost with the enclosure movement, so pivotal to the development of capitalism. It is also happening at a rapid pace throughout the world due to capitalist development.[137] This *right not to be excluded* from the use of something is one kind of individual right to property. But a system of common ownership does not include the right to exclude others. Nor does it include the right to benefit from the commons by buying or selling the commons or one's portion of it. So one has a right to use or enjoy common property, but not to dispose of it. Defenders of capitalism, from Locke on, see the restrictions on rights of ownership in common property as unjustified restrictions on individual freedom. Capitalism involves a different kind of individual right to property which includes the right to buy and sell what one owns because it is a right of exclusive ownership. This means that it is a right and freedom to exclude others. So *this kind of individual right to property entails the lack of rights and freedom of all those who are excluded*. With the predominance of the market in the modern period, the second kind of ownership has almost entirely eliminated the first. C.B. Macpherson explains that as the amount of property held in common got smaller and smaller, our concept of property has also drastically narrowed.

From the earliest ideas of property, say from Aristotle down to the seventeenth century, property was seen to include two kinds of individual rights, both an individual right to exclude others from some use or enjoyment of some thing, and an individual right not to be excluded from the use or enjoyment of things that society has declared to be for common use—common lands, parks, roads, waters. Both were rights of individuals. Both rights were created and maintained by society or the state. Both therefore were individual property.[138] Another new kind of individual property is found in programs like social security or universal medical care; individuals have the right to draw from common resources, but not to exclude others or to sell their share. Such publicly provided goods hark back to older forms and can be considered another kind of common property, particularly important for women given their role as child-

---

136 Hill 1996. Also Linebaugh 2008.
137 For a discussion of today's receding commons, see Anton 2000. The privatisation of water all over the world is particularly important.
138 Macpherson 1985, p. 77. Peter Linebaugh 2008.

bearers and primary caregivers. Legal theorist Morris R. Cohen explains that the right to exclude, which is the essence of private property, gives it the character of political sovereignty in that it gives the property owner the power to command the service and obedience of those who are not economically independent, even if this 'may be obscured for us in a commercial economy by the fiction of the so-called labour contract as a free bargain and by the frequency with which service is rendered indirectly through a money payment'.[139] Interestingly, Cohen does not infer from this analysis that private property is therefore unjustified, as he leaves open the possibility that compulsion in the economic sphere might be necessary. However, 'we must not overlook the actual fact that dominion over things is also *imperium* over our fellow human beings'.[140]

Today, in the beginning of the twenty first century, when some individuals have more wealth than that of many countries combined, and half the world's largest economies are corporations not countries, this power over things and over others extends to the entire globe. *Indeed it is the power to determine the future of life on earth.* If the defence of capitalism as an ideal rests on an expanded 'humanized' or 'compassionate' version of capitalism which would either reduce this extraordinary power or else render it benign, then everything depends on the issue of the realizability of such a reformed version of capitalism. Otherwise the defence of capitalism amounts to an apology for a very unideal system.[141] What theory of politics and social change would make this plausible?

It is time to leave the realm of theory and examine capitalism as an actually existing system.

4 Capitalism *in Reality*

4.1 *Compared to Pre-capitalist Societies*

Let us turn directly now to the question of whether capitalism in reality is good for women. One question that immediately arises is, compared to what? And in what respects? In recent discussions of capitalism's impact on women, especially discussions in the United States and Western Europe, capitalism is contrasted to less developed, pre-capitalist, traditional societies. Unless we

---

139   According to Marx, in capitalism, relations between people are perceived as relations between things, calling this the fetishism of commodities.
140   Cohen 1978, p. 159.
141   See Mills 2004.

go way back to the earliest days of human history, these societies are almost without exception patriarchal. It would seem to follow almost automatically that from a feminist point of view, capitalism would be better. But what does patriarchal mean exactly? There is a substantial and influential body of literature that problematizes the concept of patriarchy and the assumption that it is counter-posed to modernity. The definition of the concept patriarchy is male-dominated or more precisely, father-dominated, and the latter more restricted sense is how I will be using the concept, using 'sexism' or simply 'male domination' for the broader meaning. Still, even in the restricted sense, patriarchy is not a homogeneous system of male domination, by any means, but rather has many varieties. A number of writers insist that the presumptions prevailing in many feminist discussions of patriarchy are inaccurate and stress the following points about patriarchal societies:

1) Women are not in the same position in all patriarchal societies.
2) Women are not totally passive victims, respondents to external forces, but almost always have some room for negotiation in these societies.
3) Various kinds of patriarchal bargains are possible, some of which have considerable advantages for some women, particularly as they age (e.g. the infamous mothers-in-law of some societies).
4) Patriarchal bargains also exist in modern societies, e.g. the proto-typical family of 1950s middle class capitalist America of the breadwinner father and housewife mother.[142]

In my opinion, these points have considerable validity and they help us to understand why some women choose arrangements that to us today seem oppressive. Some feminists go further and argue that women are actually better off in many pre-capitalist than in capitalist societies.[143] Despite mostly being patriarchal, they maintain, subsistence economies offer more to women overall than does the globalised capitalist economy. Moreover, they say, capitalism is also patriarchal and should be described as capitalist patriarchy.

4.2   *Capitalism as Tendentially Better for Women*

Notwithstanding the validity of many of the points made above, and the variety of pre-capitalist societies, I would maintain that *as a system*, capitalism has the potential to create the conditions for better lives for women than pre-capitalist societies—in general. However, that does not entail that *in all particular cases* women will be better off in the transition from pre-capitalist to

---

[142] Deniz Kandiyoti's 'Bargaining with Patriarchy', in Holmstrom 2002, explains how the third point leads many older women to internalize and enforce patriarchy.
[143] Bennholdt-Thomsen and Mies 1999; Federici 2004.

capitalist society, particularly in the short-run, for there are many factors other than gender relations that contribute to overall well-being. Subsistence peasants, for example, are likely to be much worse off as they lose their homes and their livelihood and have to become wage workers in a capitalist economy. This is just as true, or more so, for women, as they lose the protections as well as the restrictions afforded by traditional societies. In the Philippines, for example, the destruction of natural resources has forced peasants out of their simple rural economies to living in Manila garbage dumps—literally.[144] This process is what Marx called 'primitive accumulation', a process discussed earlier in the context of seventeenth century England.

I say that capitalism is better than pre-capitalist societies for most women, over some time anyway, for two reasons, relating both to strategic and to practical gender interests. The first reason has to do with patriarchy, (i.e., father-dominated societies), the second with industrialisation. Patriarchal bargains are still patriarchal whatever their variations and even if women have some manoeuvring room within them. In most pre-capitalist societies, the father of a family has, by virtue of his position, a power that he has gradually lost in capitalist societies, and when he shares the power, it is with other men in the kinship group. In feudal societies, the most widespread system prior to capitalism, the peasant household was a work unit, and therefore, the head of the family was also the head of the work unit—the foreman, essentially. Men also monopolized military power which gave them considerable power throughout the society. In contrast, though the 1950's style arrangement of breadwinner father, housewife mother could be called a patriarchal bargain, the power of the breadwinner father in such families did not translate into power in the society at large. The work done in the family was for their immediate needs only, and was quite distinct from the dominant kind of production in capitalism. What power the breadwinner fathers had outside the family was not due to their being fathers, but rather men, mostly white middle class men. And that meant that breadwinner fathers had less total power *in* the family as well, than did fathers in pre-capitalist societies. Thus, though the arrangement of breadwinner father and housewife mother could be called patriarchal, it does not have the same overall significance for male/female social roles since it is embedded within a capitalist system. Moreover, even in the heyday of this type of family, though it was presented as the norm, it was by no means universal. Family forms varied according to class and race. I did not grow up in one, nor did most of my friends because our mothers had to work whether or not our fathers

---

144   Broad with Cavanaugh 1993.

were in the family. And historian Temma Kaplan explains that women raising their own and others' children has, for centuries, been 'the family structure of poverty under capitalism'.¹⁴⁵ Today, families where fathers work and women stay home constitute a very small minority of American families.

The fact that no particular style of family is integral to the functioning of capitalism reflects the first reason why capitalism tends to be better for women, (although for poor women, the lack of support for a family form of *any* kind can be devastating, as will be discussed later). Though capitalists are predominantly male and usually fathers, they do not have power *as fathers* but rather, *as owners of the means of production* and hence they have no necessary relationship to women. Indeed, capitalists can be women and so can political leaders. Instead of being patriarchal, capitalism, as explained earlier, is a different kind of hierarchical system which rests on a different kind of power—ownership of the means of production—that in theory at least does not absolutely require the subordination of women. Rather, the principal 'rule' or 'law of motion' of capitalism is the maximisation of profit. That is the goal of production in capitalism; that determines what is produced, how it is produced and where it is produced. In principle it does not matter whose labour power produces the profit and who gets it.¹⁴⁶ This is often cited as a reason why capitalism is good for women, but it is decidedly a mixed blessing as we shall see.

Moreover, though capitalism is gender-neutral in principle, women's subordination is sometimes useful to capitalism as well as to men—women can be paid less, for example, and they do most of the socially necessary caring work for free. (Similar things can be said about race in that capitalism is also in principle race-neutral, yet racism has been highly advantageous to capitalism. Despite similarities, however, the relationship of sexism and racism to capitalism are not identical, so I will not complicate my discussion any further.)¹⁴⁷

---

145   Temma Kaplan, 'The Disappearing Fathers Under Global Capitalism', in Holmstrom 2002.
146   On this point *The Communist Manifesto* says, 'the more modern industry becomes developed, the more is the labour of the men superseded by the labour of the women. Differences of age and sex, have no longer any distinctive social validity for the working class. All are instruments of labour, more or less expensive to use, according to their age and sex': Tucker (ed.) 2018, p. 479.
147   Indeed, a number of scholars have suggested that racism in its most virulent modern form is *due to capitalism* because on the one hand, conquest and slavery were instrumental to the development of capitalism but on the other hand, completely at odds with the new ideals of human equality. This contradiction between theory and reality required that the enslaved be reduced essentially to nonhumans, outside the pale of morality. Ellen Meiksins Wood makes this argument explicitly in 'Capitalism and human emancipation: race, gender and democracy' in 1995. It is consistent with, perhaps implicit in, Mills 1997.

Marxist, socialist and other radical feminists have debated how these competing interests within capitalism, on the one hand, towards gender neutrality for the maximisation of profit, and on the other hand, the utility of women's subordination for profit maximisation are related, and how these two tendencies have been worked out in different historical periods and places.[148] Nevertheless, overall, over time, it is clear that there has been a gradual though incomplete reduction of rigid gender roles as capitalism has developed. In Molyneux's terms, women's *strategic* gender interests have generally advanced under capitalism. This is not universally the case, however, as fully-developed capitalist countries Chile and Ireland have laws prohibiting abortion under all conditions. Though women have these rights in the United States, it is the only developed country that has not ratified the UN Women's Rights Convention CEDAW. So although there is a tendency in capitalism towards the advancing of women's strategic gender interests, this is not guaranteed and is never automatic. Capitalists can live with their denial so long as capitalist economic interests are furthered. Moreover, it remains to be seen whether progress can continue to the point of complete gender equality within capitalism or whether some gender inequities are inevitable in the system.

4.3   With Respect to Practical Gender Interests

Whether women do better under capitalism with respect to *practical* gender interests is more complicated and very much depends on which women we are talking about and what we compare it to. To the extent that practical gender interests have also advanced under capitalism, this is due to the incredible productivity of capitalism. Its inherent need to develop technology reduces labour time, provides more consumer goods and advances scientific discovery. In particular, the enormous advances in health in the twentieth century that dramatically decreased deaths throughout the world is enormously liberating for everyone, but especially for women given their role in childbirth and their responsibilities for childcare in addition to whatever other work they do. However, these are advantages for women of *development*, especially industrialisation, not specifically of capitalism, and hence is not a conclusive argument in favour of capitalism. So in pursuing the question whether capitalism is good for women, let us shift the point of comparison from pre-capitalist societies to other non-capitalist societies.

---

148   There is a large literature on this topic. See among other sources, Secombe 1973; Gardiner 1975; and Coulson, Magas and Wainwright 1975; Gough and Harrison 1975; Holmstrom 1981.

4.4 Compared to So-called Socialist Societies

Leaving aside societal forms that have not yet been realized, there have been developed societies that were not capitalist, viz. the so-called socialist societies, the Soviet Union, Eastern Europe, China, etc.[149] How does capitalism compare to them with respect to the interests of women? Immediately following the Russian Revolution in 1917, there were truly astonishing gains for women, both legally and materially. The government instituted freedom of marriage, divorce, and abortion, eliminated laws against homosexuality and the status of illegitimacy which advanced strategic gender interests beyond anything existing anywhere else in the world at that time. To appreciate just how astonishing these advances were, consider the fact that almost one hundred years later, this is still not the norm in all developed countries, much less in developing countries as Russia was at that time. Communal cafeterias, laundries, childcare all addressed women's practical gender interests in impoverished, war-torn conditions. At the end of World War I the women's movement even forced the Bolsheviks to split factory jobs between the women who had been working there and the soldiers coming back from the war. However, the Russian Revolution degenerated very quickly; indeed it underwent a fundamental transformation in the 1920s to a bureaucratic totalitarian system under Stalin. No independent political movements were allowed including of course no independent women's movement. Similar systems were constructed after World War II throughout Eastern Europe under the domination of the Soviet Union and in China after the Chinese Revolution led by Mao Tse-tung. Policies regarding women varied in all these countries according to particular state interests, but in general, the fact is that both strategic and practical gender interests were satisfied to a fair extent. Of course women were not liberated as was claimed, but neither were men as these were totalitarian societies, and the sexism of prior societies remained embedded to a great extent. Nevertheless, relative to what came before and in relation to men in these societies, women fared quite well. In some countries, like China, where women were practically slaves before the revolution, the improvements in women's lives were especially dramatic. The reason is that *like capitalists*, the ruling bureaucracies of these societies had no vested interest in women's subordination. Indeed, on the contrary, *unlike capitalists*, they had a clear vested interest in eliminating it. They needed to maximize the productivity of the whole society since they 'owned' the whole

---

149 In my opinion these societies are most accurately named 'bureaucratic collectivist', as their economies are organised collectively and property was collective, nominally owned by the whole society, but controlled totally by a bureaucracy, therefore very different from socialism as envisioned by Marx and Engels and other classical socialists.

society, not just a particular firm, so they needed to maximize everyone's input into production. Hence they instituted freedom of marriage and divorce, abortion, equal education, childcare, health care and other social supports enabling women to participate in production and society at large on an equal basis with men.[150] However, since the satisfaction of women's interests depended on their coincidence with state interests, this was unreliable. Romania, for example, had strong anti-abortion laws because the bureaucracy wanted to increase the birth rate.[151]

Today most of these societies are in various stages of transition to capitalism; the collective property has been privatized, which means that the property has been essentially stolen from the members of society, and social supports have been dismantled. Again, we see a process of primitive accumulation.[152] How have women been affected by this process? A report by the United Nations Children's Fund concluded that the position of women has 'spiraled downward … with increasing joblessness, abuse and deteriorating social services'. Most significantly in terms of overall well being, life expectancy has even declined in one third of the countries studied.[153] As for strategic gender interests, there is considerable variability, but overall the trend is backward. In terms of political influence, the number of women in government has declined by about one third. Throughout the former Soviet bloc, countless young women have migrated to work as sex workers; sometimes they are trafficked, sometimes they act in the hope it will get them a better life. In Poland, with its strong Catholic Church, women's right to abortion is threatened. In Russia and China, with no history of legally protected individual rights, and no women's movement, the switch to the market has brought sex, age and 'beauty' discrimination in employment, as employers can hire whomever they want and contract with them for whatever services they want. Market freedom for employers, but constraints for employees. As these societies are in transition, it is difficult to predict how things will evolve. It is possible that fledgling grassroots movements will succeed in regaining the strategic gender interests they enjoyed earlier,

---

150 Kruks, Rapp and Young (eds.) 1989, is a useful collection of case studies, although I disagree with their characterisation of these societies as socialist.
151 The same subordination of women's interests is common in capitalism. While the US cites the emancipation of women as a goal of its policies in Afghanistan, a little history shows that the United States was actually responsible for bringing the Taliban to power because they supported the mujahadeen, including Osama Bin Laden, against the Soviet-supported government of Afghanistan, one of whose crimes in their eyes was instituting reforms for women.
152 Holmstrom and Smith 2000, pp. 1–15.
153 '"Free Markets Leave Women Worse Off", Unicef Says', *NY Times*, 23 September 1999.

but this will be a very hard struggle in the prevailing political and economic conditions. For now it seems clear that while some women are enjoying more freedom and material goods than they ever dreamed of, primarily due to the privatization of collective property, the majority of women are worse off due to the very same cause. This deterioration in the position of most women with the transition to capitalism should not be surprising if we look more closely at what women have and have not achieved in capitalist countries around the globe.

4.5 Gains and Losses: Sweatshops and Worse

As already discussed *women's strategic gender interests* have tended to be advanced as capitalism developed although this is not always true in all respects. How women fare with respect to their *practical gender interests* is more complicated and depends on which women we focus on. In many countries around the world, both former Soviet-style economies like China or newly industrialising countries, capitalist development has taken the form of sweatshops.[154] Unlike the early days of capitalism in Europe, it is a striking fact that the majority of workers in these factories are women. Publicity about the miserable conditions in which so much of our clothing is made helped to spark an anti-sweatshop movement on US campuses and around the world, (recall the exposure of Kathy Lee Gifford and the anti-Nike campaign) and helped to ignite the global justice movement.[155]

Nevertheless, many commentators, including some feminists, have argued that the anti-sweatshop movement is misguided. Nicholas Kristof of the *NY Times*, entitled a column 'In Praise of the Maligned Sweatshop'.[156] Basically, four arguments are given in defence of sweatshops, and against struggles like

---

154 The exact definition of 'sweatshops' is not established. The US Department of Labour defines them as workplaces that violate two or more US labour laws. The International Labour Organization (ILO) has a list of eight core labour standards which ought to be met for any worker in any country no matter what the level of development. These have to do with minimum wage, maximum hours, safety conditions, right to unionize, etc. Sometimes the laws in developing countries are quite good (for example, Bangladesh has paid maternity leave), but they are not enforced. Many countries have established special Export Processing Zones expressly to avoid their own domestic labour laws, including freedom of association and right to collective bargaining, and attract foreign companies.
155 USAS.
156 6 June 2006, 'Where Sweatshops Are a Dream', 15 January 2009, among others. Mainstream economists organized the Academic Consort on International Trade (ACIT) to defend sweatshops against the critics.

those waged by the United Students Against Sweatshops (USAS) for decent labour standards, purporting to show that despite poor conditions they are actually good for their employees.

The first argument is that conditions are not as bad as critics charge, especially compared to prevailing standards and cost of living in the countries where they exist. This defence is simply not credible. Numerous independent studies have documented *worsening* conditions since the 1980s due to intense competition, particularly in the apparel industry, that has resulted in what's been called a 'race to the bottom'.[157] The International Labour Organization, ILO, has described conditions as in many cases resembling indentured servitude. We have all heard of the Triangle Shirtwaist fire in NYC a century ago; how many know that 2500 women were burned in fires in China in 1992 alone?[158] The recent economic downturn can only worsen the problems as competition to hold onto a shrinking market grows more fierce.

The second defence of sweatshops is that being exploited, even super-exploited, is better than *not* being exploited because there is no work. People in these developing countries were worse off before the sweatshops came, it is claimed, and if critics fight too hard to improve conditions, the companies will close up shop and go to other countries where they will have a freer hand, leaving their workers behind with no jobs. Kristof says, 'For those living on a garbage mountain, labour standards can hurt'. But what he does not address is how they came to be living on a garbage mountain. This brings us back to the question of whether conditions were in general worse in pre-capitalist societies. As I said earlier, it all depends ... The lives of subsistence peasants in places with adequate natural resources may be limited, but materially adequate and stable. There are no garbage mountains. The introduction of capitalism deprived those peasant farmers of means of subsistence as their farms typically were seized and consolidated into export plantations, forcing millions who can no longer survive in the countryside into cities and onto garbage mountains or migration abroad. The numbers coming into the cities makes for high rates of unemployment, poverty and desperation. *Once this process has occurred*, people are faced

---

157   Some, e.g. ACIT above, attempt to argue that there is no race to the bottom on the grounds that multinational corporations pay higher wages than those that prevail in developing countries. That could be true, but it is a different issue. Corporations have left countries with higher wages to go to countries with lower wages: from the US to Mexico, from Mexico to the Philippines, from the Philippines to China and from there to Vietnam. Neither is it a powerful moral argument since the prevailing local conditions may be truly atrocious.

158   Israel Rosen 2002, pp. 241–4. Also see extensive reports of the National Labour Committee from around the world: www.nlc.org. Terrible working conditions made worse by development are not of course confined to factories, but include mines in China.

with the proverbial rock and a hard place. A job in a sweatshop will in fact be better than its alternative, which could be starvation. Sometimes workers have no choice but to agree to whatever conditions employers try to impose, but not even to try to get better conditions through labour standards is to accept the logic of the race to the bottom.

Even if the best strategic choice sometimes appears to be to accept superexploitative conditions because it is better than the alternatives, this is hardly an argument in favour of capitalism. Rather *it is a testament to the incredible power of capitalists to impose their will.* If workers decide they have to accept sweatshop conditions, it is because it is the best of a bad lot of choices imposed by the structure of capitalism, just as a patriarchal bargain that women choose because there is no better alternative is still a patriarchal bargain, worse than a non-patriarchal one. Rather than long term investments necessary to increase prosperity, capitalism's relentless pursuit of maximum profit directs investment into sweatshops. If it is really true that the only path to growth for developing countries in the global capitalist economy is indeed factories that pay sub-poverty wages in poor working conditions, this should be seen as a condemnation, rather than a defence of global capitalism.

There are indeed very difficult practical, strategic questions regarding reform struggles within developed capitalism as well. How should American workers respond to threats either to give up some of their hard-won benefits or face losing their jobs to people across the globe who prefer sweatshops to starvation? There are no easy answers, given the power of the multinational corporations they are up against. Corporations can take advantage of the crisis to force concessions from workers even when they are not economically necessary. (For this kind of behaviour, some commentators have likened multinational corporations to the Mafia.) The auto industry is a case in point. As an economist for the Canadian Auto Workers Union explained, though the industry is in trouble throughout the world it is only in the US and Canada—where 'direct labour accounts for less than 7 percent of total auto costs',—where wage cuts are being demanded. '... ultimately it's about politics not economics'.[159] Chrysler's recent declaration of bankruptcy broke union contracts and forced autoworkers to accept lower wages and benefits. Another example is the garment industry, one of the most globalized industries, where the rich countries allow corporations like Wal-Mart to dominate the market, who then use their market power to insist on ever-cheaper prices from their producers who in turn squeeze their

---

159 Stanford 2009. Naomi Klein's *The Shock Doctrine: The Rise of Disaster Capitalism* (Klein 2007) argues that this is a dominant pattern in recent global capitalism.

workers even tighter. The rich countries also subject poor producing countries to rules, such as no subsidies to business, which do not apply to firms in their own countries and certainly did not apply in the past when their industries were first developing. Then there is the role of international lending agencies which operate like predatory loan sharks imposing harsh rules and such high interest rates that the borrowing countries become indebted for life. The game is, essentially, fixed in favour of the biggest corporations and the richest countries of the world.[160] Fighting for regional and international labour standards, such as the 'Asia Floor Wage', is one small step towards changing that balance of power and hence is in the interests of workers in both developed and developing countries. It will be a hard fight but one that should be supported by all feminists.

The third argument in defence of sweatshops focuses specifically on women, who make up an astonishing 80% of the low wage workers in developing countries.[161] Some feminists support or are ambivalent about sweatshops because they believe they liberate women from patriarchal family structures and lead to personal empowerment.[162] This argument is also offered in connection to the huge increase of women's international migration which I will discuss later. It has been well established that women's freedom to work outside the home increases their freedom and well-being, but what this proves about work in sweatshops is not entirely clear. Again, it all depends on the place and the time and the aspect of the women's lives at which we look. Women sweatshop workers should not be seen as passive victims and sometimes it is true that their work is an escape from rural poverty, gives them greater bargaining power in their families and improves their lives in various ways. But where patriarchal family structures are replaced by totalitarian working conditions backed up by totalitarian and corrupt governments, it is not clear how much the women are empowered overall by this transition. When their factories are in special export zones set up to evade labour laws and attract foreign companies, it is even less likely that women will be empowered by their work experience since one of the features of these zones is that there is no freedom of association or right

---

160 Bhattacharjee, Gupta and Luce 2009. For more detail see the documents launching the campaign for an Asia Floor Wage, forthcoming October 2009. See also the film *Life & Debt*. For more information on how poverty is reproduced in the name of development, see Bracking 2009.
161 Rosen 2002, p. 245.
162 For example, see Fernandez-Kelly and Wolf 2001. Naila Kabeer provides a detailed account of how specific social and economic conditions influence the lives of women garment workers in Dhaka Bangladesh and London: Kabeer 2002.

to organize. Moreover, paid employment only increases women's autonomy if the jobs pay living wages, and seldom do women factory workers in newly industrialising countries earn enough to support a family.[163] Their jobs seldom provide a way out of poverty; indeed conditions are sometimes so bad that their lives are cut short or they have to go back to their villages sick or almost blind, as happens to workers in electronics factories.[164] While immigrant sweatshop workers in developed countries may have reasonable hope for their children, this is not the case in poor countries. Even in the best case scenarios, which defenders like to focus on, I would simply say that capitalism is not the only means to the end of women's empowerment and often it comes at tremendous cost.

The fourth defence of sweatshops, often implicit in the previous two, concedes that things are really bad for many workers today, but argues that working women were also terribly exploited in the early days of capitalism in Manchester England or Lowell MA and look how much better off we are today. Poor conditions are inevitable in the early stages of capitalist development, it is said, but they improve greatly over time. This argument rests on the assumption that the only direction in which capitalist development works is up, that given time, capitalist countries will all look like Sweden. While logically possible, and highly desirable, this scenario is also highly unlikely. What has been called 'the Lowell model' is quite disanalogous to sweatshops today first of all because the conditions then, though bad, were actually not as bad as they are today.[165] But more importantly, the economic context was different. The wages of the young women in Lowell were supplementing the wages of their fathers, and sometimes husbands, who were earning higher wages in capital-intensive industries. By contrast, in today's newly industrialising countries, as already discussed, low wage women workers are the vast majority of the workforce. The men in their lives are not working in higher paid jobs or often, in any jobs at all. The dominant industries are not capital-intensive but low wage assembly plants. Though this division of labour may be considered less patriarchal, overall conditions for the workers are arguably worse than those that prevailed in places like Lowell. As for the future, since the early stages of capitalism in Europe and America were quite different from today's newly capitalist countries, there is no reason to think that history will repeat itself in the later stages in these countries. In

---

163   Bhattacharjee, Gupta and Luce 2009.
164   Rosen 2002, pp. 241–2.
165   Rosen 2002, p. 244; as increased competition brought worse conditions to Lowell, the native born workers protested and were replaced by immigrant workers.

particular, the newly developing countries have been forced to accept trade agreements and WTO rules which forbid them from giving the kind of supports to domestic firms that the rich countries gave when their industries were first developing.[166] We can see the results of the global garment industry's extremely inequitable power relationships in the fact that 'although Bangladesh has succeeded in developing its garment industry over the course of the past thirty years, it has not been able to significantly raise its standard of living, and their garment worker wages are still the lowest in the world. In real terms, garment wages in Bangladesh fell from 1994 to 2006, despite an enormous growth of the industry ... The structure of the supply chain ... keeps Bangladesh-based firms and workers down'. The authors of the study conclude that just as Walter Rodney showed that Europe underdeveloped Africa, the current system 'underdevelop[s] garment-producing countries with grave consequences for garment workers'.[167]

Moreover, the trajectory as capitalism develops is not necessarily up. It can remain the same, go down, or go up and then down again. In the United States, garment workers fought long and hard to get labour unions that succeeded in ending sweatshop conditions. In 1933 Frances Perkins, U.S. Secretary of Labour said 'The red silk bargain dress in the shop window is a danger signal. It is a warning of the return of the sweatshop, a challenge to us all to reinforce the gains we have made in our long and difficult progress towards a civilized industrial order'.[168] But now more than 75 years later, her warning is still apt. Sweatshops are back; in fact it is estimated that 75 percent of New York City garment firms are sweatshops.[169] So when apologists for sweatshops say wages are not bad compared to the wage standards and the cost of living prevailing in the region, they should include New York City in their calculations! The retail industry is another industry employing many women where wages and conditions have deteriorated. Unionized department stores like Macy's are in decline, replaced by non-union WalMart, which is currently the largest employer in the country. GM used to be the largest employer in the US, in the days when one out of six jobs in the US was connected to the auto industry. But the US auto industry was in serious trouble when I began this project and is now 'on life support' as some dark humourist put it. Millions of working women (and men) who had comfortable standards of living have lost them due to cap-

---

166 Early capitalist development in Europe also relied on deceit and brute force, for example, the Opium Wars. See Chang 2008.
167 Bhattacharjee, Gupta and Luce 2009, p. 76.
168 Quoted in Rosen 2002, p. 1.
169 Ibid. p. 227.

italist development and may lose their pensions as well.[170] This is in the richest country in the history of the world. We will look at the global picture later, but it should not be assumed everything is necessarily worse in the developing world, that even relatively poor people in the United States are better off than those in poor countries. In fact, African Americans, both women and men, have shorter lives than Indians in Kerala and several other poor countries.[171]

4.6   Competitive Market Constraints

Could these tendencies within capitalism be reversed? Could capitalists somehow be prevailed upon to make different choices that would be better for their employees? In the earlier discussion of freedom in capitalism, my focus was on freedom for the majority of people in capitalism, but it is worth asking: how free are capitalists? Certainly they are freer than the majority of people in capitalist societies. We have seen how much more freedom wealthy people have in their individual lives, and capitalists certainly tend to be wealthy, and we have seen how much more freedom owners of the means of production have to determine economic and political decisions than non-owners. However, this latter freedom is strictly constrained by the nature of the market system. Individuals acting in their role as capitalists *must* make decisions which they think will maximize profits. A recent report on the declining U.S. auto industry states that 'Shrinking market shares have *forced* G.M., Chrysler and the Ford Motor Company to close more than a dozen assembly plants and shed tens of thousands of workers in recent years'.[172] (my emphasis) Of course, they had choices, they made decisions, but if an individual capitalist made profit maximisation secondary to some other goal, such as maximising the well being of his employees, or the health of the planet, or some purely personal caprice, his shareholders would protest and would sell their stock in his company. Indeed such conduct would violate the fiduciary responsibility owners have to their shareholders. They believe they *must* pay the cheapest price they can in order to compete, and often they are right. The *Corporation* ... Laws are necessary to constrain them *all* so that individual corporations are not under competitive pressure to search for the lowest wage workers, perhaps even slave labourers. And these laws must be international laws, given that corporations are multinational. It

---

170   Another example of the imbalance of political and legal power between corporations and working people is that in bankruptcies, courts give priority to repayment of debts to banks and other secured creditors over repayment of workers' wages.
171   Sen 1999 p. 22 f.
172   'With Plants Shutting, the s.u.v. Lumbers Near the End of the Line', *The New York Times* 12/24/08, p. B4.

is worth struggling, therefore, for international labour standards that require living wages in all countries. Though necessary, laws are not enough, however; there are laws against slave labour but it has not been eliminated, as will be discussed later. The laws must be enforced, and competitive pressures lead to corruption. The structure of capitalism simply makes it hard for capitalists to 'do the right thing'.

4.7 Changed Gender Roles in Context

Turning back to how women are affected by capitalism, are the losses for women workers described above balanced by gains for other women workers—either here or abroad? Is this dismal picture just a piece of changing social and economic conditions in which women on the whole are doing as well or better than ever before? To some extent, of course. Women in developed countries are in positions they never were before, from doctors and lawyers to professors, corporate executives and politicians. The question then is how do we understand and evaluate the changed gender roles of the past fifty years? Have women gained *overall*, even though some have lost? If so, what have they gained?

In the United States, which I will concentrate on, the women's movement was certainly crucial in making gains for women. The gains did not come automatically with the development of capitalism but had to be fought for and won. That is the positive side of the story which feminists all celebrate. Earlier I discussed the decline of the patriarchal family—breadwinner father and housewife mother—as an indicator of the changing gender order which constituted progress for women. But not everyone was happy with this change—and those who were unhappy were not all patriarchs or conservative women—because this change has a downside. *Not many men today earn enough to support a whole family, the so-called family wage.* Though women now earn 77% of what men earn, up from 59%, this is not because women have done so well, but because men's wages have declined faster than women's.[173] Historian Nancy Maclean argues that even more important than the women's movement in explaining the changing gender relations in the post-war period was the end of the family wage.[174] More families needed more people in the workforce; to sustain the family wage, it now takes 80 hours of labour, instead of the 40 hours of the 1950s. While this has been beneficial for women *in relationship to men of their class*, it is an expression of declining conditions for most families. There has

---

173 Luce and Brenner 2006, p. 83. They also point out a recent study that shows that over their lifetime, the wage gap between women and men is actually 38%.
174 Maclean 2002.

also been a massive increase in personal indebtedness as families struggle to survive. Today's economic crisis is bringing the possibility of further changes in gender roles, but the news is not therefore good from a feminist point of view. In Feb 2009, it was reported that for the first time in American history, women may surpass men in the workforce. However, the cause is that 82% of the jobs lost had been held by men. The jobs women hold are more often part-time without benefits, and even in full-time jobs, women earn only 80% of what men earn.[175] Hence this is very bad news for most families.

If we look at the gains for women in the US since the women's movement we can see both the enormous achievements women have won under capitalism, but also the limits posed by capitalism. Essentially what women achieved is their democratic rights. The law no longer prohibits women from doing whatever men can do; in fact the law prohibits private institutions from discriminating against women. So women are legally free to contract and compete on the same basis as men. Legal restrictions on the exercise of reproductive freedom—which is fundamental to the exercise of all rights—have mostly been eliminated, though this is an ongoing struggle. Some gains have been made in protecting women from violence. These objective advances of strategic gender interests and the concomitant sea change of consciousness have allowed unprecedented freedom of opportunity for women. That is the good news.

Yet for all this, however, the wage gap between the sexes, though reduced, is still one of the largest in the world. A recent front page article in the *New York Times* reported 'Scant Progress on Closing Gap in Women's Pay' noting that for college graduates, the gap had actually increased.[176] Labour economists have shown that this is not explained primarily by discrimination, but rather by our country's 'unmatched and ever-widening levels of overall economic inequality'. One commentator described the trends of the last thirty years in the US as 'the largest transfer of wealth and income in the history of the world—far larger than what occurred during either the Russian or the Chinese revolutions'. From 1970 to 2000, the share of the total income of the richest 0.01 of Americans had gone from being 53 times the national average to 306 times the national average. Wealth is even more unequal; e.g. the top 1% has 45% of

---

175 *New York Times*, 6 February 2009. Throughout the world women tend in be in precarious work and in some places this meant that they experienced more job losses than men, e.g. Brazil. Interview with Rosane Da Silva, national women's officer for Brazil's trade union confederation. See www.ITUC-csi.org.
176 David Leonhardt, *New York Times*, 26 December 2006.

the wealth, a ratio not seen since 1929.[177] A correlate (perhaps a consequence) of this inequality is a stark decline in overall measures of human development for Americans, in the boom years as well as today. The American Human Development Index (HDI) showed a decline from #2 in the world in the 1980s, down to #6 by the mid-1990s to #15 in 2006.[178] Thus, 'American women ... were essentially swimming upstream in a labour market increasingly unfavourable to low wage workers'.[179] A similar story can be told for black Americans of both sexes.

Another piece of the explanation for the wage gap, as sociologist Johanna Brenner explains, is that the women's movement did not succeed in changing the most important aspect of the gender division of labour, viz., that women are still predominantly responsible for all kinds of care-giving: of the household, children, the elderly and disabled.[180] And neither did it succeed in winning social supports for these roles, which would have cost a lot more than the legal and policy changes they did win. As the US has the least developed welfare state of all the developed capitalist countries this means that the burden falls on individual women. This is still true today when women are becoming the majority of the workforce. Heidi Hartmann, president and chief economist at the Institute for Women's Policy Research says 'Over a long 20-year period, married men have stepped up to the plate a little bit, but not as much as married women have dropped off in the time they spend on household chores'.[181] Clearly men benefit to varying degrees from standard gender roles, and so do capitalists since they can pay less. Many families rely on take-out food, whether it is from McDonald's or gourmet restaurants. Some women can afford to buy their way out of more time-consuming household work—by employing other women as nannies, housecleaners, home health aides—but most cannot.[182] Thus, the class divide among women in our society has widened as has the gap between rich and poor as a whole. *While attention has focused on the glass ceiling, the reality is that most women cannot climb out of the basement; thus, one third of female-headed households of all races are living in poverty.*[183] The eco-

---

177 Rohatyn 2009. See also Perelman 2006. Excellent sources for figures on inequality in the US are the home page for Emmanuel Saez and the website for United for a Fair Economy (UFE).
178 Conley 2009, p. 29.
179 Blau 1993, p. 85 quoted in Maclean 2002, p. 237.
180 Brenner 2000.
181 *NY Times*, 6 February 2009.
182 This is true in Western Europe and developed countries of Asia as well. One writer describes this phenomenon in Taiwan as 'subcontracting filial duty': Lan 2002.
183 See Luce and Brenner 2006 for other important figures and analyses.

nomic crisis has taken a particularly heavy toll on African American women who were disproportionately hurt by the subprime and housing crisis. Given that most wealth in the African American community is in the form of home equity, this loss 'represents the largest loss of black wealth since the Reconstruction'.[184] People at all economic levels are working longer hours than ever before.[185] What all women would need for genuine equality with men in our society has proved much more difficult to achieve: at a minimum, free childcare, health care, shorter hours of work at higher wages, all of which require a significant redistribution of wealth. Instead, we are going backwards. So-called welfare reform, supported by Hillary Clinton, has meant that for the first time in fifty years, women and children cannot count on support if they need it. And now, in the richest country in the history of the world, many more are in need. As Johanna Brenner explains, it will take a revival of broad social movements to reverse these trends.

4.8 The Global Picture

On a global level the gap between rich and poor has also widened—to such obscene levels the figures are almost incomprehensible. Both in absolute and relative terms, poor countries are poorer today, even though the 1990s were a boom period. The most recent figures from the World Bank show that 1 out of 4 people in the developing world live on less than $1.25 per day and almost half live on less than $2.[186] One third of all annual deaths in the world can be traced to poverty. As Mary Robinson, former United Nations Commissioner on Human Rights, noted in an interview on International Women's Day 2009, poverty affects women in particular.[187] As a result of this global polarisation the middle class of the Third World now earns less than the poor of the First World, so a woman migrating to wealthier countries to be a maid or nanny may come from a family of schoolteachers in Mexico or the Philippines. Contrary to

---

184 Avis Jones-DeWeever, research director of the United Council of Negro Women, quoted in Dominique Haoson, 'Few Safety Nets for Women of Color', Interpress News Service, 4 March 2009.

185 ILO report cited in Ehrenreich and Hochschild 2002 p. 8.

186 These figures were released in September 2008 but date from 2005—*before* rising food and fuel prices and *before* the unfolding global economic crisis which almost certainly have worsened these figures. http://econ.worldbank.org/docsearch. See UN Development Reports www.hdr.undp.org/publications/papers.cfm. According to one study by the UN Development program, sixty countries were worse off in 1999 than 1980. For the 1990s, see Wade 2001, pp. 72–4, Miller 1999.

187 *Democracy Now*, 9 March 2009. Robinson was the first woman President of Ireland, the President of Oxfam and International Commission of Jurists.

the standard optimistic picture of globalisation, Saskia Sassen has shown that growth sectors of the new global economy do not only create decent paying professional jobs but also a large number of low wage dead end jobs to support the professionals at work, at home and at play.[188] In the capitalist democracy of India, studies show that sweatshop and other low wage work is perpetuated generation to generation, and even growing. Despite the growth of the Indian economy, 2.5 million children die annually, the number of underweight children has hardly declined and the number who are fully immunized has actually declined.[189] *There are now more child labourers throughout the world than ever in history.* Though capitalist development has improved the lives of many in the developing world, it has also brought growing immiseration to many poor countries, through a combination of development, massive indebtedness followed by the austerity policies imposed by international institutions like the IMF and the World Bank such as wage freezes, cuts in social services and devaluation of local currencies. Rather than improving their economies as promised, the terms of the loans are such that even though the countries have paid off their original loans many times over, many have ended up even more indebted.[190] As a result, billions of people have been left destitute (a disproportionate number of whom are women) and there has been a mass migration of women and men, mostly people of colour, from poor countries to rich countries. With men gone or unable to support them, women have had to leave their own countries and families to work in developed countries as nannies, janitors, health aides and sex workers.

Throughout history, women have migrated to do the very same jobs, but never on this scale; women now constitute about half of the world's 120 million legal and illegal migrants, and they are the majority from some regions.[191] Some have called this the feminisation of migration. In the best cases with the least abusive conditions, particularly in the care sector, migrants are able to provide for their families and achieve more personal independence than they could have achieved at home. But feminists cannot be happy about even the best case scenario because it comes at untold emotional cost to the women who migrate and to the children they have left behind. Arlie Hochschild calls it a new kind of imperialism. Instead of the male-centred extraction of gold, ivory and rubber by direct forms of coercion in the nineteenth century, today's imperialism

---

188 Sassen, 'Global Cities and Survival Circuits', in Ehrenreich and Hochschild 2002 and other works by Sassen.
189 Mishra 2006; Sengupta 2006; and 2009.
190 See Longworth 1998.
191 Ehrenreich and Hochschild 2003, p. 5.

involves the extraction of emotional resources and does not operate through the barrel of a gun. "The yawning gap between rich and poor countries is itself a form of coercion, pushing Third World mothers to seek work in the First for lack of options closer to home. But given the prevailing free market ideology, migration is viewed as a 'personal choice' ... and the consequences 'personal problems'."[192] Feminists know better than that.

In the worst cases, these immigrant workers were trafficked; even when they chose to migrate they may end up as virtual slaves. The extreme, even slave conditions of many migrant workers are not directly due to capitalism and the reforms advocated to correct them are, theoretically, compatible with capitalism. However, capitalism is *indirectly responsible* in that it creates the conditions that render workers, particularly women, vulnerable to such abuses. As scholar/activist Joy M. Zarembka explains, 'The global economic changes that push women from developing nations to migrate for domestic work have also contributed to the recent rise of domestic worker abuse'.[193] Immigrant workers outside the domestic sphere are also vulnerable to abuse as they have no legal rights. A horrific recent example comes from Greece where a Bulgarian woman unionist was blinded and almost killed to punish her for her activism against the prevailing conditions of 'medieval servitude'. Her case was ignored by the police and the press until her coworkers' protests brought it to public attention and an international petition to open an inquiry. The petition circulated about the case describes how *'gangster practices are becoming a regular part of the world of work'*.[194]

Probably the worst abuses are found in the sex industry. Thailand provides a rich case study of the good and bad consequences of capitalist development in a sexist and hierarchal society long accepting of non-marital sex for men.[195] Given its natural resources, few people starve in Thailand, except in the north where poor conditions sometimes led families to sell a girl child as a servant or slave. But today 'The small number of children sold into slavery in the past has become a flood ...' The customary ill-treatment of women combined with the relentless pursuit of profit in the new economy has brought horrendous results for women. In a country with (a conservative estimate of) over one million

---

192 Arlie Hochschild, 'Love and Gold', in Ehrenreich and Hochschild 2002.
193 Joy M. Zarembka, 'America's Dirty Work: Migrant Maids and Modern-Day Slavery', in Ehrenreich and Hochschild 2002, p. 144. There are also non-economic causes of migration such as unhappy, abusive family situations, and positive reasons like a desire for adventure and self-improvement. Research does not show the percentages in each of these categories, but what research exists shows that the overwhelming majority are driven by poverty.
194 Justicepourconstantinakouneva@gmail.com
195 The following statistics and quotes are all taken from Bales 1999.

prostitutes, about one in twenty are enslaved, again a conservative estimate. Economic development has brought both greater supply and greater demand. Prices have risen overall, but returns for agricultural products have not. Yet peasants are everywhere exposed to new and tempting consumer products. So girls are now sold not to feed a family, but 'to buy color televisions and video equipment'. The demand also can be traced to development as more men can now afford to pay for sex. 'Who are the modern slaveholders? The answer is anyone ... with a little capital to invest'. At the bottom are the pimps and brothel keepers who appear to own the girls, then there are the brokers and agents, but 'the real slaveowners tend to be middle-aged businessmen ... the slaveholder may in fact be a partnership, company or corporation' for which brothels are just one of many capital investments, often masked as part of the entertainment or tourism industries central to many countries' development plans. It is a particularly lucrative part of an investment portfolio, with low capital investment, low risk, and high turnover, as the girls are destroyed and replaced by others. Positive results of development has somewhat curtailed the supply of prostitutes from the north of Thailand, but brokers (i.e. slavers) have simply moved across the border to Burma and Laos.

Nor is slavery confined to the sex industry. Though it is illegal everywhere, the world's leading expert on modern day slavery Kevin Bales estimates that the total number of slaves today *is 27 million, more than all the people stolen from Africa in the time of the transatlantic slave trade.*[196] The population explosion and the impoverishment of millions has created a glut of potential slaves in the poorest societies. With government collaboration, slavery takes different forms and is found throughout the world, touching the lives of all of us.

'Slaves in Pakistan may have made the shoes you are wearing and the carpet you stand on. Slaves in the Caribbean may have put sugar in your kitchen and toys in the hands of your children. In India they may have sewn the shirt on your back and polished the ring on your finger ... They made the bricks for the factory that made the TV you watch. In Brazil slaves made the charcoal that tempered the steel that made the springs in your car and the blade on your lawnmower. Slaves grew the rice that fed the woman that wove the lovely cloth you've put up as curtains. Your investment portfolio and your mutual fund pension own stock in companies using slave labour in the developing world. Slaves keep your costs low and return on your investments high'.

---

196 Bales 'The New Slavery', in Bales 1999, pp. 1–33. This estimate is larger than government estimates but smaller than that offered by activist organizations. All the quotes and figures in this paragraph are from this chapter.

How should we understand the relationship of these horrors to capitalism?[197] Defenders of capitalism would say it is totally anomalous, a remnant of earlier systems and not to be blamed on capitalism. Slavery would seem antithetical to capitalism (certainly it is in theory) because capitalism rests on 'free' labour. However, as we know, slavery in the Americas played a critical role in the early days of capitalism. Through what was known as the 'triangle trade' between Africa, the Americas and Europe, slavery was an integral part of the burgeoning world capitalist economy. And indeed the very division of the world into developed and undeveloped, rich and poor, the 'First World' and the 'Third World', which most people in the former countries take as 'natural', came about through horrific violence by the powerful at crucial historical junctures.[198] Today's slavery differs in several respects from that found in early capitalism, but its prevalence and its character also have to be understood in terms of the global capitalist economy.[199] The race to the bottom, which at the high end moves jobs out of developed countries, has much worse consequences at the low end of the global economy as poor farmers have to compete with slave labour and are pushed into debt bondage themselves. The new slavery is actually more profitable than the earlier form because it is less capital intensive (the supply is closer to hand) and slaveholders are not responsible for the unproductive—the young, the old, the injured and the sick. If a slave is not productive she or he is simply disposed of. 'In the new slavery, the slave is a consumable item, added to the production process when needed, but no longer carrying a high capital cost'. *Thus capitalist development brings both freedom and slavery in its wake depending on where and at whom we look.* As Bales says, if the powerful capitalist countries and international organisations like the IMF and the WTO gave as much attention to the stealing of lives as they do to the stealing of copyright, slavery could be eliminated. Capitalism is antithetical to slavery in theory, as it is to sexism and racism, but is quite compatible with it in reality. When the values supposedly inherent in capitalism of individual freedom and equality of opportunity come into conflict with its drive to maximize profit, the latter override the former.

In theory women's practical gender interests could all be satisfied under capitalism; the Scandinavian countries come close, and the New Deal was a step in this direction. However, economic and political conditions have changed. As

---

197 Miles 1987.
198 See Davis 2001; Thomas Pogge offers arguments to show that individuals in rich countries today are responsible for *sustaining* the harm suffered by the poor.
199 Most important are the absence of legal ownership and attempts to justify it in any terms other than economic.

already discussed, the model of capitalism dominant in the US since the 80s, known as neo-liberalism, was a throwback to pre-New Deal style capitalism. As corporations searched the globe for the lowest costs, the New Deal was being dismantled, by the Democrats as well as the Republicans in the United States, and the welfare states of Europe and Japan came under increasing pressure to adapt to US-style capitalism.[200] The current economic crisis has led to a loss of credibility of that ideology, but conditions are not favourable for advancing the interests of working people and creating a less brutal form of capitalism. The mobility of transnational corporations is crucial in allowing them to influence politics in the direction favourable to them. The labour movement and other social movements are on the decline, fighting defensive battles to keep some of the gains they won under more favourable conditions; there is always someone more desperate who will take their position if they say 'no'. Could the economic crisis change this gloomy prognosis? Early in 2009 the Director of National Intelligence Dennis C. Blair described the financial crisis as the top near-term security threat facing the US, the rising unemployment rates and resulting protests all over the world are seen as a threat to stability, commentators have likened our current conditions to those preceding the rise of fascism and WW II, and there are debates on the Internet as to whether the current crisis could spawn new extremist movements as they did then.[201] It is possible that a combination of militancy, moral arguments and pragmatic fears that 'the poor will help themselves' may prevent the conditions of the majority from being worsened. However, this scenario is still a far cry from transforming all capitalist countries into Sweden. While it is logically possible, and would certainly be preferable to what we have now, a more ideal, more compassionate version of capitalism, a global social democracy, such as advocated by liberal economists like Joseph Stiglitz and Paul Krugman, does not seem to be anywhere on the horizon. Indeed the reverse seems more likely as the brutal logic of competitive global capitalism pushes down the majority of the people of the world.

4.9 *Human Interests Are Women's Interests*
Thus far my discussion of capitalism's impact on women has focused on gender- and class-related interests. But women have interests that are not uniquely gendered. As many feminists have come to recognize, women's gender interests

---

200 For example, Martin Fackler, 'In Japan, New Jobless May Lack Safety Net': 'As never before, the global downturn has driven home how a decade of economic transformation has eroded Japan's gentler version of capitalism, in which companies once laid off employees only as a last resort'. NYT, 8 February 2009.
201 Pincus and Warrick 2009; Schwartz 2009.

cannot be analysed separately from their race, class and other aspects of their identity, an approach often referred to as 'intersectionality'. I suggest that we need to go further and to give full recognition in feminist discussions not only that we are all different but inter-related in all kinds of respects, but that we are also *alike simply by virtue of being human*. This point is already expressed in the strong feminist claim that women's interests are human interests; women's rights are human rights. It is equally true and important that human interests are women's interests—whether or not they are differentiated by gender. Feminists should not limit their concerns to those uniquely or primarily affecting women. I will turn now to three reasons why capitalism is bad for women—and for all living creatures.

First is capitalism's propensity to war. Most wars in the nineteenth, twentieth and twenty-first centuries have been between capitalist countries over resources and markets. This was obscured in the second half of the twentieth century by the Cold War between the capitalist and communist countries which was used to justify massive expenditures on weaponry, particularly by the US. However, the collapse of communism did not bring a 'peace dividend' as many had hoped because 'rogue states', and 'terrorists' were used to justify the same old policies. Capitalism's inherently competitive nature makes wars inevitable as long as there are nation states as each country competes for the resources it needs for development. From colonial times, to contemporary struggles over oil and water, resource plunder is key to capitalist development which will only intensify with the expansion of capitalism throughout the globe. Wars affect all living creatures, but in modern wars, the bulk of the casualties are non-combatants, which means *mostly women and children*. Women are also subject to horrific sexual violence and are the bulk of refugees displaced by wars whose deaths from malnutrition are not counted as war casualties. Humans have always fought wars, but capitalism's inherent propensity to war combined with its inherent tendency toward technological development has resulted in weaponry that could destroy all living creatures on the globe several times over. And competition leads to self-destructive contradictions. For example, Cold War interests in Afghanistan led the United States to ignore, even to aid and abet, Pakistan's development of nuclear technology which has now been exported to other countries around the world and is widely cited as one of the greatest dangers that the US faces.[202] We need to develop a system that does not encourage the worst of human capacities and tendencies but fosters human capacities like compassion and cooperation.

---

202   Armstrong and Trento 2007.

The way we think about 'security' has to be broadened, both how to get it and what it means. As Nobel Peace-prize winner Bishop Desmond Tutu said recently 'you don't get true security from the barrel of a gun'.[203] We have to think about its meaning differently too. Especially in the United States after 9–11 security is conceived exclusively in terms of protection against intentional threats to our safety and well-being, which of course means they are threats by individuals, groups or nations. But the concept has a broader sense, of protection against threats of all kinds, whether intentional or not. These two conceptions of security are highly gendered. When we think of security in the narrow sense, (as in Department of Homeland Security) we know that it is overwhelmingly men who will be defending us against other men who are attacking us. One invariable of the sexual division of labour is that men have had the responsibility for violence. This is true today even with women in the U.S. military, especially as we go up the military hierarchy and into the realm of military technology. On the other hand if we think of security in the broader sense of Social Security and security blankets, then women enter the picture, as the other invariable piece of the sexual division of labour is that women do the bulk of the caretaking. To truly protect our well-being, we need to conceive of security in the broadest sense, as in fact the biggest threats facing humanity today are not from intentional acts. Just one example is that 'unsafe water and lack of basic sanitation cause 80% of all sickness and disease and kill more people *than all forms of violence, including war*'. It is important to note, however, that although these deaths are not the result of direct intentional acts, many intentional acts contribute to the lack of access to safe drinking water, from polluting streams and rivers to privatising water.

A second life-threatening implication of capitalist development in the age of globalisation can be summed up in the titles of two recent books: Mike Davis' *Planet of Slums* and Laurie Garrett's *The Coming Plague*.[204] Capitalist development around the globe has meant that for the first time in human history, more people live in cities than not, and the biggest are in the developing world, cities like Bangkok, Mexico City, Cairo and Nairobi. Combined with another trend of global capitalism—the growing extremes of wealth and poverty—these cities have vast slums that are potent breeding grounds for infectious disease. Centuries of capitalist development has brought us a planet of slums. The spread of industrial style agriculture throughout the world means that animals are living in vast slums too, known as CAFOS (confined animal feeding operations) with

---

203   *Democracy Now* 28 August 2009, speaking in Israel.
204   Davis 2006; Garrett 1995; Davis 2005.

horrendous consequences for our health. When we add to this equation the privatisation of everything from water to education to health care that world capitalist institutions like the IMF and the World Bank mandate, and we consider the fact that more people died in the flu pandemic of 1918–1919 than in all of WW I, we can see the catastrophic possibilities today when millions of people and things traverse the globe every minute. That most of the ingredients of the drugs used to treat disease come from China does not inspire confidence regarding either the availability or safety of the drugs we would need in an emergency.

Finally, if all countries develop along capitalist lines, life will be unsustainable on this planet. Al Gore's powerful film about global warming called 'An Inconvenient Truth' starts out with charts showing the historic rise in atmospheric temperature. It began to take off in the early nineteenth century—at the same time that capitalism developed—and is now 'off the charts', very rapidly reaching the point where human life will simply not be sustainable. And global warming is not the only threat to global survival. As the United Nations Millennium Ecosystem Assessment concluded, *almost two thirds of the natural resources necessary to sustain life* on this planet are being degraded and destroyed by human action: the oceans are being depleted of fish, deforestation is proceeding at record rates, rivers, lakes and wetlands have become toxic, 50 thousand species become extinct every year, etc., etc. 'In effect, one species is now a hazard to the other 10 million or so on the planet and to itself'.[205] Why human behaviour now threatens human survival, and how we can stop it, is not addressed. And *there is no guarantee that we can stop it*. As demonstrated by Pulitzer Prize-winning author Jared Diamond's book *Collapse*, a number of societies of the past essentially committed ecological suicide because they exhausted their natural resources and refused to make the changes in their values and ways of life necessary for survival.[206] Diamond worries that we are on the same path, but this time it is not just individual societies but the whole planet. Like Al Gore, he concludes with the usual good ideas about what we should do, from using more energy-efficient light bulbs, to lobbying, consumer boycotts, pressing corporations to adopt eco-friendly policies, and so on. But these have all been tried (with some modest successes)—and yet the problem is getting *much worse very rapidly*. The problem is that an even more inconvenient truth than global warming is that the standard measures proposed

---

205   UN, Millennium Ecosystem Assessment: Current State & Trends Assessment, 2005. The report was prepared by 1360 scientists from 95 countries.
206   Diamond 2005.

will do very little to stop it (or any of the other threats to the planet's ecosystems) as long as capitalism continues. Because capitalism is—for better and for worse—an economic growth machine. *The world economy now produces in less than two weeks the equivalent of the entire physical output of the year 1900, and global economic output now doubles every 25 to 30 years.*[207] The transition to capitalism of the Soviet bloc countries will likely increase this rate. Although communist and pre-capitalist societies were often terrible for the environment, it is ironically, the chief virtue of capitalism—its incessant need to innovate and develop—that is now the single greatest threat to our future. China, for example, plans to put as many cars on the road by 2020 as the US has now. While the economic downturn has slowed this process, it will continue if capitalism revives. Clearly this cannot go on.

Defenders of capitalism would disagree with this pessimistic prognosis. Leaving aside a rejection of the facts—which I take to be irrefutable—and the psychological need to deny such a terrifying prospect, they would likely offer two reasons for their optimism: the basic rationality of capitalists who will also be destroyed if trends continue, and the prospects for addressing the problems within capitalism, by the growth of green industry for example. To support their position, they could point to the report issued in 2006 by Britain's Treasury Secretary and former World Bank chief economist Sir Nicholas Stern which pointed out the devastating economic—as well as ecological—effects of allowing current trends to continue, concluding that it was both necessary and economically rational to intervene to reverse them. Then-Prime Minister Tony Blair agreed, urging 'radical measures'. And yet, these radical measures have not been taken. The problem, as Diamond's book shows, is that people do not always act in rational ways even when the alternative is catastrophe.

4.10   *Constrains on Rationality*

The gap between, on the one hand, the now-accepted fact that either we fundamentally change our economic practices or we die, and on the other hand, the meagre steps actually taken to address this suggests how fundamental and systemic the problem is. It is not simply that people do not want to face the difficult choices, but that *capitalism poses structural constraints on our ability to act rationally.* The subtitle of Diamond's book is *How Societies Choose to Fail or Succeed.* But is it really a matter of 'choice'? Who is it that gets to choose whether our societies continue to pursue eco-suicidal practices? Or is it rather the fun-

---

207   Porrit 2005, p. 77.

damental requirements of capitalist reproduction on a day-to-day basis?[208] Certainly all of us should do what we can to reduce our individual destructive impact on the earth. But it does not matter much whether I choose public transportation or a bicycle instead of a car if auto manufacturers are producing exponentially more cars every year. Nor, as discussed earlier, can individual corporations simply choose to promote environmental security rather than profit. The occasional CEO who seems to understand the problem is caught in a bind. For example, in the 1990s British Petroleum's CEO warned that fossil fuels accelerate global warming, adopted the slogan 'Beyond Petroleum', and invested in solar power. However, 99% of their investments remain in fossil fuels *and they are increasing*. If he did not follow this tried and true avenue to higher profits, he would be out of a job. Possibilities would seem to exist for change within capitalist terms, but they too are subject to the constraints of the market system. Wind and solar power were growing and were expected to grow more with President Obama's commitment to greener energy, but now, 'because of the credit crisis and the broader economic downturn, the opposite is happening: installation of wind and solar power is plummeting'.[209] Even if we switched to less destructive technologies, this does nothing to reduce and could even increase the overall levels of resource consumption. The basic problem is that our finite planet cannot bear the consumption of resources entailed by endless growth. Even, for example, if we were to switch to cleaner, greener cars, if we continue to produce ever more cars, the resources and materials for building, maintaining and transporting the cars would cause more pollution than we have at present.[210]

The basic problem lies in the conflict between the individual rationality enforced by the competitive market system and what is rational from a social point of view. Each firm is compelled to act to maximize its own interests, and this goes on and on—until it is too late. As economist Lester Thurow of WorldWatch Institute put it, 'Each generation makes good capitalist decisions, yet the net effect is collective social suicide'.[211] Adam Smith famously maintained that the best way to promote collective well being was by pursuit of self interest. In the eighteenth century this philosophy could not do too much harm to the natural world. But today, when 'a global engine of development of staggering

---

208 Much of my discussion here relies on the following articles: Smith 2005, pp. 294–306; Smith 2007, pp. 22–43; Holmstrom and Smith 2006.
209 'Dark Days for Green Energy', *New York Times*, 4 February 2009, p. B1.
210 John Whitelegg 'Dirty from cradle to grave' (1994), at www.worldcarfree.net/resources/freesources/DirtyfromCradletoGrave.rtf
211 Thurow 1996, pp. 302–3.

power has the capacity to melt the icecaps, transform the climate, strip mine the oceans to extinction, denude entire continents of forests, wipe out tens of thousands, if not millions, of species in a few decades, and poison the global atmosphere, all our fresh water sources, and even entire oceans', it is time to reject the theory.[212]

The environmental crisis is only the most dramatic example of the inherent conflict between the satisfaction of human needs and an economic system that has profit maximisation as its be all and end all, a system where everything has a price and nothing has a value.[213] Women's childbearing and care giving roles put them disproportionately among those who are harmed by this system.

4.11   Conclusion: What Is the Alternative? And What Should Feminists Do Now?

The burden of my argument has been that capitalism creates the conditions for genuine human liberation but at the same time it puts systematic barriers to its realisation. The same was true of the so-called socialist countries. In both systems the advances women made are those that were compatible with the interests of the dominant class; those not so compatible have not been realized. Throughout this long essay, I have argued negatively because the question was whether capitalism was good for women, not what should replace capitalism. But the critique gives us the basic guidelines for an alternative. What women need to advance their strategic and their practical interests and to lead fulfilling lives is a genuinely democratic society at all levels, economic as well as political, where they are free to organize and press for their interests as they see them and where no structural barriers stand in their way. Given the conflicts between profitability and the satisfaction of human needs in all their dimensions, we need to move to a society that aims *directly* at the satisfaction of social need. And not just individual societies, but on a global scale, because increasingly the world's people are all interconnected and ultimately one. I mean this not only in a moral sense—that every individual has equal value no matter where they happen to live—but as an urgent practical claim. Whether threats come from environmental disasters or wars or terrorism, no one can be truly secure in the world as it is organized at present. The potential conflicts between what is rational from an individual point of view and from a collective point of view require that collective rationality prevail in cases of conflict. This entails that

---

212   Smith 2007, p. 36.
213   How should we understand human needs? Most basically, as the material things necessary for survival, but also as those things necessary for *a satisfying and fulfilling life for human beings* which includes opportunities for creativity and self-development.

while there should be some role for a market, the most fundamental decisions facing society must be made by democratic planning. This is not a restriction on freedom or autonomy as some might fear. On the contrary: it is the only way that people can realize their freedom and autonomy on a collective scale. To limit our ability to plan for our social needs is to limit our freedom as well as to limit democracy. Thus rather than an inherent conflict between planning and freedom, the two coincide if planning is democratic. Social planning is the way we can expand our freedom beyond the scope of individual control in ways that matter most to us. It is the only way we can 'control our destiny'. Constraints can and should, however, be put on the power of the collectivity, which is another way of saying that there must be a recognition of certain individual rights. Women need rights both as individuals and as part of collectivities.

As Noam Chomsky has said: 'The task for a modern industrial society is to achieve what is now technically realizable, namely, a society which is really based on free voluntary participation of people who produce and create, live their lives freely within institutions they control, and with limited hierarchical structures, possibly none at all'.[214] Is this alternative socialism? The word 'socialism' has been applied to so many different, indeed incompatible models—from early utopian projects to social welfare capitalist societies to different totalitarian models of the twentieth century—that I am somewhat hesitant to use it for fear of misunderstanding. Hal Draper, the Marxist scholar and activist, has argued that the most fundamental division among the different models that have been called socialist is between what he called the 'two souls of socialism:' socialism-from-above and socialism-from-below.[215] The totalitarian 'state socialist' and the welfare capitalist models, as well as most of the utopian socialist schemes, would belong in the 'socialism-from-above' camp. But there was always another socialist tradition of socialism-from-below, of *self-emancipation as both the means to, and constitutive of, socialism*. This vision was exemplified by Marx's slogan for the First International Workingmen's Association: 'the emancipation of the working class must be the act of the working class itself'. So the vision I am projecting would be socialist in this sense.

But the word does not matter. Call it socialism, or call it eco-feminist socialism or economic democracy—or some totally new name. As the great socialist artist and poet William Morris said, 'Men fight and lose the battle, and the thing they fought for comes about in spite of their defeat, and when it comes turns out to be not what they meant, and other men have to fight for what they meant

---

214 Quoted in Albert and Hahnel 1991, p. 13.
215 'The Two Souls of Socialism', Marxists Internet Archive. See also Draper 1977–90.

under another name'. Women have always fought too; indeed early women radicals like Flora Tristan, or Eleanor Marx or Emma Goldman, Louise Michel, or Alexandra Kollontai (some of whom were 'utopian' socialists, others anarchists, and still others were Marxists) fought against capitalism, against colonialism and slavery and for women's liberation in all its dimensions. Expanding her father's famous slogan Eleanor Marx wrote 'Both the oppressed classes, women and the immediate producers, must understand that their emancipation must come from themselves'. Many anticipated the insight usually attributed to second-wave feminism, incorporating the personal, intimate, aspects of our lives as part of their liberatory vision because they understood that the economic and political and 'personal' were interrelated relations of power.[216] As discussed earlier, the Russian Revolution not only instituted such measures as communal childcare and laundries but it also eliminated laws against homosexuality and the status of 'illegitimacy'. I contend that there is a logic, a momentum, to struggles against oppression. Today that deeper vision of liberation from *all* sources of oppression, be they economic, sexist, racist, or homophobic, is widely understood on the left and in popular movements around the globe, even if there is debate about their interrelations and relative importance and some slow feet.

In defence of her neo-liberal policies Margaret Thatcher liked to say There Is No Alternative, repeating that phrase so often that it was abbreviated as TINA. An interesting thing about this claim is that if people believe it, then it becomes true; there is indeed no alternative. And then, if what I have argued above is true, humankind is doomed. I prefer to believe the slogan of the global justice movement: A Better World is Possible. That claim carries no guarantee of truth, even if we all believe it. But if enough people believe it and act on it, we have a chance of building a better world. The good news is that many people the world over are fighting for control over economic policies that dominate their lives, animated by the idea that everyone in the world who is affected by economic and environmental decisions should have some say in them. There is no grand master plan for all times and places, nor do all activists in the movement support a model of economic democracy as opposed to a reformed capitalism. Nevertheless, this is the logic of the movement which provides hopeful examples of sustainable democratic ways of living together, such as the participatory budgeting developed in Brazil, and Via Campesina an international organisation of peasants, agricultural workers, rural women and indigenous

---

216 See Taylor 1983. Excerpts of socialist-feminist 'foremothers and fathers' are found in Holmstrom 2002.

communities that fight for food sovereignty. Most are local but there are models being developed for broader global institutions and policies that are necessary to deal with our increasingly global problems and to create solidarity across local, national boundaries.[217] The goal should be to combine as much local, regional and national autonomy as possible with broad, even global, regulation as necessary, in particular to deal with environmental problems. An intriguing example comes from the world of cyberspace where the open source movement is creating what one observer calls a 'global collectivist society ... a new socialism'.[218] We need to bring this model from cyber space into real space, fusing individual creativity and autonomy with collective democratic controls necessary to protect and enhance the well being of all humankind. In the famous phrase of Antonio Gramsci, we have to cultivate pessimism of the intellect, but optimism of the will.

In the meanwhile, feminists should push to get the most from capitalism for the most women, not simply the freedom to exploit and be exploited on the same basis as men. This means they have to focus on practical, as well as strategic gender interests. For example, rather than fighting simply for the right to abortion, all feminists should embrace the concept of reproductive freedom for all women, which includes adequate medical care, childcare, decent-paying jobs for women. These cannot be separated from economic and political rights.[219] Using the terminology developed earlier, women's strategic gender interests must be united with practical gender interests. Though one cannot take on all issues at once, this is an example of how feminists must integrate the issues that affect women in all their multi-dimensionality, even ones that are not explicitly gendered. In the United States a struggle for public goods like universal medical care, childcare and elder care would enhance most all women's interests and increase the areas of society that are subject to demo-

---

217   British economist Pat Devine has developed a model of democratic, participatory planning in Devine 1988. For another model see Albert and Hahnel 1991; For more discussions, see Goldstein and Schorr 1991; Gundersen 1995; Palast et al. 2003; Fisher and Ponniah 2003; Monbiot 2003; Fox's documentary film 'Beyond Elections: Redefining Democracy in the Americas'. Also see fn. 25 for reference to Marx's discussion of the first workers' government—the Paris Commune.
218   'When masses of people who own the means of production work toward a common goal and share their products in common, when they contribute labour without wages and enjoy the fruits free of charge, it's not unreasonable to call that socialism': Kelly 2009.
219   See Rosalind P. Petchesky's 'Human Rights, Reproductive Health and Economic Justice: Why They are Indivisible', in Holmstrom 2002. The broad notion of reproductive rights was developed in the 1970s by black feminists and socialist feminists in opposition to the narrow focus on the right to abortion in the mainstream (white) women's movement. See Silliman, Fried, Ross, Gutierrez (eds.) 2004.

cratic control.²²⁰ But it is not only women in the developed world who are worthy of feminists' moral regard. And for women in the developing world, securing these rights, and even the right to food, shelter and clean water, require a struggle against global capitalist institutions like the World Bank which have imposed Structural Adjustment Programs that cut back already-meagre government services in order to pay back criminally onerous debts to the richest countries and institutions in the world. Complete cancellation of Third World debt is a necessary and just first step that all feminists must support. Aside from moral reasons, there are also selfish reasons why feminists cannot limit their concerns to their own societies. Our problems are increasingly global. As already discussed, the most important public good must be the environment which knows no national boundaries. It is striking that women have been at the forefront of environmental struggles around the world.

Finally, it is also important that feminists stress the very different values and understandings that motivate us from those that dominate capitalist culture. Individual autonomy is a crucial goal for women. But as women know better than anyone else humans are inter-dependent beings, so we should stress that autonomy is not counter-posed, but rather complementary to the values of caring, compassion, solidarity and security in the fullest sense of the term. And we should resist the capitalist logic which turns all areas of our lives into commodities, where everything has a price and nothing has a value.

To close with the optimistic words of writer and activist Arundhati Roy: 'Not only is another world possible, she is on her way. On a quiet day, I can hear her breathing'.²²¹

---

220   Anton 2000.
221   Bell 2009.

PART 4

Human Nature/Women's Nature

∴

CHAPTER 10

A Marxist Theory of Women's Nature

Debates about women's nature are very old but far from over. In fact they have acquired a new urgency with the rise of the women's movement and with the dramatic increase in the number of women in the workforce. Conservatives claim that there is a distinct women's nature that puts limits on the extent to which the traditional sexual-social roles can and should be altered. Feminists usually reject the idea, correctly pointing out that it has been used to justify women's oppression for thousands of years.

In this article I attempt to develop a Marxist approach to the question. Though such an approach is nowhere explicitly taken by Marx or Engels, it is a plausible development of their views. Marx held human nature to be determined by the social forms of human labour. I will bring out his general realist methodology and his perspective on the relation between the biological and the social. Given my interpretation of the facts about psychological differences between the sexes and the probable dependence of those differences on the sexual division of labour, this approach entails that women probably do have distinct natures. (It similarly entails that men probably have distinct natures since there is no reason to take men as the norm.) However, contrary to the usual assumption, it does not follow that sexual-social roles cannot or should not be radically altered, for men's and women's natures are socially constituted and historically evolving. Marx's approach though novel in certain respects, accords with the methodology employed in biological classifications. I shall discussion two objections: that my account underemphasizes the biological facts and that it underemphasizes social/historical factors. On my account of women's nature, this nature can change, though it will not be easy, but nothing follows about how women ought or ought not to live. I shall conclude by considering contrasts between my Marxist approach to women's nature and Marx's approach to human nature.

∵

Just as the nonhuman natural world consists of biological, chemical, and physical structures for which different sorts of explanations are appropriate, so there are many levels of explanation appropriate to human beings. The nature of a human being as a biological being would be the genotype. The philosophical question of human nature is of the nature of human beings qua social beings. According to Marx's theory, human beings have certain basic needs and capacities which are biological in origin but to some extent socially constituted: 'Hunger is hunger but the hunger gratified by cooked meat eaten with a knife and work is a different hunger from that which bolts down raw meat with the aid of hand, nail, and tooth'.[1] Some human needs and capacities are unique to human beings, but even those that are not take uniquely human forms. As new needs and capacities are continually being created, biology remains an important determining factor, but human life progressively becomes less directly tied to its biological base.

Since human needs and capacities are expressed, shaped, and even created through the activity of satisfying needs (i.e., through labour), Marx concentrated on the form of labour characteristic of the human species. Though this species can be distinguished from others on a number of criteria, Marx says that human beings in fact begin to distinguish themselves from other species when they begin to produce their means of subsistence. Because the labour of society is institutionalized into sets of social practices and social relations, by their labour people are thereby producing their whole life. The general capacity of human beings to labour in a social and purposive way takes a variety of specific forms throughout history which in turn affect and even create other human needs and capacities.

Now obviously there are biological structures that make possible the kinds of labour that human beings do. However, the relation between biology and activity in human beings differs from that in other species in two ways: first, human biology makes possible more than just a narrow range of behaviour, even within a particular historical period; and second, rather than determining the forms of human labour, human biology does no more than make possible its forms. Our large brain size, the basis of the flexibility and plasticity of human behaviour and consciousness, resulted from evolution, a major determinant of which was labour. This is the basis of Engels's remark that 'labour created man himself'. In Marx's theory, labour is the key to an explanation of social life and social change. Since this was his concern, he emphasized labour and not the biology.

Compare the methodology employed in biological classifications: animals are classified into the same or different species not simply on the basis of their

---

1   Marx 1973, p. 92. As is well known, one of the most controversial areas of Marxist scholarship is whether Marx had a theory of human nature in his later work, and, if so, whether it is significantly different from his earlier one. The interpretation I give below is consistent with both his early and his later work (as indicated by references). So there is some common theory of human nature, although there are also differences between his early and late ideas which are not relevant to my concerns in this chapter.

similarities and differences but also according to the importance of these features within biological theory. For this reason Chihuahuas and St. Bernards are classified as belonging to the same species, although there are greater differences between them than there are between many dogs and wolves. In analogous fashion. The differentiating characteristic of social beings should be determined by its importance in social theory. As the forms of human labour (and the resultant social practices and institutions) change, new mental and physical capacities are developed, some remain undeveloped, and others are destroyed. Hence different behavioural and psychological generalisations will be true of people who do different sorts of labour in different modes of production.

A nominalistic-empiricist approach would leave the discussion of human nature at that. However, I take Marx to have a realist approach to the philosophy of natural and social science. Realists maintain that the concept of nature—stripped of outmoded metaphysical assumptions—often plays an important explanatory role in answering such questions as, Why do the generalisations hold? And What is the basis of the observed similarities? Biological theories, which back up some generalisations and not others, should provide some account of the mechanisms that generate the regularities. For example, realists argue that it is not necessary to posit some underlying structure common to the things defined as one species, that generates the disjunctive set of properties defining a species and causes variations in different individuals within that species.[2] (This demand is satisfied by the concept of the gene pool.) In traditional terminology, the set of properties in accordance with laws is called the real essence.

Marx assumed the same perspective on the social world. He believed that the distinction between accidental and lawful generalisations applied to social phenomena and that certain social entities had natures, saying repeatedly that science was necessary to uncover the hidden laws of motion of capitalist society. Socioeconomic classes are not mere collections of individuals with some common economic feature-not classes simply in the logical sense. The realist methodology implies that there must be certain characteristic differences in the psychophysical structures of people who do very different sorts of labour in different modes of production to account for the observed personality and behavioural differences between them.[3] These psychophysical struc-

---

2   Hull 1970, pp. 19–54. Hull 1966–67, pp. 309–37. Hull 1965, pp. 314–26; 16.
3   By 'psychophysical' I mean to include phenomena to be explained in physical terms, psychological terms, or any mixture thereof, whatever the ultimate relation between the physical and the psychological.

tures would generate and explain a wide range of human behaviour within that mode of production, which the transhistorical features of human beings would not be able to do. To say in detail what these historically specific structures are and how they work would require a more adequate psychological theory than presently exists, one that integrates social and historical factors. However, an explanation of the varieties of human personality and behaviour requires some such hypothesis of historically specific structures. This indicates a line of future research.[4]

Talk of 'determining structures' is not inconsistent with Marx's conception of human beings as historical agents. Individually and collectively, human beings often do what they do because of their beliefs, desires, and purposes. Human beings are free in this sense. But Marx stresses that human freedom is exercised only within certain constraints. For example, we can better predict John Smith's economic behaviour by knowing that he is a capitalist than by knowing his preferences, skills, personality, and character traits.

The psychophysical structures produced by the sorts of labour that people do and the resultant social relations would constitute the nature of human beings qua social beings. Although there are certain features common to these structures, they vary as a whole from one mode of production to another. Marx is denying that there is a human nature in the traditional, trans historical sense. On his view, however, there are historically specific forms of human nature, that is, human nature specific to feudalism, to capitalism, to socialism and so on. In traditional terminology, the (variable) psychophysical structures would be the

---

4 Some fascinating work along these lines was done by the early Soviet psychologists, Lev Vygotsky and A.R. Luria, who defined psychology to mean 'the science of sociohistorical shaping of mental activity and the structures of mental processes which depend utterly on the basic forms of social practice and the major stages in the historical development of society' (Vygotsky and Luria 1976, p. 164). In a study of Central Asian peasants in the early 1930s, they discovered significant differences in the mode as well as the content of cognition between those living on a collective farm for two years and those engaged in traditional peasant agriculture. Specifically, the latter had difficulty with simple syllogisms while the former did not; and the latter classified objects according to what Luria called a 'graphic-functional' mode as opposed to the 'abstract-theoretical' mode used by the former. In attempting to give a material basis for his approach, Luria made innovative contributions to neuropsychology. Unfortunately, they did not explore the connections between social structure and noncognitive aspects of mental life. These seminal ideas have never really been developed. They were suppressed in the Soviet Union until recently and remained unknown in the West until many years later. (See also Luria, 1973. Luria, 1982). Also along these lines, Alfred Sohn-Rethel presents a convincing though speculative case for the thesis that the human capacity for abstract thinking was dependent on forms of commodity production (see Sohn-Rethel 1978.)

(variable) real essence of human beings qua social beings, and the forms of personality and behaviour to which they give rise would be the nominal essence. This acceptance of natures in the social world implies that, contrary to traditional assumptions, natures can change. Even for biological natures, however, the assumption that natures must be unchanging became less plausible after the discovery of evolution. If species can be understood as evolving sorts of things, why must natures be understood as unchanging? In Marx's view, the contrast of the social with the natural and unchanging is particularly inappropriate to human beings since they are by nature social beings with a history.

∴

Let us try to apply this approach to the question of whether women (and men) can be said to have distinct natures. Distinct sex-linked natures are supposed to account for (and to justify) the distinct social roles of women and men. It is important to see first of all that the defining biological differences between men and women cannot by themselves play this explanatory role, much less the justificatory one. A woman is defined as a typical member of the female sex, which is distinguished from the male sex by its ability to conceive and bear children. Whether these biological differences cause the social differences is an empirical question that we shall discuss shortly. However, to say that men and women have distinct natures so defined would be to utter a tautology. We are looking for the nature of women and men as social groups, not as biological groups.

Do then, men and women as social beings have distinct natures? If there are generalisations subsumable under a theory, explanatory of behaviour distinctive of a given social group, this suggests that the group has a distinctive nature. Indeed there are many generalizations we can make about a women's behaviour and roles within given cultures and many that are true cross-culturally as well. Compared to men, women spend more time taking care of children and doing other household tasks; they have less social, economic and political power in society at large and in almost every subgroup in society; their work outside the home, if any, is usually related to the work they do inside the home; they tend to cry more easily, dress and adorn themselves distinctively, trend to have distinct recreations and pleasures, and so on.

What is the explanation? Discrimination and direct social pressure are undoubtedly part of it. But are there differences between men and women themselves that underlie the behavioural differences? Many claim that biological differences between the sexes are the most important part of the explanation.⁵ However, it is highly implausible that biological differences could directly determine the social differences. If biological facts are critical determines of sexual/social roles, the connection is most likely to run through psychology; that is, biological differences cause or predispose psychological differences, which in turn cause differences between the sexes that are relevant to their respective social roles: for example, that women are more nurturant than men and hence are more appropriate caretakers of children. If there are such differences, the next question will be about their source.

Both these questions are controversial, even among the experts.⁶ Despite this and my own serious reservations about much of the research, I believe that the research to show that there exist statistically significant psychological sex differences of a sort that are relevant to the different social roles men and women play.⁷

Any position regarding the source of these differences is necessarily somewhat speculative since, by and large, the researchers look only for statistically significant relationships and do not try to establish cause and effect. The prevailing hostility among academic research psychologists to any theoretical framework makes it difficult to assess the data since the significance of the data and even what needs to be explained is to some extent dependent on a theory. But the following findings strongly support the view that social factors are the primary determinants:⁸ (1) Black males and white females, different biologically but with similar social handicaps are similar in patterns of achievement

---

5 An academic example of this point of view is Bardwick 1971. A more popular example is Goldberg 1977.
6 My reservations are based on the following objections. First, the research is confined to artificial situations and narrow cultural contexts. Second, it concentrates on statistically significant differences and ignores the magnitude, overlap and importance of the features. And third, it lacks a theoretical framework with which to evaluate the findings.
7 For example, women tend to have greater needs to be close to people (see Tyler 1965. Maccoby 1966, pp. 25–55), to be less aggressive (Maccoby and Jacklin 1974), more suggestible (Tyler 1965; Maccoby 1966), to be motivated more by a desire for love than a desire for power (Hoffman 1972, pp. 129–55), to have greater verbal and less visual/spatial ability (Tyler 1965; Maccoby 1966; Maccoby and Jacklin 1974). These differences are clearer and more significant among adolescents and adults than among young children (Block 1976, pp. 283–308.), with newborn boys and girls showing no clear psychological differences (Romer 1981, p. 7). These findings of statistically significant differences simply show that women have a trait to a higher degree than men. This is consistent with some men having it more than most women and even with a majority of women lacking it.
8 Critics of sociobiology have raised serious doubts that any specific and variable human behaviours traits are under genetic control. See in particular Gould 1977, pp. 237–42, 251–9. See also Caplan 1978.

scores and fear of success.⁹ (2) The same psychological state can yield very different emotional states and behaviour, depending on the social situation. Adrenalin produces a physiological state very much like that present in extreme fear, yet subjects injected with it became euphoric when around another person who acted euphorically and very angry when around another person who acted very angrily. Thus even if sex hormonal differences between men and women affect brain functioning, as some psychologists contend, it does not follow that there necessarily will be consistent emotional and behavioural differences between men and women. (3) Different behavioural propensities, thought by many to be biologically based, disappear given certain social conditions. In one study, when both sexes were rewarded for aggressive behaviour, the sex difference disappeared.¹⁰ (4) Studies of hermaphrodites show that the crucial variable determining their gender identity is neither chromosomal sex nor hormones administered pre- or postnatally but the 'consistency of being reared as feminine, especially in the early years'.¹¹ (5) Psychological sex differences are least pronounced in early childhood and old age, when sex role stereotypes are least powerful.¹² Furthermore, the principle of methodological simplicity supports taking environmental factors as decisive. We have at present ample evidence of environmental shaping of sex-differentiated behaviour, so ample in fact that it is sufficient to account for the cognitive and personality differences we observe in children and adults. Although it is possible that future research will discover biological factors as well, there is no reason to expect this will happen.

The social roles of men and women that are related to psychological sex differences are not universal cross-culturally, but they are very prevalent. Sex-differentiated socialisation patterns also show little cross-cultural variation, with girls being trained for nurturance and responsibility and boys for achievement and self-reliance in both developed and underdeveloped societies.¹³ This

---

9   Regarding achievement scores see Tulkin 1968, pp. 31–7. Jensen 1970. Regarding fear of success, see Weston and Mednick 1970, pp. 284–91.
10 Mischel 1966, pp. 56–81.
11 Money and Earhardt 1976, pp. 250–1.
12 Romer 1981, pp. 7, 124. Studies show that parents (as well as society) project fewer clear sex-role expectations on babies than on young children and adolescents. However, such stereotypes are projected throughout the human life: there is no time that can safely be said to be prior to socialization. Studies show that parents describe newborns in sex-stereotypic ways, even though hospital records show no objective differences, and that parents behave differently toward boy and girl babies even though they are unaware of it.
13 Barry III, Bacon, and Child 1957, pp. 327–32.

strongly suggests that many, though not all, of the psychological differences between men and woman are very prevalent, though not universal, cross-culturally. They are not universal to all women even within this culture. Something like the following is probably true: there is a common core of psychological traits found more among women than among men throughout the world, but women belonging to different cultures or subcultures have different subsets of this common core of traits. Though there is not enough rigorous cross-cultural psychological research to say for sure, this opinion accords with anthropological data we do have.[14]

There seem, then, to be several levels of generalisations (sociological, psychological, etc.) that are distinctive of women. By itself, however, this by no means implies that there is a distinct women's nature. As we saw in our discussion of taxonomy, the differences must be of a kind that is theoretically important. Following Marx's approach, we should expect psychological differences to be connected to differences in the sorts of labour that women do in society and to the resulting differences in social relations. Universally there is and has always been a sexual division of labour. Although there are some variations as to what labour each sex does, men generally have primary responsibility for subsistence activities; women's contributions to this varies. What does not vary is that, whatever else they do, women have primary responsibility for child care and most of the everyday household work. Their contribution to subsistence depends on its compatibility with child care.[15]

Several cross-cultural studies support the Marxist assumption that it is women's distinctive labour and the different social relations resulting from it that are critical in determining these personality differences.[16] Striking parallels exist between cultural and sexual differences; that is, cultures differ along the same lines as those along which men and women differ in most societies. Some cultures exhibit the sort of behaviour and personality usually con-

---

14 Margaret Mead's ground-breaking research provides dramatic examples of societies where sex roles are very different from those familiar to us. See Mead 1935.
15 For a survey of the research on sex roles and subsistence activities see Brown 1976, pp. 122–38. 'Though men typically make a predominant contribution ... there are numerous societies in which women make a predominant contribution. This variation is not random but seems to depend on two other activities which are universally sex-linked. Warfare is everywhere a predominantly male activity, and child care is elsewhere a predominantly female activity. Women do more subsistence work when men are occupied by warfare and when it is compatible with child care responsibilities. Thus societies in which women predominate in subsistence activities are those which depend almost entirely on gathering or hoe cultivation.'
16 See Chodorow 1971, pp. 173–97.

sidered masculine: everyone tends to be independent, achievement oriented, and assertive (although women still are less so than men are in the culture). In other cultures everyone tends to be compliant, obedient, and responsible—the sort of personality associated with women. Critical for us is that the difference in the 'personalities' of cultures are correlated with different economies. Where animal husbandry and agriculture are the primary sources of subsistence, obedience and responsibility are essential whereas experimentation and individual initiative would be dangerous. But societies which depend largely on hunting and fishing benefit from experimentation and individual initiative and are less threatened by disobedience and irresponsibility. Women in the latter societies tend both to fish and to have their more traditional responsibilities. Though more 'masculine' than men and women in other cultures, they are less 'masculine' than men in their own cultures. It seems plausible to say therefore that the differences between men and women can be explained by the different sorts of labour that they do.

Within our own society, certain psychological differences between young black and young white women lend support to the hypothesis. While wealthy black adolescent girls share the traditional (white) version of femininity, black adolescent girls from poor and working-class families (i.e., the majority) accept the very different values for women of strength and independence.[17] It is difficult to avoid the conclusion that the psychological differences between young black and young white women reflect the fact that black women have historically almost always been employed outside the home.

Now the Marxist view is not that there is a direct causal connection between the type of labour people do and their personality structure. Rather, the type of labour people do puts them into certain social relations, and these relations are institutionalized into sets of practices, institutions, cultural agencies, and so on. In the case of the sexual division of labour, the most important of these institutions is the family. Women are first of all raised primarily by a woman in a family. They then usually have a family of their own. Although fewer women today are full-time domestic workers than in the past, they still tend to think of their primary work role as that of a wife and mother. Their role in the family helps keep them in an inferior economic and social position. Their work outside the family, if any, is most often related to their role inside the family. Even the rare woman who has both an untraditional job and does not have a family is still shaped by the social and cultural institutions from which she is deviating. Men who for a long time do unskilled work and are treated in a pater-

---

17 Thoy 1969; Ladner 1972.

nalistic manner at work are also psychologically affected by it, but the effect is counteracted by their dominant role in the family and by the ideology of male supremacy.

The Marxist view then is that the different generalisations true of men and women can be explained by the sexual division of labour institutionalized into sets of practices and social and cultural institutions and that this in turn can be subsumed under a theory explaining the sexual/ social division of labour. The two explanations are provided by different aspects of historical materialism. In a society where there was a significantly different sexual division of labour, different generalisations would be true of men and women. In a society where there was no sexual division of labour, there would probably be few if any generalisations that were true of men but not women, except biological ones, and there would be fewer even of these. (I shall return to this later.)

The generalisations true of women and not men describe emotions and behaviour that reflect specific cognitive/affective structures more often found among women. My contention is that there is probably a common core of psychological traits found more often among women than among men throughout the world, of which women of different (sub)cultures have different subsets. The cognitive/affective structures generate the different sets of traits under different conditions. Although our knowledge at this point is too meagre to say much about these structures, an adequate explanation of the differences requires that we posit such structures. What we need is a psychological theory supplemented by social and historical considerations of the kind discussed here.[18] In the traditional terminology the cognitive/affective structures would be the real essence; the disjunctive set of traits would be the nominal essence. Although the underlying structures which give rise to the different traits would more properly be called the distinct nature of women, for ordinary purposes the nature of women could be taken to be the systematically related sets of properties to which these structures give rise.

That these properties are not universal is not a reason to reject the claim that they constitute a nature. This might seem surprising, but actually it accords with the approach used in taxonomy. Contrary to Aristotelian essentialism, classifications made in biology do not require that the defining characterist-

---

18   See Dinnerstein 1977; Chodorow 1977. Both are recent and important books that fit this approach, in that they argue that the near universal fact that women 'mother' (in a psychological as well as many physical ways) is the key to adult male and female personality structures. I disagree, however, with many of the specifics of the theories in particular, the primary emphasis put on early childhood and on the psychological aspects of the division of labour.

ics be individually necessary and jointly sufficient. The actual distribution of properties among organisms is such that most taxa names can be defined only disjunctively. Any of the disjuncts is sufficient, and the few necessary properties are far from sufficient. This makes most concepts of so-called natural kinds what are called 'cluster concepts'. There seems no reason to apply stricter criteria in the social sphere. The account given here of women's nature makes is just such a cluster concept.

There is, then, what Marxists would call a dialectical interaction between women's labour and their nature. The sexual/social division of labour is the cause of the distinctive cognitive-affective structures that constitute women's nature, and these structures are at least a partial cause of a variety of personality traits and behaviour distinctive of women, including the sorts of labour they do.

∴

Let me digress for a bit to consider the objection that my arguments show that it is the biological differences between men and women and not social factors that account for these personality differences. After all, it might be argued, it is the fact that women can bear and nurse children that is the basis of the sexual/social division of labour. So, even if the latter plays some causal role as well, it is not the most basic explanation.

The point is interesting but mistaken. Not every biological difference constitutes a difference in natures. It depends on how significant causally the difference is and hence how explanatory it is. We have already seen that women are not the same at all times and in all cultures and that cultures as a whole exhibit differences similar to those between men and women in most (though not all) cultures. The biological facts—just because they are universal—cannot explain these social and historical variations. A theory which could explain them would have to be social-historical theory. Thus, although it is obviously true that the sexual division of labour rests on the reproductive differences in the natures of men and women as social beings. The significance of the biological differences depends on the social-historical facts and, moreover, is maintained in every society by complicated social practices. Hence the difference in natures is primarily social and historical.

Consider this example (which I would claim to be analogous): suppose that the division of slaves into house and field workers was based entirely on the slaves' size and strength, bigger and stronger slaves becoming field workers, smaller and weaker ones becoming house workers. It is well known that there were differences in attitudes and, to some extent, personality between house and field slaves. What was the cause of these differences? Most writers point to these differences in work, working conditions, and social relations of house and field slaves. If different social conditions would have produced different psychological results then it would be mistaken to point to the physical differences as the cause—even though they were the basis on which house and field slaves were placed in their respective social conditions.

Now some might try to extend my argument and claim not only that the difference in natures between men and women are social and historical in origin but also that the very division into men and women is social and historical in origin. After all. There is an enormous physical variety among infants and among adults. And physical similarities and differences do not by themselves determine any particular division into groups. Rather it is the significance that society gives the physical characteristics that does this. Similar arguments regarding the classification of humanity into races are generally accepted today by informed people. Though interesting, this argument goes wrong in its assumption as to what constitutes a biological or 'natural' distinction as opposed to one that is social or historical in origin. Nothing is a 'given fact of nature' in the sense presupposed in the argument. It is true that it is the significance of the physical similarities and differences, rather than the physical similarities themselves, that determines a classification. Nevertheless, given that the sex difference is what allows for physical reproduction of most kinds of things, and that the distinction between things that reproduce sexually and those that reproduce by some other means is a very important one in biology, the division into two sexes has great importance for biological theory. The basis of the division into two sexes, then, is much the same as the division into species. Why should the sexual division not be called a natural distinction as well? Only if human beings were to cease to reproduce themselves sexually might the distinction between men and women cease to be of critical biological importance and hence cease to be a fundamental biological distinction. (Since they still could reproduce in the old way, however, it would still have some biological importance.) Even if that should come to pass, it would not show that until then the distinction between men and women was not a biological one. What is social and historical in origins is what is made of the distinction.

∴

It must not be forgotten that the similarities between men and women are greater than their differences. These similarities constitute their common human nature, as both biological and social beings. But within the sociohistorical category of human beings, I have argued that there are sex-differentiated natures. An individual woman will have this women's nature as part of her human nature. She is, of course, a particular woman and more than just a woman. Aside from being human, she is, among other things, of a particular social class, race, and culture. These are categories that cut across sex lines, and some will be as important as her sex or more important. Given the methodology I am using, this means that every individual has or is constituted by several natures. There is no contradiction in this. It simply shows that there are several different kinds of facts about people and that these require different sorts of explanations, however these facts and explanations are ultimately related. There need be no conflict between the different sort of explanations; different areas of a woman's behaviour can be explained by different aspects of her total nature. In certain conditions, however, there might be a conflict. A woman who is a wife and a mother and also a wage worker will have needs and propensities based on these social relations. These will sometimes conflict, such as when she has a union meeting and responsibilities at home at the same time. Particular conditions will also make a difference: if there is a strike going on she will be more likely to go to the union meeting than at other times. We should look for theories to explain under what conditions each factor will be most important, how factors interact, and how these correlations could change given other conditions. Our theories should also explain why all this is so. Different individuals may respond somewhat differently to the same factors because of the particular conditions of their lives and their particular socialisation experiences. The theories are about groups, not individuals. This is why many of the generalisations about the different social groups of which a person is a member are statistical and not universal.

It is important to make clear that the sense in which women have a distinct nature does not carry any of the usual implications of such a statement and is not fixed and inevitable; natures in this sense can change. Although there is a biological element as a part of its basis, the crucial determinants are not biological but social. (As we saw, even if it were entirely biological this would not make it inevitable. Not only can the biological facts be changed but also, much more important in the short run, their effects can be altered by human intervention.) That there is a distinct women's nature in my sense does not mean that every woman has this nature. The cluster of psychological traits that constitutes the nature of women as social beings need not belong to all biological females, though it would be an unusual woman to have none of the traits. Though a women's nature would explain some of women's behaviour (indeed is required for use of the concept of nature), it would not necessarily be more determinate than other aspects of her nature. Thus a woman could, overall, have more in common with a man who shared other aspects of her nature than with another woman with whom she shared this women's nature. Most importantly, a women's nature in this sense carries no moral implications about how a women ought or ought not to live. Whether a type of behaviour characteristic of women is morally or socially desirable is a normative issue. A further normative question is whether desirable traits should be divided up along sexual lines. Personally, I see not justification for this. In my opinion some traits more characteristic of women such as nurturance, are desirable for everyone, while others, like passivity, are undesirable for everyone. But any opinion about this would need argumentation independent of the facts about how men and women tend to behave. The existence of socially constituted sex-differentiated natures might be relevant to the normative questions but hardly decisive.

Though talk about women's nature does not, on my account, imply that it is immutable, it does imply that it is not easily changed. The Marxist conception of a thing's nature is of something underlying and explanatory of its observable behaviour. But being explanatory is not sufficient to be part of a thing's nature. Only those traits belong to a thing's nature that are systematically related, explain a variety of systematically related behaviour, and are subsumable in a theoretical framework. Such features do not easily and suddenly change. A sexual division of labour with resultant psychological sex differences has been near to universal, despite variations. Today, however, things may be changing. Only a small minority of Americans (11 percent) live in the tradition nuclear family of breadwinning father, homemaker mother, and two or more children. Forty-five percent of the work force is made up of women. On the other hand, the jobs that women do for wages tend to be related to their tradition and subordinate social role: they assist, nurse, teach, serve, and clean up after others in their wage work as well as in the home. Moreover, women still do most of the parenting and housework whether or not they do wage work.[19] How much this can change within capitalism is a complicated and controversial question. And how quickly the psychological differences between the sexes would disappear if the social differences were removed remains to be seen.

In neither capitalist nor non-capitalist societies has the entry of women into paid labour been sufficient to change traditional sex roles.[20] Although one part of the traditional sexual division of labour has changed, the most important part has not. Women are oppressed by their 'double duty' in both forms of soci-

---

19 A recent study showed that women wage workers work an average of sixty-nine hours per week (fort paid, twenty-nine unpaid), while make workers work an average of fifty-three hours per week (fort-four paid, nine unpaid). See Currie, Dunn and Fogarty 1980, pp. 7–32.
20 See Scott 1974. See also Molyneux 1982, pp. 56–100.

ety. That women working outside the home still do most of the childcare and housework has to be attributed in part to psychological differences between the sexes. Even women leading fairly untraditional lives still tend to hold many of the traditional assumptions, values, expectations, and self-conceptions on a deep level. So I do not think the psychological changes will be so rapid as to refute my talk of them as 'natures'. On the other hand, these psychological attributes seem to be very much dependent on the objective, economic power relations between men and women. Thus, in the working class, where women's wages are a higher proportion of family income than they are in the middle class, studies show that women gain more power from employment.[21] And even women working in low-level traditional women's jobs have more feminist consciousness than do full-time housewives.[22] Thus there is a basis for believing that, to the extent that the sexual division pf labour in society was reduced or eliminated, psychological sex differences would follow suit. As these social changes occur we are likely to see contradictions develop in the psychic structures of men and women. Using 'contradiction' in the Marxist sense of structures with incompatible tendencies, the presence of contradictions in periods of change is perfectly consistent with the idea that these structures constitute natures. The difficulty of changing male and female natures does not imply that we should not try to change them. On the contrary, if they are judged to be undesirable, as I believe they are, the difficulty of change would entail that extra efforts ought to be made.

∴

In the concluding section of this article I should like to explore a contrast between Marx's approach to human nature and my approach to women's nature. Although my perspective has been based on Marx's theory of human nature, there is an interesting difference on one point. The fact that human beings cannot, under capitalism, fulfil certain capacities unique to human beings is taken by many Marxists (and Marx) to be a criticism of capitalism. The fact that these aspects of their nature will be fully realized only in socialism and communism is taken to be a key reason why socialist and communist are in some sense better than all previous ones. Yet I have rejected any normative implications of my account of women's nature. Why is it good that human beings should fulfil their nature or aspects of their nature? And if it is good, why

---

21   See Bahr 1974.
22   Marx Ferree 1976, pp. 431–41.

doesn't it follow that women should fulfil their natures too? Or is this Marxist-feminist position I have developed lacking in any consistent theoretical basis? It says that natures should be developed when I like what is part of the natures and rejects the idea when I don't like the natures.

I think there is a consistent theoretical reason for the difference on this point. It is true that of the different historical forms of human nature, such as those feudalism, capitalism, and socialism/communism, Marx evinces a preference for the last. He often talks as if it is better than this nature should be realized and even, at times, that it is in some sense more truly human nature. What underlies this preference is not that this human nature is unique to human beings or that it differs most from the nature of other species. There is no particular reason why a group or person should develop what is unique or special to it. Rather, Marx's preference has to do with freedom conceived as the power to act on one's own belief and desires. In Marx's theory, consciousness, and much of what is taken to be human nature, is formed by the social system in which people live. This is not to say that it is formed in every detail or that human beings are more passive producers of their society. It is to say that the broad outlines, the limits, are set by the mode of production and one's place in it. Until the institution of socialism/communism, the mode of production is not under the control of people who live under it; social relations are exploitative and oppressive. Under socialism/communism, social relations are not exploitative because the mode of production is under conscious collective control. This means that the social determinants of human nature are under control. Consequently there is a basis for saying that the needs, wants, and capacities that constitute the human nature of socialism and communism are acquired more freely than are those that constitute the human nature of other epochs.

There is another reason—also having to do with freedom—why Marx had a preference for the human nature of socialism and communism. As we have seen, of all the different features of a species, Marx emphasized the characteristic form of life activity as key to the nature of the species. Free, conscious activity is a transhistorical capacity of human being that is unique to them, but it is only fully developed and realized in socialism and communism. Only when social need is the basis of production and production is under conscious collective control will there be a significant reduction of necessary labour time, beyond which, Marx says, 'begins that development of human energy which is a need in itself, the true real, of freedom'. He refers to this sort of labour which is only possible for most people under socialism and communism as 'self-realization, objectification of the subject, hence real freedom'.[23]

---

23   Marx 1974, p. 820; Marx 1973, p. 611.

Thus the human nature of socialism and communism can be said to be more free than that of previous societies in two senses: first, a key aspect of this human nature is the expression of freedom, and second, the determinants of many other aspects of human nature are under people's conscious, collective control for the first time. For this reason and because it is the most developed form of what is peculiar to human beings, Marx sometimes referred to it as the most truly human nature.[24] A higher value is put on a society in which human nature takes this form of freedom is a basic value.

The women's nature discussed in this paper is disanalogous to human nature in many respects. Most important is the fact that, while there will always be a distinctive human nature, even in socialism/communism, it seems unlikely that there will always be a distinct women's nature. Except as a remnant of the past, there seems little reason to think that there would still be a women's nature in socialism/communism, either the present one or one specific to that society. The biological differences between men and women would remain, but this does not constitute a difference in nature for reasons discussed earlier. Moreover, the biological differences do not by themselves determine the present psychological difference between men and women. Rather, it is the sexual/social division of labour and the resulting sexually differentiated social relations and socialisation that explain the differences. In Marx's theory this is determined not by biology but primarily by oppressive social, economic, and historical conditions which are not present in socialism/communism. Socialism/communism for Marx is a society of self-governing producers, the self-emancipation of the working class. Since this can come into being and survive only with the full participation of both sexes, a struggle for women's liberation is integral to the struggle for socialism. Furthermore, in a socialist society in Marx's sense there is no economic basis for women's oppression as there is in capitalism. While there might be some lingering material psychological basis in the advantages to men, the nature both of a successful struggle for socialism and of a genuinely socialist society would substantially reduce the strength, efficacy and longevity of such tendencies.

Now it is not impossible that the biological differences between men and women would still produce psychological differences under socialism/communism. Free, conscious activity will not take the same concrete form for everyone, and it is possible that these forms will differ along social lines. However,

---

24 Although this way of thinking is quite understandable, it should not be taken as negating the more relativistic analysis given earlier in the paper. For a fuller discussion of some of these issues, though with a more universalistic interpretation of Marx's theory of human nature, see Chapter 8 of this book.

since there does not appear to be a direct biological-psychological link now, why should there be then? One could say that there would always have to be some differences in men's and women's experience of themselves as physical beings, but exactly what this means or how one would determine it is somewhat obscure. In any case, unless they were expressed in social practices and institutions, such differences, if they existed, would not have the kind of importance that would warrant speaking of them as distinct men's and women's natures. The sexual and reproductive choices women make would not have the kind of profound social consequences for women as opposed to men that they do now. So women's needs and interests, in this central and currently sex-differentiated realm, would differ very little from men's.

As we saw, the reason Marx gave a preference to the human nature of socialism and communism is that it is more freely acquired than previous forms of human nature, and freedom is a key constituent of human nature. Neither of these considerations applies to the present (and past) sex-related natures. Freedom is not a constituent of (present and past) sex-related natures, and there is no abscess for saying that they were freely acquired. There is little reason to think that what is truly unique to women, bearing children, is what they would freely choose to do more than anything else. The biological differences are the abscess, along with economic, social, and historical conditions, for the sexual/social division of labour and the resulting social relations—none of which are under their control. Thus the psychological sex differences that result and that constitute sex-differentiated natures are not under their control. Furthermore, ignoring the legal restrictions that exist or that have been lifted only recently, women's traditional social role and the nature associated with it involves less freedom than men's. Being a wife and mother is supposed to be women's primary aim and self-definition, and the traits desirable for women are those that make them better able to fulfil this role-being attractive to men and able to satisfy a family's needs. Leaving aside for the moment the question of whether this life is inherently less challenging and empowering than most men's lives (hence less free in Marx's sense), the point is that this is only one choice. And though, obviously, as many men are fathers as women are mothers, men are first and foremost doctors, lawyers, tailors, and sailors. Unless this is what women would be inclined to do anyway, this implies that there are greater social pressures on women than on men. When women do take on other jobs, they are still constrained by the traditional values and expectations. Standing in the way of women's wholehearted pursuit of other options are not only the objective constraints of sex discrimination and family responsibilities but, in addition, their own conflicting feelings of obligation, conflicting desires, and even habits (for example, spending a lot of time on their personal appearance).

Women's lives are less free than men's are both because they are dependent on men and because they have children dependent on them. Traditional sexual values constrain women more than they do men. And women, being as a rule more passive oriented to other people's wishes than men are, are less able to act to realize their own desires. In all these ways the present women's nature lacks the freedom involved in the human nature of socialism/communism as envisioned by Marx.

But any women's nature or indeed any sex-differentiated nature would lack this freedom. Indeed there is a contradiction in the very idea of a society in which human nature distinctive of socialism/communism and this distinctive women's nature are both fully realized. Women (and men) are human beings. They could not simultaneously realize a limited nature determined by limiting social conditions and a nature whose essence is freedom. By definition, any sex-differentiated nature would be more limited than one not so differentiated. And while there is nothing that absolutely precludes sex-differentiated natures from being freely acquired, there seem very good empirical grounds for rejecting the idea that they could be.

CHAPTER 11

Humankind(s)

Just as the differentiation of human beings from other species has traditionally been thought to be based on some common essence or nature,[1] so has the division of humankind into certain groups, in particular, men and women and races, been thought to be based on their distinct natures. There are many similarities between the concepts of human nature, 'women's nature' (what we now call gender) and race, and how these concepts have functioned ideologically: For all three, the traditional idea was that there were fixed, natural essences determining the cognitive, moral, and emotional traits and abilities of the group in question. Some, e.g., Plato, and Herrnstein in recent years, have applied the idea to different social classes as well. I will call this view essentialism, and note that it is compatible with various metaphysical analyses. One could be opposed to metaphysical essentialism, but accept essences in this sense, as, for example, Hume did.[2] These essences have been used to explain and also, explicitly or implicitly, to justify existing hierarchical social relations of class, sex, and race. In the past century, the 'naturalness' of essences had been understood to consist in their being biologically determined, and science has been brought in to justify social hierarchies. Because of the political use to which the idea of essences or essential natures has been put, most social critics have taken an anti-essentialist position on all three concepts, though some have embraced essentialism and tried to use it for liberatory ends.[3]

What I will do in this paper is examine the debates among social critics surrounding the concepts of human nature, gender, and race. I will argue that despite their similarities, there are important and interesting differences in the

---

1 I wish to thank the other participants in the conference *Biology, Behavior, and Society: An Interdiscipliny Conference on the Social Sciences and Biology* at the University of Alberta, Edmonton, AB, 10–12 May 1991, especially Bob Ware, for their comments on an earlier version of this paper, which was given there. Thanks also to Johanna Brenner and Nancy Romer.
2 See Hume 1870, p. 123. 'I am apt to suspect the Negroes to be naturally inferior to the White'. Indeed, some have argued that the empiricism of Locke and Hume helped to justify racism, while the essentialism of Cartesian dualism makes it conceptually more difficult. See Bracken 1973, p. 116. Bracken 1978. Chomsky 1973.
3 The words 'natures' and 'natural' are extraordinarily slippery and sloppy. In this context, however, 'natures' is usually used synonymously with essences and that is how I will be using it; to mean something fixed, universal, and natural (today understood to mean biologically based), that determines the cognitive, moral, and emotional traits of the group.

usefulness of these concepts. Those differences appear in the ways they have been used and the debates surrounding them, and have to do with the differing importance of the biological and social realities the concepts address. It seemed to me in thinking about the concepts that each was examined more clearly in relation to the other two. In addition to the relative importance of the biological and the social, certain other general issues run through the debates: whether significant differences (of whatever sort) within a group make it impossible to generalize usefully about the group (i.e., whether generalisations imply some universal that precludes or makes one inevitably insensitive to differences). My answer is no. Sometimes this is a theoretical worry; in other contexts it is a political one about the necessary basis for unity. The debates surrounding all three concepts often mix theoretical, methodological, and normative issues; one of the things I try to do is to distinguish among them. My conclusions—commonsensical to me, but highly contentious—are that (a) there is such a thing as human nature and it is biologically based; (b) it is not clear whether there is such a thing as gender that differentiates men and women, but they are differentiated by sex; (c) races do not exist. Since entire books have been written about every aspect of every one of these concepts, what I can do here will necessarily be very sketchy.

∴

Few topics have aroused as much interest and controversy throughout the history of human thought as that of human nature. Philosophers, scientists, and ordinary people have puzzled over what human nature is like, what difference it makes and whether there is any such thing at all. I'm going to examine the controversy regarding human nature in and around the Marxist field, since advocates of a cooperative and egalitarian society have always been met with objections based on a view of human nature as egoistic, competitive, and aggressive, characteristics supposedly fixed and biologically determined.[4] This Hobbesian view has found support in various scientific theories, most notably Social Darwinism and today's Sociobiology, by which I mean E.O. Wilson's

---

4   In this context, the question of how to understand and whether to accept the concept of a human nature is part of a larger debate, humanism vs. anti-humanism, which is about whether history must be understood (at least partially) in terms of human purposes, and if so, whether they are collective or individual; or instead, understood solely in terms of the structures, the social relations, in which people act. Although the issues and positions overlap considerably, I will be concentrating on the narrower, more fundamental question. For a history of the debate see Soper 1986.

thesis that 'all human behaviours, social relationships, and organization are genetically encoded adaptations'.[5] Marx and Engels subjected the Hobbesian view of human nature to withering criticism, as not only reactionary but circular, since it projected onto nature features of capitalist society which it then claimed were justified because they were natural.[6] Much the same arguments have been given against Sociobiology by scientists and philosophers in exacting detail, so I will not repeat these critiques here.[7] Nevertheless, biological determinist theories of human nature have enjoyed a considerable revival in the past thirty years, and are probably hegemonic today.[8]

But while rejecting conservative characterisations of human nature, did Marx nevertheless himself accept a theory of human nature—in his mature as well as his early work? Though very controversial, in my mind, the 'ayes' in this debate clearly have it.[9] More important, however, and equally debated among Marxists, is the question whether Marx should have accepted a theory of human nature: is it consistent with his theory? is it a useful concept? (And, of course, in exactly what does the concept consist?) This debate has pretty much the same people lining up on the same sides, with Althusser the most influential exponent in the Marxist camp of an anti-humanist view of history and society, and Norman Geras, the British political theorist, providing, in my opinion, the most articulate defence on the left of the concept of

---

5   Bleier 1984. Bleier uses a capital 'S' for the Wilsonian version to distinguish it from the general study of the social behaviour of animals.
6   Though great admirers of Darwin, nevertheless, they held that 'the whole Darwinist teaching of the struggle for existence is simply a transference from society to living nature of Hobbes' doctrine of *bellum omnium contra omnes* and of the bourgeois-economic doctrine of competition together with Malthus' theory of population. When this conjurer's trick has been performed ... the same theories are transferred back again from organic nature into history and it is now claimed that their validity as eternal *laws* of human society has been proved. The puerility of this procedure is so obvious that not a word need be said about it' (Engels, 1875).
7   See, among others, Gould 1977; Caplan 1978; Lewontin, Rose, Kamin 1984.
8   Richard A. Schweder, reviewing Carl Degler's *In Search of Human Nature* writes: '[Degler] argues that the Darwinian concepts of instinct, heredity, and biological explanations of behaviour are back—this time without the racism, without the sexism, without the eugenics and without recourse to the legend of the inherent inferiority of the uncivilized and the poor. I suspect Mr. Degler is half right—biology is back' (Schweder 1991).
9   Everyone conceded he accepted a notion of human nature in his discussions of alienation in *The Economic and Philosophical Manuscripts*, but many, most famously Louis Althusser, claimed there was an 'epistemological break' between Marx's earlier humanistic, philosophical writings and his mature scientific work, noting the absence of 'humanistic' language in *Capital*. This view lost all credibility with the publication in English of the notebooks for *Capital*, known as *The Grundrisse*, in which all the early language reappears.

human nature.[10] Recently, post-structuralism has entered the debate regarding humanism with a fundamental rejection of both sides, since according to many post-structuralists, even Althusser would be a humanist because he accepts a notion of truth and rationality which they reject. For reasons of space, as well as the self-defeating character of the 'anti-rational' position, I shall not address this basic disagreement, but the influence of post-structuralism will be heard in some of what follows.

First the arguments against the concept of human nature: typically, a blend of the metaphysical, methodological, and political. In brief, the claim is that a concept of human nature—invariant, transhistorical, decontextualized—is simply too abstract to be meaningful because people always come embedded in a mode of production, a culture, a class, etc. The idea of a real essence underlying all of that is idealist. If this underlying essence is supposed to be biological, the problem is that human beings have always lived in society and everything characteristically human has been acquired in social interaction. So how could we know what was 'underlying' all forms of social life, and why would we want to, anyway? Instead, the argument stresses the changing nature of human beings due to changing social relations.[11] Some writers who deny human nature simultaneously affirm invariant biological needs and capacities. They are reluctant to use the phrase 'human nature' because of its conservative political associations, but also because the biological, in their view, has no existence apart from the social. Furthermore, they hold that whatever constants there are, are unimportant for understanding history and society. What's important, in this view, are the variations, the changes, and the social relations that transform and explain them: for example, what, how, and why different human beings eat what they do, rather than that we all must eat.[12] (Some rejec-

---

10   Some of those taking anti-humanist position are Althusser 1969; Althusser and Balibar 1970; Tucker 1961; Venable 194; Hook 1962; Suchting 1979; Seve 1978. For a defence of humanism see Geras 1983. Some others who take up the defence are Collier 1978; Heller 1976; Olman 1971; Soper 1986; Cohen 1978. They do not all agree about the precise content or its role in Marx's theories; Cohen, for example, gives it a larger explanatory role in historical materialism than some others.

11   In an earlier statement of this position, Sidney Hook said, 'If one must speak of 'the essence of man', one must find it in man's civilization, material, and ideal, and not in biology' (Hook 1936, pp. 297–8).

12   See Mepham 1973; Soper 1979. See also Holmstrom 1984, pp. 456–73. In the latter, I argued that Marx rejected the idea of a transhistorical human nature, but accepted the idea of historically specific forms of human nature (what I am calling here 'the nature of human beings'). What appears to be a substantive difference between that paper and this one is more a difference of terminology and emphasis, since I accepted the idea that human

tions of human nature are so nuanced they may be merely terminological.)[13] Moreover, many of these critics argue, this supposedly neutral view of human beings as such actually incorporates characteristics of the dominant culture, gender, class, etc., as, for example, in Hobbes.[14] In the name of a universal, it denies all particularities but one. The abstract individual of liberal theory is actually the white bourgeois male.

Marxists who defend the importance of a concept of human nature accept the truth and the importance of a great deal of what the critics say, but they reject the conclusion. While agreeing that theories of human nature have usually played a conservative political role, they argue that not all theories of human nature must do so. Nor need the idea of invariant features of human beings be idealist or abstract in some objectionable sense, even if they usually have been. Certainly the concept is an abstraction, but so is the concept of the environment or social change, which critics of human nature are happy to use. To be a useful concept does not at all require that what it is a concept to be ontologically distinct from everything else—whatever exactly that would be. Marx used the concepts of religion and government although he explicitly denied they had an independent existence. Nor need the concept of invariant human needs and capacities be understood as excluding or necessarily underemphasising the specific forms they take due to changing social conditions and relations. Indeed, Marx is most plausibly understood as offering a theory integrating the two. To avoid confusion, I will use the terms 'human nature' to designate (relatively) invariant features of human beings and 'the nature of human beings' in a broader sense to include both variant and invariant features.

---

beings had a nature *qua biological beings*, but used 'human nature' to refer to their nature *qua social beings*.

13   Consider the following remarks by the distinguished biologists Richard Levins and R.L. Lewontin, who also happen to be Marxists: 'If ideas of human nature have any value, they must be able to cope with such biologically basic functions as eating. Eating is obviously related to nutrition, but in humans this physiological necessity is embedded in a complex matrix: *within which* what is eaten, whom you eat with, how often you eat, who prepares the food, which foods are necessary for a sense of well-being, who goes hungry and who overeats have all been torn loose from the requirements of nutrition or the availability of food... A study of the physical act itself, its biological preconditions, its evolution, its similarity to that behaviour in other animals, or the regions of brain that influence it will simply be irrelevant to the human phenomenon' (Levins and Lewontin 1985, pp. 260–3). The example brings to mind Marx's statement that 'Hunger is hunger, but the hunger gratified by cooked meat is a different hunger from that which bolts down raw meat with the aid of hand, nail, and tooth' (Marx 1972, p. 92).

14   See Soper, 1986. Sopher demonstrates how often political debates have been played on this philosophical terrain.

Not only are human beings always embedded in variable social relations, as critics of the concept of human nature emphasize, but they are always embodied. They are biological beings and, simultaneously and essentially, social beings, in that their biological needs and capacities bind them into relations with others. Certainly scientists need to abstract and focus on that aspect of human beings appropriate to their study, but in order to understand the being from which it has been abstracted, much less to understand the importance for human beings of what is being studied, these aspects must be integrated into a coherent conception of the human being. Marx stressed the social and economic, as opposed to the political and ideal, or, on the other hand, the biological, first of all, because the social and economic had been omitted entirely in the dominant idealist or physical reductionist theories, respectively, and he bent over backwards in the opposite direction; but second, because he was interested in explaining history, social change, to which he believed changing social and economic conditions were key. But he did not deny other factors any explanatory role. Indeed, the biological *is* foundational to Marx's theory. This, however, does not mean the biological has epistemological primacy or greater explanatory power. Radical scientists and scientifically minded philosophers, almost all of whom reject reductionism, have discussed various alternative ways of conceptualising the relations between the biological (and physical/ chemical) and the social, one of the most popular being to understand them as non-hierarchical levels of explanation.[15]

But however precisely relations between the different aspects of human history are best understood, Marx made clear that the first premise of his view of history is the existence of living individuals with a certain physical constitution, that is, certain invariant needs and capacities. While the theory of historical materialism is, in part, about how human beings change given changes in their social relations of production brought about by their own labour, nevertheless he stressed the fundamental material needs to eat, have shelter, and the like as the bases of history.[16] Despite all the variations in what individuals eat and why (a function both of their society and their particular place in it), people need a certain minimum number of calories per day or they will die or suffer ill health. That minimum will vary due to factors such as physical condition, labour, and climate, but when the power relations of a society enter into this

---

15   See Rose 1981. A sympathetic critique and alternative is given by Barker 1981. See also Timpanaro 1970, on the importance of biology for Marxism.
16   'By ... acting on the external world and changing it, [man] at the same time changes his own nature'. (Marx 1967, p. 177). Engels suggested labour was key not only to the development *of* human beings, but also to the development *to* human beings. See Engels 1934.

determination, as they do, for example, in the belief in many parts of the world that women need less food than men do, this is simply refuted by the resulting greater rates of malnutrition for women. Moreover, even for those needs that developed only given certain productive forces and relations, 'the very fact', Geras writes, 'that [human beings] entertain this sort of relations, the fact that they produce and have a history, [Marx] explains in turn by their general and constant, intrinsic, constitutional characteristics; in short by their human nature. The concept is therefore indispensable to his historical theory'.[17] Within this integrated (some call it dialectical) conception of human beings, context and human purposes (what we want to explain and what we want to do about it) should determine which aspect should be emphasized when.

Humans share many capacities with non-humans, eating and procreating, for example, but these can take distinctly human forms, and increasingly do so with the development of the environment and humans' relations to it. Even the senses undergo this sort of transformation. In Marx's words, 'Man's musical ear is only awakened by music... The cultivation of the five senses is the work of all previous history'.[18] But of all the distinctly human capacities, the capacity to labour in a purposive way, not only from necessity, is particularly important to Marx.[19] He singles out this particular capacity as central to human nature because it is the key to historical and cultural development, which increasingly differentiates human beings from other animals.[20] The kind of labour that makes this possible would find its fullest expression in a society of freely associated producers, first of all because more individuals would be able to engage in free purposive activity than in any other society. But second, because in such a society labour would be purposive on a collective basis as well; the producers organize social production according to a democratic and rational plan instead of being ruled by it. So the nature of human beings changes to become, as Marx sees it more distinctly human. However, this is not because the human essence is finally freed from repression or because it is the telos of human history, as critics have claimed (correctly so with respect to some Marxist humanist writers), but rather, just because it is the most developed expression of what is distinctly human. Now this social/historical development is dependent on—

---

17   Geras 1983, p. 67.
18   Marx 1964, p. 161.
19   Marx 1972, p. 178.
20   'Men can be distinguished from animals by consciousness, by religion or anything else you like. *They themselves begin to distinguish themselves from animals* as soon as they begin to *produce* their means of subsistence, a step which is conditioned by their physical organization' (Marx 1978, p. 150.) My emphasis.

but not determined by—a particular feature of human biology—the brain. As Stephen Jay Gould explains, 'Human uniqueness resides primarily in our brains and in the flexibility of what our brains can do. It is expressed in the culture built upon our intelligence and the power it gives us to manipulate the world'.[21] Thus there is no inconsistency between emphasising social change and variability and rooting this in a relatively invariant biological constitution. On the contrary, it is our particular biological constitution, that is, our human nature that makes possible the changed nature of human beings.

Turning to the moral/political aspect of the controversy, it is clear that for Marx, this transformation of the nature of human beings through the development of their distinctive capacities, is an achievement with a high moral value. He refers to the full development of human creative powers as 'an end in itself' which he also calls the 'true realm of freedom', and refers to the conditions under which the associated producers organize conditions as 'most worthy of their human nature'. Despite its utopian elements, Marx's conception of self-realisation is, minimally, a plausible basis for a conception of the good life for human beings, as something each individual can aim for and many can at least partially achieve.[22] But Marx also used the concept of human nature for a more direct and simple normative purpose—to critique modes of production which do not satisfy human needs.[23] If it were impossible to speak of invariant human needs, i.e. human nature, if all needs were socially determined, then how could one make sense of a society's not meeting human needs? Even if some of the needs not satisfied in capitalism are the product of capitalism itself, such as, perhaps, the need for creative work, the most fundamental criticism Marxists make of capitalism is that even the most elementary needs for food and shelter are not met for much of the population of even the most developed capitalist societies—as we can see on the streets of our major cities. So although certain views of human nature function to support conservative political value, other conceptions provide a foundation for radical political critiques. Thus while rejecting conservative views of human nature I also reject the arguments of many left thinkers that there is no such thing as human nature. Versus leftists, there is; and it is biologically based. Versus conservatives, it does not have the content—egoistic and so forth—they usually give it; nor does it explain

---

21 Gould 1981, pp. 326; 331.
22 See Marx 1973, p. 611. See also Elster 1989.
23 Included in the concept of human needs are both things necessary for survival and things necessary for satisfaction, such as varied and challenging work. Note that this does not correspond to the distinction between biological and non-biological needs; sex is not necessary for survival at the level of the individual.

as much as they try to make it explain. This is because biological determinism is false; the biological aspects of human beings are always intrinsically interconnected with the social. A related fallacy of biological determinist theories, Stephen Jay Gould explains, is that they are theories of limits rather than potentials. As discussed earlier, the flexibility of the human brain allows human beings to adapt to different circumstances, most importantly, to both create and adapt to different sets of social relations, being more egoistic in some, and more cooperative in others. The overall nature of human beings changes in different social conditions just because, not in spite of, a biologically based human nature. Thus critics of hierarchical societies do not need to fear the idea of a biologically based human nature, but rather those who have controlled that idea. Rather than human nature precluding cooperative and egalitarian relations between people, it is human biology, on the contrary, that creates the possibility of human liberation.[24] Actually achieving it depends on other things.

∴

Ideas of women's nature or essence have functioned historically in much the same way that ideas of human nature usually have, viz. to explain and to justify existing social hierarchies: in this case, men's domination of women.[25] To speak of the nature of woman is, of course, to imply something about the nature of man, i.e. males. But as the ambiguity of the word 'man' reveals, men's nature has simply been equated with human nature while women have been defined as the Other, and their nature problematized. Both Aristotle and Kant, to take just two examples from the long and sorry history of philosophers' opinions regarding women, thought women were not complete persons. In Aristotle's view, this was because they were not fully rational; and in Kant's, because they were incapable of acting on principles. The pattern of reasoning throughout the centuries has been this: biological differences between the sexes lead to psychological differences, which lead to behavioural differences; and these are

---

24   See Barker 1981.
25   As I flag in the introduction to this volume, I wrote 'Humankind(s)' in 1991 before transsexual/transgender issues were commonly discussed. Today Trans Philosophy and Trans Studies are found in many academic departments. While I believe that my denial that sex determines gender was fundamentally compatible with thinking about transsexual/transgender issues, and affirming the legitimacy of transgender identities, when putting together this collection I was unsure how what I had written would accord with current language and sensibilities. For useful current philosophy articles see work by Talia Mae Bettcher, a philosopher and trans woman. In particular, see Mae Bettcher 2020; Antony 2020; Gleeson and O'Rourke 2021; Miles 2021.

the bases of hierarchical social roles based on sex. The concept of women's nature or essence is best interpreted as referring to these distinctive psychological traits. Though allegedly rooted in their biology and frequently conflated with it, women's nature cannot be simply identified with their biology. Otherwise, since women are by definition different biologically from men, to say that women have a distinct nature from men would be a tautology.

Feminists deny that women's and men's 'natures' account for the hierarchical relations between them, and usually deny the existence of any such essences. Feminists introduced the concept of gender, as distinct from sex, to clarify such facts as that, in our society, a woman can fail to be 'a real woman', even if she is the mother of several children. Gender is constituted by norms about how a person of a given sex is supposed to behave, think, and feel that can be called rules, since one is punished for violating them. Gender is also constituted by institutions and relations within institutions, e.g. the family; and more broadly, the sexual division of labour within society. Many feminists believe that these produce characteristic psychological and behavioural differences between men and women—and these differences are also understood as gender.

There is no necessary connection between sex and gender; a person can fail to have the psychological/behavioural traits (the gender) characteristic of their sex. Nor is there any necessary connection between sex, gender, and sexuality, that is to say, desire. While some formulations of the sex/gender distinction present the biological as an underlying substratum untouched by society, and gender as pure culture, laid on top of an inert biology (and some reject the distinction for just this reason), it should be clear from section I of this paper that this is not my understanding. Not only physical differences like musculature, but even facts about our reproductive capacities, e.g., when puberty and menopause occur, are historically and socially quite variable. So even our bodies are—in part—socially constructed. And certainly how men and women experience their bodies is socially and culturally variable. When de Beauvoir said, 'women are made, not born', she captured the sex/gender distinction and implied that gender is an ongoing social creation.[26]

---

26   Judith Butler interprets her as making the more radical claim that sex is socially constructed as well, thereby collapsing the sex/gender distinction. See Butler, 1986. Butler and other postmodern thinkers take de Beauvoir as an inspiration for their claim that gender is something of a performance, something one *does* as opposed to something one *is*. This is surely a false counterposition, unless one restricts what one *is* to biologically based essences. See also Butler 1990.

But many find feminists' social account of gender hard to swallow. Because there are biological differences between the sexes, it might be supposed that there would always be some psychological sex differences, specifically regarding sex and reproduction, even if not any particular ones. And it just seems commonsensical to suppose that these would play an important determining role in behaviour. Hence gender is ineliminable, even if any particular gender differences might be otherwise. And why should one be afraid of that possibility? After all, differences aren't necessarily inequalities and nothing follows about how we ought to treat men and women, even if the differences were inequalities.[27] It is true and very important that no normative conclusions follow automatically from psychological sex differences. And perhaps there would always be some such differences; we will have to await non-sexist social relations to find out. However, the most important problem in all biological explanations of gender differences is this: in order to know that there are biological factors pushing in the same direction as the social we would have to find some way to tease out the biological factors from all the others and determine their relative contribution, a feat quite beyond scientific capability now and in the foreseeable future. The fact is we have ample evidence of the different social/ environmental influences on men and women—evidence that is sufficient to account for whatever psychological and behavioural sex differences exist. Unless some reason is given to discount those factors, the principle of methodological simplicity bids us to reject the biological account.[28]

Moreover, as far as the existence of gender itself is concerned, as opposed to particular gender differences, the real question is the importance—theoretical and political—of any differences. Why should we suppose that psychological differences between the sexes, if they should turn out to exist, would inevitably lead to a whole host of other psychological and behavioural differences; and further, that there would be social roles based on these differences? This would happen only if the society gave a certain meaning and importance to sex differences. But even within our own society, where gender is so terribly important, the differences within each gender are greater than between the genders. The crucial point is that gender involves a number of systematically related differences between the sexes that have some structured social import-

---

27 See Midgeley 1988. Similar arguments are made regarding racial differences.
28 I take John Stuart Mill to be offering this sort of argument in *The Subjection of Women*, when he says 'I deny that anyone knows, or can know, the nature of the two sexes, as long as they have only been seen in their present relation to one another', although he can also be interpreted as taking an agnostic position (Mill 1911, p. 45).

ance. There simply are not good reasons to think that this can all be accounted for by biological differences between the sexes.

The description I have just given of the sex/gender distinction puts me on one side of what has been described as the great divide within feminism. (Actually, there are many—crisscrossing—divides within feminism, but this may be the biggest.) The conviction that men and women do not differ by nature, but rather share common needs and capacities, was the dominant feminist view until quite recently, cutting across political differences. But this was never the only voice, and as feminist thinking has evolved, this perspective may no longer be hegemonic.[29] One reason many women rejected it is that they started to notice that the conceptions of a universal human nature were all implicitly male in that they included qualities traditionally associated with men, like instrumental rationality, or in de Beauvoir's case, autonomy and aggression, and excluded qualities associated with women, like nurturance and emotionality. Furthermore, women's biology was often presented as an intrinsic obstacle to the realisation of their fully human potential. My response to this androcentric bias is simply to urge that formulations of human nature give equal status to traits traditionally associated with women. In a non-sexist society, all these common human potentialities would be developed by each individual in his/her own unique way, including some of the ways called masculine or feminine in earlier societies. Of course 'simply eliminating sexist bias' is easier said than done, since sexism is lodged not only in our institutions but in our very psyches, but the point is that the idea of a human nature shared by men and women is not inherently sexist. On the contrary, it is a conceptual obstacle to sexism.

But other feminists simply 'don't want to be like men' and react strongly against the depreciation of women's bodies and lives in some feminist thinking. Instead of minimising gender differences, these feminists embrace them.[30] Their critique, then, is of the hierarchical character of gender roles rather than of gender roles per se. While new to many of us, there was always a strong strain within feminism that accepted the conventional stereotypes of masculinity and femininity but reversed the masculine evaluation of them. The Suffragettes who argued that when women got the vote, their special needs and insights would lead to an end to war and a more caring society are the ancestors of

---

29 This perspective is variously known as equity, humanist, scientific, and minimizing feminism, depending on the details of the theory, the context, and who is doing the naming.

30 Depending on the details of their theories, the context and who is describing them, feminists on this side of the divide are known as maximizers, gynocentric, cultural, romantic, and difference feminists.

the women's peace and ecology activists today.³¹ Some of the disagreement between the two camps is political/strategic, over such issues as whether to support maternity leave or a gender neutral disability leave policy. Some feminists have worried that to support equality for two groups in conditions of real inequality will only increase the inequality. In the course of defending special treatment for women, some of these feminists have been led to embrace essentialist accounts of women's roles (although this does not logically follow). Not surprisingly, there is a strong tendency toward biological determinism on this side of the feminist divide. Cultural feminists like Mary Daly focus on what they believe to be inherent differences in male and female sexuality.³² Adrienne Rich contends that women's reproductive functions make them better able to realize a uniquely human potential of rationality and physicality, than men.³³ Even socialist feminist Mary O'Brien, while stressing that human biology cannot be separated from consciousness, nevertheless theorizes that male dominance arises from men's need to compensate for their inability to give birth.³⁴ Though few are as crudely biological as Susan Brownmiller, who argues that rape follows inevitably from male anatomy, an emphasis on universal male/female differences cannot easily avoid biological determinism.³⁵ However, biological determinist theories are no less problematic scientifically in feminist hands than anywhere else. And given that biological sex does not inevitably determine gender, i.e. sex-differentiated psychological traits, gender roles necessarily conflict with individual self development and freedom, since they prescribe what an individual ought to do simply because of his/her sex, regardless of whether he/ she has the desires and capacities prescribed for her sex.³⁶ (This is why women's oppression is properly called 'sexism', and not 'genderism', as has occasionally been suggested.)

---

31 Similarly, social purity feminists of the nineteenth century had quite similar theories and politics to today's Women Against Pornography. See Walkowitz 1983.
32 Daly 1978.
33 Rich 1986.
34 O'Brien 1981.
35 Brownmiller 1981.
36 'The ultimate goal of liberation movements ... is ... to dismantle these structures [of domination] and so release the energies of each individual for the work of active (as opposed to reactive) self-definition. In this sense a universalist politics, far from leading to 'essentialism', calls into question every 'essence' arising from social arrangements which could be amended through collective choice' (Lovibond 1992, p. 193). On questions of universalism and difference as well as postmodernism in general, see also Lovibond 1989, pp. 5–28. Rorty replies to this critique in Rorty 1991, pp. 231–58.

Aside from its tendency towards biological explanations of gender differences, a more basic criticism of gender essentialism is that there may not be the two genders these theories presuppose. The literature on psychological sex differences is extraordinarily confusing; the 'experts' (even feminists) disagree and the problem of eliminating sexist bias in the research is daunting. In any case, my judgment is that the most the research shows is that with respect to certain qualities relevant to gender roles, there are statistically significant differences between the sexes. This allows, of course, that the majority of women (or men) may not have the trait in question and that an individual man might have a trait correlated with women more highly than any woman and vice versa. It is not clear whether these facts would justify speaking of two genders; perhaps it should depend on how important the specific differences are.[37] What people ordinarily have in mind is something stronger. But there are problems even with this modest conclusion regarding gender differences. The problem is that most of the findings regarding psychological sex differences are based on research in white middle class college towns in the United States. On what grounds can we assume that what is true of white middle class American women is true of women as such—or even all contemporary American women? The justification often given for not including black women in the research is that the researcher wants to exclude any factor other than sex, such as race, from affecting the findings. But that reply assumes that white women have no race. Very little research has been done exploring how gender, race, and class intersect, but what little there is suggests that supposedly gender-typical characteristics vary along both race and class lines. For example, black adolescent girls from poor and working-class families (the majority) do not accept the 'traditional' (white) version of femininity, but rather the very different values (for women) of strength and independence.[38] But this gender difference is not just relative to racial groups, for it turns out that wealthy black adolescent girls

---

37 This, however, can only be determined within a theoretical framework. For more of these explorations and a somewhat different point of view, see Holmstrom 1982, pp. 25–42.
38 Ladner 1972. A report of a recent survey regarding girls' self esteem says 'Girls emerge from adolescence with a poor self-image, relatively low expectations from life and much less confidence in themselves and their abilities than boys'. But the report reveals this is less true of black girls (Daley 1991). No class differences are reported (or studied?). The article also reports recent work by Carol Gilligan showing that girls begin to doubt themselves at adolescence, but her sample is almost entirely white and middle class. Although her new book includes a sample of black medical students, this does not eliminate the problem because the gender difference in self confidence is not just relative to racial groups, but to class as well. See Gilligan 1990.

share the white version of femininity.³⁹ And other research shows black men sharing some of the psychological traits allegedly differentiating women from men, such as fear of success.⁴⁰

If gender, then, is inseparable from other categories like race and class, are there no (nonphysical) differences between the sexes that cut across these lines? Do the categories men and women dissolve, except as biological categories? Or dissolve completely, as some postmodern thinkers would have it? This would be too hasty a conclusion, in my opinion.⁴¹ I think it is plausible to suppose that the differences in the lives of boys and girls and men and women, of whatever race and class, particularly having to do with women's role taking care of children and others, would produce statistically significant psychological differences between the sexes.⁴² However, we should not assume the role itself to be determining; the meaning this role has for a woman may vary depending on a number of factors, such as whether it is combined with other roles and what they are, and how, for whatever reasons, it is valued in her culture. What we might find is a common core of psychological traits related to gender roles found more often among women than men (and others more common to men), but that women of different (sub)cultures have different (sub)sets. If such sex differences exist, then we could speak of two genders, i.e., sex-differentiated psychological traits which are explanatory of gender roles. On the other hand, if there are useful psychological generalisations differentiating men and women only within other groups, then we could not usefully speak of two genders simpliciter. Whether there are two genders, then, is partly an empirical question and partly a theoretical one, in that we need a theoretical context to evaluate the importance of whatever generalisations we come up with. In my opinion, that there are two genders, with class and race variations, is a very plausible hypothesis.⁴³ However, that is all it is at this point.

The sort of criticism I'm raising of theories of gender should strike a familiar chord. Just as theories of human nature have been criticized as male-biased, so theories of gender have been criticized as reflecting a white middle class and heterosexual bias. Sojourner Truth's famous question 'ain't I a woman?'

---

39   Thoy 1969.
40   Weston and Mednick 1970.
41   Even a woman who does not have children may have substantial responsibilities for the care of other dependents. And she has probably been raised (primarily) by a woman and knows that she is expected to be a mother.
42   See Nancy Chodorow 1978 and Dinnerstein 1976. See also the vast literature, both critical and supportive, their work has spawned.
43   As Jerry Fodor wrote recently in a very different context, 'Good taxonomy is about *not* missing generalizations' (Fodor 1988, p. 25).

was addressed to a convention of Suffragettes; today's white feminists are being asked the same question.[44] While Marxist feminists, as well as women of colour and lesbians, have long expressed scepticism about the idea of a universal sisterhood based on a common experience as women, recently this is coming from the centre of feminist thinking, partly because of the influence of post-structuralism's deconstructive moves.[45] Although essentialism is probably dominant in the women's movement now, the trend in academic circles has shifted against it.

The anti-essentialist conclusions I have argued for are extended to sex as well as gender by some feminist thinkers, e.g., Andrea Dworkin and Monique Wittig.[46] However, instead of reducing gender to sex, these feminists reduce sex to gender. 'Gender', writes Wittig, 'created anatomical sex'.[47] Accepting a biological determinist assumption, Dworkin believes in androgyny at a social level only because she believes in it at a biological level.[48] She writes, 'If there are two distinct sexes then it is not hard to argue that there are two discrete modes of human behaviour, sex-related, sex-determined. One might argue for a liberalization of sex-based roles, but one cannot justifiably argue for their total redefinition'.[49] She believes in androgyny at the social level only because she believes in it at a biological level. New information from various sciences, she claims, challenges the idea that there are two discrete biological sexes: not that there is one, but rather, many. Her evidence for biological multi-sexuality consists of the physical, even sexual commonalities between males and females, e.g., the fact that both sexes produce male and female hormones, and the many and varied type of cross-sexed phenomena. The point is that there are several aspects of sex identity which do not always fit together; hence not everyone fits neatly into one or the other sex. These enormous physical variations among infants and adults show that it is not the physical similarities and differences by themselves that determine the division into males and females. Rather, it is

---

44 See hooks 1981; hill 1984; Smith 1983; Hull, Scott, and Smith 1982.
45 I am thinking particularly of Spelman's very valuable book *The Inessential Woman*. See Spelman 1988. Of the (mostly non-academic) writings by Marxists and women of colour, some simply rejected feminism as a bourgeois and/or white perspective; others were more sympathetic, but critiqued what they saw as a white and/or middle-class bias and called for a greater recognition, integration, and focus on the needs of working-class women and women of colour—which largely overlap.
46 Dworkin 1974; Wittig 1981, pp. 47–54; Wittig 1982, pp. 63–8; Wittig 1989, pp. 3–12. Christine Delphy takes the same line in her writings.
47 Wittig 1982, p. 144.
48 Ibid., p. 175.
49 Ibid.

the interpretation of and the significance given to the physical characteristics. People could also be divided into groups on the basis of other physical characteristics, but greater weight is given to sex-differentiated traits because the division into two and only two sexes supports the institution of heterosexuality and the interests of a heterosexist society. In Wittig's words, 'The category of sex is the political category that founds society as heterosexual'.[50]

The flaw in this position, I would argue, is not the premises, but the presupposition about how a properly scientific classification is made. Nothing is a 'given fact of nature' in the sense presupposed here. Social elements (and sometimes social prejudices) enter into decision-making in all sciences and classifications are not so neat in other areas of biology. Biologists divide animals into species not simply on the basis of physical similarities and differences, but on the importance of those features for biological theory. The Aristotelian idea of individually necessary and jointly sufficient conditions differentiating natural kinds does not hold for species any more than it does for the sexes. Most concepts of natural kinds are what have been called 'cluster-concepts', defined disjunctively. Given that the sex difference is what allows for physical reproduction of most kinds of things, and that the difference between things that reproduce sexually and asexually is a very important one in biology, the division into two sexes has great importance for biological theory. Though not nearly as important as the division into species, why should the sexual division be considered any less a natural or biological one, taking the concepts 'natural' and 'biological' here to mean something like 'the subject of biological theory'?[51] Moreover, the political importance of the revelation that supposedly natural categories like women's nature or gender are actually social in origin is greatly reduced if everything turns out to be social. So let us assume there would still be two sexes that most people fell into, even in a non-sexist and non-heterosexist society.

Although, fortunately, this does not mean there would inevitably be two genders and roles based on them, in certain social/historical contexts it makes that more likely. Some feminist theorists give too little credence to this. For example, economist Heidi Hartmann has advanced the very influential argument that when in the last century, workers managed to secure a single wage sufficient to support a family, the fact that women became full time housewives rather than sharing wage work and housework with men was not 'natural' or

---

50 Wittig 1989, p. 10.
51 It should be clear that this in no way implies that the division of people into mutually exclusive categories of heterosexual or homosexual or bisexual is a natural or biological one. This is sexuality, not sex.

inevitable, but must be explained by patriarchal ideology and the interests of working-class men in controlling women's labour. But as sociologist Johanna Brenner has replied, given the lack of adequate contraception and sanitation and the low level of household technology, it simply made more sense for women to stay home. Although sexism played a role in creating this division of labour which then made women more dependent on men, this is not a sufficient explanation. In this particular social/historical context, the reproductive difference between the sexes was also an important causal factor. An adequate explanation of the transformation of women workers into full time housewives should include social, historical, and biological factors.[52]

What are the political/ strategic implications of these thoughts on sex and gender? An important source of the tendency to essentialist thinking among feminists may be the worry that unless there is something universal to all women—whether it be their biology or their shared oppression—then there is no basis for feminism. I think this is mistaken. There are important commonalities, though they intersect with differences. Regardless of whether and how gender is manifested in the psyches of men and women, i.e., whether or not there are two genders in that sense, gender is organized socially, particularly in a division of labour along sex lines that gives women fewer choices, more work, and less power and money. The United Nations reported in 1980 that women worldwide did 2/3 of the work for 10 percent of the income and own only 1 percent of the property.

This creates a common interest in equal pay for equal and comparable work and most radically, an end to the sexual division of labour, even though these interests will manifest themselves differently in different groups and for each individual woman. And women's biological commonality creates crucial common interests, too. Whatever their race, creed, or national origin—or their gender or sexuality—women are vulnerable to rape and unwanted pregnan-

---

52   See Hartmann 1981; Hartmann 1979; Brenner and Ramas 1984. Historian Joan Scott has argued that this division of labour was not inevitable even in that period and that assumptions about women's natural and proper role played a critical determining role, pointing out that in certain locales in France there were full time childcare facilities: Scott 1988. However, I do not believe this refutes Brenner's argument. By Scott's own account, the areas with childcare facilities had serious labour shortages. In the absence of such special circumstances that would give employers and the government an interest in increasing women's labour force participation, the reproductive differences between men and women would be—in that historical context—a critical determinant of gender roles. For an important and integrative perspective on the biological and social aspects of women's lives see also Riley 1983.

cies.⁵³ Although the implications for one's life of rape and an unwanted pregnancy may vary, all women share an interest in preventing sexual violence and in having birth control and abortion available. But having abortion available simply means having it legal if one is middle class; if, on the other hand, one is poor, it also means having it publicly funded. Regrettably, the pro-choice movement has protested threats to the legality of abortion much more vigorously than it protested the cut off of federal funds for abortion or rallied around the demand for childcare the way black women have, though childcare is an equally important aspect of reproductive freedom for women. Thus women have differences as well as commonalities and a desire for unity should not lead to the sacrifice of the interests of some.⁵⁴ On the other hand, although a universalism (based either on biology or experience) has to be rejected, neither should we overlook the real—overlapping, crisscrossing, clustering—commonalities of women. As we saw in my discussion of human nature, an appreciation of differences should not preclude an appreciation of commonalities.

∴

The concept of race is comparable to the concept of gender with one crucial difference: there is nothing comparable to sex in the case of race. The term 'race' was formerly used in a broader sense than we tend to use it today, so that, e.g., English and Irish people were considered different (and easily distinguished) races, whereas today we would consider them different nationalities. As the term is usually used today, only a small number of races, usually three, would be differentiated among the human species, most particularly between so-called whites and blacks. (It used to be debated whether blacks and whites were even of the same species.) I will be focusing on how these paradigms of race concepts have functioned in the United States and will leave unexplored to the extent to which what I say is applicable to other racially defined groups. Many people, including most of the scientific community until quite recently,

---

53   Rape is not strictly a biological matter, as is the ability to become pregnant. Rape is not found in all societies and men *can* be raped. Though it is connected to the level of misogyny and violence of given societies, I see rape nevertheless as more related to women's biology than are the above-mentioned aspects of sex discrimination. The anatomical differences between the sexes make women unable to rape men, less able to prevent being raped and, of course, liable to become pregnant if they are raped.
54   An excellent discussion of what this perspective would entail organizationally/politically is found in Combahee River Statement. See Combahee River Collective 1977.

still accept the essentialist view that each race is constituted by certain heritable traits and tendencies that all and only members of that race share.[55] And these traits are held to include cognitive, moral, and emotional traits as well as physical ones. Many more people believe this to be true on average than not, though the belief is not universal.[56] But biological accounts of race were challenged almost seventy years ago by people like anthropologist Franz Boas and by progressive sociologists, and the mainstream scientific view of race came to diverge from the popular view about fifty years ago. As Richard Lewontin, Steven Rose, and Leon Kamin, distinguished scientists in the respective fields of genetics, neuroscience, and psychology, explain, the concept of race that came to be used in biology in the 1940s was 'geographical race' ... a population of varying individuals, freely mating among each other but different in average proportions of various genes from other populations'. But since, as they explain, 'every population differs slightly from every other one on the average, all local interbreeding populations are 'races' ... [hence] race really loses its significance as a concept'.[57] When the groups conventionally considered races—the populations of Africa and Europe and their descendants—are compared for genetic variation it turns out that, except for the obvious morphological features of skin, hair, and bone, there is as much genetic variation within what is conventionally considered a race as between races. So it turns out that there really are no races in the scientific sense.

Probably most people, however, believe that the division of the species into races (usually three) is a natural or biological one because they believe people can be so classified simply on the basis of 'how they look', i.e., the gross morphological features of skin colour, hair type, and facial features. Call this the 'common sense' view of race. Some take this division to be so obvious that the only reason they can imagine anyone denying it is because they worry that racist conclusions will be drawn. But since these normative conclusions do not follow from the mere fact of difference, why, they say, should one deny the obvious fact of racial difference?[58] But this is ambiguous. When one denies the scientificity of the category race, one is not denying visible physical differences

---

55 See Gould 1981; Stepan 1982; Barker 1981.
56 A recent survey by the National Opinion Research Centre found that the majority of white people in the United States consider black people inferior and a substantial minority of black people agree. E.g., 62% of whites thought blacks less likely to be hard working; 53% of whites and 30% of blacks thought blacks less intelligent. The study, however, did not ask whether respondents believed these traits to be innate or socially acquired (AP 1991.)
57 Lewontin, Rose, and Kamin 1984, p. 120.
58 Singer 1978.

between individuals and groups that are conventionally called racial, nor that people can be so divided along these lines.

However, it does not follow that such a division is a natural or scientific one. Human beings could also be divided into two races or forty (as they are in Brazil) or one hundred and ten on the basis of these characteristics, and so could be divided into some small number of size/shape groups.[59] The arbitrariness is less obvious to us when it is based on colour primarily because we are used to it, because ours is a racist culture. The belief that colour and facial features indicate an important difference in nature because of their connections to cognitive and moral qualities has served to rationalize the differences in power correlated with colour. Notice that this argument against the scientificity of race is the same argument I rejected regarding the naturalness of sex differentiation. The difference, I contend, is the scientific usefulness of the concepts. Since we now know that differences in skin colour no more reflect genetic differentiation between the groups defined on this basis than do differences in height or weight, 'any use of racial categories must take its justification from some other source than biology'.[60]

Despite the obvious anti-racist implications of this anti-essentialist view of race, it is, however, very controversial. Recently it has been a subject of heated debate in the field of Afro-American literary theory centring around the question of how to read work by and about black writers. Philosopher Kwame Anthony Appiah and literary critic Henry Louis Gates Jr. have defended an anti-essentialist view of race, with Appiah arguing that W.E.B. DuBois, at the end of a lifelong struggle to understand the meaning and significance of the concept of race, had come to, but never fully assimilated, this same view: the idea of race has no scientific validity; it has done a great deal of damage and should be scrapped.[61] But the anti-essentialist position of Appiah and Gates has met some extremely hostile reactions, with Houston Baker, another leading critic of African-American literature, accusing Appiah of accepting 'explanations from the overseers'.[62] This debate is, of course, not new. Essentialist and anti-essentialist perspectives regarding race, from various conservative biological accounts at one end of the political spectrum to Marxist, black, nationalist

---

59 According to Marvin Harris, more than forty racial categories are distinguished on the basis of appearance; combinations of these are expressed by more than one hundred racial terms, and socio-economic status also plays a role in the classification of an individual's race. See Harris 1979.
60 Lewontin, Rose, and Kamin 1984, p. 127.
61 Appiah 1990. Appiah 1986. The principal scientific source Appiah cites is Nei and Roychoudhury 1983. See also Louis Gates Jr. 1983.
62 Baker 1986.

positions, and combinations thereof at the other end, have been argued by social scientists, political thinkers, and activists for many years.[63] While most liberal and left thinkers have been anti-essentialists, the anti-essentialist position seems to many to deny something very real and important—experientially and politically. When what is called race has had such profound and painful effects on those defined as black, it is understandable why many blacks would find it ironic, at best, to be told that race is an illusion. Houston Baker's reaction to Appiah is reminiscent of Franz Fanon's angry reaction to Sartre's description of the 'negritude' movement in literature as an anti-racist racism, an understandable but temporary stage in the eventual transcendence of race. Certainly many black nationalists would share Fanon's feeling that Sartre had 'destroyed black zeal'.[64] Moreover, in recent years anti-essentialism has sometimes been used to deny the importance of race and therefore—in a second fallacious move—to deny the importance of racism, as, for example, in many arguments against affirmative action for blacks. Thus, for familiar reasons, many embrace essentialism regarding race defensively—for antiracist ends.[65]

And one has to admit that the statement that there are no races has an air of paradox. We hear comparisons between the lives of whites and blacks in the United States all the time, but who are these groups that, for example, have differential poverty rates and life expectancies, if races are a fiction? Might they be defined by culture? Black people in the United States are often said to share a culture, but this could only serve to differentiate them from whites in the United States if the cultural differences between blacks and whites were greater than the cultural differences between Anglo Americans, East European Jewish Americans, Hispanic Americans, etc. It is far from clear that that is true. If we say simply that African Americans share a culture that differentiates them from these other groups, that is true, but then we are talking about ethnic groups, not races. And there remains the question of whom we are talking about when we talk about blacks and whites. Many black Americans, from Marcus Garvey to W.E.B. DuBois, have looked to Africa for the answer. But what they have in common with Africans cannot be a biological race, if what we have said above is

---

63   One of the more interesting writers to try to synthesize Marxism and nationalism is C.L.R. James. See James 1980; James 1977.
64   Fanon 1967.
65   For a discussion of essentialist theories of race that are strikingly similar to feminist essentialist theories, see the work of Sandra Harding. Pointing out that these commonalities refute biological determinist explanations of race and gender differences, Harding suggests they show that the real differences are between Western men and 'the rest of us' (Harding 1987).

correct. Nor can it be a culture, on any plausible definition of culture; not even all Africans share a culture. The commonality is simply that African Americans are, at least in part, of African ancestry.[66] Similarly, Greek Americans, Italian Americans, and Swedish Americans are all of European ancestry and can be called European Americans. What we call blacks are actually a population in the biologists' sense: a group living in geographical proximity, freely interbreeding, or descendants from that original group; people of European extraction are also a population.[67]

But this does not capture how the concept of race, particularly that of the black race, operates in the United States. The fact that the term 'European-American' is not used (or used only recently among the most politically conscious people), and that we only have the all-inclusive term 'African American', instead of, for example, Nigerian American or Yoruba American, reveals not only the very different history of Americans from Africa versus those from Europe, but also the different ways the groups have been perceived. A recent *New York Times* piece about retiring Congressman Augustus Hawkins described him as being 'Of such light complexion that he was frequently mistaken for white.' The phrase makes clear what defines the group we call 'black' in the US. Anyone with some minimum of (sub-Saharan) African ancestry is classified as black (unless that is, their native language is Spanish, in which case they are usually classified by their country of origin: Dominican, Puerto Rican, etc.). Until civil rights legislation outlawed racially discriminatory laws, state laws specified what percentage of African ancestry qualified a person as black; 1 / 32 was often sufficient. Much the same basis of classification still exists informally. Thus many of those who belong to the population descended from Africa are equally or more part of the population descended from Europe, but are unequivocally considered black. This usually suffices to determine a self-definition as black, but some people of multi-racial origin have expressed a distinct multi-racial identity. The racist character of the definition of 'black' is not simply the percentages, which imply that even a small amount of 'inferior' ancestry makes one inferior. A more self-confident racist criterion could be imagined according to which anyone with any 'superior' European ancestry was defined

---

66 The use of 'African-American', which Jesse Jackson has recommended, reflects this analysis. But the way the terms have changed indicates that the naming is part of a political struggle. Certainly the adoption of the term 'black' over 'Negro' was a powerful political statement.

67 Some scientists still use the term 'race' for a population in this sense, though it is agreed that populations do not differ genetically as races were defined as doing.

as white (thereby converting most 'Black Americans' into 'White Americans'). What is racist about the definition is that it has been imposed by the dominant group and used as a basis to harm people so defined.[68] Individuals are classified into other ethnic groups more straightforwardly on the basis of descent, but there is also some element of personal choice in the matter, at least for those of European origin.[69] If someone considers herself Italian American, most probably for cultural reasons, she is not going to be contradicted if she has only 3/8 Italian ancestry. And no one will insist that others, like me, whose ancestry is so mixed and homogenized that it has next to no identifiable role in the formation of a subjective identity, 'really are' of such-and-such ethnic group.

The category of 'whiteness' has received considerably less theoretical attention than has 'blackness'. The definition of 'white' (and 'non-white') is less precise than that of 'black'; in some contexts a Latino or someone from the Middle East would be classified as white, and in other contexts, non-white. While this might reflect differences in appearance, and hence probably different ancestries, it is also a matter of prevailing racial ideas.[70] In the United States, ethnic identities have been much discussed, but white has simply been taken as the norm. Even if it is losing its majority status, it has not lost dominant status. For those defined as white, race is less problematic and therefore less salient to self-definition.[71] Whites perceive 'race' as belonging to others. It is also mostly whites who have done the theorising and studying; 'blackness' has been part of the process of defining Others. But as some historians have shown, white-

---

68   Thus a seemingly more 'neutral' criterion which defines Hawaiians as those of 50% or more Hawaiian blood is bitterly resented by Hawaiians because it was decided by whites and has the effect of excluding many who see themselves as Hawaiian from the few benefits guaranteed to Hawaiians.

69   Although African Americans are the most extreme example, they are not the only 'unmeltable ethnics'. For a humorous discussion of the experience of Chinese Americans, including a debate on how they should be slotted into the irrationalities of American racial schemas, see Hong Kingston 1989.

70   For example, some people defined as black in the United States would count as 'mextizo' (mixed) or mulatto in Cuba. But even in the United States, more heterogeneous and liberal communities would probably have a more inclusive definition of white.

71   By and large, group membership is more important to an individual's subjective identity when that group is subordinated. On a psychological scale in which one selects categories that are central to one's identity, African Americans are more likely to choose 'black' than people of European ancestry to choose 'white', just as women are more likely to choose 'women' than men to choose 'man' and homosexuals to choose their sexuality than are heterosexuals. The one exception to this is class, truly the last taboo in United States society.

ness was constructed along with blackness in the early days of the American colonies, and in the nineteenth century the development of a popular sense of whiteness transcending ethnic differences was a crucial aspect in the development of the working class in the United States. Divided and conflicted ethnic groups, some very subordinated and even 'racialized', like the Irish, forged a new identity as free white men against blacks.[72] (Women were never fully part of this identity, but that is another story.)

But if the concept of race is a historical, social, indeed a political construct, obviously that does not make it unimportant—and nothing in the anti-essentialist argument I have sketched suggests otherwise. Although the referent is not a biologically defined group, in the United States the concept of race has had profound effects on those defined as black, first by legally enslaving them, then by legally segregating them. Today, African Americans still live, go to school, go to church and, to a lesser extent, work segregated from all other ethnic groups, and for the most part, subordinate to them. Though no longer enforced by law, social/economic/political power structures (and attitudes) produce the same result. All this has led to statistically significant differences between the groups defined as belonging to different races, from differential life expectancies to cultural differences to different senses of self.[73] So long as those defined as white have advantages and power over those defined as black, it would be foolish to suggest that 'race'—as it has been defined in this country should be ignored. 'Colour blind' may be an attribute of an ideal society, but not of ours; and to pretend that it is, or can immediately be made to be, is to obscure continued institutional racism. With the exception of economic class (truly the deepest taboo in American society), members of subordinated groups not only tend to have distinctive needs, but to understand them in those terms. This makes organising around the needs of that group effective as well as important.

However, while 'race' cannot be ignored, it must be reconceived. As long as racism exists, the concept of race is so powerful that the victims of racism want to seize it and use it for their own ends. As Cornel West wrote recently, 'As long as double standards and differential treatment abound ... black nationalisms

---

72 For the early period see Rawick 1972. For the nineteenth century see Roediger 1992.
73 Despite these profound differences, I don't believe there is a sufficiently distinct role that African Americans play, *regardless of their class and gender*, to justify a hypothesis analogous to the one I offered regarding gender, viz. that women's role (in all race/class groups) taking care of children and others, might generate important psychological/behavioural commonalities (i.e., gender).

will thrive'.[74] And, certainly, essentialist notions have helped to create and sustain solidarity among the oppressed as well as their oppressors. Nevertheless, essentialism is a dangerous illusion, because it has always been used to justify racial hierarchies. Moreover, it obscures differences within the group and commonalities with members of other groups. Nor is it a necessary illusion. All kinds of groups can organize around their distinctive needs, without the belief that their definition as a group is based in biology, and without even the idea that the group's unity precludes differences within the group or precludes commonalities with other groups. There are cultural differences among African-Americans (especially if we include people who have come from Africa via the West Indies); not all African Americans have the same economic interests, though they tend to cluster at the bottom of the economic pyramid; and some are women and others are men. (And as we have seen several times now, when these kinds of differences are ignored, it is the interests of the least advantaged that are ignored.) And certainly African Americans share interests with other groups. Nevertheless, the power relationships behind the social definitions of race give ample justification for organising around issues of race. In short, though most African Americans share cultural commonalities, it is not culture primarily, but rather racism that creates the group that needs to struggle against it.

⁂

In conclusion, I would like to take a very brief look at some implications of the above analyses: first, regarding the ideal; second, regarding how to get there. Try to imagine a society that was genuinely non-sexist and non-racist. In such a society, our common human nature would express itself in various different ways, based on each person's unique individual experience. Given that individuals live in groups—for example, nations and ethnic groups within nations—and engage in different kinds of social activities, we would be likely to see characteristics correlated with some of these groups and activities, though individuals vary in the extent that they manifest behaviour characteristic of their culture. Nevertheless, races, as they have been understood, would not exist. There would, however, still be two sexes, since reproductive differences are a functional difference. And as long as humans reproduce sexually, human communities will include men and women (not necessarily in any particular form of family, nor necessarily predominantly heterosexual). If any psycholo-

---

74 West 1992, p. 26.

gical/behavioural differences between the sexes (i.e. gender) should result from the biological difference, these would be within the other human groupings. This same fact—that because of biological reproduction men and women have shared communities and usually households—explains why social movements throughout history have been organized more easily on the basis of communities (from nations to ethnic groups) than on the basis of sex/gender.

Meanwhile, since we live in societies with overlapping class, race, and sex hierarchies, the analysis presented in this paper suggests the need for crisscrossing and overlapping organisational forms to combat these hierarchies: some that cut across class and sex lines, others that unite people on the basis of sex or of economic needs. Diverse interests should dictate diverse organisational forms. Since we also share common interests as human beings, for example, to save the planet, it might seem reasonable to think that the best way to further them is by all-inclusive groupings that cut across class, sex, and ethnic lines. But this only follows if no group has other interests that conflict with this common human interest, such as, one might argue, profit maximisation does. If they do, then the best way to fulfil our needs as human beings is not to organize all human beings as such, but to organize groups whose interests accord with humankind against those whose interests are divided. This is, of course, the Marxist argument.

CHAPTER 12

Alienation, Freedom and Human Nature

Many contemporary critics of capitalism, even many involved in the new social movements of the post-crisis landscape, such as Occupy, see Marx's vision of a total transformation of our political economic system as utopian.[1] Their critique is of plutocracy (government of, by and for the 1%), and their goal is to bring back or to create a more humane form of capitalism, and one that is ecologically sustainable. My view is that, on the contrary, it is the vision of an ecologically sustainable social welfarist capitalism that is utopian today. But secondly, even if it were achievable, it is not the best that humankind can do. For one reason, alienation is inherent in less brutal, less plutocratic forms of capitalism as well; in fact alienation—by which I mean workers' alienation, not just the anomie said to afflict 'modern man'—was more widely discussed as a problem in the postwar golden days of American capitalism than it is today, when economic conditions make satisfaction with a job less important than simply having one. These underlying disagreements among critics of our current system as to capitalism's inherent nature—specifically, whether or not exploitative and alienating labour and a tendency to ecological destruction are inherent in capitalism—should be seen, I believe, as crucial political questions, not merely academic. If we do not understand what it is we are opposing, we cannot figure out what we are for and how we might get there. It is in that spirit that this paper explores some interconnections between alienation, freedom and human nature in Marx's philosophy.

As *The Economic and Philosophical Manuscripts of 1844* has the most explicit discussion of alienation in all of Marx's work, it makes sense to begin a discussion of this topic with attention to this early work. But not, I think, to end there. Like some other interpreters, I do not see fundamental substantive differences on these issues between the early and the late Marx. In the quarter century between *the Manuscripts* and *Capital*, Marx developed his political economic theory, which he considered to be a science, but that does not mean he abandoned the idea of alienation in all its aspects as explained in the Manuscripts.

---

[1] An earlier version of this chapter was presented to the Philosophy Department of the New School for Social Research. I wish to thank all the students and professors for their many stimulating comments and questions.

To show the continuity I will be moving between the early and late Marx using quotations from both. The idea of a radical 'rupture' between the early and late Marx is associated with Louis Althusser in the 1970s who stressed the scientificity of the later Marx, claiming that this showed Marx had abandoned his earlier humanistic ideas.[2] This position was definitively refuted with the first publication in German of Marx's notebooks for *Capital*, known as *The Grundrisse*, the English translation of which was not published until 1973. For in *the Grundrisse* you find not only the core idea of alienation in all its aspects but much the same language. In the chapter on Capital, for example, he uses the word 'alien' eleven times on one page; as or more often in others.[3] In *Capital*, he drops some of the philosophical language—it is a work of political economy, after all—but the core ideas are still there and even, here and there, some of the language. This does not imply that the theory of alienation is unchanged, or uninfluenced by Marx's developed theory of political economy—indeed I would say it is enriched by it—much less that the theory of alienation in the Manuscripts somehow contains all of Marx's theory in embryo, as some have extravagantly claimed. However, my primary interest here is not exegesis, but in giving a plausible and attractive account of the theory of alienation and its connections to freedom and human nature that is consistent with all stages of Marx's work.

∴

In the *Manuscripts*, he describes four aspects of alienation: first, alienation from the product of labour, second, from the process/activity of labour; the third is alienation from what he calls 'man's species-being' or the human 'essence' and which I will call human nature, and lastly is alienation from other people. These four are all aspects of the one phenomenon of alienation; thus they are intrinsically interrelated, each essentially implicated in the other. As Marx understood alienation it is an objective condition, not subjective, as the term is most commonly understood. Certainly there is a subjective phenomenon of alienation when people feel disconnected, separated, estranged, other than, external to ...—whether it is from one another, their family, their work or society. And these feelings are often accompanied by unhappiness. But this is not primarily what Marx was writing about. Though the objective fact of alienation that he theorized will often, or even usually, have subjective

---

2 Althusser 1969.
3 Marx 1973, p. 390.

effects of this kind—and Marx includes workers' feelings of estrangement and unhappiness in his discussion of alienation—this is not the fundamental problem; in fact the two are not even essentially connected. That is, the subjective phenomenon could be present but not the objective and vice versa. Marx held alienation in all its aspects to be inherent, hence not eliminable, in the capitalist mode of production because it is rooted in the relations of production that define the system.[4]

The first two aspects of alienation (alienation from the product and from labour) are relatively straightforward to understand, and to see why Marx says that he 'proceeds from an actual economic fact. The worker becomes poorer the more wealth he produces'.[5] Capitalism is defined by free labour, but as Marx explains in the section of *Capital* on primitive accumulation, this is freedom in a double sense: workers are free of legal bonds, but also free of all means of subsistence except their own labour. Hence free labour means labour that can—but also that *must*—be sold to others in order to secure subsistence. He defines human labour as a process in which humans interact with Nature 'as one of her own forces ... in order to appropriate Nature's productions in a form adapted to his own wants'.[6] But as private property in Nature separates or alienates them from the natural condition of human labour, this alienation from Nature is a precondition of all other aspects of alienation.[7] Human labour power becomes a commodity, one of the means of production the owner buys, along with raw materials and machines, tables and chairs and paper clips. Because *workers* are not the owners of the means of production, they are not free to determine **what** to produce or **how** to do it. They have no control over what products they make nor over the process by which they make them, except in the same sense that a machine has control over the process. Whether blue collar or white collar or even professional, whether on an assembly line or in a fancy office, whether their product is a widget or a corporate merger, workers take their orders from the owners of the corporations they work for; their labour therefore 'belongs to another', transforming them into 'appendages of the machine'.

---

4   A short summary description of the process of capitalist production that starts and ends with the separation of the producer from the means of production is found in the section on simple reproduction in *Capital* Volume I. See Marx 1967, pp. 570–1. Numerous sections of the *Grundrisse* say the same thing, for example, one paragraph entitled 'the very concept of the free labourer already implies that he is a pauper' (ibid, p. 522.)
5   Marx 1967, pp. 271–2.
6   Marx 1967, p. 187.
7   For a powerful demonstration of this oft-misunderstood point see Bellamy Foster 2000.

Part 4 of *Capital* focuses on the development of the productive forces of capitalism and their organisation, The changes from simple cooperation to manufacture to modern industry are stages in increasing alienation, as 'the knowledge, the judgment, and the will, which, though in ever so small a degree, are practiced by the independent peasant or handicraftsman, ... are now required only for the workshop as a whole'. Each worker is made poor in individual productive power as the workshop—or office—is made rich. Since the capitalist owns this collective mechanism, its productive powers appear to be the productive powers of capital. The 'intellectual potencies of ... production, confront the worker as the property of another, and as a ruling power', transforming the workers, he says, into 'crippled monstrosities'.[8] Harry Braverman's *Labour and Monopoly Capital*[9] enriched the portrait of alienated work by providing a detailed account of the technological changes in work, e.g. Taylorism, since Marx wrote. Since technology increases productivity, it has the potential to reduce labour, but because capitalism is not only a system of material production but of production of surplus value, technology only reduces labour for those who own the technology. Technological advances under capitalism mostly increase the de-skilling of the workforce, transferring skills to the owner, cheapening production and tethering the worker more tightly to a job. In academia, where workers have an unusual degree of control over their work, consider on-line courses; professors' ideas and their work can become the property of their employer, and then anyone, or no one, can teach the course.

In the 1960s and '70s a number of liberal social scientists, most notably Robert Blauner author of the influential *Alienation and Freedom*,[10] were optimistic about the potential of technology to reduce alienation. While granting that alienation had increased under capitalist technology so far, the assembly line being the worst, they predicted that alienation would decline with the next technological stage of automation. Blauner's account, however, focused exclusively on what I have elsewhere called performance-related alienation, for example, that due to machine-pacing of work; but even if that declined, it would not affect what can be called system-related alienation,[11] due to the fact that workers do not control what, why or how they produce. Moreover, research suggests that in highly automated production, while workers may have more control over their bodily operations than on assembly lines, they make almost no contribution to production; they are spectators rather than participants;

---

8   Marx 1967, pp. 365–6.
9   Braverman 1974.
10 Blauner 1964.
11 Holmstrom 1977.

hence even performance-related alienation would be unlikely to decline.[12] As production has developed since that brief optimistic period, the machines to which workers have become appendages are increasingly electronic machines that—strikingly—allow for greater supervision and control than in factories or even slave plantations. As Barbara Garson said in *The Electronic Sweatshop*, workers now report on themselves with every key stroke. And with computers and smart phones one is never off work.

In his early work Marx spoke of workers selling their labour, which reflected the labour theory of value common at the time. Later, he changed this to labour power, a concept that was crucial in developing his theory of surplus value to explain the origin of profits in capitalism. For the moment, however, the difference does not matter. The idea that either labour or labour power is a commodity may seem self-evident to people born and raised in capitalist societies, but they are very odd commodities, to say the least. In fact, to call either one a commodity is essentially a legal fiction. And this fiction functions to support two fundamental ideological illusions offered in defence of capitalism: first, that everyone in capitalism owns something, even if it is only 'themselves' and hence their own labour power, and therefore, second, that the wage relation is a voluntary exchange between two individual commodity owners, simply a buyer and a seller. The two principal classes that constitute capitalism, with their vastly unequal power vis-à-vis this 'transaction', disappear.

Recently, for example, Philippe Van Parijs and Ann Cudd have both offered defences of capitalism on the grounds, among others, that it maximizes opportunities, defining capitalism in terms of private property and a structure of rights in which 'people in some important sense own themselves'.[13] But labour power is unlike other commodities, because it consists of mental and physical energies, capacities, potentials, and hence cannot be separated from the labourer to whom they belong. The same is true of labour, as it is the expression of these capacities, the labourer's actions. I can sell or destroy my land, my company, my stocks and bonds, my machinery or my car. My purse can be stolen or I can leave it on the bus. Whether I am happy or saddened by these separations from my property, I am still me, otherwise unchanged. But wherever my labour/labour power goes, I have to go too; whatever is done to it, is done to me. The illusion that labour power is an entity separable from the person may have come to seem more plausible after Descartes' separation of the mind (mental substance with all its attributes) from the body (the physical

---

12   See Braverman 1974.
13   Van Parijs 1995; Cudd and Holmstrom 2011.

substance and all its attributes) and his identification of the self, the 'I', with the mind. This entails both an ontological and conceptual separation of the body from the person, along with the devaluation of the body, leading to intractable sceptical problems.[14]

So when labour 'belongs to another', *the person* belongs to another. When workers 'sell their labour power' to the capitalist, they are selling their physical/mental beings, which means they are selling themselves, albeit with time and other limitations.[15] Very few people would do so if they had viable alternatives. But the structure of capitalist society sets obstacles to viable alternatives for most people. We can see then why Marx describes alienated labour as 'not voluntary, but coerced; it is forced labour'.[16] Necessarily, therefore, workers see the product of that labour as 'a stranger', Marx says. If calling the labour coerced still sounds hyperbolic, consider the fact that today in the United States, the most developed capitalist country in history, more than 150 years after Marx wrote, workers lack, on the job, the legally protected freedom to speak as they wish or even to go to the toilet when they choose. As labour activist/educator Stan Weir put it, the Bill of Rights stops at the door to the workplace.[17] The workplace belongs to the owner, so everything that's part of it belongs to him. Recall John Locke's explanation of how *labour gives the right to property*, where he says, quite unselfconsciously, 'Thus the grass my horse has bit, the turfs my servant has cut and the ore I have digged … become my property …'.[18]

Whether workers desire the products they make or despise them, whether they are proud of them, ashamed, or indifferent, in all cases, the products are separated from the producers. Workers' own products are transformed into capital, adding to the wealth of the capitalists which grows exponentially greater, both in absolute terms and as compared to that of workers. The more they use of Nature the less there is for them. (A dramatic contemporary example is the conversion of food into biofuel.) By their labour, workers

---

14 The so-called 'mind–body problem' (how these two substances could be related) which arose from Descartes' conception, did not arise in the more organic, holistic conception of the person common in earlier thinking. Matson 1966.
15 Pateman has a particularly good discussion of this, extending it to issues of prostitution and surrogacy. See Pateman 2007.
16 Marx 1967, p. 274. He says the same thing throughout his work.
17 Talk at a meeting. See Ezorsky 2007.
18 Note that this critique is not a moral critique. As morally abominable as slavery is, it is not absurd *conceptually* that people could be forced to labour, and in a commodity system, bought and sold as commodities. Hence, although slavery may be backed up by law, it is not thereby created by law in the way that something not separable in reality becomes so by legal fiat.

are also adding to the power of the capitalists—which power is power *over them* ... Marx says, the worker is related to the product of their own labour as to 'an alien object which exercises power over them'.[19] Moreover, because capitalism is a system of expanded reproduction workers reproduce, on an ever-expanding scale, not only the means of production, i.e. capital, but the relation between themselves and capital, i.e. their own alienation. Typical of Marx's many comments to this effect is the statement that 'All the moments which confronted living labour capital as alien, external powers, ... are now posited as its own product and result'.[20] By their own labour, then, workers in capitalist society create things that are the embodiment of their own physical and mental energies—but these things belong to another and they are then used against them. Workers' own activity is alien to them, turned against them. Thus, Marx says, 'The worker becomes poorer the more wealth he produces'.[21]

If one's labour is alienated, it is still possible to be un-alienated in other aspects of one's life, for example hobbies, for those who have time, or increasingly for many people, in the raising of children, as we are more able to have control over the process than in the past. Nevertheless, due to the time taken by alienated labour in our lives, its effects on the psyche in the form of reduced capacities and sense of self-worth, and most important, due to the structure of society which is at its root, alienated labour diminishes peoples' freedom in all spheres of their lives. Most importantly, it diminishes the extent to which working people are able to decide upon and to carry out the kind of life they want, a uniquely human capacity. This is alienation in a broader sense, which some writers identify as alienation, seeing alienated labour as merely an important contributor.[22]

∴

Marx calls alienation from the activity of labour '*self*-estrangement', which leads us to discussion of the third aspect of alienation. Alienation from species being, or human nature, has been seen as more problematic than the other aspects of alienation on several counts: whether it is a coherent concept, whether it fits the analysis of alienation that I've given, and finally, even if this can be defended for the early Marx, whether he maintained it in his later work.

---

19   Marx 1967, p. 275.
20   Marx 1973, p. 280. See also Marx 1967, p. 806. In the latter he describes the material conditions and social relations of capitalism as both 'prerequisites' and 'results and creations'.
21   Marx 1967, p. 271.
22   Schmitt 2003.

Marx begins his discussion of the third aspect of alienation, which he says he is 'deducing' from the first two, by saying that each species has a distinctive kind of productive activity. 'The whole character of a species—its species character—is contained in its life activity', that is, the kind of activity it engages in to satisfy its basic needs. What then is the distinctive character of human productive life? His answer: 'free, conscious activity is man's species character'. There are 2 elements, then, to human nature: freedom and consciousness—and alienated labour meets neither one. Alienated labour, as he has described it above, is clearly not free—he calls it coerced. Unlike other animals, which produce only to satisfy physical needs, humans 'produce even when free from physical need, and [he says] only truly produce in freedom therefrom'. By the phrase 'truly produces', Marx means producing in ways that are distinctively human. Like other animals, humans are immersed in inorganic nature, part of and dependent on nature, but in the human case, not only for their physical reproduction. Unlike other animals man produces universally, that is, 'in accordance with the standard of every species' thereby making all of nature his *inorganic* body. He concludes, famously, 'Man ... also forms things in accordance with the laws of beauty'.[23]

Now what does 'conscious' mean in this context? How could alienated labour not be conscious? Aren't humans—unlike machines—always conscious of their labour? Yes, or usually, in the sense of 'aware', but this is not the sense that Marx identifies as distinctive of human labour. In *Capital*, he says 'We presuppose labour in a form that stamps it as exclusively human .... What distinguishes the worst architect from the best of bees is this, that the architect raises his structure in imagination before he erects it in reality'.[24] And this purpose then directs his/her actions. So 'conscious' here has the specific sense of the labour being the carrying out, or the execution, of an idea or purpose of the worker him/herself, the agent. Alienated labour is not conscious in this sense. Instead, it is the capitalist's ideas and purposes that the worker is executing, just as a machine does. Indeed if the labour is not conscious in this sense, it may require more consciousness in the sense of attention. A machine is designed to carry out a task set by the owner; if it does not, it is replaced. The same is true of workers in capitalism. Thus since free, conscious activity is the distinctive character of the human species, its human nature, alienated labour also means alienation from this human nature.[25]

---

23   Marx 1967, pp. 276–7.
24   Marx 1967, p. 188.
25   Capitalists' freedom is much greater, but it too is constrained by the market. An owner who wanted to pay a lot more or be more ecological cannot yield competitive advantage

Though Marx does not use the word 'species being' in his later works, we find rich accounts of un-alienated labour, which clearly has the same centrality to his view of humankind as it does in the Manuscripts. In the *Grundrisse* he critiques Adam Smith's view of work as sacrifice, saying that while true of exploited labour ('external forced labour'), this is not inherent in work as such. Yes, work always involves some external goal, he says, but overcoming obstacles can be liberating when they are goals set by the individual; then work is 'self-realization ... hence real freedom, whose action is, precisely, labour'. In the same passage, he also dismisses as naive Fourier's vision of labour in a socialist society as essentially play, saying 'Really free working, e.g. composing, is at the same time precisely the most damnably difficult, demanding the most intensive effort'.[26] This description is very similar to what contemporary psychologists call 'flow',[27] an immensely rewarding experience which very few wage workers achieve.

We also see this same idea of human nature expressed in Marx's account of labour in a future socialist society in Volume III of *Capital* where he distinguishes between a realm of necessity and the realm of freedom. Even in socialism/communism, he says, there will always be some labour required by physical necessity. 'Freedom in this field can only consist of socialized man, the associated producers, rationally regulating their interchange with Nature, bringing it under their common control, instead of being ruled by it as by the blind forces of Nature; and achieving this under the least expenditure of energy and conditions most favourable to, and worthy of, their human nature. Beyond this realm, [he says] begins that development of human energy which is an end in itself, the true realm of freedom, which, however, can blossom forth only with the realm of necessity as its basis'. He concludes the passage 'The shortening of the working day is its basic prerequisite'.[28] In this passage we see what un-alienated labour would be like, though he does not use the word, and that is: free, conscious labour. It is free in the fullest sense only when free of physical need, but it is free in a more limited sense when the products and process of labour are under the control of workers themselves. Their labour is then the execution of their own ideas and purposes, not those of others. And

---

to others who lack such concerns. Thus newspapers regularly say things like 'the company *had no choice but* to close its operations in the United States, they were *forced* to cut back on benefits given the competition'.

26 Marx, 1973, p. 530. This example shows that Marx's conception of humans' distinctive kind of productive activity is not limited to material production, and is in no way 'productivist'.
27 Csikszentmihalyi 1990.
28 Marx 1967, p. 867.

he says this is most in accordance with human nature. The crucial elements of his account of alienated labour found in *The Economic and Philosophical Manuscripts* are here in Volume III of *Capital*. This account of freedom within necessity as rational collective control underscores the connection between Marx's view of human nature and his commitment to a radical democratic vision of socialism.[29]

Now the principal grounds offered for the position that Marx does not accept the concept of human nature is found in passages like the following from the beginning of *The German Ideology*—written within two years of the Manuscripts. There Marx says that the ways in which people produce their means of subsistence produce a definite 'mode of life' and he says, 'as individuals express their life, so they are .... The nature of individuals thus depends on the material conditions determining their production'. Much later, in *Capital I* he says explicitly, 'By thus acting on the external world and changing it, he at the same time changes his own nature ...' Both early and later in his work, then, Marx says two things about human nature that some see as inconsistent: first that human nature changes and yet second, that there is something called human nature from which a particular way that humans are, viz., alienated, is a deviation, and somehow less 'truly' human nature. This latter view seems to many to imply that human nature does not change; else why would a particular way humans are count as 'less truly human', rather than just another form of human nature, where no particular form is more or less *truly* human. Hence, there is an apparent inconsistency. The conclusion some critics draw from this apparent inconsistency is that Marx does not really accept the notion of human nature. A related criticism of the idea of human nature as I have explained it is that it is ahistorical (and therefore un-Marxist). Instead one should see the capacity for free conscious activity as developing within capitalism; the inability of most people to express it is one of the contradictions of capitalism.

But this argument is mistaken, as Norman Geras showed in his incisive little book *Marx's Theory of Human Nature: Refutation of a Legend*.[30] To speak of human nature—which does imply constancy—and yet to say that human nature changes is not inconsistent, any more than to say the Earth's climate

---

29   It also shows why Marx's vision of socialism is an ecological one. If human beings freely and consciously produced to satisfy their material needs collectively, their production would be sustainable; one cannot *need* to destroy the bases for the satisfaction of those needs. It is the competitive capitalist market system that needs to grow unsustainably, thus creating the catastrophic conflict with nature facing human beings today.

30   Geras 1983. McMurtry 1978.

has changed due to global warming denies that there are constants within the changes, and moreover,—and this is especially important—that there are constants that explain the changes that do occur. So having a concept of human nature and accepting changes in human nature are not necessarily inconsistent. As human nature adapts in certain ways to different physical and social conditions, the *potential to do so must already exist and moreover, explain why it develops this way and not that* ... As a materialist Marx would assume this potential is grounded in fundamental biological characteristics. Free conscious activity can certainly take different forms, some of which develop only within capitalism. However, this general capacity is true of all beings designated as human, even very early in human history, and it is expressed not only in production for subsistence but in production 'in accordance with the laws of beauty'. Consider cave paintings done by primitive humans as early as forty thousand years ago.

However the issue that arises in understanding Marx's statements about human nature is not just change versus constants, as it is in the climate case, but Marx's crediting some variations as more 'truly' human nature than others. What are the grounds for this? To explain, I have to bring in freedom, which does not apply in the climate change example. Recall that in explaining the meaning and source of alienation from the product and activity of labour, I stressed workers' lack of freedom, rooting it in their lack of control of the means of production. Instead, they are controlled by powerful others with contrary interests. The same I think can be argued in the case of human nature. In *The German Ideology*, remember, Marx says the material and social relations in which humans produce their means of production shape the variations in human nature; as they produce, so they are. The crucial question, then, is what are these social relations like? Social relations include power relations. If the conditions that shape human nature are under the control of a minority of oppressive 'others', and society is structured to support their interests, then it is plausible to say that the resulting human nature is less 'truly human nature'. Peoples' wants, beliefs, values, personalities and capacities will to a large extent reflect the interests of the dominant group in society. Thus the choosing and acting subject is constructed, in part, by a hierarchical society. Moreover, people are likely to be unaware that this is the case and hence less able to combat it. On the other hand, if the conditions shaping human nature are under the control of the majority, then human nature takes its shape without coercion, without distortion to satisfy hostile interests, but 'naturally' ... Hence it is plausible I think to describe this form of human nature formed in conditions of freedom, and expressed in conditions of freedom, as more truly human nature than those formed and expressed in oppressive social relations.³¹ (A further issue that could be explored is Marx's positive moral evaluation of this form of human nature, but this lies beyond the scope of this paper.)³²

Notice this is not to say that it is somehow uncaused, purely, inherently, inevitably what humans would be like no matter what. Not at all. In the passage from Volume III of *Capital* discussed earlier, which contrasts labour in capitalism, serfdom and slavery with that under socialism, Marx takes what would today be called a compatibilist position on the issue of freedom and determinism. Discussing two kinds of necessity and two kinds of freedom, he says that true freedom begins outside the sphere of necessary labour, in activity done for its own sake. However, within the sphere of necessity, there is still a freedom and it consists essentially of the labour being under the producers' control. Here it is collective control rather than individual control as in free will discussions, but the point is the same. The criterion is not whether actions are determined or not, but by whom/what they're determined.³³ Notice too that to speak of actions that are 'outside the realm of necessity' is not to say they are totally uncaused, but simply not caused by physical necessity. Composers' composing of music is caused by the combination of their passion to compose and their capacities, which in turn are caused by ... And so on.

Postmodern theorists also criticize the notion of human nature, stressing the differences amongst people and the biased characterisations of human nature. Though this lies outside the purview of this paper I will just say that the problem of implicit bias is very real and must be struggled against continually. However, there is no inconsistency between the concept of human nature and the recognition of its many variations, both physical and psychological. If there were, we could not use any general terms, as there are always more specific terms included in the concept. Methodologically, the critique of human nature is misguided as well. It is certain constants in human beings that allowed us to evolve differently in different physical environments. Similarly, it is the flexibility of the human brain that allows human beings to adapt psychologically to different social environments, being, for example, more egoistic in some sets

---

31 See Holmstrom 1975, pp. 423–46. Also Hirschmann 2003.
32 It is patently obvious that Marx thinks alienation and exploitation labour are bad, and their elimination in socialism is the principal reason socialism will be, as he often calls it, a 'higher' form of society than capitalism. His vision is similar to Aristotle's conception of human flourishing, as a number of authors have noted. How to square this with Marx's anti-moralism has occasioned much debate. An excellent summary of this debate is Geras 1985. My own contribution to this debate: Holmstrom 1977.
33 See Holmstrom 1975.

of social relations and more cooperative in others. Differences among humans exist *because, not in spite of*, a biologically based common human nature.

∴

The final aspect of alienation is alienation from other people, which Marx sees as following, inevitably, from the others. If the product is 'alien, hostile, powerful and independent' of the worker, it is because 'someone else is master of this object, someone who is alien, hostile, powerful and independent of him'.[34] If his activity is not under his own control, then it is 'under the dominion, the coercion, the yoke of another'. Contrary to capitalist ideology which portrays the relation between workers and capitalists as a relation between equal individuals—buyers and sellers of labour power—in reality, the vast differences in power between these two groups make it a relationship of domination, which Marx sees as dehumanising to those on both sides. Instead of the relations of community and social equality that can, and should exist between people, we see fear, humiliation, and anger on one side and on the other, a totally instrumental attitude towards their fellow human beings, as tools to be used until they are no longer needed. Relations between workers are different; they are not relations of domination, but of cooperation on the job and often outside of it given their common interests. However, this potential is hindered by the competition in which they find themselves, especially in times of crisis like today's neoliberalism: there are hierarchies at workplaces (of power and remuneration, including two-tiered wage systems for workers doing the same job), the employed are pitted against the unemployed, the unionized versus the unorganized, public employees versus private, citizens versus non-citizens, and workers of one country versus all the others, as employers close up and move to lower wage areas. In addition, there are ethnic/racial and gender differences and inequalities, which usually overlap with the other divisions. While sexism, racism and national chauvinism have a life of their own, these prejudices have always been exploited by employers to divide workers from one another. Individual workers and groups see other individuals and groups as different and threatening, and sometimes, in the short run, they could be right. In the absence of collective alternatives, feelings of solidarity and collective capacities are undermined; individualistic and defensive responses are all that seem possible. Hence alienation from other people includes alienation from other workers.

34   Marx 1967, pp. 278–9.

These alienated relations between people in capitalist society are in stark contrast to Marx's vision of ideal human relations, as expressed in this passage from the section of the *Manuscripts* called 'The Meaning of Human Requirements'. 'When communist workmen associate with one another, theory, propaganda, etc., is their first end. But at the same time, as a result of this association, they acquire a new need—the need for society—and what appears as a means becomes an end. You can observe this practical process in its most splendid results whenever you see French socialist workers together. Such things as smoking, drinking, eating, etc., are no longer means of contact or means that bring together. Company, association, and conversation, which again has society as its end, are enough for them; the brotherhood of man is no mere phrase with them, but a fact of life, and the nobility of man shines upon us from their work-hardened faces'.[35] The idea of relationships with others as a need, is also found in Marx's discussion of male/female relations. After echoing Charles Fourier's thought that the progress of civilisation is best measured by the progress of women, Marx says that 'in this relationship, is revealed too, the extent to which man's *need* has become a *human* need; the extent to which, therefore, the *other* person as a person has become for him a need—the extent to which he in his individual existence is at the same time a social being'.[36] While community and need for others has often meant sacrifice of individuality, Marx's vision of social equality combines community and individuality.

∴

So to summarize the principal thesis of this paper: alienation, as Marx understood it throughout his work, includes alienation from human nature, which can be explained in similar terms to alienation from the product, from the process of labour and from other people. Lack of freedom is central to all aspects of alienation; lack of freedom/power/control over the means of production is both its root cause and also its consequence. When Marx says that alienation makes workers poorer the more wealth they produce, he means this in many respects: it drastically reduces their capacities and sense of self worth, it severs or distorts their relations to one another and to Nature; making people 'so stupid and one-sided that an object is only ours when we *have* it;' workers have massively less power and material wealth relative to that of capitalists and in many places and times their material conditions are actually worsened

---

35   Marx 1967, p. 313.
36   Ibid., p. 296.

in objective terms. In the *Manuscripts* and in *Capital*, Marx draws on Engels' *The Condition of the Working Class in England* describing horrific living and working conditions in which not even basic animal needs for light, air and cleanliness are satisfied, much less the rich *human* needs and senses that he envisions being emancipated with socialism.

∴

In conclusion I want to draw some political implications from this analysis. First, contrary to Hegel, alienation is not a universal and inevitable ontological fact of human existence, equivalent to objectification, but a phenomenon rooted historically in capitalism. Therefore to end alienation, it is necessary to end capitalism. In good times, it might be possible to win some changes which make workers more comfortable in their alienation, but no more. Many Marxists who stress this point make what I think is a different error-because it is *rooted* in capitalism they assume that it must be *unique* to capitalism. My second point is that capitalism is merely sufficient, not necessary. Thus if capitalism is ended, alienation does not end automatically. It depends on what replaces it. As long as workers do not control the means of production, alienation will exist. This was developed both in land and in industry under capitalism, but the monopoly of land by feudal lords' also alienated the serfs from their means of subsistence. In the Soviet system although workers did not sell, i.e. alienate their labour power, but instead worked for the state, it does not follow, as Soviet 'Marxists' claimed,[37] that alienation is ruled out by definition. Property was nationalized but this is a property form, a juridical form, not a relation of production.[38] Workers did not control the state, hence they did not decide what to produce or how to do it and hence their labour was not the unity of conception and execution of un-alienated labour. Moreover, their products did not belong to them. Models of market socialism differ; whether they would involve alienation depends, I think, on the power of the market—an inhuman force—vs. human control. A democratically planned economy is the clearest example of a society without alienated labour. My third and final point: a theory of human nature is not extraneous politically. As Noam Chomsky has said, 'Any serious social science or theory of social change must be founded on some concept of human nature'.[39] This is especially important, I suggest, if one is

---

37   See Marcuse 1961.
38   See McMurtry 1973. He provides a clear discussion of the differences between these concepts.
39   Chomsky 2006 p. 126.

arguing for a radically different kind of society than currently exists. If Marx is right that most people have enormous unrealized potentials, which, if realized, would make them happier and more fulfilled, and that this can only happen in an egalitarian and free society, then I take this to be a powerful moral argument in favour of such a society, and in favour of encouraging the traits of empathy, solidarity and reciprocity necessary to achieve it.

Bibliography

Akuno, Kali and Ajamu Nangawa (eds.) 2017, *Jackson Rising*, Quebec: Daraja Press.
Albert, Michael and Robin Hahnel 1991, *Looking Forward: Participatory Economics for the Twenty-First Century*, Boston: South End Press.
Althusser, Louis 1969, *For Marx*, translated by Ben Brewster, London: New Left Books.
Altvater, Elmar 1993, *The Future of the Market*, translated by Patrick Camiller, New York: Verso.
Altvater, Elmar 2004, 'What Happens When Public Goods are Privatised', *Studies in Political Economy*, 74, 1, Autumn 2004.
Altvater, Elmar 2002, 'Obsession With Growth', in *Socialist Register 2002: A World of Contradictions*, edited by Leo Panitch and Colin Leys, London: Merlin Press.
Althusser, Louis 1970, *For Marx*, London: Allen Lane.
Althusser, Louis and Etienne Balibar 1970, *Reading Capital*, London: New Left Books.
Amsden, Alice 2007, *Escape from Empire: The Developing World's Journey Through Heaven and Hell*, Cambridge: MIT Press.
Amsden, Alice 2001, *The Rise of 'the Rest': Challenges to the West from Late Industrializing Countries*, Oxford: Oxford University Press.
Anderson, Elizabeth 1990a, 'The Ethical Limitations of the Market', *Economics and Philosophy*, 6.
Anderson, Elizabeth 1990b, 'Is Women's Labor a Commodity?' *Philosophy and Public Affairs* 19, 1 (Winter).
Anderson, Elizabeth 1998, 'Ethical Limitations of the Market', in *Economics, Ethics and Public Policy*, edited by Charles K. Wilber, Lanham md., Row man and Littlefield.
Andrews, Edmund L. 2009, 'Report Projects a Worldwide Economic Slide', *New York Times*, 9 March.
Appiah, Kwame Anthony 1986, 'The Uncompleted Argument: DuBois and the illusion of Race' in *'Race', Writing, and Difference*, edited by H.L. Gates Jr., Chicago: University of Chicago Press.
Appiah, Kwame Anthony 1990, 'Racisms', in *Anatomy of Racism*, edited by David Theo Goldberg, Minneapolis: University of Minnesota Press.
Anton, Anatole 2000, 'Public Goods as Commonstock', in *Not For Sale: In Defense of Public Goods*, edited by Anton Fisk and Nancy Holmstrom, Boulder, CO: Westview Press, 2000.
Antony, Louise 2020, 'Feminism Without Metaphysics or a Deflationary Account of Gender', *Erkenntnis*.
Antony, Louise 2020, 'Naturalized Epistemology, Morality and the Real World', *Canadian Journal of Philosophy*, 26.

Arneson, Richard J. 1991, 'Lockean Self-Ownership: Towards a Demolition', *Political Studies*, 39.

Armstrong, David and Joseph J. Trento 2007, *America and the Islamic Bomb: The Deadly Compromise*, New York: Random House.

Arruzza, Cinzia 2014, 'Remarks on Gender', *Viewpoint Magazine*, September.

Astell, Mary 2000, 'Some Reflections Upon Marriage', *Women and Men Political Theorists: Enlightened Conversations*, edited by Kristin Waters, Malden MA: Blackwell.

Aveling, Edward and Eleanor Marx 1887, 'The Woman Question', reprinted in *Marxism Today*, 1972.

Aylmer, G.E. (ed.) 1975, *The Levellers in the English Revolution*, London: Thames and Hudson.

Bahr, J. 1974, 'Effects on Family Power and Division of Labour in the Family', in *Working Mothers*, edited by L. Hoffman and F.I. Nye, San Francisco: Jossey-Bass Inc.

Bales, Kevin 1999, *Disposable People: New Slavery in the Global Economy*, Berkeley, CA: University of California Press.

Baran, Paul, *The Political Economy of Growth*, New York: Monthly Review.

Bardwick, Judith 1971, *Psychology of Women*, New York: Harper & Row.

Baker, Houston 1986, 'Caliban's Triple Play', in *'Race', Writing, and Difference*, edited by H.L. Gates Jr, Chicago: University of Chicago Press.

Barker Martin 1981, 'Human Biology and the Possibility of Socialism', in *Issues in Marxist Philosophy, Vol. 4*, edited by John Mepham and David Hillel-Ruben, Brighton: Harvester.

Barker, Martin 1981, *The New Racism*, London: Junction Books 1981.

Baran Paul A. 1975, *The Political Economy of Growth*, New York, Monthly Review.

Barry, H. III, M.K. Bacon, and I.I. Child 1957, 'A Cross Cultural Survey of Some Sex Differences in Socialization', *Journal of Abnormal and Social Psychology*, 55.

Bell, Beverley and the Other Worlds' Collaborative 2009, '"Who Says You Can't Change the World?": Just Economies on an Unjust Planet', 1 (June), at https://www.onthecommons.org/magazine/recommended-reads/who-says-you-cant-change-world-just-economies-unjust-world/index.html.

Bello, Walden 2000, 'Reforming the WTO is the Wrong Agenda', in *Globalize This!*, edited by Danaher and Burbach, Monroe, Maine: Common Courage.

Bennholdt-Thomsen, Veronika and Maria Mies 1999, *The Subsistence Perspective: Beyond the Globalised Economy*, London: Zed Books.

Benston, Margaret 1969, 'The Political Economy of Women's Liberation', *Monthly Review*, 21 (4 September).

Berlin, Isaiah 1971, *Four Essays on Liberty*, New York: Oxford University Press.

Bernard, Jesse 1971, 'The Paradox of the Happy Marriage', *Woman in Sexist Society: Studies in Power and Powerlessness*, edited by Vivian Gornick and Barbara Moran, New York: Signet.

Bernstein, Irving 1970, *The Lean Years: A History of the American Worker, 1920–1933*, Baltimore: Penguin Books.
Bernstein, Irving 1970, *Turbulent Years: A History of the Amerinan Worker, 1933–1941*, Boston: Houghton Mifflin Co.
Bettcher, Talia Mae 2009, 'Feminist Perspectives on Trans Issues', *Stanford Encyclopedia of Philosophy*.
Bindman, Jo 2002, 'An International Perspective on Slavery in the Sex Industry', in Holmstrom 2002.
Birns, Beverly 1976, 'The Emergence and Socialization of Sex Differences in the Earliest Years', *Merrill-Palmer Quarterly*, 22.
Bhattacharjee, Anannya, and Sarita Gupta and Stephanie Luce 2009, 'Raising the Floor: the Movement for a Living Wage in Asia', *New Labor Forum*, 18, 3 (Summer).
Blauner, Robert 1964, *Alienation and Freedom*, Chicago: University of Chicago Press.
Bhattacharya, Tithi (ed.) 2017, *Social Reproduction Theory: Remapping Class Re-centreing Oppression*, London: Pluto Press.
Bleier, Ruth 1984, *Science and Gender*, New York: Pergamon.
Block, J. 1976, 'Issues, Problems and Pitfalls in Assessing Sex Differences: A Critical Review of The Psychology of Sex Differences', Merrill-Palmer Quarterly, 22.
Boo, Katherine 2014, *Behind the Beautiful Forevers: Life, Death and Hope in a Mumbai Undercity*, New York: Random House.
Booth, Douglas 1978, 'Collective Action: Marx's Class Theory and the Union Movement', *Journal of Economic Issues*, 12.
Bracken, Harry 1973, 'Essence, Accident and Race', *Hermathena*, 116.
Bracken, Harry 1978, 'Philosophy and Racism', *Philosophia*, 8.
Bracking, Sarah 2009, *Money and Power: Great Predators in the Political Economy of Development*, London: Pluto.
Brandt Richard and Jaegwon Kim 1963, 'Wants as Explanations of Action', *Journal of Philosophy*, 60, 15.
Braithwaite, R.B. 1955, *Theory* of *Games as a Tool of the Moral Philosopher*, Cambridge: Cambridge University Press.
Braverman, Harry 1974, *Labor and Monopoly Capital*, New York: Monthly Review Press.
Brecher, Jeremy Ron Blackwell and Joe Uehlein 2014, 'If Not Now, When? A Labor Movement Plan to Address Climate Change', *New Labor Forum*, 1, 7.
Brecher, Jeremy 2019, 'The Clean Energy Future: Protecting the Climate, Creating Jobs and Saving Money', Labor Network for Sustainability, available at: https://www.labor4sustainability.org/articles/jobs-justice-and-the-clean-energy-future/.
Brecher, Jeremy 2019, *18 Strategies for the Green New Deal: How to Make the Climate Mobilization Work*, Labor Network for Sustainability, available at: https://www.labor4sustainability.org/wp-content/uploads/.
Brennan, Denise 2002, "Selling Sex for Visas: Sex Tourism as a Stepping Stone to Inter-

national Migration," in *Global Woman: Nannies, Maids, and Sex Workers in the New Economy*, edited by Barbara Ehrenreich and Arlie Russell Hochschild, New York: Holt/Metropolitan.

Brenner, Johanna and Maria Ramas 1984, 'Rethinking Women's Oppression', *New Left Review*, 144.

Brenner, Johanna (ed.) 2000, *Women and the Politics of Class*, New York: Monthly Review.

Brenner, Johanna and Barbara Laslett 2000, 'Gender and the State', in *Women and the Politics of Class*, edited by Johanna Brenner, New York: Monthly Review.

Brenner, Johanna and Nancy Holmstrom 2013, 'Socialist-Feminist strategy today' in *The Question of Strategy, Socialist Register*, edited by L. Panitch, G. Albo and V. Chibber, Pontypool, Wales: Merlin Press.

Brenner, Johanna 2017, 'There was no such thing as "progressive neoliberalism"', *Dissent*, 14 January 2017.

Brenner, Robert 2006, *The Economics of Global Turbulence*, New York: Verso.

Bruegel, Irene 1978, 'What Keeps the Family Going?' *International Socialism*, 2, 1.

Broad, Robin, with John Cavanaugh 1993, *Plundering Paradise: The Struggle for the Environment in the Philippines*, Berkeley, CA: University of California Press.

Brown, Judith K. 1976, 'An Anthropological Perspective on Sex Roles and Subsistence', in *Sex Differences*, edited by Michael S. Teitelbaum, Garden City, NY: Doubleday & Co.

Brownmiller, Susan 1981, *Against Our Will: Men, Women and Rape*, New York: Simon and Schuster.

Bruegel, Irene 1978, 'What Keeps the Family Going?', *International Socialism*, 2, 1.

Buchanan, Allen 1979–80, 'Revolutionary Motivation and Morality', *Philosophy and Public Affairs*, 9.

Buchanan, Allen 1984, *Marx and Justice*, Totowa, NJ: Rowman & Littlefield.

Butler, J., 1950, *Five Sermons*, Indianapolis: Bobbs-Merrill.

Butler, Judith 1986, 'Sex and Gender in Beauvoir's *Second Sex*', in *Simone de Beauvoir: Witness to a Century, Yale French Studies*, 72.

Butler, Judith 1991, *Gender Trouble*, New York: Routledge.

Caplan, Arthur (ed.) 1978, *The Sociobiology Debate*, New York: Harper and Row.

Cassidy, John 1997, 'The Return of Karl Marx', *New Yorker*, 20 October.

Chang, Ha-Joon 2008, *The Bad Samaritan: The Myth of Free Trade and the Secret History of Capitalism*, London: Bloomsbury Press.

Charnock, Greig and Ramon Ribera-Fumaz 2018, 'Barcelona en Comu: Urban Democracy and the "Common Good"', in *Rethinking Democracy: Socialist Register*, edited by Leo Panitch and Greg Albo, London: Merlin Press.

Chodorow, Nancy 1971, 'Being and Doing: A Cross Cultural Guide to the Socialization of Males and Females', in *Woman in Sexist Society*, edited by V. Gornick and B. Moran, New York: Basic Books.

Chodorow, Nancy 1979, *The Reproduction of Mothering*, Berkeley, CA: University of California Press.
Chomsky, Noam 1973, *For Reasons of State*, New York: Pantheon.
Chomsky, Noam 2006, 'A Philosophy of Language', in *The Chomsky-Foucault Debate on Human Nature*, New York: The New Press.
Church, Jennifer 1997, 'Ownership and the Body', in Diana Tietjens Meyers, *Feminists Rethink the Self*, Boulder: Westview.
Clark, Lorenne M.G. 1979, 'Women and Locke: Who Owns the Apples in the Garden of Eden?', in *The Sexism of Social and Political Philosophy*, edited by Clark and Lynda Lange, Toronto.
Christman, John 1994, *The Myth of Ownership: Toward an Egalitarian Theory of Ownership*, New York: Oxford University Press.
Cohen, G.A. 1978, *Karl Marx's Theory of History*, Princeton: Princeton University Press.
Cohen, G.A. 1988, *History Labour and Freedom*, Oxford: Oxford University Press.
Cohen, G.A. 1995, *Self-Ownership, Freedom and Equality*, Cambridge: Cambridge University Pres.
Combahee River Collective Statement 1979, in *Capitalist Patriarchy and the Case for Socialist Feminism*, edited by Z. Eisenstein, N.Y.: Monthly Review.
Combahee River Collective 1982, 'A Black Feminist's Statement' by the Combahee River Statement', in *But Some of Us Are Brave*, Feminist Press.
Cohen, Patricia 2009, 'Ivory Tower Unswayed by Crashing Economy', *New York Times*, March 5.
Conley, Dalton 2009, 'America is #...15?', *The Nation*, 23 March.
Copelon, Rhonda 1990, *From Abortion to Reproductive Freedom: Transforming a Movement*, edited by Marlene Gerber Fried, Boston: South End Press.
Coulson, Margaret, Branka Magas and Hilary Wainwright 1975, 'The Housewife and Her Labour Under Capitalism—A Critique', *New Left Review*, 89 (January).
Crenshaw, Kimberley 1989, 'Demarginalizing the intersection of race and sex: A Black Feminist critique of anti-discrimination doctrine, feminist theory and anti-racist politics', *University of Chicago Legal Forum*.
Csikszentmihalyi, Mihaly 1990, *Flow: The Psychology of Optimal Experience*, New York: Harper & Row.
Cudd, Ann and Nancy Holmstrom 2011, *Capitalism For & Against: A Feminist Debate*, Cambridge: Cambridge University Press.
Currie, E., R. Dunn, and D. Fogarty 1980, 'The New Immiseration: Stagflation, Inequality and the Working Class', *Socialist Review*, 10.
Dalla Costa Mariarosa and Selma James 1975, *The Power of Women and the Subversion of The Community*, London: Falling Wall Press.
Daly, Mary 1978, *Gyn/Ecology: The Metaethics of Radical Feminism*, Boston: Beacon .
Davenport, Coral 2019, 'Climate Panel Could Question Scope of Threat', *New York Times*, 21 February.

Davis, Mike 2001, *Late Victorian Holocausts: El Nino, Famines and the Making of the Third World*, New York: Verso.
Davis, Mike 2005, *The Monster at Our Door: The Global Threat of Avian Flu*, New York: New Press.
Davis, Mike 2006, *Planet of Slums*, London: Verso.
Degler, Carl 1991, 'In Search of Human Nature', *The New York Times Book Review*, 17 March.
Delphy, Christine 1984, *Close to Home: A Materialist Analysis of Women's Oppression*, London: Hutchinson.
Delphy, Christine and Diana Leonard 1992, *Familiar Exploitation*, Cambridge: Cambridge University Press.
Devine, Pat 1988, *Democracy and Economic Planning: The Political Economy of a Self-Governing Society*, Cambridge, UK: Polity Press, and Westview Press. Boulder, CO.
DeWaal, Frans 1996, *Good Natured: The Origins of Right and Wrong in Humans and other Animals*, Cambridge: Harvard University Press.
Diamond Jared 2005, *Collapse: How Societies Choose to Fail or Succeed*, New York: Viking.
Dickensen, Donna 1997, *Property, Women and Politics*, New Brunswick: Rutgers University Press.
Dinnerstein, Dorothy 1976, *The Mermaid and the Minotaur*, New York: Other Press.
Ditum Sarah 2014, 'Toying with Politics', http//sarahditum.com.
Draper, Hal 1970, *The Two Souls of Socialism*, available on-line.
Dworkin, Andrea 1974, *Woman-Hating*, New York: Dutton.
Eagleton, Terry 1991, *Ideology*, London: Verso.
Edel, Matthew 1979, 'A Note on Collective Action. Maximization and the Prisoner's Dilemma', *Economic Issues*, 13.
Eisenstein, Hester 2010, *Feminism Seduced: How Global Elites Use Women's Labor and Ideas to Exploit the World*, New York: Routledge.
Elster, Jon 1989, 'Self-Realization in Work and Politics: The Marxist Conception of the Good Life', in *Alternatives to Capitalism*, edited by Jon Elster and Karl Ove Moene, Cambridge: Cambridge University Press.
Engels, Friedrich 1875, 'Letter to Lavrov', 12–17 November.
Ennis, Kathy 1974, Review of Sheila Rowbotham, Women's Consciousness, Men's World', *International Socialism*, 68.
Ezorsky, Gertrude 2007, *Freedom in the Workplace?*, New York: Ithaca.
Fackler, Martin 2009, 'In Japan, New Jobless May Lack Safety Net', *New York Times*, 8 February 2009.
Fanon, Frantz 1967, *Black Skin, White Masks*, New York: Grove Press.
Farley, Melissa et al. 2003, 'Prostitution and Trafficking in Nine Countries: An Update on Violence and Posttraumatic Stress Disorder,' *Journal of trauma practice*, 2, 3/4.

Farris, Sara 2017, *In the Name of Women's Rights: The Rise of Femonationalism*, Durham: Duke University Press.

Federici, Silvia 2004, *Caliban and the Witch: Women, the Body and Primitive Accumulation*, Brooklyn: Autonomedia.

Fee, Terry 1976, 'Domestic Labour: An Analysis of Housework and Its Relation to the Production Process', *The Review of Radical Economics*, 8, 1.

Ferguson, Ann 1991, *Sexual Democracy: Women, Oppression and Revolution*, Boulder: CO, Westview.

Ferguson, Ann, Ilene Philipson, Irene Diamond and Lee Quinby, and Carole S. Vance and Ann Barr Snitow 1984, 'Forum: The Feminist Sexuality Debates', *Signs*, 10, 1.

Fernandez-Kelly, Patricia, and Diane Wolf 2001, 'A Dialogue on Globalization', *Signs*, 26, 4.

Ferree, Myra Marx 1976, 'Working Class Jobs: House Work and Paid As Sources of Satisfaction', *Social Problems*, 23, 4.

Fisher, William and Thomas Ponniah 2003, *Another World is Possible*, London: Pluto Books.

Fisk, Milton 1981, 'Determination and Dialectic', *Critique* 3.

Fisk, Milton 1989, *The State and Justice*, Cambridge: Cambridge University Press.

Fodor, Jerry 1991, 'Good taxonomy is about *not* missing generalizations', *Journal of Philosophy*, 88.

Folbre, Nancy 2009, 'Welfare for Bankers', *The New York Times Economix Blog*, 20 April.

Foot, Paul 1991, 'Poetry of Protest', *Socialist Review*, 55 (July–Aug).

Foster, John Bellamy 2000, *Marx's Ecology: materialism and nature*, New York: Monthly Review.

Frankfurt, Harry 1971, 'Freedom of Will and the Concept of a Person', *Journal of Philosophy*, 68, 1.

Frase, Peter 2012, 'The Problem with (Sex) Work', www.peterfrase.com.

Fraser, Nancy 2009, 'Feminism, Capitalism and the Cunning of History', *New Left Review*, 56, March–April: 97–117.

Fraser, Nancy 2017, 'The End of Progressive Neoliberalism', *Dissent* 2 January 2017.

Friedman, Milton 1962, *Capitalism and Freedom*, Chicago: University of Chicago Press.

Fukuyama, Frances 1987, 'The End of History', *National Interest*, Summer.

Gaa, James 1977, 'Moral Autonomy and the Rationality of Science', *Philosophy of Science*, 44.

Garrett, Laurie 1995, *The Coming Plague: Newly Emerging Diseases in a World Out of Balance*, New York: Penguin.

Gardiner, Jean 1975, 'Women's Domestic Labour', *New Left Review*, 89.

Gates Jr., Henry Louis 1986, 'Critical Remarks', in *'Race,' Writing, and Difference*, edited by Henry Louis Gates, Chicago: University of Chicago Press.

Gauthier, David 1974–5, 'Reason and Maximization', *Canadian Journal of Philosophy*, 4.

Geras, Norman 1983, *Marx and Human Nature: Refutation of a Legend*, London: Verso.
Geras, Norman 1985, 'The Controversy about Marx and Justice', *New Left Review* I/150 Mar/Apr.
Gerstein, Ira 1975, 'Domestic Work and Capitalism', *Radical America*, 7, 4, 5.
Gibson, Mary 1976–7, 'Rationality', *Philosophy and Public Affairs*, 6.
Gilligan, Carol 1990, *Making Connections: The Relational Worlds of Adolescent Girls at Emma Willard School*, Cambridge, MA: Harvard University Press 1990.
Gindin, Sam 2018, 'GM Oshawa: Making Hope Possible', *The Bullet*, 13 Dec.
Gleeson, Jules Joanna and Elle O'Rourke (eds.) 2021, *Transgender Marxism*, London: Pluto.
Goldberg, Steven 1977, 'The Inevitability of Patriarchy', in *Sex Equality*, edited by Jane English, Englewood Cliffs, NJ: Prentice-Hall, Inc.
Goldstein, Raymond L. and John K. Schorr 1991, *Demanding Democracy After Three Mile Island*, Gainesville, Fl: University of Florida Press.
Gornick, Vivian and Barbara Moran 1971, *Woman in Sexist Society*, New York.
Gough, Ian and John Harrison 1975, 'Unproductive Labor and Housework Again', *Bulletin of the Conference of Socialist Economists*, 4, 1.
Gould, Stephen Jay 1977, *Ever Since Darwin*, New York: W.W. Norton & Co.
Gould, Stephen Jay 1981, *The Mismeasure of Man*, New York: Norton.
Gowan, Peter 2018, 'A Plan to Nationalize Fossil Fuel Companies', *Jacobin*, March.
Grant, Melissa Gira 2014, *Playing the Whore*, London: Verso.
Gray, John 1980, 'On Positive and Negative Liberty', *Political Studies*, 28, 4.
Gray, John 1981, 'Hayek on Liberty, Rights and Justice', *Ethics*, 92 (October).
Gundersen, Adolf 1995, *The Environmental Promise of Democratic Deliberation*, Madison: University of Wisconsin Press.
Harding, Sandra 1987, 'The Curious Coincidence of Feminine and African Moralities: Challenges for Feminist Theory', in *Women and Moral Theory*, edited by Eva Kittay and Diana Meyers, Totowa, NJ: Rowan and Littlefield.
Harrison, John 1973a, 'Productive and Unproductive Labor in Marx's Political Economy', *Bulletin of the Conference of Socialist Economists*.
Harrison, John 1973b, 'Political Economy of Housework', *Conference of Socialist Economists Bulletin*, Winter.
Hart, Graham 2001, "Violence by clients towards female prostitutes in different work settings: questionnaire survey," *The BMJ*, 322 (3 March).
Hartmann, Heidi 1979, 'Capitalism, Patriarchy and Job Segregation by Sex', in *Capitalist Patriarchy and the Case for Socialist Feminism*, edited by Zillah Eisenstein, New York: Monthly Review Press.
Hartmann, Heidi 1981, 'The Unhappy Marriage of Marxism and Feminism', in *Women and Revolution*, edited by Lydia Sargent, Boston: South End Press 1981.
Harvey, David 2003, 'The "New" Imperialism: Accumulation by Dispossession', in *Social-*

ist Register 2004: The New Imperial Challenge, edited by Leo Panitch and Colin Leys, London: Merlin Press.
Haoson, Dominique 2009, 'Few Safety Nets for Women of Colour', Interpress News Service, 4 March.
Haug, Frigga 2015, 'Gender relations' and 'The Marx within feminism', in *Marxism and Feminism*, edited by S. Mojab, London: Zed Books: 33–102.
Hayek, F.A. 1988, *The Fatal Conceit*, London: University of Chicago Press.
Heller, Agnes 1976, *The Theory of Need in Marx*, London: Allison and Busby.
Henriksson, Lars 2015, 'Can Autoworkers Save the Planet?', *The Bullet*, 13 October.
Herman, Edward S., and Noam Chomsky 2002, *Manufacturing Consent: The Political Economy of the Mass Media*, New York: Pantheon.
Higgins, Patricia 1973, 'The Reactions of Women, with Special Reference to Women Petitioners', in *Politics, Religion and the English Civil War*, edited by B. Manning, New York: St. Martins Press.
Hill, Christopher 1996, *Liberty Against the Law*, London: Verso.
Hill, J.S. 1872, *An Examination of Sir William Hamilton's Philosophy*, London: Longmans Green and Company, Ltd.
Himmelweit, Susan and Simon Mohun 1977, 'Domestic Labor and Capitalism', *Cambridge Journal of Economics*, 1.
Hirschmann, Nancy 2003, *The Subject of Liberty: Toward A Feminist Theory of Freedom*, Princeton University Press: Princeton.
Hobart, R.E. 1966, 'Free Will as Involving Determinism and Inconceivable Without It', in *Free Will and Determinism*, edited by Bernard Berofsky, New York: Harper and Row.
Hochschild, Arlie 2003, *The Commercialization of Intimate Life*, Berkeley: University of California Press.
Hochschild, Arlie 2012, *The Managed Heart*, Berkeley CA: University of California Press.
Hoffman, L. 1972, 'Early Childhood Experiences and Women's Achievement Motives', *Journal of Social Issues*, 28.
Hollis M. and Nell E.J. 1975, *Rational Economic Man*, Cambridge: Cambridge University Press.
Holmstrom, Nancy 1975, 'Free Will and a Marxist Conception of Natural Wants', *Philosophical Forum*, 6, 4.
Holmstrom, Nancy 1977a, 'Exploitation', *Canadian Journal of Philosophy*, 7, 2, June 1977.
Holmstrom, Nancy 1977b, "Firming Up Soft determinism" *The Personalist*, 58, 1.
Holmstrom, Nancy 1977c, 'Marx, Machinery and Alienation', *Proceedings of the Society for Philosophy and Technology 11*.
Holmstrom, Nancy 1981, '"Women's work", the family and capitalism', *Science and Society*, 45, 2.

Holmstrom, Nancy 1982, 'Do Women Have a Distinct Nature?', *The Philosophical Forum*, 14, 1.
Holmstrom, Nancy 1983, 'Marx and Cohen on Exploitation and the Labor Theory of Value', *Inquiry*, 7 (Fall).
Holmstrom, Nancy 1984, 'A Marxist Theory of Women's Nature', *Ethics*, 94 (April).
Holmstrom, Nancy 1994a, 'Coercion, Exploitation and Labor', APA *Newsletter on Philosophy and Law*, Vol. 94, No. 1, Fall.
Holmstrom, Nancy 1994b, 'Humankind(s)', in *Biology, Behavior and Society, Canadian Journal of Philosophy*, supplementary, 20.
Holmstrom, Nancy 1997, 'Review of *Self-Ownership, Freedom and Equality, Philosophical Review*', 106, 4 (October).
Holmstrom, Nancy 1998, 'Feminist Perspectives on Human Nature' in *A Companion to Feminist Philosophy*, edited by Alison Jaggar and Iris Young, London: Wiley-Blackwell.
Holmstrom, Nancy 2000, 'Rationality, Solidarity and Public Goods', *Not For Sale: In Defense of Public Goods*, edited by Anatole Anton, Milton Fisk and Nancy Holmstrom, Boulder, Westview.
Holmstrom, Nancy and Richard Smith 2000, 'The necessity of gangster capitalism: primitive accumulation in Russia and China', *Monthly Review* 51, 9 (February): 1–14.
Holmstrom, Nancy (ed.) 2002, *The Socialist Feminist Project*, New York: Monthly Review.
Holmstrom, Nancy and Richard Smith 2007, 'Their Rationality and Ours', in *Toward a New Socialism*, edited by Anatole Anton and Richard Schmitt, Lanham, MD: Lexington Books.
Holmstrom, Nancy and Ann E. Cudd, 2011, *Capitalism, For and Against: A Feminist Debate*, Cambridge: Cambridge University Press.
Holmstrom, Nancy 2012, 'Exploitation', *International Encyclopedia of Ethics*.
Holmstrom, Nancy 2013, 'Is Human Nature Important for Feminism?', in *Arguing Human Nature*, edited by Eduard Machery and Steven Downs, London: Routledge.
Holmstrom, Nancy 2014, 'Sex, Work and Capitalism', *Logos*.
Holmstrom, Nancy 2020 'Marxist/Socialist Theory and Practice in the USA Today', *Marxist-Feminist Theories and Struggles Today: Essential Writings on Intersectionality, Labor and Ecofeminism*, edited by Khayaat Fakier, Diana Mulinari and Nora Rathzel, London: Zed Books.
Holmstrom, Nancy 2020, 'Democratic Socialism for a Finite World', in Gregory Smulewicz-Zucker and Michael J. Thompson eds. *An Inheritance for Our Time*, New York: OR Books.
Hong Kingston, Maxine 1989, *Tripmaster Monkey*, New York: Knopf.
Hook, Sidney 1962, *From Hegel to Marx*, Ann Arbor, MI: University of Michigan Press.
hooks, bell 1981, *Ain't I a Woman?*, Boston: South End Press 1981.
hooks, bell 1984, *Feminist Theory From Margin to Centre*, Boston: South End Press.

Hull, D.L. 1966–7, 'The Metaphysics of Evolution', *British Journal of the History of Science*, 3.

Hull, D.L. 1966, 'The Effect of Essentialism on Taxonomy: 2000 Years of Stasis, Parts 1, 2', *British Journal of the Philosophy of Science*, 15.

Hull, D.L. 1970, 'Contemporary Systemic Philosophies', *Annual Review of Ecology and Systematics*, edited by Richard Johnson, Palo Alto, CA: Annual Reviews.

Hull, Gloria T., Patricia Bell Scott, and Barbara Smith (eds.) 1982, *But Some of Us Are Brave*, New York: Feminist Press.

Hume, David 1870, 'Of National Characters', in *Essays, Moral, Political, and Literary*, London: Longmans, Green.

Hume, David 1956, 'Of Liberty and Necessity', in *An Inquiry Concerning Human Understanding*, Los Angeles: Henry Ragnery Co.

Humphries, Jane, 1977, 'The Working Class Family, Women's Liberation, & Class Struggle: The Case of 19th Century British History', *Review of Radical Political Economics*, 9, 3.

Israel Rosen, Ellen 2002, *Making Sweatshops: The Globalization of the US Apparel Industry*, Berkeley, CA: University of California Press.

Kruks, Sonia, Rayna Rapp and Marilyn B. Young (eds.) 1989, *Promissory Notes: Women in the Transition to Socialism*, New York: Monthly Review.

James, C.L.R. 1963, *The Black Jacobins*, 2nd ed., New York: Vintage.

James, C.L.R. 1977, *Selected Writings of C.L.R. James*, New York.

James, C.L.R. 1980, *The Future in the Present: Selected Writings of C.L.R. James*, London: Allison and Busby.

Jensen, A.R. 1970, 'The Race X Class X Ability Interaction', Ph.D. diss., University of California, Berkeley.

Johnson, Chalmers 1982, *Miti and the Japanese Miracle*, Stanford: Stanford University Press.

Johnson, G.T. and A. Lubin (eds.) 2017, *Futures of Black Radicalism*, New York: Verso.

Jonasdottir, Anna G. 1988, 'On the Concept of Interest, Women's Interests, and the Limitations of Interest Theory', in *The Political Interests of Gender*, edited by Kathleen Jones and Anna G. Jonasdottir, London: Sage Publications.

Kabeer, Naila 2002, *The Power to Choose*, New York: Verso.

Kaufmann, Greg 2018, 'What Farmworkers Can Teach Hollywood about Ending Sexual Harassment', *The Nation*, 24 Jan.

Kelly, Kevin 2009, 'The New Socialism: Global Collectivist Society is Coming Online', www.wired.com.

Kelley, Robin D.G. 2002, *Freedom Dreams*, Boston: Beacon Press.

Kergoat, Danièle 2009, 'Dynamique et consubstantialité des rapports sociaux', in *Sexe, race et classe. Pour une épistémolofie de la domination*, Paris: puf.

Kidron, Mike 1974, *Capitalism and Theory*, London: Pluto.

Klein, Naomi 2007, *The Shock Doctrine: The Rise of Disaster Capitalism*, New York: Henry Holt & Co.

Krugman, Paul 2009, 'How Did Economists Get It So Wrong?', *New York Times Magazine*, 6 September.

Kuttner, Robert 1997, *Everything for Sale*, New York: Knopf.

Laclau, Ernesto 1971, 'Feudalism and Capitalism in Latin America', *New Left Review*, 67.

Ladner, Joyce 1972, *Tomorrow's Tomorrow*, Garden City, NY: Doubleday & Co.

Lan, Pei-Chia 2002, 'Among Women: Migrant Domestics and their Taiwanese Employers Across Generations', in *Global Woman: Nannies, Maids and Sex Workers in the New Economy*, edited by Barbara Ehrenreich and Arlie Russell Hochschild, New York, Harry Holt and Co.

Larguia, Isabel and John Dumolin 1972, 'Toward a Science of Women's Liberation', *Political Affairs*, 51 (6 and 8 June).

Lehrman, Karen 1997, *The Lipstick Proviso: Women, Sex and Power in the Real World*, New York: Doubleday.

Lewontin, Richard C., Steven Rose, Leon J. Kamin 1984, *Not in Our Genes*, New York: Penguin 1984.

van Loon, Julienne 2019, *The Thinking Woman*, Sydney: New South Books; Rutgers University Press.

Linebaugh, Peter 2008, *The Magna Carta Manifesto*, Berkeley: University of California Press.

Locke, John 1980, *Second Treatise of Government*, edited by C.B. Macpherson, Indianapolis: Hackett Publishing Co.

Longworth, Richard C. 1998, *Global Squeeze: The Coming Crisis for First World Nations*, Chicago: Contemporary Books.

Lowy, Michael 2006, 'Ecosocialism and Democratic Planning', in *Socialist Register 2007: Coming to Terms with Nature*, edited by Leo Panitch and Colin Leys, London: Merlin Press.

Lovibond, Sabina 1989, 'Feminism and Postmodernism', *New Left Review*, 178.

Lovibond, Sabina 1992, 'Feminism and Pragmatism: A Reply to Richard Rorty', *New Left Review*.

Lucas, J.R. 1959, 'Moralists and Gamesmen', *Philosophy*, 34.

Luce R.D. and H. Raiffa, *Games and Decisions*, New York: John Wiley & Sons, Inc.

Luce, Stephanie and Mark Brenner 2006, 'Women and Class: What's Happened in Forty Years?', *Monthly Review*, July–August.

Luria, R. 1966, *Higher Cortical Functions in Man*, New York: Basic Books.

Luria, R. 1973, *The Working Brain: An Introduction to Neuropsychology*, New York: Basic Books.

Luxemburg, Rosa 1925, *The Mass Strike*, London: Merlin.

Luxemburg, Rosa 2002, 'Women's Suffrage and Class Struggle', in *The Socialist Feminist Project*, edited by Nancy Holmstrom, New York: Monthly Review.

McChesney Robert 1999, *Rich Media, Poor Democracy: Communication Politics in Dubious Times*, Illinois: University of Illinois Press.

MacIntyre, Alastair 1964, 'Against Utilitarianism', in *Aims of Education*, edited by T.H.B. Hollins, Manchester: Manchester University Press.

MacCallum Jr., Gerald C. 1967, 'Negative and Positive Freedom', *Philosophical Review*, 76, no. 3.

MacKinnon, Catherine 1979, *Sexual Harassment of Working Women*, New London: Yale University Press.

Maclean, Nancy 2002, 'Post-War Women's History: The "Second Wave" or the End of the Family Wage?' in *A Companion to Post-1945 America*, edited by Jean-Christophe Agnew and Roy Rosensweig, Malden, MA.: Blackwell.

McMurtry, John 1973, 'Making Sense of Economic Determinism', *Canadian Journal of Philosophy*, 3, 2.

McMurtry, John 1978, *The Structure of Marx's World View*, Princeton: Princeton University Press.

Maccoby, E. 1966, 'Sex Differences in Intellectual Functioning', in *The Development of Sex Differences*, edited by E. Maccoby, Stanford, CA: Stanford University Press.

Maccoby, E. and L. Jacklin 1974, *The Psychology of Sex Differences*, Stanford, CA: Stanford University Press.

Macpherson, C.B. 1962, *The Political Theory of Possessive Individualism*, Oxford: Oxford University Press.

Macpherson, C.B. 1962, *The Political Theory of Possessive Individualism*, Oxford: Oxford University Press.

Macpherson, C.B. 1977, *The Life and Times of Liberal Democracy*, Oxford: Oxford University Press.

Macpherson, C.B. (ed.) 1978, *Property*, Toronto: University of Toronto Press.

Macpherson, C.B., 1985, *The Rise and Fall of Economic Justice and Other Essays*, New York: Oxford University Press.

Magdoff, Fred and Chris Williams 2017, *Creating an Ecological Society*, New York: Monthly Review Press.

Marcuse, Herbert 1961, *Soviet Marxism*, New York: Random House.

Marx, Karl 1904, *A Contribution to the Critique of Political Economy*, Chicago: Charles H. Kerr and Co.

Marx, Karl 1933, *Wage, Labor and Capital*, New York International Publishers.

Marx, Karl 1961, *Capital* vol. 1, Moscow.

Marx, Karl 1963, *Theories of Surplus Value Part 1*, Moscow: Progress Publishers.

Marx, Karl 1964, 'Economic and Philosophical Manuscripts', in *Karl Marx: Early Writings*, edited and translated by T.B. Bottomore, New York: Prentice-Hall.

Marx, Karl 1967, *Capital*, Volume III, New York: International Publishers.
Marx, Karl 1969, *Theories of Surplus Value*, vols. 1–3, Moscow: Progress.
Marx, Karl 1970, *Capital*: Volume I, New York:
Marx, Karl 1971, *The Grundrisse*, edited by David McLellan, New York: New Harper and Row.
Marx, Karl 1972, *Capital*, vol. I, New York: Penguin.
Marx, Karl 1973, *Grundrisse*, translated by McLellan, Harmondsworth: Penguin.
Marx, Karl 1974, *Capital*, Volume III, Moscow: Progress Publishers.
Marx, Karl 1975a, *Economic and Philosophical Manuscripts*, MECW, vol. 3, London: Lawrence & Wishart.
Marx, Karl 1975b, *Grundrisse, Foundations of the Critique of Political Economy*, in *Karl Marx, Frederick Engels Collected Works*, New York: International Publishers.
Marx, Karl 1986, *The Grundrisse*, MECW, vol. 28, London: Lawrence & Wishart.
Marx, Karl 1998, *Capital III MECW*, vol. 37, London: Lawrence & Wishart.
Marx, Karl and Friedrich Engels 1967, *The German Ideology in Writings of the Young Marx on Philosophy and Society*, edited by Lloyd D. Easton and Kurt Guddat, Garden City, NY: Doubleday and Co.
Marx Aveling, Edward, and Eleanor Marx Aveling 1972, 'The Woman Question', *Marxism Today*.
Mathieu, Nicole-Claud 1990, 'When Yielding is Not Consenting', *Feminist Issues*, 10.
Matson, Wallace I. 1966, 'Why Isn't the Mind–Body Problem Ancient?', *Mind, Matter and Method: Essays in Philosophy and Science in Honor of Herbert Feigl*, edited by Paul K. Feyerabend and Grover Maxwell, University of Minnesota Press.
Mead, Margaret 1935, *Sex and Temperament in Three Primitive Societies*, New York: William Morrow & Co.
Meiksins Wood, Ellen 1988, *Peasant-Citizen and Slave: The Foundations of Athenian Democracy*, London.
Meiksins Wood, Ellen 1995, *Democracy Against Capitalism*, Cambridge: Cambridge University Press.
Mepham, John 1972, 'Ideology *in Capital*', *Radical Philosophy*, 2.
Mepham, John 1973, 'Who Makes History?' *Radical Philosophy*, 6.
Midgeley, Mary 1988, 'On Not Being Afraid of Natural Differences', in *Feminist Perspectives in Philosophy*, edited by Morwenna Griffiths and Margaret Whitford, Basingstoke: Macmillan.
Mihm, Stephen 2008, 'Dr. Doom', *New York Times*, 15 August.
Miles, Laura 2020, *Transgender Resistance: Socialism and the Fight for Trans Liberation*, London: Bookmarks.
Miles, Robert 1987, *Capitalism and Un-free Labor: Anomaly or Necessity?*, London: Tavistock.
Milkman, Ruth 1976, 'Women's Work and the Economic Crisis: Some Lessons from the Great Depression', *Review of Radical Political Economics*, 8, 1 (Spring).

Miller, Judith 1999, 'Globalization Widens Rich-Poor Gap, U.N. Says', *New York Times*, 29 June.
Mills, Charles 2004, '"Ideal Theory" as Ideology', in *Moral Psychology*, edited by Peggy Des Autels and Margaret Urban Walker, Lanham: Rowman & Littlefield.
Mishra, Pankaj 2006, 'The Myth of the New India', *New York Times*, 6 July.
Mitchell, Juliet 1971, *Women's Estate*, New York: Penguin.
Molyneux, Maxine 1982, 'Socialist Societies: Progress towards Women's Emancipation?' *Monthly Review*, 34.
Molyneux, Maxine 1985, 'Mobilization Without Emancipation? Women's Interests, State and Revolution', *Feminist Studies*, 11, 2.
Molyneux, Maxine 2002, 'Conceptualizing Women's Interests', in *The Socialist Feminist Project*, edited by Nancy Holmstrom, New York: Monthly Review Press.
Monbiot, George 2003, *The Age of Consent: a Manifesto for a New World Order*, London: Flamingo.
Moore, Barrington, Jr. 1978, *Injustice—The Social Bases of Obedience and Revolt*, White Plains, NY: M.E. Sharpe.
Moya, Paula M.L. 1997, 'Post-Modernism, "Realism" and the Politics of Identity: Cherrie Moraga and Chicana Feminism', in *Feminist Genealogies, Colonial Legacies, Democratic Futures*, edited by M. Jacqui Alexander and Chandra Talpade Mohanty, New York: Routledge.
Mullings, Leith 2002, 'Mapping gender in African-American political struggles', in Holmstrom 2002: 313–35.
Nader, Ralph, "Stop the Single Payer Shut-out," Common Dreams, 9 May, 2009, https://www.commondreams.org/views/2009/05/09/stop-single-payer-shut-out.
Nagel, Thomas 1970, *The Possibility of Altruism*, Oxford: Oxford University Press.
Nei, Masataoshi 1983, and Arun K. Roychoudhury, 'Genetic Relationships and Evolution of Human Races', *Evolutionary Biology*, 14.
Neilson, Kai 1972, 'Is Empiricism on Ideology', *Metaphilosophy*, 3, 4.
Nielsen, Kai 1974, 'Philosophy and Ideology: Programmatic Remarks for a Radical Philosophy', *Radical Philosophers Newsjournal*, 3.
O'Brien, Mary 1981, *The Politics of Reproduction*, London: Routledge and Kegan Paul.
O'Neill, Onora 1993, 'Justice, Gender and International Boundaries', *The Quality of Life*, Martha C. Nussbaum and Amartya Sen, Oxford: Oxford University Press.
Ollman, Bertell 1971, *Alienation: Marx's Concept of Man in Capitalist Society*, Cambridge: Cambridge University Press.
Olson, Mancur 1965, *The Logic of Collective Action*, Cambridge, MA: Harvard University Press.
Ostrom, Elinor 1990, *Governing the Commons*, Cambridge, UK: Cambridge University Press.
Packard, Vance 1957, *The Hidden Persuaders*, New York: David McKay Co. Inc.

Palast, Greg et al. 2003, *Democracy and Regulation: How the Public Can Govern Essential Services*, London: Pluto.

Van Parijs, Philippe 1995, *Real Freedom for All: What, If Anything, Can Justify Capitalism?*, Oxford: Oxford University Press.

Patel, Raj 2007, *Stuffed and Starved: The Hidden Battle for World Food*, New York: Melville House.

Pateman, Carole 1986, *The Sexual Contract*, Stanford, CA: Stanford University Press.

Pateman, Carole, and Charles W. Mills 2007, *Contract and Domination*, Cambridge: Cambridge University Press.

Patterson, Orlando 1991, *Freedom in the Making of Western Culture*, New York: Basic Books.

Perelman, Michael 2006, 'Some Economics of Class', *Monthly Review*, July–August.

Petchesky, Rosalind Pollack 1995, 'The Body as Property: A Feminist Re-vision', in *Conceiving the New World Order: The Global politics of Reproduction*, edited by Faye D. Ginsburg and Rayna Rapp, Berkeley, CA: University of California Press.

Pearsall, Marjorie 1986, *Women and Values: Readings in Recent Feminist Philosophy*, edited by Marjorie Pearsall, Belmont, CA: Wadsworth.

Pettit, Philip 2001, *A Theory of Freedom: From the Psychology to the Politics of Agency*, New York: Wiley.

Pincus, Walter and Joby Warrick 2009, 'Financial Crisis called Top Security Threat to US', *Washington Post*, 13 February.

Piven, Frances Fox and Richard A. Cloward 1979, *Poor Peoples' Movements: Why They Succeed and How They Fail*, New York: Random House.

Pogge, Thomas 2002, *World Poverty and Human Rights: Cosmopolitan Responsibilities and Reforms*, Cambridge: Polity Press.

Politt, Katha 2014, "Why do so many leftists want sex work to be the new normal?" *The Nation*, April 21.

Porrit, Jonathon 2005, *Capitalism As If the World Matters*, London: Earthscan.

Potter, Eliabeth 1994, 'Locke's Epistemology and Women's Struggles', in *Modern Engendering: Critical Feminist Readings in Modern Western Philosophy*, edited by Bat-Ami Bar On, Albany: SUNY Press.

Preis, Art. 1964, *Labor's Giant Step: 20 Years of the CIO*, New York: Pioneer Publishers.

Qinglian, He 2000. 'The Land-Enclosure Movement of the 1990s', *The Chinese Economy*, 33, 3 (May–June).

Radin, Margaret Jane 1987, 'Market Inalienability', *Harvard Law Review*, 100, 8.

Rasmussen Reports 2009, "Just 53% say that Capitalism is Better than Socialism," Rasmussen Reports, http://www.rasmussenreports.com/public_content/politics/general_politics/april_2009/just_53_say_capitalism_better_than_socialism [accessed September 25].

Rapaport, Elizabeth 1974, Review of Sheila Rowbotham, Women's Consciousness, Men's World, *Telos*, 21 (Fall).
Rapoport, Anatol 1974, 'Prisoner's Dilemma—Recollection and Observations', in *Game Theory as a Theory of Conflict Resolution*, Dordrecht: D. Reidel Publishing.
Rapoport, Anatol, and Albert M. Chammam 1964, *Prisoner's Dilemma: A Study in Conflict and Cooperation*, Ann Arbor: University of Michigan Press.
Rawick, George P. 1972, *From Sundown to Sunup: The Making of the Black Community*, Westport, CT: Greenwood.
Rawls, John 1971, *A Theory of Justice*, Cambridge, MA: Harvard University Press.
Reiman, Jeffrey 1987, 'Exploitation, Force and the Moral Assessment of Capitalism: Thoughts on Roemer and Cohen', *Philosophy and Public Affairs*, 16 (winter).
Rich, Adrienne 1986, *Of Woman Born: Motherhood as Experience and Institution*, New York: Norton.
Ries, Curt 2019, 'A Green New Deal Must Prioritize Regenerative Agriculture', *Truthout*, 9 May.
Riley, Denise 1983, *War in the Nursery*, London: Virago.
Richards, Janet Radcliffe 1980, *The Sceptical Feminist: A Philosophical Inquiry*, Harmondsworth: Penguin Books.
Roberts, Dorothy 2015, 'Reproductive justice, not just rights', *Dissent* Fall.
Roediger, David R. 1992, *The Wages of Whiteness: Race and the Making of the American Working Class*, London: Verso.
Rohatyn, Felix 2009, 'Saving American Capitalism', *International Herald*, Tribune, 29 June.
Romer, Nancy, 1981, *The Sex-Role Cycle*, New York: Feminist Press/McGraw-Hill Book Co.
Rorty, Richard 1991, 'Feminism and Pragmatism', *Michigan Quarterly Review*, 30.
Rose, Steven 1981, 'From Causation to Translation: A Dialectical Solution to a Reductionist Dilemma', *Bressanone Papers*, edited by Steven Rose, London: Allison and Busby.
Rowbotham, Sheila, *Women's Consciousness, Man's World*, Baltimore: Penguin Books.
Ryan, Cheyney 1997, 'Yours, Mine and Ours: Property Rights and Individual Liberty', *Ethics*, 87.
Saffiotti, Helen 1975, 'Women, Mode of Production and Social Formations', *Latin America Perspectives*, 4, 1 and 2.
Saffioti, Helen 1978, *Women in Class Society*, New York: Monthly Review.
Schachter, S. and J.E. Singer 1962, 'Cognitive, Social and Physiological Determinants of Emotional State', *Psychological Review*, 69.
Schick, Frederic n.d., 'Rationality and Sociality', Rutgers University, unpublished.
Schlick, Moritz 1966, 'When is a Man Responsible?', in *Free Will and Determinism*, edited by Bernard Berofsky, New York: Harper and Row.

Schmitt, Richard 2003, *Alienation and Freedom*, Boulder, CO: Westview.
Schwartz, Adina 1973-4, 'Moral Autonomy and Primary Goods', *Ethics*, 83.
Scott, Hilda 1974, *Does Socialism Liberate Women?*, Boston: Beacon Press.
Scott, Joan 1988, *Gender and the Politics of History*, New York: Columbia University Press.
Secombe, Wally 1973, 'The Housewife and Her Labor Under Capitalism', *New Left Review*, 83 (January).
Sen, Amartya 1970, *Collective Choice and Social Welfare*, San Francisco: Holden-Day.
Sen, Amartya 1976-7, 'Rational Fools: A Critique of the Behavioural Foundations of Economic Theory', *Philosophy and Public Affairs*, 6.
Sen, Amartya 1981, *Poverty and Famines*, Oxford: Clarendon Press.
Sen, Amartya 1999, *Development as Freedom*, New York: Alfred A. Knopf.
Sengupta, Somini 2006, 'Indian Prosperity Creates Paradox; Many Children are Fat, Even More are Famished', *New York Times*, 31 December.
Sengupta, Somini 2009, 'As Indian Growth Soars, Child Hunger Persists', *New York Times*, 13 March.
Sengupta, Somini 2018, 'Projection on Climate is Ominous. Now What?', *New York Times*, 10 October.
Sennett, Richard 1972, *The Hidden Injuries of Class*, New York: Knopf.
Seve, Lucien 1978, *Man in Marxist Theory and the Psychology of Personality*, Brighton: Harvester.
Skandier, Carla 2017, 'Nationalize the Fossil Fuel Industry', *In These Times*, 17 November
Skandier, Carla 2018, 'Quantitative Easing for the Planet', *The Next System Project*, 30 August.
Silliman Jael and Ynestra King (eds.) 1999, *Dangerous Intersections: Feminist Perspectives on Population, Environment and Development*, Cambridge, MA: South End Press.
Silliman, J. and M. Gerber Fried, L. Ross, E. Gutierrez (eds.) 2004, *Undivided Rights: Women of Colour Organize for Reproductive Justice*, Cambridge, MA: South End Press.
Singer, Marcus 1978, 'Some Thoughts on "Race" and "Racism"', *Philosophia*, 8.
Singer, Peter 2009, *The Life You Can Save: Acting Now to End World Poverty*, New York: Random House.
Smith, Barbara (ed.) 1983, *Home Girls: A Black Feminist Anthology*, New York: Kitchen Table—Women of Colour Press.
Smith, Adam 1937, *The Wealth of Nations*, New York: Modern Library.
Smith, Adrian 2014, 'The Lucas Plan: What can it tell us about democratizing technology today?' *The Guardian*, 22 January.
Smith, Joan 1977, 'Women and the Family', *International Socialism*, 100.
Smith, Joan 1978/9, 'Women's Oppression and Men's Alienation', *International Socialism*, 2, 3.

Smith, Richard 2005, 'Capitalism and *Collapse*: Contradictions of Jared Diamond's market meliorist strategy to save the humans', *Ecological Economics*, 55, 2.
Smith, Richard 2007, 'The Eco-suicidal Economics of Adam Smith', *Capitalism Nature Socialism*, 19, 2.
Smith, Richard 2016, *Green Capitalism: The God That Failed*, London, UK: World Economics Association Books.
Smith, Richard, 2016, 'Six Theses on Saving the Planet', available at: https://thenextsystem.org/sites/default/files/2018-10/RichardSmith-2.pdf.
Smith, Richard 2019, 'An Ecosocialist Path to Limiting Global Temperature Rise to 1.5°C', *Real World Economics Review*, 87.
Sohn-Rethel, Alfred 1978, *Intellectual and Manual Labor*, London: MacMillan.
Soper, Kate 1986, *Humanism and Anti-Humanism*, LaSalle, IL: Hutchinson.
Spelman, Elizabeth V. 1988, *The Inessential Woman*, Boston: Beacon.
Stanford, Jim 2009, 'The economics, and politics, of auto workers' wages', 20 April www.theglobeandmail.com.
Stepan, Nancy 1982, *The Idea of Race in Science: Great Britain, 1800–1950*, London: Macmillan.
Suchting, Wal 1979, 'Marx's Theses on Feuerbach: Notes Toward a Commentary' in *Issues in Marxist Philosophy, Vol. 2*, edited by John Mepham and David Hillel-Ruben, Brighton: Harvester.
Sweeney, Sean 2019, 'When "Green" Doesn't Grow: Facing Up to the Failures of Profit-Driven Climate Policy', *Monthly Review Online*, 3 January.
Swerdlow, Amy (ed.) 1980, *Household and Kin: Families in Flux*, New York: Feminist Press.
Taylor, Barbara 1983, *Eve and the New Jerusalem*, London: Virago Press.
Taylor, Keenga-Yamahtta (ed.) 2017, *How We Get Free: Black Feminism and the Combahee River Collective*, Chicago: Haymarket Books.
Thurow, Lester 1996, *The Future of Capitalism*, New York: Penguin Books.
Thalberg, Irving 1962, 'False Pleasures', *Journal of Philosophy*, 59.
Thoy, C.B. 1969, 'Status, Race and Aspirations: A Study of the Desire of High School Students to Enter a Profession or a Technical Occupation', Dissertation Abstracts International 2.
Tilly, Louise 1989, 'Gender, Women's History and Social History', *Pasato e Presente*, 20–1.
Timpanaro, Sebastiano 1970, *On Materialism*, London: Humanities Press.
Tucker, Robert 1961, *Philosophy and Myth in Karl Marx*, Cambridge: Cambridge University Press.
Tucker, Robert (ed.) 1978, *The Marx-Engels Reader*, 2nd edition, New York: W.W. Norton & Company.
Tulkin, S.R. 1968, 'Race, Class, Family and School Achievement', *Journal of Personality and Social Psychology*, 9.

Tyler, L.E. 1965, *The Psychology of Human Differences*, New York: Appleton-Century-Crofts.
Varikas, Eleni 1995, 'Gender, Experience and Subjectivity: The Tilly-Scott Disagreement', *New Left Review*, 211, May/June.
Venable, Vernon 1945, *Human Nature: The Marxian View*, New York: Knopf.
Veroff, Joseph and Sheila Feld 1970, *Marriage and Work in America*, New York: Van Nostrand Reinhold.
Vygotsky, Lev, A.R. Luria 1976, *Cognitive Development: Its Cultural and Social Foundations*, Cambridge, MA: Harvard University Press.
Vygotsky, Lev 1982, *Thought and Language*, Cambridge, MA: MIT Press.
Vogel, Lise 1983, *Marxism and the Oppression of Women: Toward a Unitary Theory*, New Brunswick, NJ: Rutgers University Press.
Wade, Robert 2001, 'Global Inequality', *The Economist*, 28 April.
Wainwright, Hilary 1975, 'The Housewife and Her Labour Under Capitalism—A Critique', *New Left Review*, 89.
Wainwright, Hilary 2003, *Reclaim the State*, London: Verso, 2003.
Wainwright, Hilary 2015, 'Why I became a feminist socialist', *Jacobin*, 28 December.
Wainwright, Hilary 2016, 'Radicalizing the Party-Movement Relation: From Ralph Miliband to Jeremy Corbyn and Beyond', in *Socialist Register 2017: Rethinking Revolution*, edited by Leo Panitch and Greg Albo, London: Merlin Press.
Wainwright, Hilary 2018, 'Forging a "Social Knowledge Economy"', in *From the Streets to the State*, edited by Paul Christopher Gray, Albany: State University of New York Press.
Waldron, Jeremy 1988, *The Right to Private Property*, New York: Oxford University Press.
Walkowitz, Judith R. 1983, 'Male Vice and Female Virtue: Feminism and the Politics of Prostitution in Nineteenth Century Britain', in *Powers of Desire*, edited by Ann Snitow, Christine Stansell, and Sharon Thompson, New York: Monthly Review Press.
Warren, Paul 1994, 'Self-Ownership, Reciprocity, and Exploitation, or Why Marxists Shouldn't Be Afraid of Robert Nozick', *Canadian Journal of Philosophy*, 24.
Weeks, Kathi 2011, *The Problem with Work: Feminism, Marxism, Antiwork Politics, and Postwork Imaginaries*, Durham: Duke University Press.
Weinbaum, Batya and Amy Bridges 1979, 'The Other Side of the Paycheck: Monopoly Capital and the Structure of Consumption', in *Capitalist Patriarch and the Case for Socialist-Feminism*, edited by Zillah Eisenstein, New York: Monthly Review.
Weston, P. and M. Mednick 1970, 'Race, Social Class and the Motive to Avoid Success in Women', *Journal of Cross-cultural Psychology*, 1.
Whitelegg, John 1994, 'Dirty from cradle to grave', at www.worldcarfree.net/resources/freesources/DirtyfromCradletoGrave.rtf
Williams, Eric 1966, *Capitalism and Slavery*, New York: Capricorn.

Winstanley, Gerard 1973, *Winstanley: The Law of Freedom and Other Writings*, edited by Christopher Hill, Harmondsworth: Penguin.
Wittig, Monique 1981, 'One is Not Born a Woman', *Feminist Issues*, 1.
Wittig, Monique 1982, 'The Category of Sex', *Feminist Issues*, 2.
Wittig, Monique 1989, 'On the Social Contract', *Feminist Issues*.
Wood, Ellen Meiksins and Neal Wood 1997, *A Trumpet of Sedition*, London: Pluto.
Xinran 2003, *The Good Women of China: Hidden Voices*, New York: Anchor.
Young, I.M. 1997, 'Socialist feminism and the limits of dual systems theory', in *Materialist Feminism*, edited by R. Hennessy and C. Ingraham, New York: Routledge: 95–106.
Zaretsky, Eli 1976, *Capitalism, The Family and Personal Life*, New York: Harper & Row.
Zimmerman, David 1981, 'Coercive Wage Offers' *Philosophy and Public Affairs*, 10.

Index

abortion 25, 62, 166, 169, 171, 174, 178, 199–200, 225, 266
absolute monarchy 159, 164, 178
abuse 28, 37, 200, 213
accumulation strategy 111
Afghanistan 154, 200, 217
Africa 214–15, 267, 269–70, 273
alienation 6, 8, 32, 36–38, 91, 111–12, 123, 156, 165, 167, 275–89
Allison, Dorothy 187
Althusser 250–51, 276
Altvater, Elmar 111–12
Anderson, Elizabeth 38, 168, 179
Appiah, Kwame Anthony 268–69
Aristotle 66, 104, 153, 191–93, 256
Astell, Mary 164
autonomy 60, 64, 155, 166–167, 172, 188, 205, 223, 225–26, 259

Bangladesh 201, 204, 206
bankruptcies 203, 207
banks 68, 145, 184, 186, 207
de Beauvoir, Simone 257, 259, 294
Bellamy Foster, John 277
Bello, Walden 186, 292
Benston, Margaret 17, 43, 61
Blauner, Robert 278
Buchanan, Alan 81, 83, 87, 91
Bureaucratic collectivism 67, 69, 199
bicycles 100, 110, 221
biological determinist theories 250, 256, 260
biological differences 233–34, 239, 245–46, 256, 258–59, 274
biology 230, 238, 240, 245, 248, 250–51, 253, 257, 264–68, 273, 300
    human 230, 255–56, 260, 292
    women's 259, 266
body 20, 32, 35–37, 100, 118, 154, 160, 165–69, 195, 257, 279–80
bondage 71
    debt 39, 215
brains 7, 235, 252, 255
    human 256, 286
Braverman, Harry 278–79
Brenner, Johanna 23, 140, 208, 210–211, 265

bureaucracy 14, 16, 190, 199–200
Butler, Judith 257

capital 2–3, 13–15, 42–47, 49, 52, 54, 57–59, 62, 101, 103, 250, 275–78, 280–84, 286
capitalist democracies 66, 71, 113, 152, 154, 212
capitalist development 15, 193, 201, 205, 212–13, 215, 217–18
Charnock, Greig 78, 102
childcare 3, 23, 39, 50, 174–75, 198–200, 225, 243, 266
children 37, 51–52, 55, 57, 148, 150, 168, 178, 181, 210–14, 217, 233–35, 246–47, 262
Chibber, Vivek 15
Chodorow, Nancy 52, 236, 238, 262, 294
Chomsky, Noam 66, 154, 155, 223, 248, 289, 295, 299
Clark, Lorenne 164
class 7, 15, 17, 20–23, 51, 61–62, 120–24, 154, 251–52, 261–62, 271–72, 274
class societies 13, 57, 66, 69, 117, 121, 123, 125, 127, 131, 133–38
climate 5, 16, 72–73, 98–99, 108–111, 222, 253, 284–285, 293
Cohen, Gerald A. 93, 95, 155, 166, 171, 173, 251
Cohen, Morris 194
collective action 4, 5, 81, 82, 84, 86–87, 89, 92–93, 96, 103, 136, 296, 305
Combahee River Collective 22, 266, 295
commodities 20, 27, 32, 38, 44–45, 47–50, 131, 133–34, 166, 168, 277, 279–80
communism 94, 123–27, 135–36, 140, 168, 217, 243–47, 283
Communist Manifesto 140, 156, 197
communities 8, 108–9, 147, 149, 154, 164, 167–68, 179, 187–88, 287–88, 295
competition 132, 202, 217, 250, 283, 287
    global 140
    increased 205
    intense 202
condoms 29, 35, 37, 40
conflict 21, 72–73, 82, 95–96, 104, 118, 120, 149, 215, 221–22, 241

contract   36, 49, 59, 152, 159, 162–167, 190–91, 194, 200, 203, 209
contradictions   124, 162, 197, 241, 243, 247, 284
critique   2, 4, 6, 8, 34, 91, 94–95, 138, 178, 180, 259–60, 295
Cudd, Ann   5, 6, 23, 279

Delphy, Christine   18, 263
democracy   65–68, 70–71, 109, 112, 151–55, 186, 191, 197, 211, 218
democratic socialism   4, 65–75
destruction   22, 70, 97, 103, 105, 196, 275
Diamond, Jared   219
dictatorships   68, 151–52, 176
Dinnerstein, Dorothy   52, 238, 262
division of labour   54, 59, 74, 180, 205, 238, 265
divorce   199–200
domestic labour   17, 19, 42–49, 51, 53–59, 62
domination   32, 36, 38, 121–22, 147, 153, 155, 177, 190, 192, 195, 199, 256, 287
Draper, Hal   67, 72, 223
Dworkin, Andrea   263

Eagleton, Terry   176
ecology   70, 109, 220, 282, 284
economic conditions   25, 49, 191, 201, 208, 253, 275
economics   4, 66, 92, 153, 203
education   40, 100, 102, 109, 142, 183, 219
Ehrenreich, Barbara   211–13
emancipation   26, 29, 63, 67, 70, 80, 83, 123, 148, 200, 223–24
employers   19, 31, 45, 55, 163, 173–74, 177–78, 189, 200, 278, 287
energy   16, 33, 69, 73, 109, 112, 192, 260, 283
  human   33, 69, 112, 123, 192, 244, 283
Engels, Friedrich   67–68, 120–21, 123–24, 152, 156, 199, 230, 250, 253, 289
equality   1, 42, 149, 156, 159–60, 164, 172, 184–85, 215, 295, 300
essentialism   248, 260, 263, 269, 273
evolution   143, 145, 230, 233, 252
exploitation   2–3, 13–14, 16, 18–19, 32, 35, 52, 54, 56–57, 62, 299–300, 307
Ezorsky, Gertrude   31, 171, 173–74, 178, 280

false consciousness   80, 121–23, 126–27, 129, 135–37
family   19, 30–31, 42–43, 49–53, 55–62, 86, 92, 134, 141, 164, 174–75, 183–85, 187, 196–97, 204–5, 208, 211, 213–14, 237–38, 242–43, 246, 257, 264, 274, 276
fathers   2, 99, 167, 196–97, 205, 224, 246
femininity   237, 259, 261–62
feminism   17–18, 36, 143, 259, 265
  radical   62, 164, 295
feudalism   13–14, 16, 20, 24, 54, 66, 69, 90, 92, 126, 157, 165, 190, 232, 244
Fisk, Milton   24, 43
food   27, 47–48, 162, 170, 176, 183, 189, 193, 210–11, 252, 254–55
forced labour   33, 69, 189–90, 280
fossil fuels   66, 102, 105, 108, 110, 113, 221
Frankfurt, Harry   118
Frase, Peter   31
freedom   1, 5–6, 29–31, 33, 69–71, 117–19, 122–23, 149, 151–52, 154–57, 162, 164–65, 169–79, 182–93, 223, 244–47, 281–83, 285–86
free rider problem   80, 82–84, 86–87, 95, 97, 103–4
Friedman, Milton   152, 156
Fukuyama, Francis   140

Gauthier, David   89–91, 94
gender   7–8, 15, 23, 216–17, 248–49, 252, 256–58, 260–66, 272, 274
gender differences   258, 261, 269, 287
gender roles   31, 198, 209, 259–62, 265
Geras, Norman   251, 254, 284, 286
Gibson, Mary   79, 95
Gotha Program   56, 94
Gough, Ian   45, 47, 48, 59–62
Gramsci, Antonio   126
Gray, John   172–73
Green New Deal   106, 108–9, 113, 293, 307
Grundrisse   33, 250, 276–77, 283

Hahnel, Robin   223, 225
Harrison, John   45, 47–48, 59, 61–62, 198
Hartmann, Heidi   18, 210, 264–65
hierarchies   7, 20–21, 186, 274, 287
Hirschmann, Nancy   162, 171, 175–76, 191, 286

Hobbes, Thomas   124, 159, 163, 252
Hochschild, Arlie   36, 143, 211–13
households   43, 61, 148, 210, 274, 309
housewife   46–48, 54, 61, 295, 308, 310
humankind   102, 224–25, 248–75, 283
human nature   5–8, 33, 90, 117, 119, 122–27, 136, 186–87, 229–30, 232, 243–56, 259, 275–89
Hungarian Revolt   67, 154

identity   22, 26, 146–47, 217, 235, 263, 270–72, 305
identity politics   15, 22
ideology   4, 52, 55, 58, 95, 121–22, 186, 216, 238, 296
Imperialism   25, 72, 212
industries   28, 37, 39, 50, 57, 109, 145, 161, 203–4, 206
inequalities   52, 58, 66, 178, 184–87, 191, 210, 258, 260, 287

James, C.L.R   25, 269
James, Selma   25, 44, 54

Kaplan, Temma   197
Kidron, Mike   45
Krugman, Paul   141, 150

labour power   4, 14, 32, 42, 55, 122, 189, 197, 279, 287, 289
Levellers   158–59, 163–64, 167
Lewontin, Richard   250, 252, 267–68
liberation movements   169, 260
libertarians   38, 119, 173, 189
Locke, John   124, 159–66, 179–80, 193, 248, 295
Lovibond, Sabina   260
Lucas Aerospace Plan   107
Luce, Stephanie   204–6, 208, 210
Luria, R.   232
Luxemburg, Rosa   19, 45, 74, 83, 88

MacCallum, Gerald   172, 192
machines   34, 36, 49, 167, 277, 279, 282
   an appendage of the   34
Macpherson, C.B.   101, 153, 159, 162–63, 178, 193
Magna Carta Manifesto   158, 302
market   48–50, 70, 94–95, 111–12, 140, 144–45, 151, 179–80, 183, 200, 203, 289
market socialism   70, 289
market system   16, 70, 159, 162, 166, 168, 207, 221
Marx, Eleanor   63, 224
Marx, Karl   1–2, 13–14, 18–19, 32–34, 44–48, 53–57, 67–69, 73–75, 80–81, 90–96, 120–26, 134–36, 191–92, 229–33, 243–45, 250–55, 275–78
Marx's vision of socialism   70, 112, 284
Meiksins Wood, Ellen   143, 153, 159, 161
Mills, Charles   143, 165, 167, 194, 197, 258
Mode of production   16, 18, 19, 43, 45–47, 57–62, 120, 152, 232, 244
Molyneux, Maxine   148, 198
Morris, William   223
money   43, 46, 66, 73, 93, 157, 161–62, 171, 177, 185–86, 188
monopoly   32, 145, 180, 189, 289, 310

neuropsychology   232, 302
Nozick, Robert   156–57, 166, 173, 174, 179, 180–81, 183–84, 190

Obama, Barack   146, 184
Olson, Mancur   80–81, 83–84, 86–87, 91
Ostrom, Elinor   102, 111–12

Pateman, Carole   27, 35, 36, 38, 167, 180, 191, 280
patriarchy   18, 20–21, 23, 30, 195–96
Patterson, Orlando   151, 170, 306
Petchesky, Rosalind   167–68, 225
planning   4, 5, 70, 73, 111–13, 133, 223
Plato   129, 153–54, 191–92, 248
population   52–53, 65, 151, 156, 250, 255, 267, 270
poverty   6, 30, 39, 171, 181, 187, 197, 202, 204–5, 210–11, 213, 218, 269
   extreme   147
   rural   204
power   29, 47, 84, 152, 156, 176–78, 184–86, 189–92, 194, 196–97, 203–4, 222–24, 243–44, 281, 287–89
power relations   20, 55, 58, 94, 159, 224, 253, 285
primitive accumulation   20, 157, 196, 200, 277

private property   101–2, 105, 144–45, 156–62, 168–69, 177, 179, 183, 186, 191, 194, 277, 279
producers   13–14, 16, 20, 48, 54, 59, 94, 113, 190–92, 277, 280, 286
productivity   45–46, 162, 179, 199, 278
profit maximisation   15, 93, 110, 198, 207, 222, 274
profits   14–15, 19, 35, 40, 45–46, 69, 74–75, 93, 197–98, 213, 221
prostitutes   27–31, 35–40, 46, 191, 214
prostitution   27–28, 34–40, 166–67, 191, 280, 296, 310
psychological differences   229, 234, 236–37, 242–43, 245, 256, 258, 262
public goods   5, 80, 82, 100–101, 103, 105, 111–12, 142, 144, 291, 300

Qinglian, He   101

race   7–8, 21–23, 25, 186–87, 196–97, 202–3, 215, 217, 240–41, 248–49, 261–62, 265–74
racism   8, 18, 20–21, 25, 197, 248, 250, 269, 273, 287, 291
Rapaport, Elizabeth   26, 62
rape   35, 37, 38, 169, 171, 176, 260, 265–66
rational choice theory   103
rationality   4–5, 73, 77, 79, 81–82, 84–85, 89–97, 99–100, 103–5
Rawls, John   31, 79, 95, 149, 171, 181, 185
reproduction   18, 44, 47, 49–51, 74, 186, 258
revolt   67, 80–81, 162
revolution   4, 71, 79–97, 123, 143, 145, 148, 153
Ribera-Fumaz, Ramon   108
Rich, Adrienne   260
Robinson, Mary   211
Robinson Crusoe   92, 180
Rodney, Walter   206
Romer, Nancy   234–35
Roosevelt, F.D.R.   109, 182–83
Rowbotham, Sheila   59, 61–63
Russian Revolution   67, 154, 199, 224

Sartre, J.P.   269
Sassen, Saskia   212
Schmitt, Richard   281
scientists   219, 249–50, 253, 270
Secombe, Wally   46–47, 54, 198

self-ownership   156–57, 164–70
Sen, Amartya   79, 86, 94, 103, 162, 181, 207
Sengupta, Somini   110, 212
sexism   18, 20–21, 23, 45, 52, 58, 61–62, 175, 195, 197, 199, 259–60, 265
sexual division of labour   54, 56, 148, 218, 229, 236–39, 242, 257, 265
sex work   3, 26–27, 29–31, 34, 19
slavery   6, 13–14, 20, 28, 39, 165, 169, 189–91, 197, 213–15, 280, 286
Smith, Adam   33, 144, 221, 283
Smith, Barbara   22, 170, 176
Smith, Richard   16, 107, 109–110, 209, 300, 308, 309
So-called socialist societies   61, 199, 222
socialism   8, 16, 53, 56, 65–73, 75, 93–94, 112–13, 120–21, 124–25, 127, 135–36, 140–41, 223, 245, 286
socialist feminists   17, 22, 26, 38–39, 75, 108, 225
social welfare   145, 152, 181, 183
Sohn-Rethel, Alfred   95, 232
surplus value   19, 43–44, 47–49, 53–54, 59, 74, 95

Taylorism   278
Thatcher, Margaret   140, 187, 224
Thunberg, Greta   110
transphobia   28

unemployment   52, 73, 111, 150, 183, 188, 202
United States   18–19, 65, 74–75, 140, 142, 145, 150–56, 177, 180–84, 186–87, 198, 206–8, 216–18, 266–67
utopian socialist   8, 33, 67–68, 91, 224, 275

Varikas, Eleni   146
violence   37, 171, 175, 180, 190, 209, 215, 218, 266, 296, 298
Vygotsky, Lev   232

wage labour   13, 18, 32, 34, 45, 58–59, 74, 144–45, 157, 159–61, 167
wage work   19, 33, 50, 52, 57–58, 61, 242
water   98, 100, 102–3, 111–12, 193, 217, 219
whiteness   271–72
Williams, Eric   165
Winstanley, Gerard   158, 177, 182
Wittgenstein, Ludwig   92

Wittig, Monique   263–64
women's movement   63–64, 170–71, 176, 199–200, 208–10, 225, 229, 263
World Bank   140, 211–12, 219, 226

Young, Gary   134

Zarembka, Joy M.   213